THE CAMBRIDGE ILLUSTRATED HISTORY OF

Germany

THE CAMBRIDGE ILLUSTRATED HISTORY OF

Germany

MARTIN KITCHEN

CAMBRIDGE
UNIVERSITY PRESS

Published by the Press Syndicate of the University of Cambridge
The Pitt Building, Trumpington Street, Cambridge CB2 1RP
40 West 20th Street, New York, NY 10011-4211, USA
10 Stamford Road, Oakleigh, Melbourne 3166, Australia

First published 1996

This book was produced by
CALMANN & KING LTD
71 Great Russell Street
London WC1B 3BN

Project editor: Liz Wyse
Picture research: Bella Grazebrook
Layout: Andrew Shoolbred
Cartography by Hardlines, Charlbury, Oxford

Printed in Italy at New Interlitho

A catalogue record for this book is available from the British Library

Library of Congress cataloguing in publication data
Kitchen, Martin.
The Cambridge Illustrated History of Germany / edited by
Francis Robinson
p.   cm. – (Cambridge illustrated history series)
ISBN 0-521-45341-0
1. German-History
I. Title. II. Series: Cambridge illustrated history.
DD89.K55 1996
95-38062   943-dc20   CIP

ISBN 0 521 45341 0 hardback

Contents

Acknowledgements

Although it is impossible to list all the people and institutions who have helped me either directly or indirectly in this project, I would especially like to thank Rosemary Bradley and Mary Scott, my editors at Calmann and King; Peter Richards and Pauline Graham at Cambridge University Press; the picture editor Bella Grazebrook and the project editor Liz Wyse. All have given me invaluable help, encouragement, constructive criticism and timely prodding. I am particularly grateful to T.C.W. Blanning for saving me from many errors, clichés and split infinitives. The German Academic Exchange (DAAD), a true friend of foreign scholars of Germany, gave me a generous grant which enabled me to do much of the research.

Introduction

No country is fonder of historical debates than Germany, sometimes over topics which to outsiders hardly seem important. The question of when German history began is still a matter of discussion, often with strong political overtones. Did it begin in 843 when the Treaty of Verdun gave Louis the German the lands east of the Rhine? Or did it begin in 887 when Arnulf of Carinthia partially restored the territory of the Carolingian empire? Some historians have suggested 911, when Conrad I was elected king, while others suggest the coronation of Otto the Great in 936, or the imperial coronation of Otto in Rome of 962. Those who wish to stress the continental role of Germany begin with Charles the Great, an emperor who was described as the father of Europe (*Pater Europae*); or the eastward expansion and violent conversion of the Saxons and the creation of bishoprics in Münster, Paderborn, Hildesheim, Osnabrück, Bremen, and Hamburg.

The first use of the word German (*theodiscus*) was in a report by the papal legate in England. The council of Tours in 813 referred to *teotisca*. But it was not until the end of the tenth century that mention was made of the 'land of the Germans' (*terra teutonica*) and the expression 'kingdom of the Germans'. The empire was once again described as the Holy Empire (*sacrum imperium*) in 1157, but there was nothing German in the title until 1512 when, under Maximilian I, it became the 'Holy Roman Empire of the German Nation', a phrase which bemused contemporaries and which even the most ingenious scholars have been unable to decipher.

In 911 the four East Frankish peoples – the Franks, Swabians, Bavarians, and Saxons – formed the kingdom of Germany. In 925 were added the Lotharingians, some of whom were French-speaking. The kingdom corresponded roughly to the former West Germany and lay on the eastern borders of Christian Europe. With the conversion of the Slavs, Scandinavians, and Hungarians, Germany found itself culturally and politically central in Europe, a development that was to have a profound effect.

Under the Ottonians, Salians, and Hohenstaufen, Germany was clearly the predominant power in Europe. The east was Christianized and colonized, and agriculture and mining developed, and the universities became great cultural centres. But this empire was fundamentally weak. It was too large to be effectively controlled and its component parts constantly threatened to break off. It had no capital and the German emperors were embroiled in Italian politics, for Rome legitimized their rule. The rivalry between the Welf and the Hohenstaufen dynasties further undermined the empire and, from the beginning of the thirteenth century when France grew pre-eminent in Europe, Germany became a power vacuum dominated by the territorial princes.

Representatives from the Slavs, Germany, Gaul and Rome approach Otto III's throne with gifts for the heirs to the Caesars. From Otto III's Gospel-book, Reichenau school c.1000, in the Bamberg treasury.

The *Germania* of the Roman historian Tacitus was first published in Germany in 1497, and had an immense effect on the Germans' image of themselves at a time of nascent national identity. They relished the description of their forebears as morally upright, unshakably honest, chaste, patriotic, modest, brave, and hospitable, and the painful realization that they did not quite live up to such exacting standards they attributed to the baneful influence of the corrupt Roman Church. Freed from this degenerate control, the Germans would return to their natural condition and, with their closeness to nature and moral discipline, would recover their former greatness. German national feeling was thus based on an intense hatred of the frivolous French and the venal Romans. It is therefore hardly surprising that foreigners delighted in quoting those passages of Tacitus which the Germans prudently overlooked, in which he spoke of their drunkenness, greediness , ill-manners, and their brutality.

The Reformation further weakened the empire and offered fresh opportunities for the princes to increase their power. The fragmentation of Germany was formally recognized in the Peace of Westphalia of 1648 which brought an end to the Thirty Years War. Germany was now a loose federation of virtually sovereign states, some of which provided the framework within which modernization and reform could take place. Coincidentally, in 1789 there were 1,789 such entities ranging from the European powers of Austria and Prussia to minute abbeys and imperial villages with autonomous rights. Constitutional reform within the empire could only take place with the agreement of all the signatories to the Treaty of Westphalia, which included Russia after the Treaty of Teschen in 1779.

Napoleon put an end to the empire and reorganized Germany, creating the Confederation of the Rhine out of sixteen states, of which Bavaria, Württemberg, and Baden were the most important. The impulse for reform in these states came from France and they adopted the progressive *Code Napoléon*. In Prussia, reforms were designed to enable the state to cast off the French yoke and laid the foundations for German strength in the nineteenth century.

Xenophobia is an important ingredient in nationalism and modern German nationalism was born of an intense hatred of the French, confirmed by the unacceptable behaviour of Napoleon's occupying forces. A feeling of national identity was first clearly articulated in the eighteenth century and was centred on the distinct cultural and linguistic characteristics of the Germans. It was cosmopolitan, apolitical and rarefied, and only began to turn sour under the impact of the French revolutionary wars. Cosmopolitanism gradually turned into an arrogant sense of cultural mission; the apolitical became a reactionary obsession with a romanticized Germanic past; and the rarefied became an escape into metaphysical obscurities. Nationalist hopes that had been awakened by the struggle against Napoleon were frustrated by the Congress of Vienna which sacrificed German national aspirations to the imperatives of diplomacy.

Most German patriots in 1815 had hoped that the empire would be restored and strengthened, but Britain and Russia preferred the to their minds feeble compromise solution of a German Confederation. It was a loose association of the thirty-nine remaining German states without a government or head of state but with a federal assembly (*Bundestag*). Although Germany seemed outwardly powerless it had immense potential. The Customs Union (*Zollverein*), founded in 1834 under Prussian leadership, created an economic association which soon challenged British supremacy. All that was needed was political unification to make Germany the greatest power on the continent. With a fleet it could threaten Britain.

Parliamentarians who gathered in Frankfurt in 1848 had to tackle the fundamental questions 'who is a German?' and 'where is Germany?' There was general agreement that Germans were people who spoke German and that Germany was, in the words of the nationalist poet Ernst Moritz Arndt, 'wherever German is spoken' (*Soweit die deutsche Zunge reicht*). But the problem could not so easily be solved. Were German-speaking Alsatians Germans, even though they were French citizens? Were Prussian Poles Germans simply because there was no Polish state?

Bohemia was part of the German Confederation, but what rights should be accorded to Czechs? Should Jews be treated as equals, or should the German people be protected against such threatening outsiders?

Most of the delegates to the Frankfurt parliament wanted a greater Germany (*Großdeutschland*) which included Austria, a dominant power with a fleet that could rival the Royal Navy. United Germany would be a world power. The liberals hoped to build an integrated community which was strong enough to protect itself against its neighbours and could afford protection to German minorities on its borders. Germans in France, Luxembourg, the Netherlands, Schleswig, and Switzerland would be reabsorbed into the nation. There was little discussion of Alsace and Lorraine in Frankfurt because the parliamentarians were understandably fearful of French reactions, but there were few such inhibitions about the Polish question. Whereas liberals had traditionally been enthusiastic supporters of Polish national aspirations against Tsarist autocracy, such sentiments were now denounced as treasonable attempts to hand over the German minority to a backward people. Similar arguments were used in discussions of the future of Bohemia, Schleswig-Holstein, and northern Italy. The interests of healthy national egotism took pride of place over concern for the rights of other peoples to national self-determination. There were very few liberals who realized that the failure to recognize the rights of others posed a threat to their own, and that victories over insurgent nationalities merely strengthened the forces of reaction. This fatal mistake was the result of insisting that nations should be based on ethnicity rather than shared values and a common law. Even today a Russian, born of parents who can claim descent from Germans but who cannot speak a word of German, has an automatic right to German citizenship. A child of Turkish parents, born in Germany, fluent in German and attending a German school does not.

At the time Bismarck's unified Germany did not seem as menacing as it became subsequently. That it was founded on 'blood and iron' made it no different from Italy, Greece or Serbia. It was a constitutional monarchy in which parliament was a great deal more than a 'fig leaf for absolutism' as the socialist leader August Bebel claimed. On the other hand, Germany was united in the course of three wars which came in rapid succession and in which the Germans fought without assistance. The German empire was almost overnight the most powerful nation on the continent, and was soon to overtake Britain as an industrial power. The population grew from 38 million in 1871 to 64 million in 1914, increasing the dynamism of the new nation state. Its geographical position at the centre of Europe meant it shared common frontiers with France, Austria-Hungary, and Russia and only a short expanse of sea separated it from England. Bismarck declared that Germany was 'saturated' but he knew that the great powers would always be watchful and suspicious of this powerful newcomer.

The new Germany acted as a powerful magnet to German minorities elsewhere. In Austria-Hungary Germans were a minority who felt threatened and powerless, and were increasingly attracted to a radical *Großdeutscher* (Greater Germany) nationalism and racism. Adolf Hitler came from such a background. Soon the call was heard that all Germans should be united, and the Pan-German League (*Alldeutscher Verband*), formed in 1890, attracted even liberal intellectuals such as Max Weber. He proclaimed in his inaugural lecture in Freiburg that if Germany did not begin imperial expansion, the unification of 1871 was merely a 'prank'. The programme of bringing all Germans together, including German-speaking Swiss and Netherlanders, as well as imperial expansion overseas, could not be achieved without a major war. Many sober people in responsible positions began to prepare for the final battle, viewing the prospect with equanimity.

Bismarck's domestic policy was as divisive as his foreign policy was dangerous. He rallied support by painting a lurid picture of the threats posed to the infant state by determined enemies. First and foremost came the Socialists but almost as pernicious were the Poles, French, Alsatians, Danes, Catholics, and Jews. A majority of citizens were thus denounced as enemies of the Reich and it seemed only Prussian Protestant conservatives could be true Germans. The remarkable cohesion of the nation in August 1914 showed that in extreme situations these old hostilities could be overcome and nationalism work its magic, but the divisions and antagonisms always remained beneath the surface.

Germany's war aims during World War I became increasingly excessive the less likely its final victory seemed. The rapid collapse of the western front came as a rude shock and was carefully concealed from the people by the army supreme command which blamed the democratic parties in the Reichstag. The Treaty of Versailles took away all those frontier areas where the majority of the population was non-German, but the powers would not permit Austria and the German-speaking Sudetenland to join Germany, knowing that this would make it the strongest power in Europe. Given Germany's truculent and offended mood, it was likely sooner or later to attempt to undo the decisions of 1918/19. The Versailles Treaty was unacceptable to the vast majority of Germans; it was harsh enough to make them deeply resentful and determined to defy the *Diktat*, but was too feeble to prevent them from overthrowing it. Few seemed to have realized that even within the frontiers laid down at Versailles, Germany was still the strongest power in Europe.

The Treaty of Locarno of 1925 and Germany's subsequent permanent membership of the council of the League of Nations was recognition that Germany counted among the great powers. But this was not enough for most Germans. A chronic economic crisis coupled with a political stalemate allowed Adolf Hitler to agitate with increasing effectiveness. His programme met with the approval of the overwhelming majority of the people. First he established a one-party dictatorship; those who did not support it were terrorized into submission. Then he began to tear up the *Diktat* of Versailles finding a *Grossdeutsche* solution to the German problem in 1938, one which was accepted enthusiastically by Britain and France in the Munich agreement. Bit by bit the Treaty of Versailles was undone. Military service was introduced in 1935, the Rhineland occupied in 1936, Austria and the Sudetenland annexed in 1938. In March 1939 Hitler occupied Bohemia and Moravia, and the Memel was then taken from the Lithuanians in the last annexation before the war.

The Nazis provided a radical answer to the perennial question 'who is a German?' Bismarck's 'enemies of the Reich', among them Socialists, politicized Christians, and left-liberal politicians were forced into exile or locked up in concentration camps. The German 'racial community' had to be purged of all alien and debilitating elements. The mentally and physically handicapped, homosexuals, habitual criminals, Gypsies, and Jews, were segregated, sterilized and murdered.

Hitler did not want a global confrontation and would have preferred to gobble up eastern Europe, but only through a major war could he hope to realize his long-term racial and imperial fantasies. Many in the Nazi leadership thought the declaration of war by France and Britain on 3 September 1939 a disaster, but a series of brilliant victories followed which silenced the sceptics. The campaign against the Soviet Union, the culmination of Hitler's strategy, at first went like clockwork. The defeats at Stalingrad and El Alamein in 1942 spelt the beginning of the end, but it was too late for the millions of Jews who had been murdered in a crime of unfathomable horror. This combination of ideological madness and bureaucratic efficiency was the policy of which Hitler was proudest.

In 1945 Germany once again became a power vacuum to be filled by the occupying forces, a little Germany between the Rhine and the Oder, divided up into four zones. As a result of the Cold War, Germany was divided into a Stalinist totalitarian East and a democratic capitalist West. In the East, a planned economy was introduced which emphasized heavy industry, and the country was ruthlessly exploited by the Soviets. Whole factories were dismantled to be rebuilt in the Soviet Union. The reparations collected far exceeded the amount agreed upon by the wartime allies. Almost one quarter of the East German population fled to the west before the building of the Berlin wall in 1961.

The western powers treated 'their' Germans leniently, re-educated them in the ways of parliamentary democracy, and encouraged a liberal market economy. The Germans responded enthusiastically and pragmatically, their economy boomed, and they were soon accepted as equal partners in the western alliance. Remarkable steps were made to confront the Nazi past, and no country has ever made such an effort to atone for the sins of its history. The division of Germany was accepted and the East German dictatorship was appeased in the hope that conditions for the ordinary people in the East might improve. But by 1983 East Germany was virtually bankrupt. Economic statistics were fiddled, machinery was hopelessly out of date, massive investments were made in unproductive enterprises, the cost of social welfare was excessive, and the country could only survive with massive loans from West Germany. As the Soviet empire began to collapse East Germany was hopelessly isolated, the last remaining post-Stalinist dictatorship. The fortieth anniversary of the foundation of East Germany was celebrated on 7 October 1989, but the guest of honour Mikhail Gorbachev refused to support the East German leader, Erich Honecker, and gave every encouragement to the reformers. Honecker was forced out of office on 18 October. The government of Lothar de Maizière, formed after the first free elections since 1932 on 18 March 1990, worked out the details of the unification of the two German states which took place on 3 October 1990.

The West German political class was taken completely by surprise by the rapid course of events. The vast mass of West Germans did not want unification, largely because they knew it would cost them a great deal. After the initial euphoria when the wall fell on 9 November 1989 and the sparkling wine flowed, came the massive hangover. Westerners speculated against the east mark, easterners moved to the West. Chancellor Helmut Kohl cast caution aside and, against the advice of most experts, did the only sensible thing: ignoring the staggering costs involved, he introduced the mighty Deutschmark in the East and united the two countries as

A view through the Berlin Wall of the frontier strip and East Berlin. The 'Wall-Woodpeckers' (Mauerspechte) chipped away at the wall with hammers and chisels provided by enterprising Poles, the fragments sold as souvenirs.

quickly as possible. The gulf between the two Germanies soon became painfully apparent. Few had appreciated the full extent of the East's economic backwardness in industry and agriculture, its massive ecological destruction, the wretched state of public health, and housing, its antiquated infrastructure. Profound psychological damage had been caused by fifty years of dictatorship, secret policing, censorship, and repression. 'Ossis' were treated as the embarrassingly poor relatives of the affluent 'Wessis', and East Germans felt that their country had become a colony for greedy Westerners.

The task facing Germany is awesome, the 'German question' still open. The walls that have been built since 1989 in peoples' heads and hearts have to be broken down and, for the first time in the thousand-year history of Germany, national unity based on democratic principles has to be combined with a responsible exercise of its immense power. A democratic and prosperous Germany, securely integrated within Europe, free from any territorial ambitions, and prepared to subordinate its national interests to those of other nations, would be a threat to none and a benefit to all. There is so much of which the Germans can justly be proud, it is to be hoped that this is sufficient to prevent the resurgence of those dangerous ambitions that have intoxicated them in the past and have proved so disastrous.

CHAPTER 1

The Beginnings of German History

The answer to the question 'Who were the Germani?' used to be simple. They were the people who spoke the Germanic language and who lived in a clearly defined geographical area. The Roman historian Tacitus, writing at the end of the first century AD, defined Germania as the land between the seas and the Danube, from the Rhine to the Vistula. The Germani were, he claimed, a pure blooded folk who had lived there since time immemorial. According to their legends their god Tuisto was born of their soil. Tuisto's son Mannus (the origin of the word 'man') had three sons from whom sprang the three original Germanic tribes. This belief in the racial purity of the Germanic peoples, so dear to later nationalists and racists, is reflected in the Latin word *germanus* and the English word 'german' meaning 'having the same parents', 'closely connected' or 'sprung from the same stock'.

CONFLICT WITH ROME

Julius Caesar felt it necessary to explain why he had not conquered and colonized Germania as he had Gaul. It was, he reported 150 years before Tacitus, a country inhabited by barbarians, its thick forests teeming with unicorns and other mysterious animals. Such a country could never be colonized and was best ignored. This remained the prevailing wisdom on *Germania libera*, even though Roman merchants travelled the length and breadth of the area and conducted profitable business with its barbarians. Amber from the Baltic was particularly prized in Rome, and merchants travelled along the 'amber roads' from Marseille or Venice to Hamburg, or from Aquileia to Danzig bringing back tons of the material which Roman craftsmen made into exquisite objects.

That Germania was a region with a quite distinct history and culture from western Europe was a belief cherished by the otherwise so cosmopolitan German humanists in the 18th century. Their hero was Arminius the Cheruscan, to whom they gave the German name Hermann, who in AD 9 utterly defeated the Romans in the 'Teutoburg Forest', which is assumed to be near Detmold. Hermann thus became the hero of the movement of national liberation from Roman tyranny and foreign influence. By contrast French historians argued that their national history was rooted in the glorious classical civilization of Greece and Rome.

Augustus (63 BC–AD 14) established Rome's strategy towards Germania which was to be followed for centuries. Defensive positions were taken up along the Rhine and the Danube and a *limes* (defensive frontier) was built from Koblenz to Regensburg during the reign of Domitian (AD 51–96). In the third century AD the empire was attacked by Goths, Franks, and Alemanni – polyethnic groupings and alliances as their names 'the free' and 'all men' suggest. The Franks concentrated their efforts against the Roman garrison in Cologne, while the Alemanni were active around Mainz. It is for this reason that when the Romans abandoned the *limes,* they called the Germanic peoples of the Upper Rhine Alemanni, and those of the Lower Rhine Franks.

There are accounts of numerous clashes between Germanic tribes and Roman troops during the fourth century. When the Roman frontier troops were recalled to deal with problems at home, the tribes raided the border provinces for plunder and tribute. The result was a confusing series of skirmishes and battles with various feuding tribes who were led by a multiplicity of kings, army commanders, and nobles of varying rank. Once the political situation stabilized in Rome, the Germani were driven back across the frontier and new treaties were signed. Thus in 357 the Alemanni were defeated near Strasburg and forced to abandon their settlements west of the Rhine. The Romans restored one of the emperor Trajan's old forts east of the Rhine which, under the terms of a treaty with the Alemanni, had to be supplied at the expense of the locals.

In 368 the Alemanni captured Mainz, but in a counter-offensive under the emperor Valentinian I, were pushed back across the Rhine. In the following year the emperor tried to crush the Alemanni but the operation was unsuccessful. In 374 the emperor signed a treaty with Macrian, king of the Bukinobanti, but Rome's new ally was killed in battle against the Franks in 380. Macrian had met his end facing the army of the Frankish king Mirobaudes, who was also a high Roman officer. Mallobaudes was thus both the enemy and the servant of the Roman emperor. He was one of a number of powerful Frankish officers in Roman service who fought against the Alemanni and Goths, but was unique in that he never severed his ties with his own people nor betrayed them to Rome as others often did.

For many, service in the Roman army led to assimilation. The native Germani had worshipped the god Wotan and looked forward to a hero's life in Valhalla, attended by virgin Walkuries. Under Roman influence, many adopted the sophisticated neo-Platonic paganism of the Romans, others converted to Christianity, or became Jews. Gradually, the tribal religions and social structure of the Germani along the Rhine and the Danube disappeared.

The Danubian Goths were the first to encounter Christianity. Seriously short of manpower, they had raided the Balkans in search of prisoners and brought back Christians from this most Christian region of the Roman empire. Their captives set about 'turning their masters into their brothers'. The most notable among them was 'Little Wolf', Wulfilas. He was born north of the Danube in about AD 310, but his family had originated in Cappadocia, in eastern Anatolia. He was ordained bishop of the 'Land of the Goths' at Antioch in 341, a clear indication that the area was already partially Christian. Wulfilas translated the Bible into Gothic. He subscribed to the Arian heresy, which denied that the Son was co-equal and co-eternal with the Father, and claimed that he was merely the best of human beings, a teaching condemned at the Council of Nicea in 325. The Nicean creed insisted

This bronze statue of a Roman soldier carrying a military emblem once formed part of a horse's armour and dates from the first century AD. This was the period when the emperor Augustus first established Rome's attitude towards the Germanic tribes people, and Roman soldiers took up defensive positions along the rivers Rhine and Danube.

A detail from the column of Marcus Aurelius in Rome showing Roman legionaries crossing a river on a pontoon. The Roman army took up a defensive position on the frontier (*limes*) along the Rhine and the Danube and was involved in a series of border skirmishes with the Germanic tribes. Many from *Germania libera* served in the Roman legions, but their loyalty was often questionable.

upon the 'homoousian' dogma, which held that the Son of God was of the same essence as the Father. Wulfilas was instrumental in spreading the Arian heresy among the Goths.

Christian Goths were persecuted by the pagan elite and were forced into exile. The Roman emperor Constantine II welcomed them and granted them land in present-day Bulgaria. Wulfilas was their bishop until his death in 383, the emperor compared him to Moses: he had led his people into the promised land. The Christians continued to be persecuted and were denounced as allies of the Romans, but nevertheless their number and their influence increased, and some pagan leaders (*Reiks*, as in the German *Reich* or empire) converted.

Faced with the growing threat from the Huns to the east, the Goths made an alliance with their old enemies, the Gothic Christians who had become friends of Rome. Many Goths emigrated to the Roman empire, where they laid down their arms, declared their allegiance to the emperor, and paid taxes, following the example of many Alemanni and Franks in the west. By 376 the Goths were arriving in such numbers that local officials were unable to disarm them and there were severe food shortages. Much of the Roman army in Thracia had been withdrawn to fight the Persians, leaving the region open to attack by the Goths. On 9 August 378 the Roman army was routed at Adrianople and the emperor Valens killed in battle. The Romans were then forced to recognize the importance of assimilating immigrant groups. The new emperor, Theodosius, granted the Goths certain autonomous rights within the empire, thereby making it easier to defend Christendom against pagan invaders.

GERMANIC INVASIONS AND MIGRATIONS

In 375 the Gothic tribes of southern Russia were overrun by the Huns, a collection of Asiatic tribes rather than a distinct people. The Huns absorbed many of the Germanic tribes, and their greatest leader, Attila, had a Gothic name. Even Attila was unable to unite the Huns or extend his power over all the subject tribes, and many independent Hunnish chieftains defied his sovereignty. The invasion launched a great movement of peoples. The Huns expelled the Ostrogoths from the Crimea and the Ukraine. The Ostrogoths in turn forced the Visigoths back to the Danubian frontier of the Roman empire. After the Roman defeat at Adrianople, the Visigoths settled in Greece, plundered Italy, and sacked Rome under Alaric I, moving on into Aquitaine and then to Spain. Vandals, Sueves and Alans from Silesia and the Theiss valley, crossed the Rhine at Mainz in 406 and ravaged Gaul for three years before crossing the Pyrenees and settling in Spain.

An engraving, made in about 1820 by Ludwig Buchorn (1770–1856) of the Hunnish king Attila (c. 406–453), the 'scourge of God'. He became joint king with his brother in 434 and, heading a collection of tribes, controlled a vast region stretching from China to the Rhine. In 447 he conquered the area from the Black Sea to the Mediterranean, defeating the Emperor Theodosius in three engagements. In 451 he invaded Gaul but was checked at the Battle of the Catalaunian Fields. He ravaged northern Italy in 452 and died the following year.

Having murdered his older brother Bleda in 444/5, Attila became the undisputed leader of the Huns. In 447 he laid waste to the lands between the Black Sea and the Mediterranean, and, having received tribute from the emperor in Constantinople, settled in the area between Belgrade and Christowa. In 451 the new emperor Marcian stopped the annuity payments to Attila, who promptly marched westwards along the Danube, collecting allies among the Germanic tribes as he went. Attila's army crossed the Rhine and attacked Gaul, engaging the Romans and their allies, mainly Visigoths under Aetius, at the Battle of the Catalaunian Fields, between Troyes and Châlons-sur-Seine. The battle was not decisive, but Attila's aura of invincibility was lost. Contemplating suicide he withdrew to the Danube; a Hun leader who was unsuccessful in battle was doomed.

In the following year, 452, Attila was again on the march, invading northern Italy and holding court in the emperor's palace in Milan. Pope Leo the Great sent an envoy to Attila begging him not to attack Rome, warning him that the Goth Alaric, who had sacked Rome in 410, had died shortly afterwards. The Huns had no need of such dire warnings; Attila's army, ravaged by sickness, was forced to withdraw from Italy and return to Pannonia. In 453, in the arms of a Germanic beauty Ildiko (immortalized in Germanic legend as Kriemhild), Attila died of a stroke. It was the last of his many wedding nights.

The fratricidal rivalries of Attila's numerous sons left the Huns leaderless, and they were conquered by a coalition of tribes under the leadership of Aldarich and the Gepidae. The victorious coalition now controlled eastern Hungary and signed a treaty with the Byzantine empire, ruled from Constantinople. The Huns soon lost their ethnic identity and were absorbed among the local peoples.

From 470 to 485 Euric, king of the Visigoths, was one of the most powerful figures in western Europe. He had seized the throne by the time-honoured method of murdering his brother, conquered most of Spain, and crossed the Rhône to occupy Provence. Euric appreciated the superior culture of the Romans of Provence, preserved and encouraged their efforts, and appointed Romans to high office. He was the first Visigoth king to codify the law, and one of the few to die a natural death, in 484 at Arles. Euric's son, Alaric II, was no match for his powerful rival, the Frankish king Clovis. In 507 Alaric II fell in battle near Poitiers, according to legend at Clovis' own hand, and the Frankish king captured Bordeaux and Toulouse.

THE MEROVINGIANS

Clovis had been converted to Christianity by his Burgundian wife, Saint Clotilda. Most of the Germanic kings had accepted the Arian heresy, but Clovis was rigorously orthodox, following the creed agreed at the Council of Nicea. The common people of Gaul and Spain were also orthodox and thus welcomed the Franks. The bishop and historian Gregory of Tours wrote a century later: 'Everyone fervently and lovingly longs for the domination of the Franks'. Alaric's death was seen as God's judgment on the Arian heresy.

The Merovingians traced their royal lineage back to a legendary ancestor Merovech, and through a mythical sea monster to the gods. It was therefore a sacral monarchy, but their authority was enhanced by the more convincing demonstration of military prowess. Clovis became pre-eminent among the Frankish chiefs by defeating Syagrius, the last Roman governor of Gaul, near Soissons in 486 and then crushing the Alemanni in 496, and the Visigoths in 507. He consolidated his power by slaughtering all rival Frankish chiefs, and was formally acknowledged as sole king of the Franks by being raised upon his warriors' shields. Clovis was thus both a sacral and a military monarch.

Clovis was checked by the armies of the Ostrogoth Theodoric, Alaric's father-in-law and ally, at Arles and Carcassonne, and died in Paris in 511. Clovis had been the first of the Merovingian kings to control most of Gaul, and his conversion to orthodox Christianity allied the Franks with the Gallo-Romans. Intermarriage between the two peoples was now far from exceptional, and the Germanic and the Roman were inextricably entwined. Although tribal elements remained, the Franks were no longer a Germanic tribe, but a European people.

When Clovis died, all his sons inherited his kingly grace. It was believed that the blood in their veins gave them magical powers: they could make the crops grow by walking across the fields; they could interpret bird-song and the calls of the wild beasts; and they were invincible in battle, provided they did not cut their hair. The kingdom was effectively divided up, and the sons set about murdering one another. The people saw no reason to object to this practice. They believed that the more people who held magical powers the better, and that when some were killed, this merely proved their magic to have been weak. By contrast, the Vandals, whose name has unjustly become synonymous with wanton destruction, were the only Germanic tribe which favoured primogeniture to ensure an orderly transfer of power. The Merovingians only began to accept this notion 200 years after their conversion to Christianity.

The Franks were defined as free men, and only free men had any legal status. The Frankish people (*populus Francorum*) were nevertheless divided according to a hierarchy of dependency, and included both ethnic Franks and Gallo-Romans. Slaves were excluded from membership. Between the king and the people stood the nobility, an aristocracy of both blood and service. Kings consulted these powerful magnates who gave their consent in the name of the people, and who also executed the royal will. Strong kings made use of the nobility to keep the people in line, while weak kings were obliged to make concessions to the noble ruling class.

THE IMPACT OF CHRISTIANITY

When Clovis was baptized, his people, according to Germanic custom, followed suit. His kingdom was now religiously uniform, the Church cooperated fully with the state, and fellow-Christians welcomed his occupation of Visigothic territory. The Merovingian kings ruled a national Church. They called councils, nominated bishops (most of whom initially came from the Roman senatorial nobility, like Gregory of Tours), and made use of ecclesiastics in the royal service.

Merovingian Christianity amounted to little more than a belief in the miraculous, and many pagan elements remained. In this, the Franks were no different from many other contemporary Christianized people, and the practical effects of conversion were minimal. Clovis continued to murder and plunder without moral scruples. Although pagan gods were demoted to the level of evil spirits, they still received sacrifices from their erstwhile devotees to ensure that

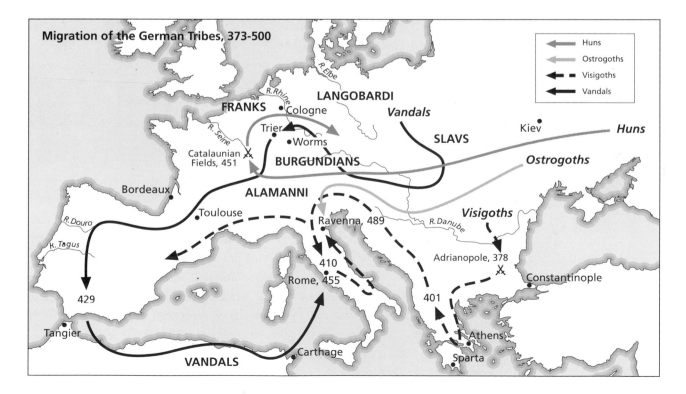

Migration of the German Tribes, 373–500

Saint Boniface (c.680–c.754), originally known as Wynfrith, was an Anglo-Saxon from Wessex. The 'Apostle of the Germans' went to Germany as a missionary in 718. He was consecrated bishop in 723 and became archbishop in 732. In 754 he resigned the archbishopric of Mainz, resumed his missionary work, and was murdered by pagan Frisians.

they did not get up to any mischief. Barbarous practices such as trial by ordeal continued for centuries.

The Frankish nobility founded monasteries and churches on their estates as capital investments and sources of income over which they maintained strict control. They could appoint and dismiss priests, a practice often attacked by the Church. There was, however, a vigorous popular Christianity whose hero was Saint Martin of Tours, an ordinary soldier who became a monk and a bishop. It was believed that Christ, who had taken on the form of a beggar, had met him and shared his cloak, which subsequently became revered as the Merovingian kings' most powerful relic.

The organization and ministry of the Merovingian Church declined, but it remained within the orthodox faith, and enough survived to be rapidly revived by the Carolingians, a dynasty which came to power in 751. Above all, the Church upheld the tradition of classical education. Few had mastered the Latin language; these *literati* were mostly clerics, and later a handful of educated women. Nobility and commoners were mostly classed as *illiterati* with no access to classical culture. Christianity had absorbed a great deal of classical culture, first Greek and then Latin, from the time of Saint Paul, and the process was to continue in medieval scholasticism. The Church fathers taught that faith and reason coexisted happily, and thus the seven liberal arts (grammar, dialectics, rhetoric, arithmetic, geometry, music, and astronomy) were seen as prerequisites of the higher, theological truths.

The Franks also absorbed the practical culture of the Gallo-Romans. They learnt how to bake bread and make wine, cultivate fruit and vegetables, make and lay bricks, blow glass and fashion iron implements for agriculture. They learned advanced techniques of administration, economics, and jurisprudence. While the

ET SYRIAM SOBAL · ET CONVERTIT
IOAB · ET PERCUSSIT EDOM IN VAL
LE SALINARUM · XII MILIA ·

Carolingian cavalry are represented in an Irish manuscript from the library at St. Gall, c.750. The heavily-armed cavalry formed the core of the Frankish army. Protected by a light chain-mail tunic and metal helmet and armed with a shield, short sword and lance, all of the highest quality, they were a formidable force.

practical problems of daily life were tackled in a manner which saved the Merovingians from complete atrophy, the resilience of paganism to Christianity was leading to cultural and intellectual decline. An impetus from outside was needed for the Christian and classical tradition to take firm root.

A number of Irish monks, following the lead of the first and greatest of the Irish missionaries, Saint Columban, had established important foundations in Europe. The Anglo-Saxon missionaries who followed, led by the English Benedictine, Saint Willibrod, in 690, had an even greater impact. The Anglo-Saxons, unlike the Irish, had been converted by the Romans and were rigorously orthodox. Theirs was a far richer and more advanced culture, with a remarkable literature in both Latin and the vernacular, and the intellectual achievements of Anglo-Saxon clerics placed them far above the other Germanic churchmen.

Saint Boniface of Crediton arrived in Frisia in 718. In the following years he established a number of monastic foundations in Hessen, Thuringia, Bavaria, Westphalia, and Württemberg, and he did much to reform the Frankish Church. He was murdered by heathen Frisians in about 754, and was buried in Fulda, his tomb soon becoming a popular shrine. The monastery at Fulda became a major missionary centre; the Franks no longer needed help from outside to propagate the gospel, and the Church thrived on the foundations laid by Saint Boniface.

THE CAROLINGIANS

It was a fortunate historical coincidence that the missionary activities of the Irish and the Anglo-Saxons corresponded with the rise of the Carolingians. The Merovingians were in steady decline, but the magical royal blood still ran in their veins. The Carolingians were 'mayors of the palace' or governors of Austrasia, an area comprising north-eastern France and parts of western and central Germany. They became the most powerful of the Frankish noble families and they soon were kings in all but name; foreign powers and the papacy dealt with them rather than with the Merovingians. Thus, the Carolingian Pepin of Héristal, who styled himself duke and prince of the Franks, was the effective ruler during several weak Merovingian reigns. His bastard son Charles Martel defeated the Alemanni and the Bavarians, drove back the Moslems in a ferocious battle in 732 in the region between Tours and Poitiers, and five years later liberated Burgundy and Languedoc from the Moslems.

Having first convinced a popular assembly that the Merovingians had lost their kingly grace, Charles Martel's son Pepin III 'the Short' made the decisive move to depose them. He had also secured the consent of Pope Zacharias, who used his apostolic authority to command that Pepin be made king. In 751 he was named king in place of Childeric III, and was anointed by the Frankish bishops. Pope Zacharias had assured Pepin that he supported his claim to the throne on the Augustinian grounds that 'it is better that he who has the power should be king, rather than he who lacks kingly power'.

Pepin was elected king in the manner of the Franks, but he lacked the magical powers inherent in royal blood. He therefore sought the Church's blessing, which was given in a unique form of unction designed to show that his kingship came not through his blood, but from God. Pepin was thus the first monarch to rule by the grace of God. To underline the importance of this act, Pepin was anointed on two occasions, the second time, with his two sons Charles the Great and Carloman, by Pope Stephen II in 754. The second unction married the new concept of monarchy by divine right with the Germanic concept of magic power carried by blood. To insure against any weakening of the hereditary principle, the Frankish magnates were threatened with excommunication if they dared to choose a king from another family. The Carolingians had created a hereditary dynasty that ruled 'by the grace of God'.

For the Carolingian monarchy to work effectively it was essential that the aristocracy should accept the king's leadership. Both the king by the grace of God and the nobility, were subject to the same law, they were partners in government; royal absolutism was precluded. Authority centred on the Carolingian court, which provided the model for medieval Europe. Lay and spiritual magnates attended the court to offer advice, receive orders, or promote their individual causes. A permanent staff of royal servants had originally domestic functions as their titles suggest: treasurer, steward, cup-bearer, and marshal. The office of mayor of the palace was abolished by the Carolingians, since they had used this position to usurp the crown. These officials' functions soon extended far beyond the royal household. The treasurer became responsible for administration of the royal estates and finances. The marshal, who was later called constable (*comes stabuli*), was originally the supervisor of the stables, but later administered the army. The offices of steward and cup-bearer became honorary, and by the time of Otto the Great, all four offices were symbolic of the nobles' subservience to the king, for example on official occasions like the coronation.

The monarch and the Church were mutually dependent. The king's clerical entourage was organized by Pepin III in the royal chapel (the word originating from the Carolingians' most sacred relic, the cloak – *capella* – of Saint Martin). By the time of Charles the Great, all the scribal and archival duties of the administration were handled by these clerics, for hardly any laymen knew Latin, or were even literate. The scribes were headed by the chancellor who, although subordinate to the arch-chaplain or head of the king's chapel, was soon to become the most powerful of the royal officials; the title and importance of the office survives to this day.

Both the Merovingians and the Carolingians had tried to unify their kingdoms by requiring personal allegiance from all their subjects, but they failed in the attempt. Many noblemen had ancient rights and privileges which left them immune to these demands. Kings therefore coopted the nobles by giving them power and wealth, and raising them above their peers. These imperial aristocrats served the king because they knew that it was in their best interests to do so. It was only when the monarchy declined in the late ninth century that they broke loose to pursue their own ends.

Local administration was centred on the ancient Germanic districts (*Gaue*) in the east, and on the Roman administrative districts (*civitates*) in the west. In the *Gaue* the local nobility presided over the courts of law, in the *civitates* the king's agents, the *comites,* acted as judges and looked after the crown's interests. The royal official with judicial functions was known by the Latin title *comes* (count), or by the Germanic *grafio*. The counts managed large estates, often with ancient rights and privileges. Many treated their counties as their own fiefdoms, helped themselves to parts of the royal demesne and passed their positions on to their sons. The nobility gradually became hereditary.

CONQUEST AND CONVERSION: THE EMPIRE OF CHARLES THE GREAT

Charles the Great, 'Charlemagne' (768–814) revived the Roman empire and united much of Europe. His Frankish empire created a diverse European community in constant tension between the monarchy and regional aristocracies. He presided over the Carolingian renaissance, a revival of cultural life within the Frankish Church after the decline under the Merovingians. He was fully aware of the state's need for educated people, and combed Europe for intellectuals to bring to his court, surrounding himself with a brilliant assembly of Lombards, Visigoths, Irish, and Anglo-Saxons. He practised what he preached and attempted, at an advanced age, to learn to read and write. The court school, founded by Pepin III, was converted into an imperial academy, in which gifted pupils were given exceptional training. However, the ability to write was largely confined to the monasteries, so monks played an important role in the administration and the law; it was not until the end of the eleventh century that merchants learned to read and write in order to

An idealized reliquary bust of Charles the Great (Charlemagne) made of gold and silver and encrusted with semi-precious stones, made in Aachen in 1349.

A fourteenth-century manuscript depiction of Charles the Great and his soldiers in a massive wooden carriage.

conduct their affairs efficiently. Although the Franks regarded themselves as the true heirs of the Romans, studies were made of the linguistic and ethnic characteristics of the Germanic peoples, of whom the Franks were considered to be the most developed. In 786 the first mention was made of the German language (*lingua theodisca*), and Charles the Great ordered that a Grammar be written. In 794 it was announced that this language, old high German, was the equal of Hebrew, Latin and Greek, and Latin literature was translated into the vernacular. However, German was not generally accepted as a literary language until the twelfth century. The 'Hohenstaufen classics' were written in a common language, free from dialect

Charles the Great fought more than fifty campaigns, which he saw as crusades for the unity and protection of Christendom. For three years he shared power with his younger brother Carloman, and became sole king in 771. In the following year he embarked on his campaigns against the Saxons, which were to have profound effects on the course of German history. The Saxons, despite their fierce resistance, were forced to submit to the king; in 777 the imperial Assembly met on Saxon soil at Paderborn, and Charles the Great prematurely proclaimed Saxony part of the Frankish kingdom. The Saxons renewed their efforts to drive out the invaders, but eventually were defeated in a bloody battle in 782, after which 4,500 Saxon warriors were beheaded. The survivors were forcibly converted to Christianity, and whole populations were dispossessed, their lands settled by subjects loyal to the Frankish king. By 804 all resistance had ended and the Frankish kingdom extended as far as the River Elbe. The Saxons were gradually absorbed among the Franks and came to share the same faith. A century later Widukind of Corvey put an optimistic gloss on this process: 'The Saxons who once were comrades and friends of the Franks have become their brothers and, by virtue of the Christian faith, virtually one people with them'.

In 774 Charles the Great, at the behest of Pope Adrian, had annexed Lombardy, and was recognized by the pope as protector of Rome (*patricius Romanorum*), an important step towards attaining the imperial throne. In 788 he deposed Tassilo III, duke of Bavaria and son-in-law of the Lombard king Desiderius, and in 791 he defeated the Avars in the south-east, who had allied with the Bavarians.

Charles the Great then attacked the Arabs in Spain and, having defeated their divided forces, established a military frontier which extended as far as the River Ebro. Similar frontier zones, or marches, were established in the south-east as far as Lake Balaton and across the Elbe south of Magdeburg. He was now master of Europe, his only rivals being the distant Byzantine emperor and the even more remote Harun-al-Raschid, caliph of Baghdad, with whom he exchanged an amicable correspondence. On Christmas Day 800, he was crowned Emperor of the Romans in a dramatic ceremony at Saint Peter's Basilica.

Charles the Great did not want to be known simply as Emperor of the Romans, and was concerned lest the title cause problems with the rival emperor in

A magnificent ivory carving representing the Archangel Michael fighting a dragon. This Carolingian masterpiece from the Rhineland once formed part of a book-cover and was carved in about 800.

Constantinople. After lengthy deliberations he arrived at an ingenious circumlocution, describing himself as 'emperor governing Rome' (*imperator Romanum gubernans*) and also as 'king of the Franks and Lombards'. His right to rule was emphasized by the insistence that he was 'crowned by God'. By this means the Frankish, Christian, and Roman aspects of his monarchy were combined in a formula that was also acceptable to the Byzantines. In 812 the two emperors recognized one another, the Byzantine was Emperor of the Romans, the Frank simply emperor. Soon the two empires were described as the eastern empire (*imperium orientale*) and the western empire (*imperium occidentale*). This clear distinction was underlined by Charles the Great's court scholars, who described him as the 'father of Europe'. The Frankish empire, the west, and Europe were now seen as one and the same.

THE RISE OF THE EAST-FRANKISH GERMAN EMPIRE

The fact that Charles the Great was both king and emperor made the question of the succession particularly vexing. Kingship was divisible, but the imperial office was not. In 806 he divided the realm into three parts for his three sons, but he made all three responsible for the defence of the Church. The youngest Pepin died in 810, the oldest Charles in 811. In 813 Charles the Great ordered his remaining son, Louis the Pious, to be crowned co-emperor in the imperial chapel at Aachen. Charles the Great died the following year and in 817 Louis the Pious decided that the empire, like the Church, could not be divided. Divine guidance was sought in three days of fasting and prayer, and Louis' eldest son Lothar was designated co-emperor. Lothar's two brothers, Pepin and Louis the German, were then appointed as subordinate kings.

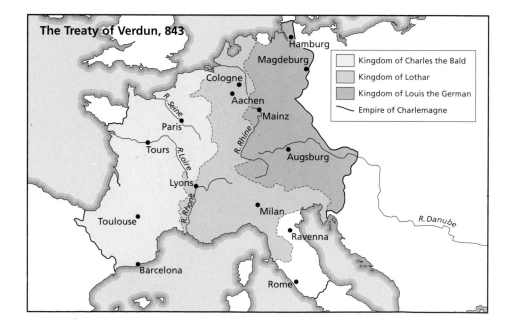

In 823 Louis' second wife Judith gave birth to a son, known to history as Charles the Bald. She was an ambitious woman who persuaded her husband to change the imperial ordinance of 817 and divide the empire into four parts. Lothar, Pepin, and Louis were enraged at this diminution of their inheritance and were supported by the majority of the aristocracy and the episcopate. They rose up against their father and there followed four years of civil war. The father died in 840, and Lothar's attempt to force his brothers' submission ended in disaster on the battlefield at Fontenoy in 841. Skirmishes continued between the brothers until the nobles, tired of continual strife, forced them to accept the Treaty of Verdun in 843.

The treaty granted Lothar the Frankish heartland from the North Sea to Italy, and from the Saône and Rhône to the Rhine. Louis the German was given the eastern territory, Charles the Bald the western. As emperor, Lothar claimed precedence over his brothers, but they freed themselves as far as possible from his control. The empire was further divided on Lothar's death in 855, when his share was subdivided among his sons. Louis II became emperor and received Italy. Charles was given Provence and parts of Burgundy. Lothar II was given the remainder, including the Frankish capital Aachen, and the area was later called Lotharingia (Lorraine) in his honour. When Charles of Provence died, his share was divided between his two brothers.

As a result of these divisions the empire no longer coincided with the Frankish kingdom, but was confined to Italy. North of the Alps Charles the Bald and Louis the German ruled virtually independent kingdoms. When his brothers died, Charles III (the Fat), the youngest son of Louis the German, restored the territorial unity of the empire. The west Frankish line then died out, except for an

The entrance door, known as the 'King's Hall', to the monastery at Lorsch dates to the second half of the ninth century. This Benedictine monastery was elevated to the status of imperial abbey by Charles the Great and was the burial place of some of the East-Frank Carolingians.

under-age grandson of Charles the Bald, and Charles the Fat was thus able to add their lands to his kingdom. In 881 he was made emperor, and Charles the Great's empire restored, but Charles the Fat proved unable to defend it against the ravages of the Norsemen. In 887 he was deposed, and the Carolingian empire was divided into five kingdoms, of which only East Francia remained under a Carolingian, Arnulf of Carinthia, Charles the Fat's nephew. The other kings were usurpers and obliged to pay homage to Arnulf, not because they respected his dynastic claims, but because he forced their submission. He was almost the last of the Carolingians to wear the imperial crown, but imperial unity was now a thing of the past. Arnulf was crowned emperor in 896, died three years later, and was succeeded by Louis the Child. The imperial crown had become an empty symbol fought over by insignificant Italian nobles. No-one north of the Alps seemed to be interested in this worthless title.

Europe was now beset with civil war between rival nobles and was invaded by Vikings from the north, Arabs from the south and Hungarians from the east. Louis the Child was unable to offer his unfortunate subjects any protection. Tribal leaders took matters into their own hands and struggled for prominence. The Hungarians plundered Moravia and Saxony, and defeated Luitpold of Bavaria at Pressburg in 907. Three years later they decimated Louis the Child's army near Augsburg. The wretched king died in the following year without issue.

The Lotharingians elected the Carolingian Charles the Simple, a great-grandson of Charles the Bald, as Louis' successor, but this was unacceptable to the nobles to the east of the Rhine. They had become immensely powerful in the long period of civil war and border raids, and had established themselves in Saxony, Bavaria and Franconia. They elected as their new king a non-Carolingian, Conrad I, who had recently become duke of Franconia. Conrad was determined to crush his rivals, but died in 918 as a result of the wounds he received during a campaign against Arnulf of Bavaria. The Franconian and Saxon nobles, meeting in Fritzlar, elected the most powerful among them, Henry of Saxony, known as 'the Fowler', to be their new king. Henry knew he could not count on the Church's support, so, to demonstrate his independence, he refused to be anointed by the Archbishop of Mainz. He promptly set about making the nobles pay him homage, uniting the Franconians, Saxons, Swabians, Bavarians, and the dissident Lotharingians in a feudal contract which recognized their tribal powers. Henry prudently left the nobles well alone, realizing that he was dependent on their loyalty and had little influence over them. He was, however, determined that this newly united polity, the Kingdom of the East Franks, soon to be called the Kingdom of the Germans, should not fall apart on his death. In 929 he issued an ordinance appointing his second son Otto sole king, so breaking with the Frankish tradition of sons sharing their inheritance, and establishing the German principle of impartibility.

Henry negotiated an armistice that lasted nine years, and used the breathing-space to build a strong defensive frontier and strengthen his cavalry. After a

The richly ornamented 'Tassilo chalice' was presented by the Bavarian Duke Tassilo and his Lombard wife Liuitberga to the abbey at Kremsmünster, which the duke founded in 777. Tassilo was the independent Duke of Bavaria who was eventually forced by Charles the Great, intent on centralizing his kingdom, to renounce his duchy, and entered a monastery where he spent the rest of his life.

The coronation of Otto the Great

Otto I, known as 'the Great', ascended the throne on 7 August 936. His father, Henry 'the Fowler', had formally designated Otto as his successor at a court assembly in Erfurt during his final illness. Otto's coronation at Aachen was described in detail by the aristocratic monk Widukind of Corvey. Outside the church, the great lords met in the hall to swear allegiance, while inside clerics and laymen waited to give Otto their formal acclamation. Archbishop Hildebert of Mainz presented him to the assembled people with the words 'Behold, I bring you here King Otto, chosen by God, designated by the mighty lord Henry, and elevated to the throne by all the princes. If you are satisfied with this choice show it by raising your right hands to heaven!' The people unanimously greeted their sovereign with unbounded enthusiasm.

Otto was then led to the altar and presented with the insignia: the sword with which he was to ward off the enemies of Christ and maintain peace among the Frankish people; the cloak and bracelets symbolic of Christian kingly power; and the orb and sceptre. He was then anointed and crowned. He heard mass from Charles the Great's throne, so underlining the fact that he was reviving the Carolingian empire. The ceremonies concluded with a sumptuous banquet, at which the powerful dukes of Lorraine, Franconia, Swabia, and Bavaria officiated in their symbolic roles of chamberlain, steward, cupbearer, and marshal. Otto's guests

The imperial crown designed for the coronation of Otto I, 'the Great' (912–73). The plaque shows King Solomon as the symbol of wisdom. West German, c.962.

received luxurious presents and gracefully retired.

This splendidly theatrical ceremony left a vivid impression on contemporaries and remains one of the most dramatic events in medieval history. All the great dukes were there except Siegfried of Merseburg, the Saxon leader, who was defending the eastern borders of the empire. The ceremony was designed to demonstrate that Otto inherited his throne from his father, that his coronation depended on the consent of the magnates and the people (*populus Francorum atque Saxonum*), and on the grace of God.

The coronation was a direct response to Louis IV's coronation in Laon on 19 June and defied any future West Frankish claims to the empire, as well as being a show of unity at home. Furthermore, it implied that Otto would follow in Charles the Great's footsteps and be crowned emperor in Rome. His sacramental anointing raised him above the stem-dukes (clan-leaders), while emphasizing that they were integral to the kingdom. A distinction was made between the indivisible kingdom and the family estates of the king, which could be divided up among his heirs.

number of campaigns against the Slavs across the border formed by the rivers Elbe and Saale and the Bohemian forest, he built a forward defensive area by fortifying such towns as Merseburg and Meissen, which he had taken from the Slavs. In 933, after only six years, Henry broke the armistice with the Hungarians at the battle of Riade. The Magyars fled rather than engage a superior force, and Henry won a victory which gained him admiration throughout Christendom. He contemplated travelling to Rome to claim the imperial crown, but in 936 died of a stroke.

THE OTTONIANS

Henry's son Otto, known as 'the Great', ascended the throne on 7 August 936. By his father's ordinance of 929, he had formally been designated successor. However Otto's brothers, Thankmar and Henry, did not accept the impartible succession, and were supported by the dukes of Lorraine and Franconia, who resented the king's attempts to strengthen the monarchy. Soon they were joined by members of the Saxon aristocracy whom they had successfully bribed. The kingdom was plunged into a protracted civil war which Otto was fortunate to survive. Thankmar died in 938, the quarrel with Henry was settled, and Otto made his brother duke of Bavaria. One by one the dissident dukes died off, and Otto gave their duchies to members of his own family; Swabia was awarded to his elder son, Liudolf, and his son-in-law, Conrad the Red, was given Lotharingia.

Soon the royal dukes began to behave like their predecessors. Conrad the Red joined Liudolf in 'Liudolf's Rebellion' in 953, which was supported by many nobles. The Hungarians supported the rebels, with the result that many of the rebels abandoned the cause, for the plundering Magyars filled them with understandable alarm. In 955 Otto crushed the Hungarians at Lechfeld, the greatest battle of the century, and resistance was broken. Germany was freed from the Magyar menace, and the Hungarians ceased to be freebooting marauders and became a sedentary people. The bishopric of Passau began the conversion of the country, which was successfully completed under Otto III, so Hungary, unlike Russia, culturally became part of western Europe. Otto learnt a bitter lesson from the rebellion: he could not rely on his own family to shore up his power. Now he turned to the Church for support.

Otto relied on the statesmanlike advice of his youngest brother, Bruno, who had taken holy orders and served as chancellor, arch-chaplain, and archbishop of Cologne. When Conrad the Red was deposed, Bruno was also made archduke of Lotharingia, a new title combining the roles of archbishop and duke. In the royal chapel Bruno trained selected clerics, who were then appointed to high positions in the Ottonian Church. This new elite combined lay and spiritual functions; the bishops and abbots were given jurisdictional powers, as well as the right to collect taxes, mint coins, and control local markets. Church and state now became inextricably intertwined

Church lands, capably administered by loyal clerics, provisioned the court as it travelled the country. The Church also financed the bulk of Otto's armies. Although the system worked admirably under Otto, it bore within it the seeds of conflict. Otto and Bruno helped to make the Church rich and powerful and thus more worldly, a fact that was soon to fill zealous reformers with horror. Otto strengthened the monarchy, but in doing so superseded the pope. Ambitious popes were soon to claim the supremacy of the spiritual over the temporal.

Henry I's victories against the Slavs and Magyars had not been decisive enough to secure the frontier from marauding bands. Otto was therefore determined to reinforce the marches. His army was defeated by the Bohemians and it took a long time before this powerful nation was subdued. To the north he asserted German hegemony over the Slavs as far as the River Oder, and formed two vast marches. The Trans-Elbian March, covering approximately Holstein and Mecklenburg, was conquered by Hermann Billung, one of Otto's closest lieutenants, whose family were later to become dukes of Saxony. The Great March of Gero to the south was much larger and when the Margrave Gero died in 965, the march was divided up into more manageable units.

Otto's eastern policy depended not only on the sword but also on the cross. The heathen Slavs were forcibly converted, their princes usually the first to be baptized. New bishoprics were founded in Brandenburg, Havelberg, and Oldenburg to supervise this missionary work. The Danes were converted and further bishoprics founded in Aarhus, Ripen, and Schleswig. Magdeburg was elevated to an archbishopric to supervise missionary work in the east, and Russia might well have come under the Roman Church had not the Grand Duchess Olga's son, somewhat to her chagrin, showed a preference for Byzantine missionaries. This gesture of filial defiance was to have profound consequences, in that Russia was henceforth bound to the eastern rather than the western Church and thus never became an integral part of Europe. German missionaries were also active in Bohemia once Duke Boleslav I had submitted to Otto in 950, and the new bishopric of Prague was placed under the archbishopric of Mainz.

Thirteenth-century stone statues from the cathedral in Magdeburg of Otto 1 'the Great', with his first wife, the English princess Edgitha. The emperor holds an orb and sceptre. Magdeburg was the centre of missionary activity in the East and Otto the Great had made it an archbishopric.

Otto I, the small figure on the left, presents Christ with a model of Magdeburg Cathedral. He is accompanied by Saint Mauritius and an angel, and observed by Saint Peter, the two patron saints of the cathedral. The ivory carving (c.975) is probably from northern Italy.

The East March, roughly the equivalent of present day Austria (Österreich – from *regio orientalis* or *Ostarrichi*), was reorganized in much the same way as the marches of Gero and Billung, except that the area was fully Germanized. After the annexation in 1938 Hitler renamed Austria the East March (*Ostmark*) to emphasize its historical origins as a border province of the German empire.

In 951 Berengar of Ivrea (forty miles north of Turin) seized the throne of Italy, and Adelheid, the young widow of Lothar, the previous king, appealed to Otto for help against the usurper. Otto seized the opportunity, conquered Lombardy, married Adelheid, and proclaimed himself king of Lombardy. Otto made approaches to Rome about the imperial crown but was snubbed. Since he had pressing matters to attend to in the north, he returned to Germany, but came back to Italy ten years later when the pope begged for help against Berengar.

Pope John XII crowned Otto emperor on the feast of the Purification of the Virgin, 2 February 962, in a magnificent service in Saint Peter's. Although his empire was consciously modelled on that of Charles the Great, Otto did not claim to be ruler of the west, and the emperorship was now closely linked to the German monarchy. Henceforth German kings travelled to Rome to be crowned emperor by the pope. This required a special relationship with the pope and involvement in Italian politics. Initially, the emperor was senior partner in the dual rule with the pope. Under the *Ottonianum*, the pact that Otto made with the papacy, the emperor was given decisive influence over the election of the pope, who was obliged to swear allegiance to the emperor. The emperor was king of Germany and also king of Italy, and the two kingdoms were separate, but linked in a personal union. After 1032 the emperors were also kings of Burgundy, which likewise remained separate under the personal union.

In order to assert his authority over the pope and the Romans, Otto deposed John XII and forced the Romans to submit to his will. As soon as his back was turned, the Romans elected another pope. During his third visit to Italy, beginning in 966, Otto extended his influence to the south, confronting the Byzantines in the process. After a series of battles, Apulia was ceded to Byzantium and Capua and Benevento to Germany. Peace was concluded and Otto's son, the co-emperor Otto II, was married in Saint Peter's to Princess Theophano of Byzantium, who proved to be a remarkable empress. Most important of all, the German empire was now formally recognized by the Byzantine emperor.

Otto I died in 973, not long after a majestic ceremony at Quedlinburg at which he received delegations from the lay and spiritual princes, and delegates from Byzantium, Rome, Russia, Hungary, Bohemia, Poland, Denmark, and even Africa. It was a splendid culmination to an extraordinary reign. But his kingdom was far from secure. His successor Otto II was faced with a series of nobles' revolts, which started in southern Germany under Henry the Wrangler of Bavaria, spread to Swabia and Lorraine, and then to Poland and Bohemia. The West Franks were intent on winning back Lotharingia. They raided Aachen, but Otto II narrowly escaped, counter-attacked, and reached Paris. Having stabilized the situation, both at home and against the Franks, Otto now turned to Italy to support the pope in his struggles against the Roman aristocracy. When the pope's position was secured, he rashly decided to attack both the Byzantines and the Arabs, who had begun to raid Sicily in 976. After a successful campaign against the Byzantines in Apulia, he marched south against the Arabs in Calabria. He suffered a crushing defeat at Cape Colonne, and only just escaped with his life. Then Otto received the shattering news that the Slavs had taken advantage of his absence in Italy to win back everything they had lost east of the Elbe to Otto the Great, and that the Danes had begun to raid northern Germany. While still in Italy, Otto II contracted malaria and died in 983 at the age of twenty-eight. He was the only German emperor to be buried in Saint Peter's.

CHAPTER 2

From the Ottonians to the Salians

In 983, Otto III was still a minor but the empire was in the capable hands of his grandmother Adelheid, his mother Theophano, and their advisors, the archbishops of Mainz and Worms. They managed to secure the north, hold the Slavs in check and persuade Hugh Capet (king of France) to abandon the gains of his predecessors in Lotharingia. In 994 Otto III reached his majority at the age of fifteen and immediately announced ambitious plans for Italy and the empire. He was a charming, fascinating, intelligent, cultivated young man, and determined to emulate his greatest forebears.

A detail from Otto III's *Gospel-book* (c.1000) shows the emperor seated in majesty, receiving the homage of the nations, surrounded by archbishops and dignitaries carrying his arms. Elsewhere, representatives from the Slavs, Germany, Gaul and Rome approach the throne with gifts for the heir to the Caesars.

THE END OF THE OTTONIAN DYNASTY

In 996 Otto travelled to Italy to receive the homage of the
nobles. While on his way to Rome for his coronation the pope
died, and Otto appointed his cousin and personal chaplain,
Bruno of Carinthia, to the holy see as Gregory V. Empire and
papacy were now closely associated and Otto was proclaimed
emperor of the Romans. But as soon as Otto travelled north to
his beloved palace at Aachen, the Romans elected an anti-pope
and expelled Otto's cousin. Otto returned to Rome and suppressed the rebellion with extraordinary brutality. He built a
palace on the Palatine Hill, and by making Rome an imperial
city he ignored the Donation of Constantine which gave Rome
to the pope, brazenly insisting it was a forgery. This was unacceptable both to the popes and to the people of Rome, and
when the Romans revolted in 1001 the emperor was forced to
flee the city. Otto was convinced that this was divine judgment
for his failures and declared that he would shortly renounce
the imperial Roman crown and live the life of a hermit. His
sincerity was never put to the test. He died childless in the following year at the age of twenty-two.

Christ crowns Henry II and
Kunigunde, flanked by the
apostles Peter and Paul, from
an illuminated manuscript of
the Gospels of Bamberg,
c.1010. In the lower portion,
representatives of the peoples
and tribes pay homage to the
royal couple. The central
crowned figure, symbolising
Rome, offers the emperor the
symbol of worldly rule.
Coronations were acts of
immense symbolic signifi-
cance which underlined both
the spiritual and temporal
powers of the emperor.

Otto's successor, Henry II, was the son of Henry the Wrangler of Bavaria. He
realized that the key to the empire lay in Germany and not in Rome and that any
attempt to revive the Roman empire was bound to fail. He was crowned in Mainz
and then made his royal progress throughout Germany. Secure at home, he
turned his attention to the powerful Duke Boleslav Chobry of Poland, who had
become duke of Bohemia and was creating a vast kingdom in the east which
rivalled his power in Germany. Although he was troubled by severe pangs of conscience, partially assuaged by founding a magnificent church in Bamberg, Henry
allied with heathen tribes who refused to convert to Christianity. There followed
a series of campaigns which held Boleslav in check, although he retained the
Silesian march (frontier zone) of Lusatia as a fief of the empire.

Henry campaigned in Italy in 1004 and was crowned king of the Lombards in
Pavia. It was not until ten years later that he went to Rome for the imperial
coronation. He suppressed a revolt in Rome and, in 1022, campaigned against the
Greeks in southern Italy and brought Salerno, Benevento and Capua back into the
empire. Henry II revived the Ottonianum (an affirmation of the Donation of
Constantine made by Otto the Great in 962), thus rejecting Otto III's attempts to
separate Rome from the Church.

Henry II's policy towards Burgundy was also similar to Otto the Great's. Otto had
married the king of Burgundy's sister and Henry was the nephew of Rudolf III of
Burgundy. Rudolf was childless and appointed Henry II his heir, promising to hand
over Basel as a guarantee of the seriousness of his intent. The Burgundian nobility,

Statues of Henry II and his wife Kunigunde decorate the doorway of Bamberg Cathedral. Henry II founded the magnificent cathedral at Bamberg, and was buried there. The foundation was in part an attempt to assuage his pangs of conscience for having allied with heathen tribes in order to defeat Duke Boleslav Chobry of Poland, who was posing a direct threat to Henry's power in Germany.

wishing to preserve their independence, objected vigorously to Rudolf's policy and Henry led two campaigns into Burgundy to assert his rights, but died before his uncle. His energetic successor, Conrad II, was to absorbthe kingdom of Burgundy into the German empire.

Henry II restored the territorial integrity of the Reich and strengthened the monarchy by paying close attention to Church affairs. He supervised the selection of bishops and was able to secure the appointment of many outstanding church-men. He encouraged Church reform and reformed a number of monasteries, for he was a deeply religious man and keenly aware of the important role played by the Church in educating imperial administrators. He was ever mindful of the economic potential of the efficient ecclesiastical estates which were an important source of revenue.

Henry II died on 13 July 1024 and was buried in his beloved cathedral in Bamberg. Since he had no heir, his remarkable wife Kunigunde – to whom Henry had often entrusted the affairs of state during his absences – took his place until a new king was elected. When Conrad II, the first of the new Salian dynasty, was given the imperial insignia, Kunigunde retired to a Benedictine nunnery.

THE SALIANS

The dynasty had changed, but Conrad II ruled according to Ottonian principles. In a famous episode in Constance in 1025, he received a delegation from Pavia which had come to plead forgiveness for having razed a royal castle on the death of Henry II. The envoys argued that when Henry died there was no king whom they could have offended. Conrad clearly distinguished between the kingdom and the king when he replied: 'The kingdom remains when the king is dead, just as the ship is still there when the helmsman falls'.

The transpersonal concept of statehood began when the Frankish custom of dividing their kingdoms among their sons ceased, but Conrad II was the first to enunciate clearly this principle. It implied that he laid claim to the entire Ottonian empire. This claim was rejected by many Italian nobles who offered the throne to the son of the king of France, Robert II. When Robert refused, they then offered it to the son of William of Aquitaine, who also refused. The Italian episcopate remained largely loyal to Conrad, and Conrad's campaign in Italy, which began in the spring of 1026, started in auspicious circumstances. Within a year he had subjected the kingdom of Italy to his will, and subdued the southern marches. He was crowned emperor at St Peter's at Easter in 1027. The coronation was a magnificent affair attended by King Canute of England and Denmark, and King Rudolf III of Burgundy. Conrad II was thus recognized as the equal of his illustrious predecessors, Otto the Great and Henry II.

As Henry II's successor, Conrad claimed to be the heir to the throne of Burgundy. Rudolf III, who favoured another candidate, felt obliged to give way after Conrad's remarkable successes in Italy. Conrad had showed his determination to win Burgundy by seizing Basel, but when Rudolf died in September 1032 Conrad was fully occupied in Saxony, and Count Odo II of Champagne, Rudolf's nephew, claimed the crown, winning the support of a significant section of the Burgundian aristocracy. Conrad, who had already been given the crown by a delegation from Burgundy, acted quickly and was crowned in February 1033 in a church built by the Empress Adelheid in Payerne (Peterlingen). Although he concluded alliances with the king of France and with the archbishop of Milan which reinforced his extremely powerful position, it took him almost two years to bring Burgundy under his control.

The kingdom of Burgundy, as distinct from the duchy of Burgundy which was part of France, stretched from Luxeuil and Basel to Marseille and Nice, and represented a significant territorial gain, but it was difficult for the emperors to subdue. Although the virtually independent Burgundian aristocracy proved to be unruly subjects, the German emperors were determined to hold Burgundy for strategic reasons. As long as Burgundy was in German hands, however tenuously, the western Alpine passes to Italy were secure. The kingdom was vital to German interests in Italy.

Conrad did much to strengthen the position of the minor knights, whose military contributions he appreciated and whose support he needed against Aribert, the powerful archbishop of Milan. Aribert had sided with the aristocrats against the minor knights, who were demanding the right of inheritance over their estates, which could be taken away from them at the whim of their feudal lords. When Conrad travelled to Italy to settle the dispute which had reached a critical phase with the victory of the minor knights in the battle of Campo Malo in Lombardy, the archbishop chose to challenge the emperor.

Having made an unsuccessful attempt to storm Milan, on 28 May 1037 Conrad promulgated the *Constitutio de feudis* which made all fiefs, however small and insignificant, heritable. The new law applied initially only to Italy, but was soon adopted in Germany. It did much to strengthen a new class which stood between the mighty aristocrats and the peasantry. In Italy this class was made up largely of the minor knights, while in Germany they also included civil servants, the *Ministeriales*, who, although they were not free, possessed land and virtually became the lower aristocracy, serving their lords, both lay and episcopal. *Ministeriales* were the strongest supporters of the crown.

The emperor was forced to abandon the siege of Milan and Archbishop Aribert, thinking that Conrad was on the run,

A relief portrait of the emperor Henry II (973–1024) on a one-sided coin (*bracteate*) made in Augsburg.

The nave of the cathedral at Speyer, founded by Conrad II (990–1039).

Christ is depicted healing a paralytic in an illustration from Saint Mark's gospel in Henry III's *Golden Gospel-book*, c.1050.

Opposite: The Emperor Henry III (1017–56) hunting with a falcon. Hunting was the most popular pastime of the medieval elites. Superb and highly trained animals were both outward signs of wealth and prestige as well as means of demonstrating to the full their owners' skill and prowess. Hunting was seen not only as an art but as a science, and many treatises on hunting are also significant contributions to zoology and ornithology.

offered the Italian crown and even the imperial throne to Conrad's old rival in Burgundy, Odo of Champagne, who had taken advantage of Conrad's absence to attack the imperial palace in Aachen. The local nobles under the leadership of Duke Gozelo I, remained loyal to the emperor and on 15 November 1037 Odo's army was smashed in a bloody encounter at Bar-le-Duc, one of the the largest and most brutal battles of the age. Odo was killed and his banners were sent to the emperor in Italy.

Although he had failed to subdue Milan, Conrad II was no longer in any danger from the alliance between Aribert and Odo, and was therefore free to assert his authority in southern Italy. On his return to Germany he devoted himself mainly to Church affairs. Despite being damned as a simonist for the sale of benefices by his powerful ecclesiastical rivals, such as Aribert of Milan, Conrad nonetheless gave his full support to the reform movement, and did much to strengthen the imperial Church.

After a brief second and final campaign in Italy, Conrad II died in Utrecht in June 1039 at the age of forty-nine. He was buried in the magnificent cathedral in Speyer which he had begun and which was to be the greatest monument of the Salian dynasty, and the burial place of subsequent German emperors.

HENRY III

Conrad had made careful preparations for the succession of his son Henry III, who was elected king in 1027 at the age of ten. He was given an exceptional education by Bishop Brun of Augsburg and Bishop Egilbert of Freising, assisted by the court chaplain Wipo, and his able and energetic mother Gisela. He was made duke of

Bavaria in 1026 and when he reached his majority at the age of fourteen he ruled the duchy independently. In 1038 he became duke of Swabia and was crowned king of Burgundy. By the time of his father's death Henry was thus well prepared for the succession, and his election passed without difficulty.

According to custom, Henry travelled the length and breadth of the country to demonstrate his power and authority. Germany had no capital and the emperor had no official residence. Successful emperors were constantly on the move, and it is hardly surprising that the two most remarkable medieval statues, the equestrian figures in Bamberg and Magdeburg, show the monarch in the saddle. Queens were also without permanent residence and therefore accompanied their husbands on their journeys, playing an important part in the affairs of states as genuine partners with considerable power and influence.

Important decisions were taken at Assemblies (*Reichstage*) attended by high ecclesiastical dignitaries and the mightiest aristocrats. These Assemblies varied in size and duration and were only genuine *Reichstage* when matters of great national importance were under consideration. Church affairs were discussed at synods at which the king acted as an honorary president, although the meetings were chaired by the archbishop of Mainz as the primate of the German Church, or a papal legate, or sometimes the pope himself. Kings held courts wherever they travelled so that ordinary people could appeal for justice.

Medieval kings were desperately short of revenue, so this court on horseback made economic sense. The court could reside with the tenants of the royal demesne, whether lay or clerical, and took hospitality as payment. The primitive state of communications made this style of government effective both economically and politically. Excess production did not have to be shipped off to imperial granaries, and the court was always on the move, often travelling ten to twenty miles a day, keeping an eye on the kingdom. When emperors established a permanent court they soon lost control over the empire. Such charisma attached to the emperor that his visits were seen by ordinary folk as a guarantee against bad weather, poor crops, or the plague. He was the Lord's anointed, endowed with atavistic magic powers.

On his accession, Henry III was faced with a very dangerous situation in the east. Poland was in a state of chaos when Duke Mieszko II died in 1034, and his widow and son Casimir sought asylum in Germany. Similar confusion existed in Hungary on the death of King Stephen in 1038. Duke Bretislav I of Bohemia seized the opportunity to attack Poland, sacked Cracow, and captured the Polish capital Gnieszno. He returned to Prague with the highly prized remains of Saint Adalbert, the first Czech bishop of Prague, hoping to make Prague an archbishopric independent of Mainz. Henry, who was protecting the Polish heir, demanded that Bretislav hand over the booty. When this was refused he sent his armies against Bohemia and their Hungarian allies in 1039. Although Henry's forces initially suffered a serious reverse, the campaign reached a successful conclusion in

September 1041. Bretislav attended the Assembly at Regensburg where he begged for mercy. His duchy was restored and he proved a loyal vassal. Casimir returned to Poland and successfully established his authority, becoming known as Casimir the Renewer. Hungary still remained a thorn in Henry's flesh.

In 1041 the Hungarians deposed King Peter who committed himself to Henry III. In the third campaign against Hungary, in which Henry was assisted by Bretislav's Bohemians, the Hungarian usurper Aba was defeated and Peter was once again crowned king, in a spectacular ceremony in Székesfehérvár. Henry III now had loyal liegemen in Poland, Bohemia, and Hungary so that the eastern marches of his empire were secure. He was firmly established in Germany and ended his father's feud with Aribert of Milan. His marriage to Agnes, the daughter of Duke William V of Aquitaine, strengthened his position in Burgundy and after seven years of marriage and the birth of three daughters, a male heir was born – the future Henry IV.

In 1046 Henry went to Rome for his coronation. The ecclesiastical reform movement, which called for a more spiritual and apostolic life, had not had any effect on the see of Saint Peter. No fewer than three popes – Benedict IX, Silvester III, and Gregory VI – awaited Henry's arrival, each supported by powerful clans. Silvester replaced the deposed Benedict who, tired of his clerical career and anxious to become a respectable married man, had sold his pontifical office to John Gratianus, who was supported by the immensely rich Roman family, the Pierleoni. As Gregory VI he at once showed that he intended to take his duties seriously and won the approval of Peter Damian, prior of Fonte Avellana and leader of the reform movement in Italy. In blissful disregard of the circumstances of Gregory's ascension to the apostolic throne the prior proclaimed that the 'thousand-headed poisonous snake of simony' had been crushed underfoot and that a new apostolic golden age had begun. Gregory VI was not quite so certain. He knew that Henry III was a profoundly pious man, fully committed to the reform movement, and was uncertain whether he would accept his pontificate.

The king, who saw himself as Christ's deputy and as a latter-day David, could not overlook the scandalous circumstances of Gregory VI's appointment, and at the synod of Sutri both Gregory VI and Silvester III were deposed. A further synod was held in Rome at which Benedict IX was removed from office. Henry III was determined to find a non-Roman pope so that the Holy Father would not be entangled in Roman politics, to emphasize the universality of the Church, and to ensure that the Church was reformed at the centre. Bishop Suidger of Bamberg had no desire to move to Rome, but bowed to his liege lord's will and was crowned Clement II. He remained bishop of Bamberg, which gave him a handsome income and a comforting insurance policy, and as such was bound in allegiance to the king.

The new pope celebrated the coronation mass in Saint Peter's on Christmas Day 1046, the day after his own enthronement. By condemning simony the new pope placed himself at the head of the reform movement, but his sudden death in

October 1047 meant that he could achieve little. Once again Henry selected the pope, the Alsatian aristocrat, Bishop Brun of Toul. As Leo IX he proved to be an outstanding pope. He was a highly cultivated, charming, eloquent man of exceptional strength of character, and totally devoted to reform. Leo IX copied Henry III's style of government. He travelled tirelessly throughout Europe visiting bishoprics and monasteries, and holding synods to make sure that reforms were carried out and to assert the authority of the papacy over the national churches. But his reforming efforts were not a total success. His determination to assert the authority of the see of Rome over all of Christendom led to a serious breach in relations between the Eastern (Byzantine) Church and Rome. His territorial ambitions caused him to march against the Normans in southern Italy with a rag-tag army of cut-throats and vagabonds in an adventure which Henry III refused to underwrite. His army was defeated and he was taken prisoner and died in Rome shortly after his release in 1054.

His chosen successor, Gebhard of Eichstätt, was fully committed to the emperor and, as Victor II, abandoned Leo's ambitious plans for the papacy. Henry III's empire was also beginning to fray at the edges: Hungary left the empire; relations with France deteriorated; there was unrest in Lotharingia and Flanders; and the Slavs raided the eastern marches. By the time of his death in 1056, at the age of thirty-eight, Henry III had lost much of his popularity, and there were widespread

Canossa

The struggle between the emperor and the papacy came to a dramatic climax at the meeting between the emperor Henry IV and Pope Gregory VII at Canossa in 1077. The pope had been invited by the German princes to Germany in order to settle their dispute with the emperor. Henry undertook a dangerous winter journey to Italy in order to forestall the pope's visit. When the pope heard that the emperor had crossed the Alps he felt it prudent to seek the safety of the margravine Matilda's castle at Canossa. Matilda, known as the 'daughter of Saint Peter', was an immensely rich and powerful widow, her detested husband having died in the previous year. She maintained a magnificent court and surrounded herself with silver-tongued sycophants and hair-splitting theologians.

The Lombard nobility, hoping that Henry had come to liberate them from the power-hungry pope, welcomed him, expecting that he would travel on to Rome for his coronation and replace Gregory VII with a more pliant pontiff. They were prepared to assemble an army to make sure that Henry succeeded in this mission. The king, however, would hear none of this, as he desperately needed the papal pardon in order to restore his authority in Germany. He moved on to Canossa where he waited in a hair shirt, barefoot in the snow at the castle gates until the pope granted him an audience. Gregory VII was in an awkward situation: if he gave Henry absolution he had nothing to hold over him; if he refused, he would be charged with vindictiveness and lack of Christian compassion. After three days he gave in, and Henry was received back into the arms of the Mother Church. Henry promised that he would respect the pope's judgment in his struggle with the German princes and guarantee him safe conduct throughout his realm. Henry then prostrated himself in front of the pope, his arms stretched out in the form of a cross, and received the eucharist. A reconciliation feast followed, but the king ate nothing, said nothing, and morosely scratched the table with his nails.

Henry, whom the pope had recognized as king, still hoped to stop the pope from meeting with the German princes. On the other hand Gregory had humiliated Henry, even if he had not won a decisive victory. The German princes felt that the pope complaints that he was no longer the pious, just, and peace-loving monarch he had seemed to be at the beginning of his reign. He was the last of the theocratic emperors, ruling both over and through the church, but he was still essentially a warlord. The institutions of his empire remained rudimentary and his favourite palace in Goslar was neither a capital nor an administrative centre. The treasurer, steward, cup-bearer, and marshal attended to the personal affairs of the emperor, supervised the court staff and were responsible for the monarch's safety. The royal chapel was of enormous importance, for it provided the personnel for the chancellery, as well as clerks and notaries. Although the chapel and the chancery were at the centre of Ottonian and Salian government, they produced fewer written documents than under the Carolingians. Most of these documents concerned Church affairs. There was no archive, no register of documents, and the treasury did not even keep accounts. Since the court was constantly on the move, there was no place for an elaborate bureaucracy and it was not until the middle of the twelfth century that an effort was made to bring some kind of order into this haphazard administration.

had betrayed them by restoring the monarchy, and they no longer saw him as a useful ally. The Lombard aristocracy took the opposite view. They felt that the king had behaved unworthily, failing to protect the Church against a dangerously ambitious pope, and had suffered a crippling humiliation. Henry's enemies were weakened, but his prestige among his supporters had suffered a severe set-back, and it soon seemed that his humiliation had been futile.

Canossa was thus a shattering experience for contemporaries and it remains symbolic of the prostration of the powerful to the point of becoming a cliche. Otto von Freising wrote that the Church had destroyed the empire by treating the king of Rome not as a mighty ruler, but as a common outlaw.

In May 1872, at the height of the struggle with the Catholic Church, Bismarck told the Reichstag that he would never go to Canossa 'either in body or in spirit!'

Henry IV, on bended knee, begs Mathilda of Tuscany and his godfather Hugo, abbot of Cluny, to intercede on his behalf with Pope Gregory VII.

HENRY IV AND THE ROAD TO CANOSSA

Henry IV was only six years old when his father died, but he had already been elected and crowned king. His mother Queen Agnes acted as regent, a fact which exasperated the fractious nobility. She had always been regarded as an outsider by the German aristocracy and her support came exclusively from the princes of the Church. During her regency a number of powerful dukes were able to assert their independence from the crown and some of those whom she favoured, such as Rudolf of Rheinfelden, duke of Swabia (who had kidnapped Henry III's twelve-year-old daughter and was thus in a position to blackmail the queen), Otto of Northeim, duke of Bavaria, and Berthold of Zähringen, were to become her son's most dangerous rivals.

Civil strife was widespread in Germany, particularly along the lower Rhine, where the rivalry between Archbishop Anno of Cologne and Henry, Count Palatine, led to numerous bloody engagements. When the German army intervened in a dispute over the succession to the Hungarian throne and was defeated, the result was a disastrous loss of prestige. Burgundy and Italy were largely ignored during the regency. The papacy asserted its independence, urged on by the increasingly powerful grey eminence, Hildebrand, who had served the deposed pope Gregory IV as well as Leo IX, and was a member of the college of cardinals. When Victor II, the last of the popes loyal to the emperor, died in 1057, the new pope, Frederick of Lotharingia, abbot of Monte Cassino, was elected without the knowledge of Queen Agnes. As Stephen IX he pursued an anti-imperial policy, but reigned for less than a year. The Roman aristocracy then secured the election of Benedict X. The cardinals had fled the city, and their leader Hildebrand was in Germany as papal legate. Hildebrand returned to Italy and secured the appointment of the bishop of Florence, who took the name Nicholas II. In his conciliar decree of 1059, *In nomine Domini,* he asserted the right of the college of cardinals to choose their candidate for the papacy, thus excluding the Roman aristocracy from the process, though the emperor's rights were left undecided.

On his death in 1061 the cardinals, guarded by Norman troops, exercised their new rights. They selected the bishop of Lucca who ascended the papal throne as Alexander II. Agnes refused to accept their choice, and attempted to reassert the imperial power of papal selection by supporting Bishop Cadalo of Parma as anti-pope (Honorius II). Civil war broke out in Rome as the two pontiffs struggled for power, and Honorius was driven out of the city, ending his days in Parma.

The opponents of Queen Agnes decided to act: they were concerned about the security of the empire, resentful that the affairs of state had been entrusted to a mere woman, and jealous of Bishop Henry of Augsburg, her closest advisor and rumoured to be her lover. In 1062 Archbishop Anno of Cologne kidnapped the young king by luring him on board ship and sailing down the Rhine to Cologne. The imperial insignia were also captured in the 'coup d'état of Kaiserswerth'. Queen Agnes resigned as regent and Archbishop Anno took her place. The arriviste

Anno was soon locked in rivalry with Archbishop Adalbert of Hamburg-Bremen, a member of the ancient aristocracy whose ambition was to be the 'northern pope'. He was also obliged to share the regency with Archbishop Siegfried of Mainz. The bitter struggle for power between the German bishops reached a dramatic climax during the Whitsun mass at the imperial chapel in Goslar attended by the young king. Armed troops of the Abbot of Fulda and the bishop of Hildesheim hacked one another to pieces during the service, and the king fled to his castle.

On 29 March 1065 the fifteen-year-old king received the accolade in Worms. He was a sickly youth, surrounded by young men of humble birth, unable to free himself from the influence of Archbishop Anno of Cologne and his powerful allies. In 1066 Anno and his coalition partners drove Adalbert of Bremen from court, ridding themselves of their most powerful rival. Henry was obliged to marry the fourteen-year-old Bertha of Turin, whom his father had chosen. Whether from spite or libidinal deficiency the marriage was unconsummated. Henry treated his child bride shabbily and demanded a divorce in 1069, a plan that was frustrated by Peter Damian, the papal legate. The papacy thus won a significant victory, and the monarchy suffered a further loss of prestige. Henry accepted this verdict and did his duty. The following year a daughter was born.

The overthrow of Archbishop Adalbert of Bremen led the heathen Slavic Liuitzi to slaughter Christians, abandon the faith, resume their pagan practices, and defy the king. Godfrey the Bearded was the mightiest prince of the day, controlling the axis from Lotharingia to Tuscany in the interests of the monarchy. When Godfrey died in 1069, Henry was faced with difficulties on the frontiers of his kingdom, but he survived these setbacks. The campaign against the Slavs in 1069 was little more than a demonstration, but it saved Henry's face. Godfrey the Bearded's successor, his son Godfrey the Hunchbacked, proved to be a ferocious warrior and loyal subject, and he stabilized the western and southern regions.

During Henry IV's minority and in the early years of his reign the nobles had steadily eroded the power of the crown by seizing crown lands and rights. Prompted by Archbishop Adalbert, the young king decided to stop the rot. Henry set out to create a royal demesne in the Harz south-east of Goslar (as the Ile de France was to become for the French kings) protected by a series of mighty fortresses. To the Saxon aristocracy this amounted to the tyrannical denial of their rights, a challenge to their status and a threat to their security. The castles were given to upstart outsiders, mostly Swabians, who exploited the local peasantry. The Thuringians and Saxons complained that they were being reduced to slavery. Both the aristocracy and peasantry wished to challenge the monarchy, and they temporarily sank their differences to make a common front.

When the king called for troops to fight the Poles in 1073, it was rumoured that he really intended to march against Saxony. The Saxons demanded that the king disband his army, destroy his castles, and restore the rights and lands which they felt were theirs. Henry IV refused these demands and the Saxons marched against

Goslar. The king fled to the fortified castle at Harzburg where he was besieged. In a dramatic escape he made his way to Hersfeld to meet the army he had prepared for the Polish campaign.

The king was heavily outnumbered and waited six months before he dared march against the Saxons. His opponents were hopelessly divided between the peasantry and the aristocracy whose real interests were diametrically opposed. The Saxons could not risk a royal victory over their divided forces and so decided to negotiate while they still had the upper hand. On 2 February 1074 the Peace of Gerstungen was concluded. It was a peace which Henry found hard to accept. He agreed to destroy his castles in Saxony and Thuringia, abandon Goslar, hand back the property he had seized, acknowledge the ancient rights of the Saxons, and grant the rebels a general amnesty.

It was agreed that the church at the Harzburg should be spared, as the king's brother and son were buried there, but the local peasantry stormed this symbol of Salian despotism, razed it, and desecrated the royal graves. This was a clear breach of the peace treaty and Henry IV had no difficulty in raising an army to punish the Saxons. On 9 June 1075 the two large armies clashed near Homburg. Henry IV won the day in a fierce battle in which Godfrey the Hunchbacked distinguished himself. The Saxon nobility fled the field on horseback, leaving the peasant infantry to be slaughtered by loyalist troops. The king was not especially happy about the outcome of the battle: the Saxons had lost thousands of peasants, but he had lost some of his most devoted nobles.

The royal army went on the rampage in Thuringia and eastern Saxony, but the proud Saxons refused to sue for peace. They ended the campaign only when the king appeared with a fresh army in October 1075. Most of the Saxon leaders were imprisoned; only the most powerful of them, Otto of Northeim, was pardoned and took part in a ceremony in Goslar at Christmas in which it was promised that on his death Henry's two-year-old son Conrad would be elected king.

THE STRUGGLE BETWEEN THE POPE AND EMPEROR

Henry IV seemed to be at the pinnacle of his power, but he was soon to suffer one of the worst humiliations in history. On New Year's Day 1076 a message arrived from Hildebrand, who had been elected pope Gregory VII in 1073, warning Henry that if he did not do penance for continuing to associate with courtiers who had been excommunicated, he too would be denied the sacraments. The pope further admonished the king for having installed bishops in Milan, Fermo, and Spoleto without consulting him. The pope insisted that since he was the direct successor of Saint Peter, the king must obey his commands; he pointed out that Henry's recent successes were solely due to the grace of God.

Henry IV was not the man to buckle to such impertinence and decided to challenge the pope. He called the German bishops to a meeting in Worms on 24 January 1076. Twenty-six bishops signed the 'Negative Reply of Worms' in which

Saint Michael's Hildesheim, a Romanesque masterpiece begun by Bishop Bernward in 1010. Although it was badly damaged in World War II, it remains a striking example of the richness of Ottonian and Salian architecture.

they told 'Brother Hildebrand' that they no longer accepted his authority and accused him of all manner of wrong-doing, including consorting with a married woman. Henry IV, as ruler of Rome, ordered Hildebrand to step down. The king's letter was copied and posted to all corners of the empire and a massive propaganda campaign was mounted against the pope.

Gregory VII refused to be intimidated. On receiving the letter from Worms he excommunicated the primate of the German Church, Archbishop Siegfried of Mainz, suspended all the bishops who had subscribed the letter, and excommunicated all the pro-German Lombard bishops and a number of French bishops who, for various reasons, met with his displeasure. As if that were not enough, he denied Henry's right to rule in Germany and Italy, released all Christians from their allegiance to the king, and excommunicated him.

The Church was undergoing fundamental reforms and was ready to struggle for supremacy over the temporal powers. With almost megalomaniac energy, Gregory VII set about establishing the absolute and unquestioned authority of the papacy, not only over the Roman Church, but over all the worldly powers. The emperor was undoubtedly the greatest of these worldly powers and a victory over him would thus be decisive. Gregory had little doubt that he would succeed; the theocratic powers of the Ottonians and Salians had been diminished, and the papacy had broken loose from imperial control.

The struggle between the pope and the emperor was complicated by the aspirations of the Italian cities for communal self-rule and the right to appoint bishops. Nowhere was the struggle more violent than in Milan, where the archbishop and the minor knights who controlled the city were loyal to the empire. The pope opposed them, supported by a mass movement fired by religious fanaticism. The struggle between the emperor, the pope, and the Milanese culminated in a terrible massacre of the religious fanatics, and the papal faction was beaten.

Very few of the German bishops were prepared to support the emperor in his struggle with the pope, and the south German and Saxon nobility seized the opportunity to revolt when the pope released them from their oaths of loyalty to the king. The two groups made an alliance to overthrow the imperial constitution and to elect a new king. Otto von Northeim, an archetypal trimmer, once again changed sides and rejoined the rebellious Saxons now that they seemed likely to succeed. An increasing number of German bishops joined the Gregorian camp.

Henry IV's throne was saved because of rivalry between Otto of Northeim and the other leading personality among the rebels, Rudolf von Rheinfelden, and also because Gregory VII wanted a submissive Henry, not a new king who might prove even more difficult to control. The German princes invited the pope to attend an Assembly in Augsburg to adjudicate in their struggle with the king. Gregory VII accepted the invitation and began the long and difficult journey north.

Henry IV decided to forestall the pope for he desperately needed the papal pardon to restore his authority in Germany. He travelled through Burgundy, celebrating Christmas in Besançon, and from there to Geneva and the Mont Cenis. The weather was terrible, the pass exceptionally dangerous, but there could be no delay: the pope was due to meet the German princes on 2 February.

News that the king had crossed the Alps filled the pope with alarm and he fled to the security of the margravine Matilda's castle at Canossa which was deemed impregnable. Henry waited barefoot in the snow at the castle gates for the pope to grant him an audience. After three days Gregory VII relented and Henry was received back into the arms of the Mother Church.

The German princes reacted to the news from Canossa by calling an Assembly on 13 March 1077 in Forcheim, where they elected a new king, Rudolf of Rheinfelden, duke of Swabia. The new king was obliged to accept certain conditions: the monarchy was no longer hereditary and he was forced to accept the canonical election of bishops. Henry IV marched against the anti-king, who fled to Saxony. Although Henry ruled in central Germany, Rudolf was still in control of Saxony. The pope played a waiting game while a series of bloody engagements took place between the forces of the two kings. It was not until January 1080 that Henry IV finally defeated Rudolf at Flarchheim near Mühlhausen in Thuringia, and he

promptly demanded that the pope excommunicate his rival. Henry threatened to appoint an anti-pope if Gregory VII failed to oblige. Gregory accepted the challenge, excommunicated Henry a second time and acknowledged Rudolf as king of Germany. In total disregard for political reality the pope proclaimed that he possessed judicial power over all secular rulers. Gregory later prophesied that if Henry did not do penance before him by 1 August, he would be destroyed.

This time Gregory VII had gone too far. The excommunication was so blatantly politically motivated that few could take it seriously. Henry organized a synod of loyal bishops in Brixen at which the 'impertinent Hildebrand' was accused of blasphemy, murder, heresy, necromancy, and sundry other misdemeanours and was declared deposed. Archbishop Wibert of Ravenna was appointed pope. He was a decent and honourable reformer who chose the name Clement III.

There were now two kings and two popes; Church and state were hopelessly divided. In October 1080, Henry's army was defeated on the White Elster, but Rudolf of Rheinfelden's right hand was hacked off in the battle and he died on the following day. The rebels had lost their outstanding leader and it was seen as a divine judgment that Rudolf had lost the hand with which he had once sworn allegiance to Henry IV.

Meanwhile, Henry IV marched towards Rome, seeking revenge for Canossa. In May 1081 he reached Rome, but the citizens remained loyal to Gregory VII and the king felt obliged to retreat. Unmoved by the news that the new leader of the rebels, Hermann of Salm from the ducal house of Luxembourg, had been crowned in Goslar at Christmas, Henry laid siege to the Eternal City. Once more he failed, only to try again in the spring of the following year. This time he was partially successful, but the pope held out in a strongly fortified position.

Gregory VII demanded another Canossa, but his position was far from enviable. His strongest ally the Margravine Matilda was unable to give him much assistance.

In a detail from an allegorical miniature from the 'Maiden's Mirror' (*Jungfrauenspiegel*) of Conrad von Hirsau (c.1200) widows are shown sowing and reaping. The women are elegantly dressed, the work purely symbolic.

Hermann von Salm was a man of little consequence. Otto von Northeim, the papal faction's most talented commander, died in January 1083. Gregory hoped to win the support of the Norman Robert Guiscard, but he was fully engaged in an over-ambitious attempt to seize Byzantine territory in Greece Deprived of his only promising ally, the pope's position began to crumble. The Romans grew tired of Gregory's intransigence, which had brought them nothing but misery. They opened the gates of the city and on Maunday Thursday 1084, Henry IV entered Rome in triumph. On Easter Sunday he was crowned emperor in Saint Peter's by the anti-pope, Clement III.

Henry had little time to enjoy his triumph. Gregory VII was still in Rome. Robert de Guiscard returned bloodied from Byzantium and, joined by Saracens from Sicily, marched on the city. Henry prudently retreated, leaving Rome to the mercy of the Normans and their Moslem allies. An orgy of rape and plunder followed; the city was set on fire and thousands of Romans were dragged off into slavery. Rome had not witnessed such horrors since the barbarian invasions.

Gregory VII had been completely discredited by calling upon the plundering Norman hordes, and he fled the city to establish his court in Salerno. From this safe distance he once again dismissed his hated rival and called upon all of Christendom to destroy him. Shortly afterwards he died, unforgiving to the last, much to the distress of his spiritual advisors. His last words were: 'I loved righteousness and hated injustice, hence I die in exile'.

Henry IV was rid of his rival, but he could never free himself from the shadow of excommunication and the humiliation of Canossa. After his flight from Rome Henry asserted himself in Germany, excommunicating a number of Gregorian bishops and chasing Hermann von Salm into exile among the Danes. In southern Germany the Gregorian opposition was led by the Welfs (Guelphs). In 1089 the seventeen-year old Welf, son of Welf IV, duke of Bavaria, married the forty-three-year-old Margravine Matilda of Tuscany. This politically motivated marriage created a powerful anti-imperial alliance which included significant parts of southern Germany, Lotharingia and Tuscany.

Henry returned to Italy in 1090 to smash this threatening new alliance. He seized a number of Matilda's castles, forcing her to retreat to the safety of Canossa. Matilda then persuaded Henry's son Conrad to betray his father and he was crowned king of Italy by the archbishop of Milan, who also changed sides at this opportune moment. Conrad committed himself to Pope Urban II, who promised him the imperial crown if he proved his devotion to the Church. The pope then further bound Conrad to his cause by arranging his marriage to the daughter of Roger I of Sicily. Milan, Cremona, Piacenza, and Lodi formed the first alliance between Italian cities, and joined the anti-imperial forces. Henry IV was now in a critical position and was unable to retreat to Germany, as his opponents controlled the Alpine passes. The emperor suffered a further humiliation when his Queen Praxedis, a young Russian widow of dubious morals who had fallen under

Matilda's sway, appeared before the reform synod in Piacenza and accused her husband of startling sexual perversion.

Henry IV was given a respite when Urban II turned his attention to the reform of the French Church and called for a crusade to save the eastern Christians from the advance of Islam. Young Welf's marriage to Matilda was not a success, and when the alliance fell apart, Welf IV was prepared to treat with the emperor. In 1097 Henry was able to return to Germany after seven frustrating years in Italy.

At an Assembly in Mainz in the following year Henry deposed Conrad, his faithless son, who died two years later in Florence. His younger brother Henry was elected king in 1099. Urban II's successor, Paschal II, was as determined as his predecessors to strengthen the papacy, and he reaffirmed the emperor's excommunication. Henry attempted to reconcile with the pope by promising to go on a crusade if he could receive the sacraments, but the pope remained adamant.

Henry IV supported the minor knights and burghers and furthered their economic interests. By doing all he could to stop civil unrest he won the support of all those who were disillusioned with the endless feuds among the aristocracy and who longed for peace and order. He avenged the Jews by punishing those responsible for the pogroms in 1096 and by protecting those who had been forcibly baptized and wished to return to their faith. Such a policy was anathema to the clerical and lay princes, who persuaded young Henry that his inheritance was endangered by his father's foolish policies. The pope freed the boy from the oath of allegiance he had made to his father. An Assembly was called in Mainz in 1105 to settle the quarrel, but young Henry did not want to risk losing his case. He took his father prisoner, seized the imperial insignia, and was crowned Henry V by the archbishop of Mainz in January 1106.

Henry IV, who had suffered so many setbacks, still refused to give up. He escaped from his dungeon and prepared to fight for his crown. Many sympathized with his plight and the Lotharingian princes drew their swords on his behalf. But Henry IV died on 7 August 1106, before the bloody civil war could begin, having forgiven all his enemies including his treacherous son. He was a genuinely popular king and there was widespread grief at his passing. Although he had been excommunicated, the poor clergy prayed for his soul while the cathedral chapter of Liège was held at bay by common soldiers and the armed populace. The earth of his grave was held to have magic properties; even though kings failed to satisfy the longings of the people for peace, prosperity and justice, they were still attributed a certain magic and remained the focal point of the hopes and aspirations of the ordinary people.

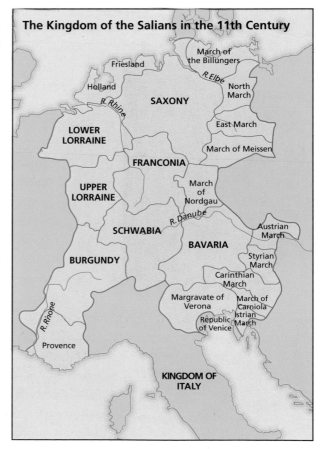

The Kingdom of the Salians in the 11th Century

HENRY V AND THE END OF THE SALIANS

Henry V proposed a compromise with the pope by which he would have a veto right over episcopal appointments, give new bishops their ring and their staff, and the bishop would then swear allegiance to the king. The king would thus forswear simony and his control of elections but not his control of appointments. This was unacceptable to the pope, who insisted that the Church would still be subservient to the king.

In 1110 Henry V assembled a vast army and marched into Italy to force the pope to accept lay investiture and Henry's coronation in Rome. He had recently become engaged to Matilda, the nine-year-old daughter of Henry I of England, and had received a substantial subsidy from his new ally. Henry met with no resistance in northern Italy and even the Margravine Matilda prudently avoided any engagement. The pope now proposed a separation of Church and state. The king would have no say in the appointment of bishops, but the Church would hand over its vast estates to the crown. Henry V, uncertain how the nobility would react to such an accumulation of wealth by the crown, announced that he would agree provided this arrangement was accepted by both the Church and nobility.

The clerics were appalled by the pope's suggestion, for they would lose most of their wealth and power. The nobility were likewise opposed since they too would lose estates they held as fiefs from the Church, and they had no desire to strengthen the monarchy to such an extent. When Henry V arrived in Rome and the pope made his remarkable suggestion public, blood ran in the streets. Henry V promptly ordered the pope's arrest along with a number of prominent churchmen and leading Roman citizens. The pope was helpless without the intervention of his Norman allies and felt obliged to accept Henry's original conditions. He therefore swore that he would never excommunicate him and a treaty to that effect was signed on 11 April 1111 on the Ponte Mammolo. Two days later Henry V was crowned in Saint Peter's. To complete his victory, the emperor obtained the pope's permission to give his father a religious funeral in the cathedral in Speyer.

Many powerful churchmen promptly denounced the treaty, ignored the pope's objections, and excommunicated the emperor. At about the same time, the German princes revolted but were defeated by the imperial forces and then humiliated. Outraged by the emperor's treatment of his enemies and by his lofty political ambitions, the aristocracy of Saxony and Thuringia rose up and decisively defeated the imperial army at Welfesholz near Mansfeld in February 1115. In order to re-establish his position in Germany, when the margravine Matilda died in July of that year, Henry V decided to take possession of her vast estates and establish a power base in Tuscany from which he could challenge both the pope and the German princes. He took Matilda's estates without difficulty, but in Rome the Gregorians had prevailed and forced the pope to renounce the treaty with the emperor. Henry V celebrated Easter and Whitsun 1117 in Rome and his

A fight between crusaders and Saracens. The Moslems were well equipped and skilful soldiers who frequently got the better of the crusaders, although the Christian forces were usually better organized and supplied.

young English wife was crowned empress by the archbishop Mauritius of Braga. The archbishop was promptly excommunicated by the pope who had fled the city after a violent dispute between the leading Roman families, in which he had backed the losing side.

The pope died in the summer of 1118 and his successor Gelasius II refused to renew the treaty of Ponte Mammolo. Henry promptly made the faithful Mauritius of Braga pope. He chose the name Gregory VIII, but was known in Rome as the 'Spanish donkey'. Henry V then returned to Germany, which was riven by the strife between the imperial and the papal parties, and marched against Mainz whose archbishop, Adalbert, was the leader of the papal faction. A Saxon army was put at Adalbert's disposal, but a battle was avoided thanks to negotiations at Würzburg, where it was agreed that imperial and Church property be respected and anyone breaking the peace executed.

The investiture controversy was not settled until the new pope, Calixtus II, a wily diplomat, sent a delegation to Worms which reached an agreement that henceforth the emperor would give the bishops a sceptre as a symbol of their worldly rights and powers, but would not give them the ring and crozier, since these were purely religious symbols. The spiritual was now clearly separated from the temporal, and the monarchy had finally lost the last vestiges of its religious powers. After the proclamation of the Concordat of Worms (1122) a mass was celebrated, and Henry V received the Eucharist and the kiss of peace from Cardinal Lambert of Ostia, the leader of the papal delegation. The chronicler Ekkehard of Aura wrote that Christ's rent tunic was now repaired.

In 1124 Henry V, allied with Henry I of England, decided to go to war with France. William, the heir to the English throne, had drowned when the White Ship sank in the channel, so Henry V's wife, William's twin sister, was now heir to the English throne. The emperor hoped that a successful campaign in France would confirm her claim. The German princes, whose appetite for wars of conquest had yet to be whetted, showed no enthusiasm for a foreign adventure that, if successful, would further strengthen the king. Faced with the firm resolve of the French to defend their country against the invader, handicapped by his own minuscule army, and suffering from a mortal illness, Henry V retreated. He died in Utrecht on 23 May 1125. The empress Matilda returned to England, married Godfrey of Anjou and struggled vainly against Stephen of Blois for the English crown. Their son ascended the throne as Henry II, the first of the Plantagenets.

A crusading knight at prayer. A similar suit of chain-mail was worn by most crusading knights, an attire that had changed little since the days of Charles the Great. A simple helmet decorated with a cross would be worn in battle.

<table>
<tr><td>CHAPTER 3</td><td></td></tr>
</table>

The Hohenstaufen and the Late Middle Ages

Henry V was the last of the Salian dynasty and he died without a son. There were three candidates for the throne: Frederick of Swabia, Lothar of Saxony, and Leopold, margrave of Austria. The meeting of the electors was rancorous and violence was only narrowly avoided before the choice fell upon Lothar. The new king gave his daughter in marriage to the duke of Bavaria, Henry the Proud, who was a Welf, an ancient family dating back to the eighth century. In return, Lothar received the support of the Bavarians. Frederick of Swabia, a Hohenstaufen, refused to hand over the royal estates which he had inherited from his uncle, Henry V. The Salians had combined their private estates with the royal demesne in an attempt to form a territorial kingdom, and Lothar III was determined to regain control of them. The Swabians countered these efforts by electing Frederick's younger brother Conrad III anti-king in 1127. This was the beginning of a prolonged struggle between the Hohenstaufen and the Welfs.

The lengthy war between the king and his powerful rival ended in 1135, when Conrad was obliged to renounce his crown and the emperor left him in possession of his estates. When Lothar died two years later, the electors chose the Hohenstaufen anti-king Conrad. The election took place with unseemly haste, and Conrad III was crowned in Aachen by the papal legate without the regalia, which were held by the Welfs. Conrad III, a man of immense physical strength, soon established his authority. Having dealt with his Welf rival, Henry the Proud, he turned his attention to international affairs. In 1144 the Moslem leader Zengi seized the crusader state of Edessa in south-eastern Anatolia. Inspired by the preaching of Bernard of Clairvaux, the charismatic founder of the Cistercian order, Louis VII of France and Conrad III, along with many members of the German aristocracy, took the cross. Conrad decided to secure the election of his son as king before leaving for the Holy Land, which took place after he had allowed the Saxons to mount their own crusade against the heathen Wends in Pomerania, Mecklenburg, and Brandenburg. This was an important step towards the German colonization of the east.

The second crusade was an unmitigated disaster. The crusaders suffered a series of defeats in Asia Minor and failed to take Damascus. In 1149 Louis VII and Conrad III returned to Europe. Conrad was soon locked in battle with the Welfs, who had allied with the Norman Roger II and then with Louis VII of France. Conrad withstood the Welfs, but he died in February 1152 before his coronation could take place in Rome. He was the first German king since 962 who had not been crowned emperor.

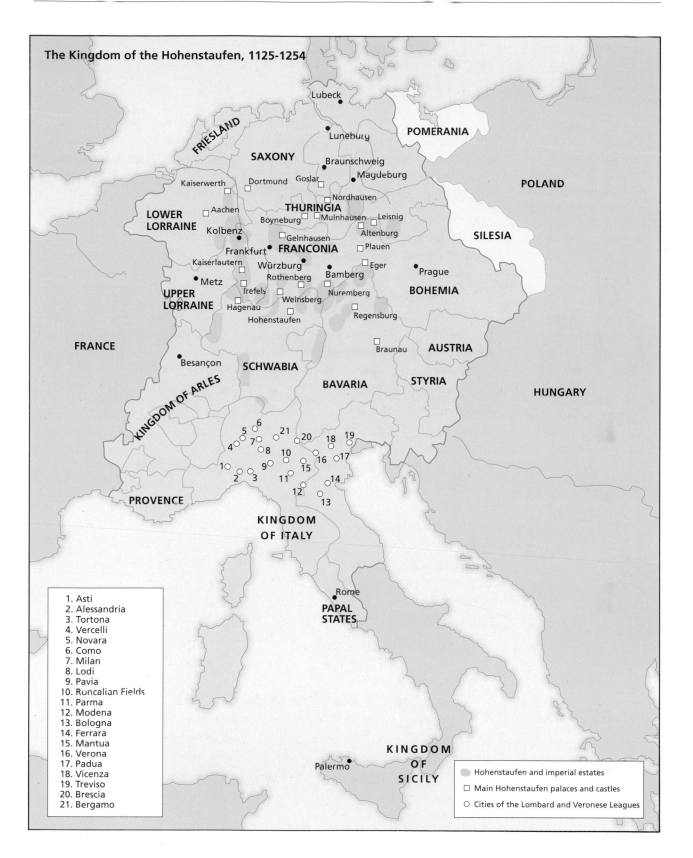

The Kingdom of the Hohenstaufen, 1125-1254

Lubeck

FRIESLAND

Luneburg

POMERANIA

SAXONY

Braunschweig

POLAND

Kaiserwerth   Dortmund   Goslar   Magdeburg

Nordhausen

LOWER
LORRAINE   Aachen   THURINGIA   SILESIA

Boyneburg   Mulnhausen   Leisnig

Kolbenz   Altenburg

Gelnhausen

Frankfurt   FRANCONIA   Plauen

Kaiserlautern   Würzburg   Eger

Metz   Rothenberg   Bamberg   Prague

Trefels   Nuremberg   BOHEMIA

UPPER   Weinsberg
LORRAINE   Hagenau   Regensburg

Hohenstaufen

FRANCE   Braunau   AUSTRIA

Besançon   SCHWABIA

KINGDOM OF ARLES   BAVARIA   STYRIA   HUNGARY

6
5   21
4   7   20   18   19
8   10   16   17
PROVENCE   1   9   15
2   3   11   14
12
13

KINGDOM
OF ITALY

Rome

PAPAL
STATES

1. Asti
2. Alessandria
3. Tortona
4. Vercelli
5. Novara
6. Como
7. Milan
8. Lodi
9. Pavia
10. Roncalian Fields
11. Parma
12. Modena
13. Bologna
14. Ferrara
15. Mantua
16. Verona
17. Padua
18. Vicenza
19. Treviso
20. Brescia
21. Bergamo

KINGDOM
OF
SICILY

Palermo

⬤ Hohenstaufen and imperial estates

☐ Main Hohenstaufen palaces and castles

◯ Cities of the Lombard and Veronese Leagues

Hildegard of Bingen

Hildegard was born of aristocratic parents in Bermersheim near Alzey in 1098. At the age of eight she was sent to be educated by the abbess Jutta of Spanheim whose small community of nuns was attached to a Benedictine monastery at Disibodenberg near Bingen. She spent her entire life in the nunnery, of which she became abbess about 1141. About 1150 she refounded Saint Rupert's monastery on the Rupertsberg near Bingen, which had been destroyed by the Normans, and moved there with her nuns. She died in 1179.

Her fame as a mystic, poet, naturalist, musician, apothecary, politician, and diplomat spread throughout the empire. Although her Latin left much to be desired, and she needed the assistance of a faithful scribe, she maintained an extensive network of correspondents including Frederick Barbarossa, Bernard of Clairvaux, emperors, popes, and archbishops. The 'Sybil of the Rhine' offered advice on all manner of topics from herbal medicine to heresy.

On her promotion to abbess she had a mystical experience of Pentecostal flames descending from heaven and encircling her. In the next ten years she made a compilation of her numerous visions in *Scrivias* ('Know the Ways') and produced two major scientific works, *Physica* and *Cause et cure*. Her morality play, *Ordo Virtutum* ('Play of the Virtues'), was written a century before any similar works. Her considerable output of poetry and music was collected in the *Symphonia armonie celestium revelationum* ('The Symphony of the Harmony of Celestial Revelations').

Today she is best known as one of the most remarkable composers of her day. Her music expresses her mystical longings and profound spirituality. Her songs, although written in the vocabulary of the Middle Ages, are extremely complex and range in mood from the contemplative to the declamatory, always controlled by the restraints of plain chant.

Four popes requested that she be canonized, none with success. Her life provides a striking example of the extent to which women could pursue successful careers in the Middle Ages. Excluded from the priesthood, she showed little interest in theological problems or philosophy, but concentrated on the mystical and the practical, combining both in a manner which was typical of her age. In spite of her piety and modernity she shared the social prejudices of her times. When asked why she only admitted aristocrats into her community she replied: 'Who would keep all his animals in one barn — ox, donkey, sheep, and goats?' Social inequality was ordained by God, the call for equality therefore blasphemous.

An illustration from *The Book of the Divine Works of Ordinary Men*, c.1230, representing the vision of Saint Hildegard of Bingen.

A fourteenth-century French illustration from *Le rommans de Godefroy de Bouillon et (...) de tous les autres roys qui one estre outr mer jusques a Saint Loys* shows Moorish cavalry getting the better of the Crusaders. Godfrey of Bouillon (c.1060–1100), known as the 'Protector of the Holy Sepulchre', was made duke of Lower Lotharingia by the Emperor Henry IV. He was the energetic leader of the First Crusade (1096–99) and became the first Christian ruler of Jerusalem.

FREDERICK 'BARBAROSSA'

Conrad's son Henry was only eight years old; Conrad had proposed that his nephew, Frederick III of Swabia known as 'Barbarossa', should succeed him. The choice had much to recommend it. Not only was Barbarossa an outstanding personality, his mother was a Welf, and thus he bridged the rival houses of Welf and Hohenstaufen.

Barbarossa concentrated principally on Italy. There were good reasons for this: it was vital that he be crowned emperor, for without the prestige of the title his position in Germany would be further weakened; and he could not afford to leave northern Italy to his opponents for the prosperous Italian towns were an essential source of revenue. In March 1153 he made the Pact of Constance with Pope Eugenius III, promising his support against the Normans, who had occupied the south of Italy since the late eleventh century. He also promised his support against the rebellious Romans, and agreed to prevent the Byzantine emperors regaining a foothold in Italy. In return, the following pope, Hadrian IV, agreed to crown Barbarossa and acknowledge the rights of the empire.

The coronation took place in Saint Peter's on 18 June 1155, the ceremonies interrupted by violent attacks from dissident Romans. Barbarossa returned to Germany having failed to fulfil his part of the Constance bargain. He had been unable to pacify Rome and had not marched south against the Normans. However, the pope made his own peace with the Normans, and was no longer so dependent on Barbarossa. Relations between the emperor and the pope became more strained when a message from Hadrian IV to Barbarossa was translated from the Latin for

A Bavarian illustration of 1188 shows Frederick I 'Barbarossa' (1122–1190) dressed as a crusader. When Saladin (1169-1193) captured Jerusalem in 1187, he became master of most of Syria. This was taken as proof that Christian Europe had strayed from the paths of righteousness and at the Diet of Mainz in 1188 Frederick I swore to take the cross in the Third Crusade (1189–1191). Saladin withdrew his forces from the frontier posts as the emperor approached, but Barbarossa was drowned crossing the river Saleph. An Arab chronicler wrote: 'Had not Allah had the mercy to destroy the King of the Germans just as he was about to enter Syria one would now write: Syria and Egypt once belonged to Islam.'

the benefit of the illiterate aristocrats gathered in Besançon in October 1157. The translation of the ambiguous word 'beneficium' – which the emperor's party insisted meant 'fief' and the pope later argued simply meant 'benefit' or 'good deed' – suggested that the pope regarded the emperor as his vassal, a view echoed in a controversial mural in the Lateran Palace showing the emperor leading the pope's horse. The nobility was so outraged, that the two papal delegates, one of whom was to become pope Alexander III, came within a hair's breadth of being murdered. Hadrian IV died in 1159 and was succeeded by two popes, Alexander III and Victor IV, who promptly excommunicated one another. Barbarossa was unable single-handedly to overcome the papal schism, and neither the king of England nor of France was willing to support him.

In a world of emerging national states, the emperor was no longer accepted as the heir to the universal Roman empire. John of Salisbury, the English prelate and scholar, asked on whose authority such a vulgar and uncivilized people as the Germans could claim to judge over the nations. He pointed out that his sovereign lord, Henry II (whose own bitter conflict with the Church climaxed in 1170 with the murder of Thomas Beckett, Archbishop of Canterbury), regarded himself as king, papal legate, patriarch, emperor, and whatever else he chose to be in his own kingdom. John of Salisbury regarded the situation as undesirable and essentially tyrannical, but it was the shape of things to come. The fact that Germany could not completely abandon the traditions of two and a half centuries, and follow the lead of England and France, was partly due to the papacy's need for a universal empire.

In 1162 Barbarossa defeated Milan, which led the opposition to the assertion of imperial prerogatives over nothern Italy. The highly coveted relics of the Three Kings were taken back to Cologne Cathedral. Five years later he entered Rome in triumph, and Alexander III fled the city disguised as a humble pilgrim. The triumph was short-lived, for his men were decimated by malaria, and Barbarossa was forced to abandon plans for a campaign in southern Italy. The northern cities banded together and built a common fortress named Alessandria in honour of the pope. It was uncertain whether the emperor would be able to make his way back across the Alps. After a number of hair-raising adventures and narrow escapes, he reached Germany with a small band of trusted knights. In 1174 he returned to Italy and laid siege to Alessandria. Failing to take the fortress, Barbarossa agreed to a provisional treaty at Montebello. Hostilities resumed when it proved impossible to reach a compromise agreement between the Lombard cities and the emperor. Barbarossa appealed for help to his cousin, Henry the Lion, but Henry refused. Barbarossa's small force was defeated by the Milanese, and the emperor fled the field, narrowly escaping capture. He had no choice but to make peace with the pope. The cost was high: he had to abandon the anti-pope Calixtus III, renounce his right to rule Rome, resign the margraviate of Tuscany, and establish truces with the Lombards and the Normans.

In Germany, Barbarossa concentrated on strengthening the territorial monarchy by increasing the royal demesne, making his estates more profitable, and building a series of impressive castles. He was reluctant to act against his great Welf rival Henry the Lion, and was slow to respond when the north German princes registered a series of complaints against him. When Henry refused to appear in court he was automatically outlawed. In 1180, at the Assembly of Gelnhausen, the imperial princes, led by the emperor, decided that Henry the Lion's offices in Germany should be divided. Westphalia was given to the archbishop of Cologne; the area roughly corresponding to present-day Lower Saxony was given to Bernard of Anhalt; and Bavaria was given to Otto von Wittelsbach. These decisions had a lasting effect: the Wittelsbachs were to rule in Bavaria until 1918; the future kingdom of Hanover and duchy of Brunswick were to result from this decision; the boundaries of the present-day provinces of North Rhine-Westphalia and Lower Saxony exist in part because of the judgment made at the Assembly of Gelnhausen.

Henry the Lion was forced into exile at the court of his father-in-law in England. The Welfs retained only their estates around Brunswick and Lüneburg, over which they held rights of absolute ownership. These estates later became a Duchy which was to be partially absorbed by Prussia in 1866. Barbarossa needed powerful allies in his struggle against Henry the Lion, and they had to be rewarded. The division of Germany into a number of small states was the result of this imperial weakness.

Barbarossa's second wife Beatrice of Burgundy bore eleven children, but only five survived infancy. Henry, his second son, was crowned king at the age of three in 1169, and, at the age of nineteen, was engaged to the thirty-year-old Constance, the king of Sicily's aunt. The Sicilian king died in 1189 without an heir, so Barbarossa's successor claimed Sicily. His other children were engaged to the sons and daughters of the emperor of Byzantium, of the kings of England, Castille, Denmark and Hungary, and to the niece of the king of France. Few of these engagements ended in marriages, due to the numerous deaths in the imperial family.

In 1188, at an Assembly in Mainz, Barbarossa proposed a crusade to the Holy Land. This crusade was carefully prepared as a military operation rather than an expression of religious zeal. A large army was assembled in Regensburg in 1189 and began the long march to Jerusalem. On 11 June 1190 Barbarossa was drowned while bathing in the river Saleph in Asia Minor. His death on his way to Jerusalem gave him a mythical status which he otherwise would not have obtained, notwithstanding his remarkable popularity.

Before Barbarossa left for the Holy Land, Henry the Lion had returned from England in an attempt to win back his estates. Barbarossa's son, who was left in Germany as regent and who had by then succeeded as Henry VI, was unable to defend the city of Lübeck, the only part of northern Germany under royal control. Henry VI was obliged to make a compromise peace with Henry the Lion. He then left for Italy, made a number of important concessions to the papacy, and was crowned emperor by the aged pope Celestine III.

Late twelfth-century monument to a crusader, possibly Hugues I de Vaudemont, who died in 1154. The crusading knights were often swashbuckling careerists, but others were inspired by a genuine if misguided piety, and many grew to appreciate and respect Islamic culture and thus enriched European civilization.

Tancred, the Norman crusader, had seized the throne of Sicily and captured the new emperor's queen. Henry's troops were decimated by the plague while campaigning against Tancred in Naples, and were forced to return to Germany. The Guelphs organized the anti-imperial forces, including many south German princes and some powerful bishops. Henry's position was precarious in the extreme, but he was saved by an unusual stroke of luck. Richard Coeur de Lion, Tancred's ally, was shipwrecked near Venice while returning to England and tried to complete his journey in disguise through Germany. He was taken prisoner in December 1192 by Duke Leopold V of Austria, whom he had grossly insulted during the crusade. The duke handed his royal prisoner over to the emperor, who began to negotiate the terms of his release. The huge ransom demanded for Coeur de Lion financed Henry VI's second successful campaign against Tancred in Italy. Tancred died and Henry was crowned king of Sicily in Palermo cathedral at Christmas 1194. The following day his son Constantine was born, who became known to history as Frederick II.

The German princes initially refused to elect his son king, and he had to abandon the idea of an hereditary monarchy. The Sicilian aristocracy plotted to murder the king, and when the attempt failed the ringleaders were executed in an unspeakably brutal manner, and the queen was forced to witness the deaths of those whom she had befriended. The emperor then prepared to go on a further crusade, but he contracted malaria and died in Messina on 28 September 1197 at the age of thirty-one.

FREDERICK II AND THE END OF THE HOHENSTAUFEN

Henry VI's three-year-old son Frederick was made king of Sicily, but in Germany two rival kings were elected. The Hohenstaufen party chose Philip, Barbarossa's younger son, while the Welfs chose Otto IV, a son of Henry the Lion. In the same year, 1198, Innocent III became pope. He was a man of enormous ambition who admitted to being less than divine, but insisted that he was superior to any other mortal. He was determined to adjudicate between the rival kings. At first he pretended to be an honest broker, then he demanded a price. The Welfs made the best offer and received the papal blessing. The pope now claimed the right to select the emperor, and suggested that the German princes, if left to their own devices, might well elect a heretic or an idiot.

Most of the German princes supported Philip, but when he was murdered by Otto of Wittelsbach, they quickly changed to the side of the rival king, Otto of Brunswick. The great poet, Walter von der Vogelweide, who had written a number of verses in praise of Philip, now put his pen at Otto of Brunswick's service. The pope, who initially had favoured Otto, was beginning to have second thoughts, but Otto had the full support of the German aristocracy and had a large army. Innocent III, ever the political realist, reluctantly agreed to crown Otto emperor. Otto then proceeded to march against Sicily, forcing the young King Frederick to prepare to flee to Africa. Frederick was the pope's ward and he therefore felt himself obliged to

Frederick II

Few figures in medieval history are as fascinating as Frederick II, few lives so packed with adventure, few reputations so distorted by exaggerated propaganda campaigns both for and against. Speculation about this extraordinary man began with his birth. His mother was forty years old, and had been married for nine years without producing a child. Even though it was claimed that the queen delivered her heir in the market-place under public scrutiny, it was still rumoured that he was the changeling son of a butcher. That he was born in a town called Jesi in this unusual manner was said to be proof that he was the anti-Christ.

His legitimacy was questioned because of his precarious inheritance. He was crowned king of Sicily at the age of two, and was only three years old when his father, Henry VI, died. Powerful forces opposed the union of Sicily with the Holy Roman Empire: Sicily was a hereditary kingdom and

Frederick's mother Constance, who loathed the Germans, was solely concerned that he should reign in Sicily; the pope disliked the Hohenstaufens who, by seizing the crown of Sicily, had encircled the papal states; in Germany the Hohenstaufens were opposed by a powerful group of nobles. Tuscan and Lombard towns formed an anti-Hohenstaufen alliance and forced Philip of Swabia, the younger brother of Henry VI who had been put in charge of the margravine Matilda's estates, to flee to Germany.

Frederick II's heroic efforts to restore the unity of the empire took on mythical proportions. It was said that he had not died, but was sleeping on a mountain top, ready to return when the empire was in need. The more modern myth about Frederick II is that he was the first truly modern emperor, a man who overcame the limitations of the Middle Ages and pointed the way to the Renaissance. He was a remarkable

figure who had absorbed the cultures of both Europe and the Orient. He was a patron of the arts and sciences, and was himself the author of a treatise *De arte venandi cum avibus* ('The Art of Hunting with Birds') which was the definitive work on ornithology for several centuries. His tolerance towards Moslems was such that many Christians feared that he might convert to Islam, but he was brutally harsh in the pursuit of heretics and discriminated against the Jews, forcing them to wear special clothing. Although he was a man of immense culture and learning, he was also a suspicious and mean-spirited despot. It is because of these contradictions that the *stupor mundi* ('wonder of the world') is still as fascinating as he was to his contemporaries.

Frederick II with his master falconer, the dedication page of Frederick II's *The Art of Hunting with Birds*, 1232.

The 'Bamberg Rider' in Bamberg Cathedral. This magnificent equestrian statue, dating from the early thirteenth century, represents a proud royal figure, in simple attire, gazing into the distance and seated on a splendid horse. Such equestrian statues are symbolic of the itinerant German court and of the Emperor's concern for his people. This figure is not representative of any specific emperor, and it has been suggested that it might be an idealized portrait of Constantine the Great.

excommunicate the emperor and to support the claim of a Hohenstaufen, a house which he detested. In September 1211 a small group of German princes, prompted by the French and by the pope, once again elected Frederick.

The eighteen-year-old Frederick II at once undertook the hazardous journey to Germany to establish his authority, even though he had the support of only the pope and the French. He had a number of narrow escapes. Otto IV was allied with the English but the French victory over the English at Bouvines on 27 July 1214 amounted to a victory of Frederick over Otto IV in Germany. Frederick II was crowned in Aachen in 1218. Otto still claimed to be king until his death in 1218, but there was little of substance to his claim. Frederick promised to take the cross and free the Holy Land. In 1225 he solemnly swore that he would begin his crusade in the summer of 1227. The pope, Gregory IX, correctly suspected that Frederick intended to establish himself in continental Italy, and seized the opportunity offered by Frederick's delays in mounting the crusade to excommunicate his dangerous rival. In a calculated challenge to the pope, Frederick assembled his crusaders in Brindisi. Once again the plague struck, the emperor sickened, and the crusade was called off.

Frederick II again ignored the pope, and against his orders began his crusade the following year. Having treated with the sultan of Cairo, he entered the Holy City in triumph and crowned himself king of Jerusalem. Meanwhile, a papal army invaded Sicily and combined with the anti-Hohenstaufen forces on the island. Frederick returned to his kingdom and quickly defeated his enemies, although his attempts to subject the northern Italian cities were unsuccessful, and the pope excommunicated him once again in 1239. There followed a long and increasingly acrimonious propaganda war between the two sides, the pope accusing the emperor of having said that the three greatest swindlers in history were Moses, Jesus Christ, and Mohammed.

In order to get his son Henry elected king, Frederick II had in 1220 been obliged to grant the prince bishops sovereign rights, including the right to levy customs duties and to mint their own money. When the lay princes complained that the regent, Frederick's son Henry (VII), had granted the towns too many privileges, these rights were also granted to them in decrees in 1231 and 1232. The emperor hoped that these concessions, further steps towards the creation of the territorial principalities, would end his struggles with the princes, but Henry was determined to extend the power of the crown. The struggle between father and son grew increasingly bitter. Henry allied with the anti-imperial Lombard princes and approached the French. In 1235 Frederick II returned to Germany after a fifteen-year absence, travelling with an exotic retinue of Saracens and Ethiopians along with a menagerie of leopards, apes, and camels. Henry was arrested and died in prison seven years later, probably by his own hand.

Having proclaimed the peace (*Landfrieden*) at Mainz, Frederick II had to deal with his son's principal ally, Duke Frederick the Pugnacious of Austria. The

The Golden Bull

The Golden Bull of 1356 was the nearest medieval Germany came to a constitution; not in the modern sense, but rather a bundle of proposals debated at two Diets, which established clear procedures for electing a king.

Before, kings had been elected by the nobility and acclaimed by the populace. Most elections were unanimous, suggesting the king's unique political qualities, with the sacramental anointment emphasizing his religious status.

According to the Golden Bull at least four of the seven electors had to be present, and a simple majority was sufficient. If one of the electors was also a candidate, he was permitted to vote for himself. On the death of an emperor the archbishop of Mainz was to call all the electors together to meet within three months. They were to be given a free passage to Frankfurt, whose citizens were to finance them. Each elector was allowed 200 knights, of whom no more than 50 could be armed. No outsider was permitted to enter the city while they were in session and the city was responsible for maintaining law and order, a dubious privilege.

The proceedings began with a mass in the church of Saint Bartholemew. If the electors did not reach a decision within thirty days, they were put on a diet of bread and water. The archbishop of Mainz summoned votes in order of precedence: the archbishops of Trier and Cologne, the king of Bohemia, the elector palatine, the duke of Saxony and the margrave of Brandenburg. The archbishop of Mainz had the final say and so could decide a tied vote.

The Golden Bull also clarified the rights of the other estates. The 'citizens beyond the pale' (*Pfahlbürger*), those living outside the towns, lost their rights and only town-dwellers enjoyed the protection of the law, a principle that applied well into the nineteenth century.

The Germany of the Golden Bull was not an incipient nation-state. The electors were virtual sovereigns within a loose confederation. Article 31 formally recognized this diversity in 'laws for different nations with distinct customs, habits and languages'.

The Golden Bull of 1356 with
Charles IV's imperial seal.

Austrian refused to appear before a royal court, was outlawed, and his imperial fiefs were seized. Frederick II was determined to bring Austria under imperial control. He travelled to Vienna, which he made an imperial city, and where his son Conrad had been elected king in place of the imprisoned Henry (VII). The emperor's victory was short lived. It proved impossible for him to control Austria from Sicily, and two years later he was obliged to restore Austria to Frederick the Pugnacious, with Vienna ceasing to be an imperial city. Frederick the Pugnacious died in battle against the Hungarians in 1246, and Frederick II seized his estates. After the emperor's death in 1250, Austria was taken by the king of Bohemia, and it was not until 1273 that a Habsburg was able to regain it.

In 1244, Pope Honorius III had fled to Lyon where he held a council to depose Frederick II, but he could not find a convincing anti-king. After Frederick's death in 1250 his son Conrad IV continued the struggle against Pope Innocent IV, and when he died in 1254 his illegitimate brother Manfred had himself crowned king of Sicily in 1258. In 1265 Pope Clement IV, in an attempt to frustrate the Hohenstaufen, gave Sicily as a fief to Charles of Anjou, the French king's brother. In the following year Manfred died in battle against Charles of Anjou. Conrad IV's son, Conrad, known as Conradin or Corradino, continued the fight against Charles. At first he was successful, but in August 1268 he was defeated at Tagliacozzo. He fled but was captured and, with his execution in the Naples marketplace, the Hohenstaufen dynasty came to an end.

Meanwhile, on Conrad IV's death, William of Holland tried to assert his claim in Germany and was supported by the League of the Rhine, an association of Rhenish towns which was formed in 1254 and which rapidly expanded to include more than seventy, stretching from Lübeck to Zürich. When William died in battle against the Frisians in 1256, the League of the Rhine claimed the right to rule until a suitable king had been elected.

The election of 1257 was conducted by a small group of electors who later were to be known as the electoral princes (*Kurfürsten*): the archbishops of Mainz, Cologne and Trier, the king of Bohemia, the margrave of the Rhine (later called the elector palatine), the duke of Saxony, and the margrave of Brandenburg. The archbishops of Mainz and the margrave of the Rhine favoured Richard of Cornwall, the second son of King John of England, and brother-in-law of Frederick II of Hohenstaufen. The other electors favoured King Alfonso of Castille who was also related to the Hohenstaufen through his mother. Alfonso, although he had invested a considerable sum in bribing the electors, was unable to leave his kingdom to claim his crown because of the opposition of the Castillian estates. Richard had no such problems and was crowned king in Aachen. He remained in Germany for almost four years, staying by the Rhine in the heartland of his support, but he was obliged to return to England where his brother Henry III was struggling with the barons led by Simon de Montfort. He died in 1272.

KINGS, PRINCES AND CRISIS

The period which Friedrich Schiller (1759–1805), speaking as a poet rather than an historian, described as 'a terrible time without an emperor', ended with the election of Rudolf of Habsburg in 1273. He was the most powerful prince in south-western Germany but, at fifty-five years old, was ancient by the standards of the day. Perhaps he was seen as a provisional monarch, and one from whom concessions could be wrung. King Ottokar of Bohemia was not present at the election and refused to accept Rudolf as king. Rudolf was obliged by feudal law to banish his rival and prepare for war. He prudently arranged the marriages of one daughter to the duke of Bavaria, another to the duke of Saxony, while a third was engaged to the king of Hungary. With the support of such powerful allies, Rudolf marched confidently against Ottokar and won a decisive victory at Dürnkrut near Vienna on 26 August 1278. The fleeing Ottokar was captured and killed. Rudolf

The Wartburg was the castle of the Landgraves of Thuringia. Between 1190 and 1217, during the rule of Hermann I, it was a great musical and literary centre modelled on the French courts of the period. The two greatest German poets of the age, Wolfram von Eschenbach (c.1170–c.1220) and Walther von der Vogelweide (c.1170–c.1230) met at the Wartburg. Luther sought refuge in the Wartburg, and it was here that he translated the Bible. In the nineteenth century the Wartburg became a national monument, symbolic of the glories of the medieval and Protestant traditions.

then married his daughter Guta to Ottokar's son Wenzel II, who was confined to Bohemia. The Austrian lands taken by the king of Bohemia in 1250, were given to Rudolf's sons. This was the beginning of the Habsburg empire.

Otto, the margrave of Burgundy, also refused to pay homage, arguing that he owed allegiance to the emperor but not to the king, and Rudolf was yet to be crowned emperor. Rudolf would have none of this. He assembled a sizable army and marched on Besançon. Otto gave up the unequal struggle and duly pledged allegiance. Next, Rudolf turned his attention to Thuringia, which was in a state of chaos; the local aristocracy were indulging in an orgy of feuds, vendettas, and murders. Rudolf descended upon the region, destroyed more than fifty castles, and celebrated the return of law and order in the Assembly of Erfurt in 1289. He died in Erfurt on 15 July 1291 aged seventy-three.

If it had been the intention of the electors in 1273 to choose an elderly and weak king, they had seriously miscalculated. In 1291 the archbishop of Cologne wished to see his creature, Adolf of Nassau, elected in place of Rudolf's son Albrecht, and he was supported by the archbishop of Mainz, who also hoped to extend his territorial power under a weak monarch. But once again things did not turn out quite as the electors had hoped. The new king continued his predecessor's policies in Thuringia to great effect, and the archbishop of Mainz allied with the king of Bohemia and Rudolf's son Albrecht of Austria to call a meeting of the princes in Frankfurt and declare the king deposed. Albrecht was elected king and promptly took the field against Adolf. On 2 July 1298 a decisive battle took place at Göllheim in the Palatinate in which Adolf was killed.

Albrecht made an alliance with the king of France and married his eldest son to his new ally's daughter. The Rhenish electors were troubled by this policy, which greatly strengthened the king's position in the west, and again they plotted his overthrow. But Albrecht was militarily far too powerful for the electors, and their common front soon collapsed. Pope Boniface VIII proved to be a more impressive opponent. Albrecht's proposal that the pope give him Tuscany was dismissed, and after lengthy secret negotiations, Boniface pronounced Albrecht a renegade and rebel. In 1302 the pope threatened to excommunicate Philip IV of France for imposing a tax on the Church. On the same day he published the bull 'Unam sanctam' in which he quoted Jeremiah 1:10: 'See, I have this day set thee over the nations and over the kingdoms, to root out, and to pull down, and to destroy, and to throw down, to build, and to plant'. It was a remarkable claim to papal supremacy, which could only be realized by reaching a compromise with Albrecht I. The pope recognized Albrecht's election and told the king of France that he was subject to the emperor. Albrecht agreed that the power of the electors and the office of emperor were dependent on the pope. It seemed that the pope had thus finally won the ancient struggle over the German king and emperor, and was in an advantageous position to bring the king of France under his sway.

Boniface did not enjoy his triumph for long. On 7 September 1303 William Nogaret, a close associate of the French king, and Sciarra Colonna, from a powerful anti-papal family, stormed the pope's summer residence and took him prisoner for two days. He was so badly treated by his captors that he died shortly after his release. This proved to be a disaster for the Germans, because the papacy had now fallen under the control of the French. In 1309 Clement V moved the papal court to the city of Avignon in southern France, where it was to remain in the 'Babylonian Captivity' until 1417.

Albrecht died in 1308, and Henry of Luxembourg was elected King Henry VII by the spiritual electors, one of whom, Balduin, was archbishop of Trier and Henry's brother. The new king and his episcopal brother were forceful personalities who quickly made the house of Luxembourg the equal of the Habsburgs. Having established his power in Germany, Henry left Bohemia in the capable hands of Peter Aspelt, the archbishop of Mainz, and departed for Italy.

Although, thanks to the long absence of an emperor, the north Italian towns had become increasingly independent, the area was clearly divided into two main factions. The Ghibellines (those parties within the Italian city-republics who tended to support the imperial cause) invited Henry VII to come to Italy; among those who gave him an extravagant welcome was Dante, who had been condemned to death by the Guelphs and forced to flee Florence. It was almost two years before Henry VII was eventually crowned in Rome. He was unable to reach Saint Peter's because of Guelph opposition, so instead was crowned in the papal basilica of St John Lateran in 1312. The subsequent coronation banquet was rudely interrupted by a shower of Guelph arrows. The new emperor was determined to assert his authority over all other monarchs, but his ambitions came to nothing. He died in August 1313 and lies buried in a magnificent tomb in Pisa.

It proved a difficult task to find a successor, and it was not until 19 September 1314 that Duke Frederick the Fair of Austria was elected king. The following day Ludwig of Upper Bavaria was also elected. Both sides were extremely reluctant to risk a pitched battle, and their armies did not clash until 1322 at Mühldorf, where Ludwig was victorious.

Three years of negotiations followed before the two kings agreed to form a joint monarchy. They soon found themselves confronted by a powerful opponent in Pope John XXII, who was elected in 1316 at the age of seventy-two as a compromise candidate unlikely to live long. To the electors' dismay he lived to be ninety-one, and proved a most vigorous pope. He was determined to increase the wealth of the Church by demanding annates, the first year's income of minor ecclesiastics on appointment to a benefice, and also one-third of the income of all bishops appointed by the pope. This prompted a heated discussion about the wealth of the Church. The pope declared that all those who argued that Christ and the apostles had no property were heretics.

The quarrel between Ludwig and John XXII escalated to the point where the pope excommunicated the king, denied him all political rights, and henceforth called him simply 'the Bavarian'. Ludwig ignored the pope, went to Rome, and was crowned emperor by an excommunicated bishop. Ludwig appointed an anti-pope, Nicholas V, whose authority vanished as soon as Ludwig left Rome.

John XXII died in 1334, but his successor Benedict XII was a close associate of the French king and intended to assert his authority over the German Church. This prompted a vigorous reaction from the German princes, and when the pope tried to remove the archbishop of Mainz, the electors met at Rhens near Koblenz in 1338 and asserted they alone had the right to choose the king by majority vote. They made no mention of the imperial title, but Ludwig announced that although the pope had the right to crown the emperor, this was a purely confirmatory act.

Ludwig's territorial ambitions towards Brandenburg determined the princes to remove him. His co-king Frederick had died in 1330, and in 1346 the electors chose Charles, the son of the blind King John of Bohemia. Charles was a man of exceptional ambition and cunning who had been educated at the French court, becoming a friend of future pope Clement VI, who did much to secure Charles' election to the throne. Charles' chances of establishing his claim were greatly diminished when the English long-bow men destroyed the French knights at the battle of Crécy in 1346. King John of Bohemia was killed in the battle. Charles was wounded and narrowly escaped, his reputation in ruins after this crushing defeat. He was crowned in Bonn, since Aachen, like most imperial cities, sided with Ludwig. He was widely regarded as little more than the pope's puppet, but his chance was soon to come. On 11 October 1347 Ludwig died of a stroke while out bear-hunting.

The Black Death

Historians are uncertain about the causes of the plague. The Avignon pope's private physician, Guy de Chaualiac, a man generally regarded as the greatest practitioner of his day, claimed it was caused by a particular conjuncture of the planets. Others suggested it was spread by wandering Jews, a theory warmly endorsed by the Nazis and perpetrated today in the most popular German historical atlas produced by a highly regarded publishing house. Perhaps it was brought to Europe by the crusaders, although there is little evidence of widespread epidemics in the Middle East at that time. It seems more probable that the plague originated in India, carried by rats with fleas, and brought to Europe by the merchant ships which travelled to and from the Black Sea.

Whatever the cause of the plague the people were helpless in the face of this horrific epidemic. Physicians who dabbled in astrology and superstition, wandering magicians in search of the gullible, and bloodsuckers with their leeches had no idea that the plague was spread by rats and insects and were at a loss for a cure. The mere sight of someone infected was said to be enough for one to contract the disease. Death was omnipresent and omnipotent, the grim reaper was the dominant icon of the age. In Mainz and Cologne about a hundred people died each day. As many as twenty-five million people died in Europe, possibly over half the population.

The chronicler and Dominican Heinrich von Herford reported that in 1349 in Germany and elsewhere in Europe, Jews were put to death 'in the most horrible and inhuman manner, by iron and fire'. He did not believe that the Jews were guilty of poisoning the wells and causing the plague as their torturers claimed, and he felt that the massacre was the result of envy of their wealth — debtors had chosen a good opportunity of getting rid of their creditors.

With no medical help and without Jews to slaughter, people were either resigned to their fate or joined the processions of flagellants who stripped to the waist, confessed their sins amid prayers and hymns, and were flogged. The Church took a dim view of these public confessions, for it was determined to maintain its monopoly over the forgiveness of sins. The fear of hell and the desire for divine forgiveness were central obsessions at the time. Sin was palpable and had to be extirpated, punishments were remarkable for their sadistic brutality. Adulteresses were buried alive, traitors quartered, blasphemers had their tongues ripped out, and murderers were skinned alive.

A procession of flagellants at Doornik in 1349.

A CENTURY OF CRISIS

Politically, the first half of the fourteenth century was probably not significantly worse than other periods in the Middle Ages, but it is remembered as a time of terrible natural disasters. A devastating famine started in 1315 and lasted for three years. Twenty years later the crops in southern Germany were destroyed by swarms of locusts, and there were a number of serious earthquakes. On top of these horrors, there were outbreaks of the plague: in 1351 an epidemic throughout Germany is estimated to have killed one-third of the population. Subsequent famines and plagues meant that the population did not begin to grow again until a century later, and did not regain its previous level until the beginning of the sixteenth century.

These disasters were seen as signs of divine retribution, and amidst widespread manifestations of mass religious hysteria, many bizarre heretical sects were formed and Jews were brutally murdered throughout Germany. It was widely rumoured that the Jews had poisoned the wells and that this had caused the Black Death. The swarms of locusts were said to be God's punishment because Jews had desecrated the Host. Although the Church authorities frowned on such practices, flagellants marched through the towns in elaborate processions, and sins were confessed in public. In many instances, such as the pogrom in Nuremberg in 1349 in which 560 Jews were burnt at the stake, Jews were murdered simply for their property.

There was a significant movement of population away from the land and into the towns, resulting in the abandonment of many villages and a sharp reduction of agricultural land. The dramatic fall in population meant that agricultural prices fell, as did rents and dues. The incomes of landowners, whether aristocratic or not, were drastically reduced. Many aristocrats partially made up for this loss by serving the increasingly powerful territorial princes. By contrast, wages in the towns rose sharply and the golden age of the wage-earner began. Towns benefited from the availability of cheap grain by building granaries, and so eliminated famine, while in the countryside, when the crops failed the people still went hungry. Although most were content to blame all these disasters on the machinations of the Jews, some spoke out against an explanation which allowed many to slaughter their creditors. Some clerics argued that the plague was God's punishment for Christian sinners, while others suggested that natural disasters might have natural explanations.

Charles IV was in an exceptionally precarious situation on accession. He faced the opposition of the estates in Bohemia who feared a powerful monarch, and even the death of his rival Ludwig did not leave him undisputed king. The rival electors

The gigantic figure of the Landgrave of Thuringia, assisted by his soldiers, servants, and women, fends off attackers who are besieging the Wartburg. From the Manesse Codex (1305–40).

offered the crown to the English king Edward III, the victor at Crécy, as his replacement. Charles moved cautiously. He won over a number of important towns and negotiated with Edward, who had no particular interest in the German crown.

Charles' position in Germany was soon strong enough to allow him several years in Bohemia. The bishopric of Prague had become independent from the archbishopric of Mainz in 1344 and became an archbishopric, an important step towards Bohemian independence. Prague University was founded in 1348, the first in the German empire, so German scholars no longer had to go to France and Italy. The magnificent Charles Bridge over the River Moldau is testimony to the importance of his capital, as was the rebuilding of the cathedral and the foundation of many lesser churches. Charles added a number of territories to Bohemia, including Lusatia and Silesia, Moravia, the bishopric of Olmütz, Troppau, and much of the Upper Palatinate. Bohemia thus extended almost as far as the important financial centre of Nuremberg, and Erlangen was founded as a Bohemian town.

Once Charles was firmly established in Germany and Bohemia the call came for him to seek the imperial crown. Charles IV set out for Rome and was crowned in April 1355. He only stayed for one day and hastily returned to Germany. Charles wisely avoided becoming embroiled in Italian politics or in conflicts with the pope, and paused only to fill his coffers with tax money from the imperial cities. He thus returned to Germany as the uncontested emperor, his power and his wealth considerably enhanced.

A university professor delivers a lecture to his students, Strasburg, 1502. The earliest universities were associations of private academic schools which were protected by emperors, kings or popes and given a certain amount of autonomy, academic freedom, self-governance, and freedom from taxation. The first German universities were founded in Prague (1348), Vienna (1365), Heidelberg (1386), Cologne (1388), and Leipzig (1409).

At the Assembly of Nuremberg in 1356 a number of important issues were discussed, among them the question of the election of the king. It was agreed that the electors should be the archbishops of Mainz, Cologne, and Trier along with the king of Bohemia, the elector palatine, the duke of Saxony, and the margrave of Brandenburg. Election was to be by a simple majority. No mention was made of the pope's right to approve the choice. These proposals were accepted at a second Assembly in Metz and published as the Golden Bull, so named because the seal was made of gold rather than wax.

Charles IV died in 1378 leaving a powerful inheritance, but his son Wenceslas was not a success. He was an impetuous, short-tempered, and brutal man who soon faced the opposition of the Bohemian aristocracy and Church. He captured the vicar-general of Prague, John Nepomuk, and had him tortured and drowned in the Moldau. The citizens of Prague revolted, and in southern Germany the towns rose up against the nobility. Wenceslas got no support from his brother Sigismund, whose hold on the Hungarian throne was tenuous and who led a disastrous crusade in 1396, losing most of his men and almost his life. In 1400 the four Rhineland electors deposed Wenceslas, a decision which he did not even contest with arms – the final evidence of his weakness.

SCHISMS AND COUNCILS

The new king, the Elector Rupert of the Palatinate, was determined to correct the mistakes of his predecessor, but his ambitions were unrealistic. Rupert wanted to depose the Visconti (one of the most prominent Ghibelline families who ruled Milan), end the schism in the Church between Rome and Avignon, and be crowned emperor in Rome. But the southern German merchants who had financed his election did not want to bear the cost of an expedition to Italy. The Florentines, eager to humiliate the Milanese, supported the expedition but were unable to finance it.

Rupert was deeply concerned about the schism, and had founded the University of Heidelberg in 1386 as an intellectual support for the Roman pope and a haven for scholars who had fallen foul of his rival at Avignon. In 1409 the cardinals from Avignon and Rome called a council to meet in Pisa, without consulting the two popes or the emperor. The council deposed both popes and elected a third, Alexander V, who died shortly afterwards and was followed by John XXIII. When Rupert died in 1410, the electors chose two kings: Wenceslas' brother Sigismund and his cousin Jobst. Since Wenceslas was still alive, there were now three kings, just as there were three popes, but Jobst died shortly after his election, Wenceslas had no support, and Sigismund's claim was virtually unchallenged.

Although his early career was far from glorious, Sigismund proved to be a remarkable king. He had a highly developed political intelligence, was enormously energetic, and was a skilled diplomat. Admittedly, circumstances were in his favour; France counted for little during the reign of Charles VI (known as 'the Foolish'), who lost the battle of Agincourt and died completely insane. As king of Hungary, Sigismund was seen as the champion of Christian civilization against the Turks. Pope John XXIII was deposed at the Council of Constance for his spectacular sexual misdemeanours and his incorrigible venality. The Avignon pope Benedict XIII was also deposed, and the Roman Gregory XII resigned. In 1417 Martin V was crowned and the schism temporarily ended.

The appalling state of the Church during the schism gave ample grounds for fundamental criticism, and it is hardly surprising that Prague, the prosperous capital of the empire and a great intellectual centre, should have been home to many reformers. The prominent theologian, Hieronymus of Prague, spoke in 1409 of the 'most holy Bohemian nation' and this modern concept of nationality was used by King Wenceslas to change the constitution of the University of Prague in the Kuttenberg Decree, whereby the Bohemians were given three votes in the university council, the other nations only one. Previously the foreigners had had three votes, the Bohemians one. By balancing the council in the Bohemians' favour, Wenceslas hoped to win the support of the university for the Pisan pope, the

German scholars being in the Roman camp. The Germans responded to the decree by moving to Meissen, and the margrave built them a new university in Leipzig in 1409. Prague never recovered from the loss of these scholars and was soon under attack as a centre of heresy.

Jan Huss, the greatest Bohemian reformer, was born in about 1370. A charismatic preacher, he was also a professor at Prague University. When, in 1412, he was called to Rome, he refused to go, and announced that Jesus Christ was head of the Church, not the pope. One of Sigismund's men guaranteed Huss safe conduct to and from the Council of Constance. In spite of this guarantee, Huss was condemned to death and burnt at the stake after a lengthy trial in which he was allowed no defence. The reformers now had a martyr, and the explosive mixture of religious, political, and economic demands led to a bloody Bohemian revolt. The Hussite armies went on the rampage in central Europe, their brutality doing little to communicate the reforming message to their hapless victims.

The Council of Constance had secured the unity of the Church, addressed the Bohemian heresy, and acknowledged the need for reform. But reforming zeal soon gave way to an unedifying power struggle between the pope and the council. By 1437 there were two councils and soon, two popes. Sigismund died in the same year. In the last twenty years of his reign he had been unable to repeat the success of the Council of Constance, and he concentrated instead on his Hungarian kingdom, although it brought him little. Bohemia was rent apart by Hussite violence. His position in Germany had been weakened by his father who had alienated many areas. It was clear that the empire was as much in need of reform as the Church.

The German princes had found that the income from their sovereign rights (*Regalien*), such as customs dues and coin-minting, was not enough to meet their immediate needs. They therefore called upon their subjects for assistance in the form of taxes. For this reason the German word for tax (*Steuer*) implies aid and assistance. The princes invited representatives of the aristocracy, the Church, the towns, and in some instances the free peasants, to discuss such requests. This was the beginning of parliamentary institutions, for these representations of the estates soon did more than merely apportion taxes: they also began to make demands of the princes.

The territories and the larger towns were more successful than the emperors at introducing efficient administrations, codifying their rights and privileges, and recruiting a skilled bureaucracy. The Reich still had no supreme city. Kings established their capitals in their own territories – Ludwig the Bavarian in Munich, Charles IV in Prague, and Frederick III in Graz. These courts were small by later standards, but they provided much needed additional income for an aristocracy suffering from the agricultural crisis.

In order to counteract the power and influence of the Rhineland electors, Sigismund had granted the electorate of Brandenburg to a Hohenzollern, the count of Nuremberg, who was his diplomatic advisor and agent. He soon departed from

Brandenburg, a sandy waste populated by a fractious nobility, and was the first of a house that was to rule Prussia and then Germany also until 1918. Sigismund also granted Saxony to the margrave of Meissen, establishing the Wettins as the ruling house.

In 1438 the electors gave the throne to Albrecht of Habsburg, a choice which was as momentous as the promotion of the Hohenzollerns and the Wettins, for the Habsburgs were to provide emperors in Germany until 1806 and in Austria until 1918. Albrecht's election was unanimous, but since he was already king of Hungary and Bohemia, he was reluctant to accept the throne. He was never to be crowned; in the year following his election he died of dysentery while fighting the Turks.

The oldest surviving Habsburg, the twenty-four-year-old Frederick III, was unanimously elected in 1439. He was in a particularly strong position in that he inherited Carinthia, Styria, and Krain. All the remaining Habsburg lands were in the hands of two minors who were wards of the new king. The election seems to have excited little interest and was uncontested, yet it was of enormous consequence. Frederick III was to reign for fifty-three years. His death was perhaps somewhat premature, caused by the amputation of a burnt leg. His doctors assured posterity that it was due to the convalescent's over-indulgence in fresh fruit. His reign is chiefly memorable for his astonishing longevity.

Frederick III supported the Roman popes against the Basel council, which met from 1431 to 1437 to discuss questions of Church reform and their anti-pope, Felix V. In return, he gained control over the churches in his empire and was provided with sufficient funds to secure his coronation in 1452; he was the last of the German emperors to be crowned in Rome. By this time the council in Basel had been disbanded and the anti-pope had resigned.

In the following year Constantinople fell to the Turks, but Frederick III was reluctant to defend the Christian world against Islam. In the east the Teutonic Knights, a religious-military order formed in Acre in 1190, had been granted all the heathen lands they had conquered to the east of the empire, and so controlled the Baltic, Prussia, and East Pomerania. From 1440 an association of Prussian estates were demanding a voice in the affairs of state and received support from the king of Poland. In 1454 war broke out when the estates seized most of the castles of the Teutonic Knights. The civil war dragged on for thirteen years, finally ending with the Treaty of Thorn in 1466 which forced the Teutonic Knights to give up most of their territory, the emperor being unable to give them the assistance they requested.

Frederick III was equally unsuccessful in Bohemia and Hungary. In Hungary the estates appointed Matthias Corvinus king in 1458, and his reign, one of the most remarkable if controversial of the late Middle Ages, was to last until 1490. Ladislaus Postumus, the heir to these crowns, was the emperor's ward, but George von Podiebrad was proclaimed king of Bohemia by the estates, and ruled from 1458 to 1471. He was to prove an exceptionally energetic monarch. George von Podiebrad, a moderate Hussite, was determined to uphold the compact of Prague

of 1433, which permitted the Bohemians to receive the Eucharist in both forms. Pius II annulled the compact and threatened to try the king for heresy. The Bohemian king then called for a European crusade against the Turks, and for a reform of the empire. Frederick III supported George of Podiebrad, whom he treated as his deputy in the east, but his position remained precarious and worsened when the Bohemian king died in 1471. Matthias Corvinus, who had fought against George of Podiebrad on his excommunication in 1466, took Moravia, Silesia, and Lusatia from his successor in 1478. The Hungarian king had already defeated the Turks and seized Bosnia in 1462, and Moldavia and Wallachia in 1467. In 1482 he declared war on the emperor, and in 1485 he captured Vienna, where he resided in magnificent style. Frederick III was now driven out of his hereditary lands and resided in Graz under the shadow of his mighty rival. But he had managed to save and enhance the inheritance for his successors. Matthias Corvinus had no legitimate heir, and in 1463 had signed the Treaty of Pressburg. When Ludwig, king of Bohemia and Hungary, died at the Battle of Mohács in 1526, Austria, Bohemia, and Hungary went to the Habsburgs under the terms of the Pressburg Treaty. The three kingdoms were to remain united until 1919.

In the west, Frederick III's great rival was Charles the Bold, duke of Burgundy, a ruler who was richer than the emperor, or the kings of England and France, and who was in many ways more powerful than all of them. But Charles' ambitious plans came to nothing because his magnificent host of armoured knights was no match for the Swiss infantry armed with lances. At the battles of Grandson and Murten in 1476 and Nancy in 1477, where Charles was killed, the Swiss inflicted crushing defeats on the Burgundians, and proved that the knight-in-arms was now a romantic anachronism. Charles the Bold's assault on Germany was also a disaster. He attacked the archbishopric of Cologne and laid siege to Neuss, but Frederick was able to assemble a large imperial army, the first since the Hussite wars, and force the Burgundians to abandon the siege. An appeal was made to German national interest and met with a remarkable response. The German princes made common cause against a brutal invader, and the concept of nation, first used to classify students at the universities, then more broadly by the Church councils, was now used in its modern sense.

MAXIMILIAN I AND THE HABSBURGS' RISE TO POWER

In 1473 Charles the Bold hoped to marry his daughter Maria to Frederick III's son Maximilian. The emperor broke off the meeting at the last moment and it was not until after Charles' humiliating defeat by the Swiss at Grandson that he agreed to the engagement. When Charles the Bold was killed at Nancy and French forces invaded Burgundy, Frederick III acted swiftly and decisively. He enfeoffed Maximilian and Mary with Burgundy, and arranged their marriage by proxy. Four months later, on 19 August 1477, the pair were united. Ten months afterwards an heir was born. Mary died in 1482 as the result of a riding accident.

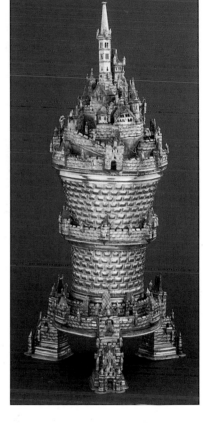

A gold and gilt metal-covered beaker in the shape of a fortified town. This late fifteenth- or early sixteenth-century masterpiece is by a German goldsmith.

Opposite: An illustration in the Hamburg municipal by-laws of 1497 shows merchants and sailors in Hamburg harbour. Hamburg was one of the principal members of the Hanseatic League, an association of 150 north German towns, designed for trade and mutual protection. The Hansa did much to colonize Eastern Europe, controlled trade between the North Sea and the Baltic, and mounted a number of successful military campaigns from 1350–1450.

The Medieval bath house

Personal hygiene was not a matter of pressing importance in the early Middle Ages. The humble peasant who only had one set of clothes saw no point in washing. Many of the early churchmen objected strongly to bathing. Some argued that water was bad for the body, others that the sight of one's own naked body might inspire lewd thoughts. Saint Augustine thought that bathing was permissible for Christians, but that it should not be done more than once a month. In 973 Caliph al-Hakam II's envoy to the Franks reported that he could think of nothing more revolting than a Frankish knight. They washed once or twice a year and never washed their clothes until they fell to pieces. For a Moslem, obliged to wash five times a day before prayers, such filth was unimaginable. Other observers reported that the Slavs at least had primitive steam baths in which they flogged themselves almost to death and then revived themselves with cold water.

In Bavaria the farmers had steam baths as early as the seventh century, and the German word for room (*Stube*) derives from the spray (*Stieben*) of the steam. It is probably due to the salubrious influence of the Orient that wealthy Europeans began to build in their castles and town palaces bathrooms with tubs of wood or metal. It was a sign of hospitality to offer a distinguished guest a bath. The hostess would bathe and massage the more illustrious among them, and sometimes even the host would perform this menial function.

In the finer steam baths knights were massaged, scrubbed and dried by nimble-fingered female attendants (*Badwibel*). Such luxury was extremely expensive and Tannhäuser reported that his habit of bathing twice a week cost him a fortune, largely because of the cost of the additional services performed by the female attendants. By the twelfth century public baths in many towns provided a more economical alternative. By the fourteenth century there were four bath houses in Mainz alone. These were very sociable establishments: Men and women bathed together, engaged in energetic conversation, ate and drank, enjoyed the music of strolling minstrels, and retired to neighbouring bed chambers for more intimate delights. It is hardly surprising that the old English word for a bath ('stew') later meant a brothel.

In the later Middle Ages public baths were denounced as dens of vice, the attendants as whores, and the operators as exploiters of immoral earnings. Medical men warned of contracting syphilis, the 'French disease' (*malum frantzosen*), and other unpleasant illnesses. Jealous spouses murdered their faithless wives whom they caught *in flagranti* in the tub. Patrons were frequently robbed of their belongings while bathing. Those who worked in bath houses were seen as pariahs — when Albrecht III of Wittelsbach secretly married the beautiful Agnes Bernauer, daughter of an Augsburg bath house operator, his father was so outraged that he had the unfortunate woman murdered.

Bath houses were most frequently visited on Saturday nights, or the night before a feast day. With their firm belief in astrology, people felt that it was inauspicious to bathe during the dog days of July and August, when the sun was in Leo. Special family occasions were celebrated in the bath houses: a *balneum nuptiale* was held before a marriage, and similar bathing parties were held after a birth or a funeral.

People in the Middle Ages tended to pay more attention to their hair than to their bodies. Hair was worn long and loose and had to be carefully groomed and regularly washed to avoid lice. Teeth were cleaned in the morning using a cloth and salt or powder, although this had little effect and most people lost their teeth at an early age. Most men were shaved only after a bath, and thus irregularly. Monks were shaved once a week, their tonsures every fortnight. Bathing had far less to do with hygiene than with sensual pleasure. A German proverb said: 'If you want a hearty laugh, go and take a cheery bath' (*Wiltu eyn tag fröhlich seyn? geh, ach geh in pad hinein*). Many emerged from the bath house much less clean than when they entered.

A bath house in the late Middle Ages from a manuscript written
for Antoine of Burgundy, c.1470.

landum eciā luxuria
malum cū accusare
aliquto facilius est
quā vitare opert nō inferat² Non
quidem ut nūllū honorem rapiat
sed ut seipm recognoscens ad
penitencia impelli possit iunctaȝ
illi libido qui eo hysdem vicioruȝ
pncipit oritur neqȝ q a reprehende

aut ab emendatione separentz geiō
mentis errore cōnexe· translateur
En ceste partie valerius commence
son vjᵉ liure qui est de dit z des
faiȝ dignes de memoire de la cite
de romme z des estrangiers· ouql
apres ce que valerius ce vij liure
precedent a determine de vertu z
operations vertueuses· en ce vjᵉ

In 1490 Maximilian obtained the wealthy duchy of Tyrol from his spendthrift cousin Sigismund. In the same year he defeated the Hungarians and under the Treaty of Pressburg was granted the title of king of Hungary, the succession being guaranteed should the joint-king Wladislaw die without heir. Maximilian was not yet master of Burgundy, and embarked on fifteen years of war against the French and against the estates in the Netherlands. In 1488 he was captured by the Netherlanders and once again Frederick III managed to assemble an imperial army which forced both the Netherlanders and the French to submit, at the Peace of Senlis in 1493. Maximilian was now secure in Burgundy and recognized in Artois and Flanders. A few months later Frederick III died.

Maximilian, often dubbed the 'last knight', enjoyed the sport of jousting, but realized that knights were militarily worthless and that the future belonged to the *Landsknecht*, the mercenary pikeman, and to the artillery. The brutal commander who laid waste to the Netherlands was also a great patron of the arts and literature, and the complexity of his character was captured by the greatest of his court painters, Albrecht Dürer. In 1494 Maximilian married Bianca Maria Sforza, the daughter of the duke of Milan, and shortly afterwards he allied with Pope Alexander VI, Venice, Milan, and the Spanish to drive the French from Italy. In 1495 the Reichstag in Worms agreed to imperial reforms in return for a modest grant towards Maximilian's Italian campaign against the French. An Eternal Peace was proclaimed, feuds were outlawed, and it was decreed that all disputes be settled in an imperial court (*Reichs-Kammergericht*) composed of nominees of the emperor and the estates. But it was unclear how the decisions of the court could be enforced or an imperial tax collected, so it was opposed by most of the territorial princes.

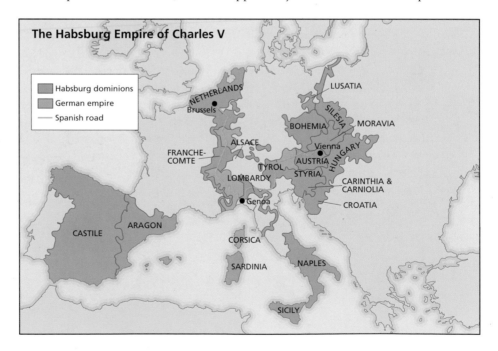

The Habsburg Empire of Charles V

Maximilian's campaign in Italy was not a success and had to be abandoned, in part because of the insufficient support of the Reich. In 1499 at the Treaty of Basel, Maximilian recognized that he no longer had any authority over Switzerland, whose forces had defeated the Swabian League and the emperor's armies. The Reichstag grudgingly granted him the funds to travel to Rome for his coronation, funds which were never provided; but he would have been unable to do so, for the French controlled northern Italy. In return for the money that was never paid, the emperor agreed to a Reich Government (*Reichsregiment*) made up of representatives of the lay and clerical princes and the towns. The government was to guarantee the peace (*Landfrieden*), and control the administration of the imperial court and army. The government could make decisions when the king was absent, but the king could do nothing without its consent. The emperor was thus theoretically rendered powerless, but he retaliated, and the government was no more able to put its decisions into effect than had been the monarch. It was further weakened by rivalries among the estates, and ceased to function in 1502. Local district organizations (*Reichskreise*), designed to ensure the peace, were far more effective and served as intermediary bodies between the Reich and the individual territories. The cause of the estates against the emperor was weakened even more by the deaths of Berthold von Hennenberg, archbishop of Mainz, and Philip Elector Palatine, two of the most influential reformers.

Since the Diet had only granted him the funds for a very modest army which was unable to fight its way to Rome, Maximilian was crowned emperor in Trent in February 1508, and he thus broke the tradition of a coronation by the pope. His successors were crowned simultaneously king and emperor. Maximilian's involvement in Italian politics ended in failure. In 1516 he made peace with Francis I and abandoned the German possessions in Italy. But Habsburg losses through war were to be amply compensated by gains through fortuitous marriages. Ferdinand of Aragon had married his daughter Joanna to Maximilian's son Philip. Maximilian's daughter Margaret was married to the heir to the Spanish throne Juan, son of Ferdinand of Aragon and Isabella of Castille. Three heirs to the Spanish throne died, so in 1517 Philip and Joanna's son Charles, jointly with his insane mother 'Juana la loca', inherited Spain, Naples, and Spanish America. In 1515 Charles had inherited the Low Countries and Burgundy from his father, and in 1519 he was elected emperor on the death of his grandfather. His grandfather's dream of a universal empire seemed finally to have been realized.

CHAPTER 4 | # *The Reformation*

Opposite: The Emperor Maximilian and his family were painted by Bernhard c.1515 on the occasion of a double engagement in the Habsburg family – 'others may fight wars, but fortunate Austria prefers marriages!'

Throughout much of Europe the sixteenth and early seventeenth centuries were characterized by the growth of the authoritarian, assertive, and self-confident nation state. Tudor England with its rich culture and pugnacious navy, Spain and Portugal with their daring explorers and overseas empires, the Versailles of Louis XIV, and the armies of the Swedish kings were all typical expressions of this new spirit. In Germany the situation was quite different. The old trans-national Holy Roman Empire was in decay, its component parts struggling to assert their sovereign independence. Could the empire be restructured to form a federal Germany able to meet the challenges of the new age of the nation state, or would the empire dissolve into a collection of small states, with the German language as their only common denominator? It was not until the eighteenth century that the future of Germany seemed likely to be decided, by the outcome of the struggle between two states of new European significance, Austria and Prussia.

GERMANY'S ECONOMIC MIRACLE

Although Germany in the early sixteenth century lagged far behind much of the rest of Europe in its political development, economically it was second to none. During the Middle Ages, the Hanseatic League, an association for the mutual protection of 150 German towns, had dominated east-west trade from the Atlantic to the Baltic. By the sixteenth century, the Hanseatic towns were already in decline, their privileges gradually eroded by the claims of the new nation states, but in other areas the German economy was growing at an impressive rate. In mining and metals the Germans were at the forefront and as bankers they were replacing the great Italians. International trade, particularly with the Orient, was flourishing, and industrial production, based on a system of sub-contracting to home-based labourers, was making impressive advances.

The leading sector of the German economy was mining, particularly in the ore deposits of the Harz, the Erzgebirge, the Thuringian Forest, and the Alps. This was an age of innovation; the need for capital stimulated banking; new ways of organizing production were developed; engineers found ingenious solutions for complex technological problems. Most of the larger metal works, particularly those around Mansfeld, were organized as limited liability companies whose investors came from all walks of life, from wealthy merchants to housemaids. Germany was the world's largest producer of silver until the Spanish began importing it from the New World in the mid sixteenth century, and since silver became the standard unit of payment, this made Germany the financial centre of Europe. Gold coins such as the guilder and the florin were replaced by the silver taler, named after the town of Joachimsthal in the Erzgebirge where Count von Schlick first minted a large silver coin.

Jakob Fugger 'the Rich' (1459–1525) was the most important of Germany's financiers. He is depicted in a characteristically brilliant portrait by Albrecht Dürer, painted c.1518.

CLEOPHAS · FRATER · CARNALIS · IO=
SEPHI · MARITI · DIVAE · VIRG · MARIAE ·

JACOBVS · MINOR · EPVS · MARIA · CLEOPHAE · SOROR
HIEROSOLIMITANVS · VIRG · MAR · PVTATIVA · MA
TERTERA · D · N ·

IOSEPH · IVSTVS · SIMON · ZELOTES · CONSO=
BRINVS · DNI · NRI ·

Frederick III the 'Wise' of Saxony (1463–1525) was Pope Leo X's favoured candidate for emperor, and the protector of Martin Luther. This portrait, by Lucas Cranach the elder, emphasizes his strength of character and piety (c.1515).

A woodcut from Augsburg, dated 1531, shows a farmer and a Jewish money lender, seated at his counting-board. For the Jews in Germany the Reformation brought no relief. Luther had at first imagined that his version of Christianity would be acceptable to Jews, but a counter-offensive by proselytizing Jews dashed his hopes. In *Concerning the Jews and Their Lies* (1543), he relapsed into the crude rhetoric of the Middle Ages, denouncing the Jews as ritual murderers and usurers, and announced that both Calvinism and Catholicism were 'Judaic' heresies.

Among the bankers (known as 'financiers') such as Ehinger and Schad in Ulm, or Fugger, Höchstetter and Welser in Augsburg, the Fuggers were by far the most important. Emperors and princes pleaded for credit with Jakob Fugger, wittily nicknamed 'the Rich'. The Fuggers had begun as textile manufacturers and merchants in the fourteenth century and then started to lend their own money. As this banking business expanded they accepted deposits from princely and aristocratic investors on which they earned fixed interest. The Fuggers were also involved in the metal industry and owned virtually all the mines and metal works in Hungary. As the bankers of the emperors Maximilian and Charles V they were granted mining rights in the Habsburg domains which gave them a virtual monopoly over silver, copper and mercury. The emperors owed their election, as Jakob Fugger did not hesitate to remind them, to huge loans from his house. In 1519, when the electors had to choose between Maximilian's grandson Charles V of Spain and Francis I of France, Charles oiled their palms with 851,918 guilders, of which 543, 585 came from the Fuggers. This was a staggering sum: at that time a housemaid earned 1.5 guilders per annum, a school teacher 3.75, and a princely councillor between 80 and 200.

The fortunes of the Habsburgs and of bankers like the Fuggers and the Welsers, were intimately connected. When the emperors faced financial ruin, the bankers saw their capital drain away. Gradually they turned their backs on such bourgeois pursuits and became mighty princes who tended their estates and protected their commercial capital. Eventually, the Fuggers were no longer bankers, but princes of Babenhausen, indistinguishable from many other German nobles.

Although the economy made impressive advances in the sixteenth century, the benefits for the ordinary people were lost by rapid population growth and inflation. Real wages sank dramatically and in many professions continued in a more or less steady decline for 200 years. The aristocracy and the wealthy burghers prospered, and this was the age of the 'prayer, booze and guzzle princes' (*Bet-, Sauf- und Freßfürsten*), tipplers and trenchermen of quite staggering capacity. The Saxon court set such high standards of gluttony that it was said that one arrived as a human being and left as a pig. Luther claimed that each country had its own devil and that 'our German devil is to be found in a good wineskin and is called booze'. Throughout the sixteenth century the average Hamburger consumed nearly 200 gallons of beer yearly. His sober descendants in 1993 drank a mere 33 gallons.

Although the social position of the aristocracy was unchallenged, the sixteenth century was in many respects the century of the bourgeoisie. They controlled the economy, set cultural standards, and exercised considerable political influence. Society was divided according to estates based on rank, status or caste, rather than the modern divisions of class as defined by economic criteria, but this did not mean that there was no opportunity for social advancement.

LUTHER

Martin Luther's father, Hans Luder, was first a peasant, then worked as a miner. Thanks to his marriage to Margaretha Lindemann, the daughter of a prosperous burgher, he was able to start a copper-smelting business in Mansfeld from which he made an excellent living. At the behest of his father, Martin began to study law, a passport to prestige, wealth, and influence. Luther abruptly ended his legal studies in July 1505 when he was travelling home from university in Erfurt. He was so terrified by a lightning bolt, he swore by Saint Anne that he would become a monk. Much to his father's distress, he promptly entered the Augustinian order in Erfurt, well known for the extreme severity of its observance. Luther outdid his fellow monks in the intensity of his prayer, the length of his vigils and the ferocity of his self-chastisement, all in the hope of finding salvation in the eyes of the stern and merciless God of the Middle Ages. In 1512 he was appointed professor of biblical studies at the University of Wittenberg. He studied the text of the Bible rather than turning to learned exegeses, and it was this intense critical examination of the original texts which led him to reject the current doctrine of salvation.

The critical passage for Luther was Romans I verses 16 and 17: 'For I am not ashamed of the gospel of Christ: for it is the power of God unto salvation to every

Johannes Gutenberg

Johannes Gutenberg was born about 1397 under the name Henne Gensfleisch zur Laden, the son of a burgher from Mainz. He was forced to leave Mainz in 1430 when a struggle broke out between the burghers and the guilds and he moved to Strasbourg where he made his first experiments in printing. He returned to Mainz by 1448, when he borrowed 150 guilders and, in 1450, a further 1,600 guilders from one Johannes Fust in order to set up his press and print the Latin Bible. This was an immense sum of money, the equivalent of several hundreds of thousands of pounds. In 1455 Fust demanded his money back and as the result of the ensuing court case Gutenberg went bankrupt.

He began printing books again on a much more modest scale. In 1457 he printed a Psalter and, in 1460, Johannes Balbus' *Catholicon,* a Latin dictionary. In 1462 the elector Adolf II of Nassau seized Mainz and the burghers were driven out of the city. Gutenberg moved further down the Rhine to Eltville where he helped build another press. In 1465 Adolf of Nassau honoured Gutenberg and granted him a small pension. He died on 3 February 1468.

Gutenberg was not the 'inventor of printing' as was claimed in his eulogy. His great invention was the use of moveable metal type. First the 296 typefaces, based on contemporary calligraphy, were engraved on steel dies. The dies were then pushed into a softer metal to make negative forms. The cast was made with a mixture of lead, antimony, bismuth, and tin in an ingenious hand-held instrument which was Gutenberg's unique invention. The typefaces were stored in a specially constructed case, the most often used letters being nearest to hand. The printer slotted the letters into the composing stick and then transferred them to a frame, known as a chase, which contained one page of print. Gutenberg made his own ink and the press was based on the principle of contemporary wine presses. The printing technique invented by Gutenberg remained in use until the eighteenth century.

The printing of the Bible was a mammoth task. It was 1,292 pages long, with forty-two lines to the page — hence the code-name B42 - and 180 copies were printed. The task took three years to complete, using six typesetters and twelve printers. Gutenberg's aim was to produce a book that looked exactly like a hand-written manuscript. Thirty Bibles were printed on parchment, the remaining 150 on paper specially produced in Italy. Only forty-eight copies have survived to this day.

In spite of the enormous cost of printed books – a Gutenberg Bible cost the equivalent of four years' income of a skilled worker such as a clerk – an amazing number of books were produced in the following years. Five million volumes of *incunabula* (books printed before 1500) were produced; the 1,100 printing shops located throughout 260 European towns were responsible for a staggering total of 27,000 titles.

Left **Johannes Gutenberg (c.1397–1468) in a steel engraving c.1840 by J. Kern.** *Below* **Psalms 1-4 from the Gutenberg Bible.**

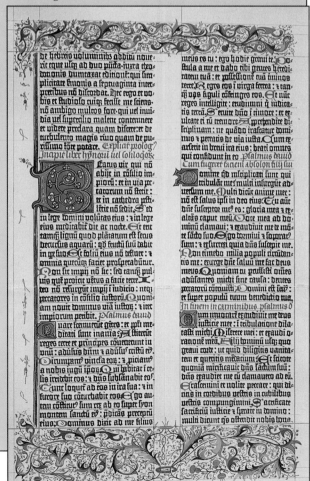

one that believeth; to the Jew first, and also to the Greek. For therein is the righteousness of God revealed from faith to faith: as it is written, the just shall live by faith.' Luther now believed that salvation came not from good works and self-chastisement, but solely from faith which would be strengthened by studying the Bible. Salvation came only from the Bible, from grace and from faith: '*sola scriptura, sola gratia, sola fide*'. Although Luther now rejected the vision of God as a merciless and avenging judge, he still believed that man and his world were fundamentally tainted by original sin and did not share the humanism of Catholic reformers such as Erasmus who believed that the world could be put in order by men of good will.

Luther's next major development was occasioned by the sale of indulgences, a practice that strengthened his belief that the temporal world was deeply tainted with sin. In the fifteenth century the Church permitted sinners to avoid increasingly elaborate acts of contrition by the purchase of indulgences. Indulgences could also be bought which shortened one's time in purgatory, or the time the dead needed to spend in purifying fire. The Medici pope, Leo X, whose pontificate began in 1513, was a cultured friend of Erasmus and the hope of the reform party, but was obsessed with grandiose schemes for rebuilding Rome. In order to finance these plans he exploited the credulity of the masses by proclaiming a jubilee indulgence in 1517. A sales force of hundreds of businesslike ecclesiastics was sent throughout Christendom to rake in the money.

Martin Luther, in one of many portraits by Lucas Cranach, whose brilliant draftsmanship and psychological penetration illuminate the complexity of the reformer's character.

One of the most talented of these travelling salesmen was the Dominican monk Johannes Tetzel who made extravagant claims for the efficacy of his indulgences. Luther heard of Tetzel's promises in the confessional where penitents told him that their past and even future sins, however horrendous, could be wiped away on payment of a suitable sum. Outraged by these reports, he composed his ninety-five theses which he sent to the archbishop of Mainz and the bishop of Brandenburg in November 1517. The story that he nailed the theses to the door of the castle church in Wittenberg is almost certainly apocryphal, originating several decades later.

The archbishop of Mainz, Albrecht von Brandenburg, was a mighty prince of the Church, one of the three spiritual electors, and responsible for the sale of indulgences in Germany. Albrecht was also archbishop of Magdeburg and administrator of Halberstadt, an accumulation of offices which was strictly forbidden by canon law. The papacy was generously prepared to overlook this irregularity on immediate payment of the princely sum of 24,000 ducats in gold. The archbishop had borrowed the money from the Fuggers and was consequently hopelessly in debt. He received 50 per cent of his income from indulgences in Germany and needed this money to pay his debts and acquire capital. He was not going to tolerate criticism from a monk. Receiving no reply from the archbishop, Luther gave copies of his theses to a number of associates to test their reactions. Some published them without the author's permission and they soon became the subject of fierce debate throughout the empire and beyond. German translations from the Latin appeared within six weeks. In December the archbishop of Mainz pronounced the anathema on Luther and proclaimed him a heretic. An official trial for heresy was initiated by the court of the papal see early in 1518, a remarkably swift reaction by the standards of the time. Luther's criticism of the sale of indulgences and his doctrine of salvation attacked the foundations of the Church. The idea of a priesthood of all believers denied the distinction between the lay and the clerical and made a privileged priesthood irrelevant. The sale of indulgences was difficult to justify, but if Luther's strictures were not countered, the worldly splendour of the papacy was called into embarrassing question.

The Augustinian Luther was cross-examined by Cardinal Cajetan, a member of the rival Dominican order, at the Diet of Augsburg in October 1518, but nothing more was heard of the case for two years. The emperor Maximilian had fallen ill in late 1518 and the papacy wished to prevent the election of his grandson Charles, the king of Spain. Leo X's candidate was Elector Frederick the Wise of Saxony, who supported his troublesome subject Luther. The papacy decided to soften the attack on Luther until the new emperor was elected.

Luther's attacks on the Church became increasingly radical. By 1520 Luther had concluded that the Roman Church was a gigantic pseudo-Christian fraud and that the pope was the anti-Christ. The reformer of 1517 was now a revolutionary, and his message was heeded by hundreds of fellow Augustinians, priests, and

An illustration from Luther's translation of the Bible shows the seven-headed serpent described in the Book of Revelations. Luther was not the first to translate the Bible into German, nor did he establish the norms for modern high German. On the other hand Luther's Bible with its forceful language had a profound impact on the development of the German language.

theologians throughout Germany. Luther's revolutionary theology was the product of the soul-searching of a lonely monk. He was preoccupied with the intimate relationship between man and God, and, unlike Zwingli and later Calvin, he felt that political and social concerns were extrinsic to this discourse, though affected by it. But for the majority of Germans, Luther's appeal for religious freedom and his attack on the Church implied a call for political freedom and an attack on political structures. His rousing pamphlet, *On The Freedom of a Christian*, was published in 1520, a time of economic and social uneasiness, and had an immediate and widespread political effect. On 10 December 1520 Luther and the humanist Philipp Melanchthon orchestrated a remarkable happening in Wittenberg. They built a bonfire on which they burnt the papal bull threatening his excommunication, along with a number of theological works which upheld the authority of the pope. Luther was by now a figure with a huge popular following both among scholars and the illiterate. Few understood the theological ramifications of Luther's concept of freedom, interpreting his individualism in political terms. The Reformation thus became not only a question of religious renewal but also a powerful social and political movement in which the various estates pursued their particular interests.

Silver coin representing Charles V (1500–58).

The new emperor Charles V, was crowned in Aachen on 23 October 1520 in a curiously bungled ceremony; even part of the regalia was missing. In January 1521 Charles attended his first Diet at Worms at which some important reforms were initiated. The empire was divided up into a number of administrative districts, intermediate instances between the states and the empire which had responsibilities for taxation, military policy, economics, and law and order. The imperial court and other institutions were strengthened. As part of this ambitious reform many complaints about Church abuses were heard. But the Diet of Worms is primarily remembered for the meeting between the twenty-one-year-old emperor and the thirty-seven-year-old theology professor from Wittenberg. Charles hoped Luther would renounce his heresy, but was disappointed.

On the contrary, Luther delivered an uncompromising and fearless attack on the authority of the Church. Christianity for Luther was a personal matter between the individual and his God, and no worldly institution, however magnificent and powerful, could stand in the way. He is reported to have said: 'I shall remain true to the words I have written unless I am clearly contradicted by writings or a convincing argument. I do not believe the pope and the councils, for it is obvious that they have often erred and contradicted themselves'. He concluded: 'As long as I am bound by conscience to the word of God I cannot and will not retract anything, because to do anything against one's conscience is to risk one's salvation. God help me. Amen'. Luther's words were enthusiastically received by the crowd, but the propagandists' versions of these final words had an even greater impact. According to the broadsheets Luther had concluded with the defiant words: 'I cannot act in any other way. Here I stand. God help me. Amen.' Luther won precious little support for his position at Worms and an imperial edict was issued demanding that all who helped him in any way were to be arrested. Charles V promised to devote all he had to the struggle against heresy: 'My kingdoms and powers, my friends, my body, my blood, my life and my soul'. On 3 January 1521 Luther was excommunicated, but he still enjoyed the protection of the elector of Saxony and was safely housed in the Wartburg in Eisenach.

THE REFORMATION TURNS VIOLENT

The new message was spread by the minor clergy and the Augustinians, who had houses throughout Germany. These men were to form the core of the Protestant ministry. Many had close contacts with humanists who instinctively found Luther's teaching attractive, as long as they could ignore his pessimistic view of mankind as hopelessly corrupt and sinful. Some abandoned Luther when Erasmus, the greatest of all the humanists, published the pamphlet *De Libero Arbitrio* in 1524, which upheld his belief in free will against Luther's grim determinism.

Though oral propaganda remained important, none of this would have been possible without Gutenberg's printing press, invented some seventy years before. The Reformation had an extraordinary effect on the book trade. Only 200 titles were produced in Germany in 1518; there were 900 in 1519. Luther's writings were peddled at the Frankfurt book fair and were exported in large numbers throughout Europe. In 1521, when the Diet of Worms ordered that all Luther's writings be burnt, there were already half a million copies of his works in circulation. If Luther had been active a century earlier he would quickly have been forgotten. The diffusion of printing rendered the Church powerless against these intoxicating theories. Luther published his translation of the new testament in 1522 and the old testament in 1534. By the time of his death in 1546 about one million copies had been sold, an astonishing figure by the standards of the day, especially as these Bibles cost up to a year's wages for a housemaid. The fact that the Bible, the source of all religious truth for Protestants, was now readily available for study by ordinary people, was an important factor in making the Reformation possible.

First among the lay supporters of the Reformation were the imperial knights, a minor aristocracy who owed their titles directly to the emperor. They had seen their privileges eroded and were resentful of the Church in whose service many of their fellows had grown rich. In August 1522 the imperial knight Franz von Sickingen presided over a meeting of 600 knights from the lower Rhine at Landau. They swore 'brotherly association' to preserve their rights in the newly forming states, and to defend their new faith. Arguments between them were to

The Emperor Charles V is shown enthroned in a garden, with a crown, orb and sceptre representing temporal and spiritual power. A clerk, a knight, and a dreamer people the foreground.

be settled not by violence or even law, but by their own courts of arbitration. In the spirit of their new piety they abjured excessive drinking and swearing.

In one respect the imperial knights were ahead of their time. The idea of a nationwide and religiously sanctioned confederation was later to have a revolutionary impact in England and the American colonies. But the imperial knights were a declining class, both economically and politically, and they could no longer play their traditional role in society. Blown out of the saddle by gunpowder, the once proud knights could either seek their fortunes on foot as mercenary officers, take up the uncertain profession of robber-baron, or swallow their pride and enter the service of the lay or spiritual princes. Their traditional means of seeking justice by bloody feuds had been outlawed at the end of the fifteenth century and their illegality was underlined by the Peace of Nuremberg in 1521, but gang wars and vendettas still continued.

Most of the imperial knights lived in relative poverty in their decrepit castles, their lives constantly at risk. Ulrich von Hutten claimed that life was so dangerous that he had to wear armour when hunting or fishing. The landowning aristocracy of northern Germany, although they too had grievances, were much more prosperous. Their different economic and political aspirations made a nationwide alliance virtually impossible. The Knights' War of 1522–23 was thus confined to central, western, and southern Germany and was more of a feud than a war. The poorly organized and badly equipped knights had little chance against the princely armies. Only in Trier was Franz von Sickingen initially successful, but the elector, Richard von Greiffenklau, found powerful allies who forced Sickingen back into his castle in Landstuhl where he was killed on 7 May 1523, his fortress shot to pieces by the artillery of Philip of Hessen and the elector palatine.

Sickingen's death marked the end of the revolt and the princes proceeded to raze the knights' castles and seize their lands. But this was not the end of the imperial knights as an estate. They reorganized into local associations, rather than on an imperial level, and defended their interests as best they could. From 1540 the emperors saw the imperial knights as useful allies against the princes, and jealously protected them. When the empire reached its inglorious end there were still 1,700 imperial knights, many of proud independence and considerable influence.

THE PEASANTS' REVOLT

Two years after the knights' revolt was crushed, the peasantry rose up. They too had seen their ancient rights encroached by the early modern territorial state. They were hurt by inflation, and saw the profits from increased agricultural production going to the landlords, who were now often paid in cash rather than kind. They were the victims of greedy fiscal policies and capricious administrators. Conditions varied throughout Germany from serfdom to relative independence, but in most areas the peasants were increasingly threatened economically, politically and socially. Only those who could market their own produce profited from the

Thomas Müntzer

Thomas Müntzer, an early and enthusiastic follower of Luther, was probably born on 21 December 1489 in Stolberg in the Harz mountains. He was active in Thuringia as a theologian and preacher. His thought was strongly mystical, stressing the obligation of individual Christians to struggle for the heavenly kingdom. Luther, with his theory of the 'two kingdoms' clearly distinguished between theology and politics, between heaven and earth. Müntzer, whom Luther denounced as a fanatic, refused to draw such a distinction and announced that the apocalypse was near, the thousand-year-kingdom about to begin.

Having wandered around Bohemia, Franconia, and southern Germany as an itinerant preacher, he was elected by his radical followers to be minister in the Thuringian imperial town of Mühlhausen. He seized the opportunity offered by the Peasants' War to take up the 'sword of Gideon' and under a flag made of thirty yards of white silk, emblazoned with a rainbow, he assembled his troops to fight the 'fat cats' (*grossen Hansen*), the princelings and the wealthy, the petty, greedy anti-Christs whose egotism blinded them to his millenarian vision.

After the disaster of Frankenhausen, when Müntzer's troops were massacred by a royal army, he was taken prisoner and, after excruciating torture, called upon his followers to abjure violence and 'to beg mercy of your lords, whom I trust will forgive you'. After further torture he confessed to the error of his ways and was beheaded on 27 May 1525.

By mixing millenarianism with the justifiable grievances of the peasants, Müntzer enabled the opposition to discredit the entire movement. When the peasants began to seek scriptural justification for their political demands, Luther spoke out against them in his pamphlet *Against the Murderous, Thieving Hordes of Peasants*. The tragedy of Frankenhausen was caused by the fact that Müntzer had no understanding of the political and economic aims of the peasantry, who in turn could not understand his brand of militant mysticism. His hopes of punishing the wicked and establishing the kingdom of God on earth were bound to be a miserable failure, as are all such enterprises, especially in their secular Utopian form.

The result was a hardening of the fronts. Luther was now solidly on the side of the princes and sanctioned the appalling slaughter of tens of thousands of mostly innocent peasants. Luther wrote: 'Dear Sirs, whoever can should stab, smite and strangle. If you die thereby you could not die a more blessed death, since you die in obedience to God's order... The peasants have a bad conscience and an unjust cause and any peasant who dies thereby is lost, body and soul, and belongs to the devil for all eternity'. Luther was later to feel a little ashamed of such outbursts and wrote: 'I killed Müntzer just as I killed Erasmus. Death is upon my head. But I did it because he wanted to kill my Christ'. Luther's reaction to Thomas Müntzer and the Peasants' War marks the end of the Reformation and the beginning of Protestantism, a politically sanctioned religion.

A scene from the Peasants' War shows a surprise attack by crudely armed peasants on an imperial soldier's camp.

increase in agricultural prices. Communal village rights were denied as the states pursued their centralizing policies. Many free peasants were reduced to serfdom.

Although these were hard times for the majority, it would be a mistake to imagine that the Peasants' War was the frustrated outburst of the desperately poor. It was the rich and middle-income peasants who struggled to protect their rights to self-determination in the village and in the Church, not the impoverished serfs. The peasants wanted to elect their own priest and ensure that their tithes remained within the parish. They wanted to restore their rights to use common lands, to hunt and fish, and to exploit the communal forest. They wanted abolition of the onerous death duties owed to the *Leibherr* (a lord with jurisdiction over serfs). These demands to restore the community were couched in Christian terms. The aim was not to do away with lords and masters but to ensure that the relationship between lord and peasant was based on brotherly love, and that the community was built on Christian principles. These lofty ideals were proclaimed by insurgent Swabian peasants in Memmingen in March 1525, where the 'Christian Association' was formed from three rebel groups. Their ambitions were given the sanction of divine law, thanks to Luther's propagation of the gospel and the new theology of liberation. The princes had little difficulty in suppressing the revolt. Under the command of Georg Truchsess von Waldburg, the emperor's mercenary army crushed the peasants in Swabia. In Wurttemberg, where Duke Ulrich sided with his peasantry against the Habsburgs, with whom he was involved in a dynastic squabble, the rebels were defeated at Böblingen in May and brutal reprisals were meted out to their supporters.

Despite these early victories by the imperial army, the revolt continued. Among the imperial knights and burghers the peasants found allies such as Tilman Riemenschneider, who had been mayor of Würzburg and was regarded as Germany's greatest sculptor. The attempt to call a peasants' parliament at Heilbronn to discuss fundamental reform of the empire was frustrated by the arrival of troops from the Swabian League, emboldened by their recent victory at Böblingen. Since the imperial and princely authorities had no intention of negotiating with the insurgents, the struggle became increasingly violent on both sides. The peasants were guilty of a number of atrocities and the princes' forces repaid them one-hundredfold. The imperial army won several further battles.

The leading figure in this later, radical phase of the Peasants' War was Thomas Müntzer. He was an explosive mixture of mystic, activist and charismatic harbinger of the apocalypse. He preached a bloody crusade against the anti-Christ which would end with the triumphant thousand-year rule of Christ the saviour. Müntzer's fiery rhetoric found a ready echo among the peasants, artisans, miners, and urban poor of Thuringia, and he soon assembled an army of gullible devotees, 5,000 of whom soon lay dead at Frankenhausen. The royal army lost all of six men in this massacre. Müntzer was captured and encouraged by experienced torturers to call upon his followers to abandon the unequal struggle and beg mercy from the princes. He was shown none, and was beheaded along with fifty-three of his followers on 27 May 1525.

Luther was appalled by the Peasants' War and particularly by the activities of Thomas Müntzer, whom he described as his 'false brother'. He was convinced that the devil was on the side of the peasants, and that their struggle was aimed against the divine truths which he had discovered. He thus placed himself firmly in the camp of the princes whom he realistically saw as the best guarantors of the Reformation. Like so many other fanatics, dictators and starry-eyed idealists who feel they alone have discovered the truth, he was quite prepared to condemn thousands to their death. In his pamphlet *Against the Thieving and Murderous Hordes of Peasants* Luther urged the princes in God's name to slaughter the insurgents. Some 75,000 died, most of them unnecessarily, at the hands of those who acted in this spirit.

The peasants never had any chance of realizing their political programme since their Utopian vision of a communal, Christian brotherhood could not be implemented in the manifold small territories where they were strongest. Only in Tyrol did the insurgents have a clear political programme, a fact which was not lost on the authorities, who promptly suppressed the uprising for fear of another Switzerland. Nor were the peasants sufficiently developed politically to spearhead such a fundamental social reform. The long-term effects of the war were disastrous. The ruling classes were now convinced that no concessions whatsoever should be made to the peasantry, beyond a few token gestures such as granting them a limited voice in local government. Thus the position of the aristocracy was strengthened. Nevertheless the peasantry did not lose their determination to stand up for their rights, and legal reformers did much to find non-violent

In a sixteenth-century engraving of a German village, a group of pious church-goers are contrasted with boisterous villagers who are over-indulging in drink, food and amorous pursuits.

ways of solving the problems of rural society. The peasants have often been portrayed as depressed, humble and deferential creatures, but in fact they remained active subjects.

The Reformation was especially welcomed in the towns. About 30 per cent of the urban population was literate, as opposed to a mere 5 per cent in rural areas, so Luther had a far larger potential readership. The educated burghers (*Bildungsbürgertum*) of the towns were the most receptive to the new ideas and, together with Protestant clerics, propagated them among the illiterate from the pulpit, in taverns, and in the market place. During this period towns were small enough for there to be a real sense of community, both secular and religious, and so were particularly responsive. Only two cities, Cologne and Augsburg, had populations of over 40,000. The Roman Church was never fully integrated into the small urban communities, for the priests owed their primary allegiance to Rome, and the cathedrals were self-governing bodies which enjoyed all manner of privileges, exemptions, and immunities. Efforts had been made to bring the Church and its charitable institutions under the control of the town councils, but this could only

Mounted patrician youths enjoy chasing apprentices in Nuremberg on 3 March 1560, the occasion of the annual 'Apprentice-Sticking' (*Gesellen-Stechen*). Painting by Jost Amman (1539–91).

succeed up to a point. The Protestant Church had immediate ties to the community; a committee of laymen appointed and dismissed ministers, controlled finances, and supervised the social services. The minister, with his wife and family, lived an exemplary bourgeois life amid his fellow burghers, something which the celibate priest could never do.

The imperial cities and hundreds of smaller towns were centres of republican virtues. In theory, all citizens were protected against wilful arrest and taxation. They had equal responsibilities and duties. Their common interests were represented in a series of committees which dealt with all aspects of town life. Members of the political elite were seen as equals, their ranks were open to men of talent and achievement, and they formed a benevolent oligarchy which jealously protected the independent rights of the towns against princely ambitions to dominate them. In practice, there had been a tendency from the fifteenth century, particularly in the imperial cities, for these civic oligarchies to become self-serving tyrannies claiming a God-given right to exploit the citizenry like any corrupt monarch. The towns were also under attack from the princes who were determined to absorb them into their territories. The struggle of the towns to free themselves from local tyrannies and to protect themselves against the princes had resulted in a number of uprisings in the early sixteenth century, just as there had been widespread local unrest among the peasants in the years before the Peasants' War. In many instances these political disputes had strongly anti-clerical overtones. The ideas of the Reformation were thus eagerly taken up in the towns, for they gave religious sanction to this political, social, and economic struggle.

Münster was the most radical of the German towns. In 1525 there had been riots against the town council, but the bishop had been able to keep the population under control. The town became Lutheran in 1532 and was officially recognized by the bishop as such in the following year. In January 1534 a baker from Haarlem, Johann Matthys, arrived in Münster and proclaimed that the age of slavery was over, the Lord was about to return, that the children of God should be baptized, and that unbelievers must be put to the sword. Münster was particularly receptive to these ideas, as many citizens had heard of the Biblical exegeses of Melchior Hoffman, who announced that the end of time would occur in 1534, in Münster. Some 1,500 citizens including clerics, laymen, patricians, artisans and merchants, were baptized and awaited the Second Coming. The unbaptized fled the town and pleaded with the bishop and princes to restore the old order. Jan Matthys announced that Münster was the New Jerusalem which alone would be spared from God's avenging angels, who would destroy more than 90 per cent of the population. Thousands prudently moved to Münster to await the end of the world, which was expected to occur before Easter.

On 24 February an anabaptist council was elected which promptly ordered the destruction of statues, paintings, illuminated manuscripts, musical instruments, games of chance, and other such devilish objects. The bishop assembled an army

The courtyard of Innsbruck Castle, in a watercolour by Albrecht Dürer (1471–1528). Durer was born and lived in Nuremberg, and made lengthy visits to Italy and the Netherlands. He was court painter to both Maximilian I and Charles V and met Erasmus and Luther. Although a masterly draftsman and painter he is best known for his engravings and woodcuts, and he invented etching. His masterpieces included engravings on the Apocalypse, detailed and tender sketches of everyday life, topographical paintings such as this illustration, and official portraits.

which besieged the town in March. This only served to make the inhabitants of the New Zion even more radical. They indulged in mass acts of penitence, performed wildly ecstatic dances, practised polygamy, and established a primitive communism by pooling their belongings.

Easter passed without the apocalypse. Jan Matthys called for God to act and, with a handful of followers, left Münster and charged the bishop's army. He was promptly cut down by the mercenary soldiers (*Landsknechte*). Back in the town, Johan Bockelson, a tailor's apprentice from Leiden, appointed a new council of elders. Shortly afterwards, he secured his coronation as King Johan the Just and,

A German burgher family seated at table in an engraving entitled 'Concordia'. The quotations on the wall are from Deuteronomy 6: 'You must love Yahweh your God with all your heart, with all your soul'; and Matthew 22 'Love thy neighbour as thyself'. This painting has an ironical flavour. Only the father is listening as his son says grace. The women have already started their meal and inhabit a separate space. With incomes in the towns rising faster than agricultural prices, townspeople enjoyed a relatively comfortable material life, and devotional practices were often taken lightly.

with his six wives and elaborate court, he ruled Münster like an old testament king. The bishop was determined to put an end to this nonsense and after a long siege the town was stormed on 25 June and the leading anabaptists killed. This brief period of extremist Protestantism immunized Münster against the Reformation. The town returned to the traditional Church and remains to this day staunchly Catholic.

THE ORIGINS OF THE WARS OF RELIGION

The princes, far more than the peasants, knights or townspeople, were prompted to become Protestants by self-interest. The Reformation gave the princes the opportunity to seize or tax Church lands. On the other side, the powerful princes of the Church, including the electoral bishops of Mainz, Cologne and Trier, the abbots of the imperial monasteries, and the lesser bishops, were determined to uphold the privileges of the Church and to resist the reformers. After the Knights' War, many a minor aristocrat realized that the Church offered the best opportunity for social advancement. Thus the Schönborns, Greiffenklaus, and Dalbergs became prince bishops and electors. The Bavarian Wittelsbachs clung to the old religion and became virtually hereditary bishops of Cologne, Germany's richest bishopric and largest town. However neither Catholics nor Protestants were motivated solely by money and many Catholics were open to the new humanism of Erasmus. Reforming zeal was by no means a Protestant monopoly.

Although Charles V had every reason to uphold the Catholic Church and to resist the reformers, his European ambitions were such that he spent little time in Germany and left the government in the hands of his brother Ferdinand. The

German princes took advantage of the emperor's absence to assert their power, and since Charles and Ferdinand badly needed the princes' support to finance their foreign wars, particularly against the Turks, they were unable to resist their encroachments. Furthermore, the princes had shown their strength by crushing the knights, defeating the peasants, and dealing with the anabaptists. At the Diet of Speyer in 1526, the Edict of Worms was in effect annulled and the princes were permitted freedom of conscience. In 1529 the emperor, strengthened by his victories in Italy, reaffirmed the Edict of Worms. The 'Protest' made at Speyer by the five evangelical princes and the fourteen cities opposing this attempt to assert imperial authority, gave the new religion its name.

Charles V attempted to stop the rot by attending the Diet of Augsburg in 1530, the first Diet he had attended since Worms ten years before. He hoped to bring the heretics back into the fold of the Mother Church, but it was far too late. Philipp Melanchthon, Luther's close associate and friend, produced the Augsburg Confession (*Confessio Augustana*), an important exposition of Lutheran theology (though designed to a create a bridge to the Zwinglians). Luther, who was still under the imperial ban, could not risk going to Augsburg, but he remained in close contact with Melanchthon and supported the document.

The Catholics responded to the *Confessio* with their *Confutatio*, and reaffirmed the Edict of Worms, announcing that all who opposed it were guilty of a breach of the peace. The Protestants were understandably alarmed and, on 27 February 1531, they met at Schmalkalden in Thuringia to form a defensive league against the emperor. Germany was now divided into two armed camps and war was only avoided because Charles V was once again embroiled with the Turks who were marching towards Vienna. In August 1532 he proclaimed the Nuremberg Concession, in which he agreed to a temporary religious truce in return for Protestant support for the campaign against the Turks.

For the next ten years Charles V was almost exclusively concerned with his foreign wars, and the German princes profited from his absence to strengthen their position. In 1542, once he was free from these entanglements, the 'Emperor's Decade' began, in which he concentrated on Germany. His attention turned first to Jülich-Cleves, a rich and powerful state centred on Düsseldorf which had absorbed the estates of Geldern in 1538. In 1541 the Diet of Regensburg proclaimed that these estates, contiguous with the Habsburg lands in the Netherlands, rightfully belonged to the emperor. The imperial army marched against the duke of Jülich-Cleves, William V (known as 'the Rich'), who vainly hoped for help from the French king and the Schmalkaldic League. In signing the humiliating Venlo treaty in September 1543, William was forced to lose a considerable amount of territory, to renounce his tolerant Erasmian attitude, and to support the Counter-Reformation. The result of this swift campaign was that a power vacuum was created in north-western Germany. Jülich-Cleves could never become a powerful state like Brandenburg-Prussia, Bavaria, or Saxony.

Emperor Charles V is shown receiving a copy of the Augsburg Confession, an important exposition of Lutheran theology, at the Diet of Augsburg, 25 June 1530.

Efforts to reach an accommodation with the German Protestants failed. Pope Paul III and his legate, Cardinal Contarini, were prepared to make concessions, but their efforts were frustrated by the German hard-liners who had influence in the Curia, the court of the papal see. By the time the Diet met in Regensburg in June 1546, the emperor was ready to move against the Protestants. The pope promised him 12,500 soldiers and a huge subsidy. He had won the support of William of Bavaria and Maurice of Saxony, to both of whom he promised the electorates which were held by other less pliable members of their families.

The Schmalkaldic War began before the pope's troops arrived from Italy and initially did not go well for the emperor, but the League soon proved to be a quarrelsome coalition unable to coordinate its strategy. Maurice of Saxony seized the opportunity to invade the territories of his cousin John Frederick who raced back to defend them. Abandoning an excellent defensive position in order to retreat to Wittenberg, John Frederick's troops were defeated at Mühlberg. This easy victory brought the war to an end. John Frederick was captured, and Philip of Hessen was arrested and rendered homage to the emperor, even though his freedom had been guaranteed. Both leaders were imprisoned in the Netherlands.

Although the emperor was at the height of his powers, the religious problem remained a threat. He sought its solution in an imperial ecumenicism, a middle way between the reactionary Catholics and inflexible Lutherans. This 'Interim', produced by the Diet of Augsburg between 1547 and 1548, satisfied neither side and quickly became the object of general ridicule. In 1555 the experiment was formally ended.

At the same time the emperor tried to create a centralized federal state in which the princes would act only in consultation with him, and which would ensure adequate revenues for the imperial army, administration, and justice. This the princes were determined to resist. Maurice of Saxony, who owed his electoral throne to the emperor, had no intention of bowing to his will. The princes were appalled by the treatment meted out to Philip of Hessen and John Frederick of

Saxony and complained of the 'bestial Spanish servitude' which Charles V was attempting to impose on Germany. Maurice of Saxony, although weak and isolated, ruthlessly used his exceptional diplomatic skills to dupe Charles V by laying siege to Lutheran Magdeburg on behalf of the emperor, an elaborate masquerade in which he admitted to the mayor that his intention was to hoodwink the emperor, win time, and then form an anti-Habsburg alliance with the disgruntled German princes. The opposing German princes then signed the Treaty of Chambord on 15 January 1552 with Henry II of France, who now played the role of protector of German liberties. In return the French king received the towns of Cambrai, Metz, Toul, and Verdun which straddled the 'Spanish Road', the supply route between the Habsburg domains in Italy and the Netherlands.

The Treaty of Chambord was hardly signed before the inveterate intriguer Maurice of Saxony began to negotiate with King Ferdinand I, whom Charles V had left in charge of German affairs. On 11 July 1553 Maurice of Saxony died in battle against the Margrave Albrecht Alcibiades of Brandenburg-Kulmbach, a swash-buckling adventurer who had broken the peace and attacked Nuremberg, Bamberg and Würzburg in an attempt to expand his modest territories. Thus the German princes lost one of their most effective leaders, a modern Machiavellian prince who fell at the hands of an old-style robber-baron and mercenary general.

The religious peace of Augsburg of 1555 was largely the work of Ferdinand I, who realized that Charles V's Catholic and imperial plans were unrealistic and that the empire could not be held against the wishes of the princes. The principle of 'Cuis regio, eius religio', that religion should be determined by the princes, rather than being a matter of individual conscience, was coupled with the 'beneficium emigrandi' – the right of subjects to emigrate to states where their religion was tolerated. The Peace of Augsburg guaranteed the rights of the princes over their states and the empire was now formally a political union of assorted territories rather than a federal state. Responsibility for taxation and for mustering an army rested not with the emperor but with the estates represented in the Diet (Reichstag) and in the imperial districts. Each territory paid taxes and provided soldiers according to its size and wealth. The Peace of Augsburg created a loose federal construction which lasted for 250 years and enabled its member states to achieve a remarkable degree of independence, diversity, and modernity.

The religious solution at Augsburg showed that both Luther and Charles V had failed. Luther, who died in 1546, wanted the Reformation of the existing universal Church, not the division of the Church into confessions – Catholic, Lutheran, Calvinist. Charles V had struggled to preserve the universal Church but had excluded the reformers. The old Church, now known as Catholic, was never again to be a homogeneous body, but was to adapt itself locally and make concessions to national requirements. The universality of medieval Europe was giving way to the particularism of the modern. Charles V's vision of a universal empire sanctioned by a universal Church could not be realized.

CHAPTER 5

The Counter-Reformation and the Thirty Years War

In October 1556 Charles V, disillusioned, prematurely old, and suffering from gout, abdicated the throne of Spain in favour of his son Philip II, and handed over the empire to his brother, Ferdinand king of Rome. He retired to the isolated monastery of San Jerónimode Yuste in the Estremadura where he died in 1558.

RELIGIOUS CONFLICT

In the years immediately following the Peace of Augsburg, Catholics and Protestants coexisted in relative harmony in Germany. In many places they shared the same churches and cooperated in local representative bodies. Inter-denominational marriages were common. But soon the fronts began to harden. The conclusions of the Council of Trent (1545–63), the *Tridentinum*, which were published in January 1564, made a sharp distinction between the Catholic and Protestant Churches. The Latin Bible, the vulgate, was proclaimed the only true version and placed on an equal footing with the teachings of the Church fathers and the decisions of previous councils as the source of divine truth. Luther's *sola scriptura* was firmly rejected and his translation of the Bible pronounced unacceptable. The Council insisted that redemption could come only through God's grace and that this divine grace was transmitted through the sacraments. The Church and its hierarchy was clearly distinguished from the laity by this sacramental function and remained the essential intermediary between God and man. Whereas the Protestants accepted only the three sacraments ordained by Christ – baptism, the Eucharist, and absolution – the Council of Trent affirmed four further sacraments – marriage, confirmation, ordination, and extreme unction. For the Catholic Church the attitude of the recipient of these sacraments had little effect on their healing grace, whereas for Protestants the faith of the individual was decisive and the sacraments had a negative effect on the unbeliever. Tridentine doctrine on purgatory, the veneration of the saints, holy relics, and indulgences made the gulf between Catholics and Protestants still wider. Ignatius Loyola, the founder of the Jesuit order, opened the Collegium Germanicum in Rome, where German-speaking priests were trained according to strict Tridentine orthodoxy in an attempt to bring the Protestant Germans back into the fold.

Germany was now divided into three exclusive religious blocks: Catholics, Lutherans, and a smaller group of Zwinglians and Calvinists in the reformed churches. Reformation and Counter-Reformation helped bring about national unity in Scandinavia, France, and Spain; in Germany it further divided the princedoms and towns along religious lines, creating differences of mentality and culture which are still noticeable today. Duke Albrecht V of Bavaria (1550–79) was the forceful leader of the Catholic party, combining enthusiasm for the Tridentine reforms with a determination to further Bavaria's interests. When the archbishop and elector of Cologne, Gebhard Truchsess von Waldburg, became a Protestant in 1582 it seemed likely that the Catholics would lose this important territory's voice in the electoral college, and that its citizens would be forced to accept the new religion. Albrecht V's successor, William V 'the Pious' immediately sided with the Spaniards to oust the Protestants in the Cologne war of 1583–85. As a result, William's brother Ernst became archbishop at the age of twenty-nine, even though under canon law he should have been at least thirty. He had already had a remarkable career in the Church: in 1566, aged twelve, he was made bishop of Freising; in 1573 he was given the bishopric of Hildesheim; in 1581 Liège. His experience and his extravagant life-style were hardly in the spirit of the Counter-Reformation, but they well served the political and territorial interests of Bavaria's ruling family, the house of Wittelsbach. He also pleased the Church, for most of western Germany thus remained Catholic.

There were important islands of Lutheranism and Calvinism in this region. The count palatine, Johann Kasimir, had converted to Calvinism while in Paris, and his university in Heidelberg became the centre of German Calvinism; its theologians produced the Heidelberg Catechism of 1563, in which the fundamentals were laid out in 129 questions and answers. Most of the other Calvinist states were small territories bordering the Palatinate or Calvinist Holland. Two important exceptions were Hessen-Kassel and Brandenburg, where the elector Johann Sigismund converted to Calvinism in 1613 but was unable to reform most of his subjects. The Calvinist states allied, fearful that the Counter-Reformation might get out of hand and that there would be a Saint Bartholemew's Night massacre of Protestants in Germany, as there had been in France in 1572. They sided with the anti-imperial forces while the Lutherans, who did not take the threat of the Counter-Reformation so seriously, believed that the religious peace could best be preserved by strengthening the authority of the emperor.

The Reformation not only deepened the political divisions within Germany, it also emphasized the cultural differences. Nowhere is this more noticeable than in architecture. The great Catholic princes and bishops like the Prince Bishop Julius Echter von Mespelbrunn of Würzburg and Archbishop Wolf Dietrich von Raitenau of Salzburg turned their towns into flamboyant Baroque monuments to the Counter-Reformation. Others followed with less ambitious projects, such as the Jesuit church of St Michael in Munich, remarkable for its restrained magnificence. Protestant architecture of the period accurately reflects the austere piety of the Zwinglians and Calvinists, and many of their churches were little more than dreary lecture halls, since the sermon was the focus of the service, not the Eucharist. Only in the north of Germany, where the influence of the prosperous Dutch was felt, was this simplicity combined with a certain grace and lightness of touch. The New Church in Emden, for example, copied the Noorderkerk in Amsterdam.

The Lutherans were not iconoclasts like the Reformed Church. They preserved the decorated altars and paintings of the old Church and added new paintings illustrative of their catechism. Lutheran princes were every bit as eager as their Catholic rivals to rebuild their towns and erect impressive buildings as testimony to their power and wealth. Wolfenbüttel, rebuilt by Duke Julius of Brunswick-Wolfenbüttel in the mid sixteenth century, was the Lutheran equivalent of Würzburg. The church of the Blessed Virgin Mary, a strange combination of the Gothic, Renaissance, and Baroque built early in the early seventeenth century, is the first masterpiece of Lutheran ecclesiastical architecture. In the spirit of the Lutheran emphasis on scholarship, Duke August the Younger of Brunswick-Wolfenbüttel built a magnificent library which by 1666, the year of his death, contained more than 100,000 volumes.

Although architecture thrived in Germany in the late sixteenth and early seventeenth centuries, painting and sculpture were in serious decline, in part because of a rejection of the fine arts by many Protestants. The early sixteenth century had been something of a golden age. The wonderful carvings of Tilman Riemenschneider and Veit Stoss combine Gothic piety with Renaissance humanism in works of great power and beauty. Matthias Grünewald's painting on the altar in Isenheim is a most moving representation of Christ crucified. Albrecht Altdorfer set his paintings of religious and mythical subjects in remarkably detailed and romantic settings, and was the first European artist ever to paint a landscape without figures. Albrecht Dürer is the best known of these great artists and produced a wide range of works which were appreciated internationally. Hans Holbein the younger first achieved fame with his detailed and realistic portraits

The stone bridge at Frankfurt, engraved by Matthaeus Merian (1593–1650). Frankfurt was a free city which welcomed refugees from the Netherlands escaping religious persecution. They contributed significantly to making the city one of the leading trading, banking and manufacturing centres of the age.

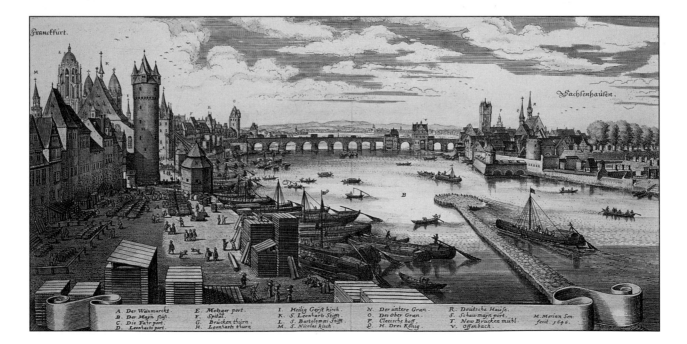

when he moved to England in 1532. Lucas Cranach, like Altdorfer a member of the 'Danubian School', was brought to Saxony by Frederick the Wise and produced a number of remarkable portraits of the Wittenberg reformers. His fluid draughtsmanship foreshadows the mannerists.

The notable decline of German painting by mid sixteenth century is due in part to economic factors. The princes, Catholic or Protestant, could afford fashionable Italian or French masters such as the surrealist Giuseppe Arcimboldo, the favourite painter of Rudolf II. His court at the Hradschin castle was not only a great centre of mannerist art, it also hosted Tycho Brahe and Johannes Kepler, along with an assortment of astrologers, alchemists, and charlatans. On the other hand, the German bourgeoisie lacked the funds to sponsor the genre painting which thrived in Holland, so were forced to make do with indifferent family portraits produced by local hacks.

Most of the literature of the age was still written in Latin. Only in Protestant Germany were efforts made to reach a wider public by producing literary works in the vernacular. Catholics not only regarded Latin as a superior and more dignified language, they also felt that high German, with its roots in Saxony and Thuringia, was essentially a Protestant language. The effects of this prejudice were long-lasting. At least until the nineteenth century most German literature was produced by Protestants, many of the writers being the children of Protestant ministers. To this day the inhabitants of Catholic areas are more likely to speak in dialect rather than standard German.

The 'Study for the hands of an apostle' by Albrecht Dürer (c.1508) is a striking and much-loved image of private piety.

Music was profoundly affected by the Reformation. Whereas Calvin loathed music for its sensuality, Luther saw it as one of God's greatest gifts to man, and made it a central part of the Church service. The first great German composer, Heinrich Schütz, was a Protestant who only wrote vocal music, most of it sacred. He was sponsored by John George of Saxony and became his *Kapellmeister* in Dresden in 1619. He remained there until 1635, when the elector could no longer afford musicians because of the expense of the Thirty Years War.

There was little place for music in the Catholic Church of the Counter-Reformation, and most of the music produced in Catholic areas was secular. Although the Habsburg emperors were keen sponsors of music, it was not until the eighteenth century that the Catholic south produced composers of genius.

THE GERMAN STATE

The administrative history of the German states after the Peace of Augsburg was less affected by religious differences. In Protestant states it was easier for princes such as the elector of Saxony to control the Church by appointing a governing

An engraving by Wenzel Hollar entitled 'The Marketplace' shows scenes from women's lives in a German town in the middle of the seventeenth century.

body, made up of theologians and lawyers, which was independent from the estates. In Catholic Bavaria a Spiritual Council with a similar function was appointed in 1570 with clerical and lay members. The papal see accepted the sovereign powers of the dukes of Bavaria over the Church in the concordat of 1583 and reaffirmed this position at Salzburg in 1628 and Augsburg in 1631. Although the dukes, who became electors in 1623, had fierce struggles with the Church, the Spiritual Council gave them wide powers and its formation was an important step towards a modern centralized state.

Bavaria was administratively the most advanced of the German states. Albrecht V had brought the aristocracy into line and dealt with the Protestant threat. His successor William V, who combined piety with brutal political realism, had brought the bishopric of Cologne under Bavarian influence. His son, Maximilian I, the best of the Wittelsbachs, had considerable abilities as an administrator, statesman and diplomat, but these have often been overlooked on account of his dour, ascetic personality.

Bavaria was divided into four administrative districts whose bureaucracies acted as intermediaries between the duke and the estates. Although these districts were headed by aristocrats whose status and wealth gave them almost complete independence from the duke, the administrators were increasingly drawn from the middle class. These highly qualified professionals were completely subservient to the state and their authority increased at the expense of the estates – the nobility, clergy and burghers – which complained frequently, and fruitlessly.

At the centre of the administration was the council of state (*Hofrat*) from which a treasury (*Hofkammer*) was separated by Albrecht V in 1550. Financial affairs were conducted by middle-class specialists since such sordid business was deemed to be beneath the dignity of the aristocracy. The treasury liaised closely with the administrative districts to itemize budgets and make financial projections.

Revenues increased steadily, partly due to a state monopoly on salt and beer, and expenditure was carefully controlled giving Bavaria the resources to finance her ambitious territorial policy.

During the Cologne War and the Thirty Years War a War Council was formed. The administrative details of mustering troops, logistics, and the building of fortresses was left to the middle-class experts, while military operations were the preserve of the aristocracy. The Privy Council (*Geheimer Rat*), also staffed by professionals, worked closely with the duke and supervised the entire administration, much to the annoyance of the estates, who felt the mere existence of the Privy Council was a slight upon their abilities and integrity. All these objections were studiously ignored.

The power of the princes over the estates was also enhanced by the codification of the law, even though in many instances the initiative for such action came from the estates themselves. In Bavaria a team of middle-class lawyers worked for fifteen years on the new code, published in 1616. Traditional law was respected but where it was ambiguous, or where there were gaps, the principles of Roman law were applied and Roman law upheld the power of the princes. The opportunities for appealing decisions of a local court to a court outside the principality, such as an imperial court, were greatly reduced. The law was modified and interpreted to meet the needs of the early modern state.

In the German states the law was used to a far greater extent than anywhere else in Europe to regulate all aspects of public and private life. Laws were enacted on economic activity, professional ethics, religion, medicine, the social services, sexual behaviour, and begging. The concept of 'the common good' was not based on a consensus reached after struggle between social groups, but was enforced from above by princely decree. This was to have unfortunate effects upon the political development of Germany.

The princes found it impossible to finance the ever-increasing bureaucracy, mercenary armies, and judicial administration from the revenues of their own domains. Increasingly therefore, taxes had to be assessed and regularly collected. According to a decision of the Diet of Augsburg in 1555, the princes, not the emperor's agents, had to collect imperial taxes. Taxes were raised to pay for an imperial army to destroy the Turkish enemies of Christendom. This greatly benefited the princes, who collected far more money than they gave to the emperor. The bishop of Würzburg, for example, collected 294,166 guilders in the 'Turk Taxes' of 1566, 1576 and 1582, but paid only 163,268 guilders to the emperor.

Local parliaments (*Landtage*) asserted their rights to impose new forms of taxation including income and property taxes, hearth taxes, and poll taxes, and demanded a say in how the money was to be spent. Excise (*Akzise*), such as the tax on beer, did not have to be approved by the parliaments and thus soon became the most common form of taxation. As the state's demands for greater revenues increased, and the princes' ambitions for absolute rule grew, the parliaments were gradually pushed aside. The emergency situation of the Thirty Years War gave the princes the opportunity to collect taxes without consulting parliament. In Bavaria, parliament met thirty-three times between 1514 and 1579 and six times between 1579 and 1612, but did not meet at all between 1612 and 1669.

GERMAN SOCIETY IN THE SEVENTEENTH CENTURY

Aristocracy, clergy and burghers formed three estates, each divided into a multiplicity of sub-castes, and each bound by a strict imperial dress code so that the social divisions were clearly visible. Yet the Reformation did have an effect on this social structure, in that both Luther and Calvin insisted on hard work, education, and professional expertise, middle-class values accepted by all Christians. The aristocracy too accepted middle-class values, in as much as they ran their estates as enterprises, built factories, and exploited mineral resources. In the seventeenth century there was an aristocratic counter-attack against this capitalist spirit, with a reassertion that birth and honour were above economic success. The sovereign state with its rapidly growing bureaucracy offered exceptional opportunities for social advancement. The sons of burghers, artisans, and even peasants could secure employment within the princely administration. If successful, they were ennobled and became the social equals of those disgruntled aristocrats who resented the princes' rise but were too lazy to study for a political career.

The fluidity and uncertainty of the sixteenth century gave rise to a conservative reaction. The aristocracy realized that it had to make concessions to the modern age or it would be pushed aside by the middle class. Town guilds, threatened by modern manufacturing, demanded that their privileges be respected. Middle class pastors, doctors, lawyers, and professors made sure that their sons followed in their footsteps, so that the professions became almost hereditary. Yesterday's parvenus became the pillars of today's establishment.

The Reformation and Counter-Reformation also affected the family and the status of women. Luther stressed the importance of love between parents and children, and the Tridentine decree on marriage insisted it should be based on mutual respect and love. Society remained patriarchal: an analogy was drawn between the family and the state, with the husband and father as sovereign power. But the status of wives was changing: servants regarded them as equal to their spouses, and the new office of pastor's wife amounted almost to an independent profession, so many parish demands were being made of her.

The sixteenth century began in an atmosphere of confident optimism. European ships explored the world, religious reformers provided a humanistic alternative to a corrupt and worldly Church, farmers profited from the increased demand for agricultural produce, and the towns prospered as the economy expanded. By mid century the mood had changed. Silver from the New World fuelled an alarming inflation. The religious fronts had succumbed to intolerance, internecine squabbling, and violence. Agriculture's failure to meet the requirements of a rising population caused further inflation, unemployment, and hunger. In the towns, although the rich continued to prosper and there was a remarkable building boom, per capita incomes were falling. In Augsburg three-quarters of the population were classified on the tax-rolls as being without means (*Habnits*). A worsening climate caused a number of catastrophic harvests. And the plague was rampant: in various epidemics in Nuremberg between 1561 and 1585, of the population of 45,000, more than 20,000 died.

Economic difficulties and resistance to the encroachments of the absolutist state caused a number of peasants' revolts between 1575 and 1630, particularly in southern Germany and in the Habsburg lands. Throughout the empire the towns were in revolt as their rights and privileges were curtailed. In many places these urban revolts took the form of anti-Semitic pogroms, the most famous of which were the Fettmilch riots in Frankfurt between 1612 and 1616. Vinzenz Fettmilch, a demagogic gingerbread baker, led a popular protest against the city council which he held responsible for the economic and social problems besetting the city. Frankfurt's artisans and shopkeepers were bitterly resentful of the influx of refugees from the Netherlands and of Jews, whom they blamed for the mid-century depression. They unleashed their fear and anger in the pogrom of 21 August 1614. The Jews were driven from the city and their houses plundered, dispersing Germany's largest Jewish community among a number of neighbouring towns and villages. In 1616 the city authorities stamped out this popular movement and Fettmilch was executed. In the following year an imperial edict guaranteed the safety of Frankfurt's Jews, many of whom returned. Individual states took over responsibility for protecting Jews, and allotted them different economic and social functions, enabling many to prosper.

Witch-hunting, like the outbursts of violent anti-Semitism, was part of a complex social-psychological response to the uncertainties and problems of a changing society. The new and violent reaction to witchcraft was systematically laid out in the *Malleus maleficarum* written by the inquisitor and Dominican prior, Jakob Sprenger and his fellow Dominican Heinrich Institoris. The book was published in Strasburg in 1486 and went through twenty-eight editions by 1669. The basic assumption of this popular text was that since all misfortune and evil was the work of the devil, it should be possible to combat the Evil One by hounding downs his minions, witches. A witch was defined as a woman who made a pact and had sexual intercourse with the devil. She was able to fly in order to attend a witches' sabbath at which she and her kind worshipped the devil. A witch had the power to do all manner of evil, such as afflicting her enemies with disease, causing hailstorms or turning milk sour.

Witches were tried by civil courts and the sentence was usually a foregone conclusion. Confession and repentance did not save them, nor did a test by ordeal, since innocence could only be proved if the victim died in the process. Some courts merely exiled the witches, some merciful judges ordered their execution, but most were burnt at the stake. Considerable efforts were made to get the accused to denounce fellow witches, giving them an excellent opportunity to seek revenge on those they wished to harm. In some instances confessions were carefully arranged so that local dignitaries could get rid of their political or economic rivals. Thus the 'witches mayor' of the Westphalian Hanseatic town of Lemgo, Hermann Cothmann, established a reign of terror in the 1660s and 1670s. As prosecutors, judges and executioners, he and his cronies condemned countless rivals to the stake. Finally, one Maria Rampendal, a barber's wife, refused to denounce anyone and miraculously survived the excruciating torture. Having been expelled from Lemgo she successfully appealed to the imperial court. The witch-hunters were subsequently removed from office.

In times of crisis, such as the years between the 1580s and the end of the century, or during the Thirty Years War, the number of trials of witches increased dramatically. The last German witch was executed in 1775, by which time some 100,000 unfortunates had lost their lives. The abolition of witch hunts was a triumph for the new spirit of rationalism, and vindicated the efforts of enlightened theologians and philosophers who had bravely spoken out against this madness.

THE ORIGINS OF THE THIRTY YEARS WAR

The obsession with witches and with astrological prediction were signs of a general crisis. Politically the fronts were hardening between Catholics, Lutherans, and Calvinists. In 1607 there were riots in the imperial city of Donauwörth when the Protestant majority attacked a Catholic procession on Saint Mark's day. The emperor, Rudolf II, under whose patronage the procession was to have taken place,

Astrological predictions of forthcoming disasters, presaged by the appearance of a number of remarkable comets, including Halley's comet in 1614, were signs of a general crisis as the fronts between Catholics and Protestants hardened.

felt personally insulted, and ordered the duke of Bavaria to enforce the imperial ban by outlawing the Protestants. The duke was subsequently granted the city in gratitude for his services for the Catholic cause. This was manifestly illegal, since Donauwörth was Swabian, not Bavarian, and the ban should have been enforced by the Lutheran duke of Württemberg.

In January 1608 the Imperial Diet met in Regensburg in an attempt to meet the debts the emperor had incurred in the war against the Turks. Events in Donauwörth forced most moderate Lutherans into the radical camp of the elector palatine, who wanted greater Calvinist and Lutheran representation in the major imperial bodies. The Saxons tried to reach a compromise, but when the Elector Palatine's representatives walked out of the Reichstag most of the moderates followed their lead. The imperial court and the Reichstag were thus unable to perform their function of reconciling the two sides, and the old system of ensuring imperial peace failed. On 14 May 1608 the radical Protestants under the leadership of the elector palatine agreed a military union at a meeting in a monastery at Auhausen near Nördlingen. On 10 June 1609 the Catholic League was formed in Munich. The empire was now divided into two hostile military blocks.

The Catholics were in the stronger position. They had political differences but none of the doctrinal divisions which plagued the Protestant Union. Their finances were also on a much sounder footing. Bavaria had a full treasury and the League could rely on subsidies from the pope. The duke of Bavaria also had a superb general in Johann Tserclaes Tilly; it was said that he had learnt to pray with the Jesuits and learnt to command with the Spaniards.

In Bohemia, the emperor Rudolf II was widely considered to be mentally unstable and incompetent. Protestants and the estates had seized the opportunity to win new freedoms offered by the lax regime of Rudolf II and by the squabbles between the emperor and his brother Matthias. Matthias, who was elected emperor in 1612, was determined to put an end to this drift. The Protestants had built two churches on ecclesiastical land, one in the grounds of a Benedictine monastery in Braunau, the other at Klostergrab on land belonging to the archbishopric of Prague. They had assumed that the emperor's permission granted to Protestants to build churches in 1609 was without restrictions, but it was now claimed that this only applied to the imperial domain and not to the lands of the Catholic Church. The Protestant leadership in Braunau was flung into jail and the Klostergrab church demolished. The governor of Prague, acting on the instructions of Archbishop Khlesl of Vienna, then forbade a meeting of a Protestant grievance committee, the *Defensoren*. In protest against this move, some twelve notables under the leadership of the Calvinist Count Heinrich Matthias Thurn and the Lutheran Joachim Andreas von Schlick, marched into the Hradschin castle on 23 May 1618, grabbed Wilhelm von Slawata and Jaroslaw Martinitz, the reactionary officials seen as responsible, and threw them out of a window. The two landed unharmed forty-five feet below.

When Matthias died in March 1619, the Bohemian Landtag provocatively elected the Calvinist Wittelsbach elector palatine, Frederick V, as their new king. The sixteen-year-old Frederick V had married Elizabeth Stuart, the daughter of James I, in February 1613 and, prompted by an ambitious wife and greedy advisors, he impetuously decided to accept the crown of Saint Wenceslas. It was immediately shown to be an over-hasty move. He had virtually no support, not even from his father-in-law the king of England. Maximilian of Bavaria put his fine army at the service of the new emperor, Ferdinand II, and it was Tilly and the Bavarian troops who were largely responsible for the resounding victory over the Palatine and Bohemian armies at the battle of the White Mountain outside Prague on 8 November 1620, almost exactly one year after Frederick's coronation.

This was a decisive victory, and Frederick, now contemptuously christened the Winter King by the Catholics, lost his electoral seat, which the emperor had given to Maximilian of Bavaria as a mark of gratitude. In 1618 Don Balthasar Zúñiga became Philip III of Spain's chief minister. His predecessor, the duke of Lerma had established a 'Pax Hispanica' with England and the Netherlands. The new minister rejected his predecessor's policy, arguing that it had enabled the Dutch to grow too powerful. The Spanish now subsidized the emperor Ferdinand, and sent troops into the Palatinate, which the hapless Frederick was unable to defend. It looked as if Spain would now annexe these lands and gain extra protection for the strategic Spanish Road, the north-south route used to supply the Spanish forces in the Netherlands. But statesmen in Brussels and Madrid urged caution; the Spanish army in the Netherlands had been weakened by operations in the Palatinate, and

In the pogrom of 1614 the Jews of Frankfurt were driven out of the city. This engraving by Matthaeus Merian (1642) illustrates the plundering of the Judengasse.

England and France might feel obliged to intervene. The Spaniards therefore occupied only the left bank of the Rhine, while Tilly besieged Heidelberg, which fell in September 1622. The centre of German Calvinism was now firmly in Catholic hands, and the magnificent Bibliotheca Palatina, the finest collection of Protestant scholarship, was shipped off to Rome. The Winter King and his queen wandered haplessly around Europe, objects of Catholic derision.

The victory at the White Mountain made mercenaries and fortune-hunters flock to the imperial side. The emperor had the money, the lands, and the booty for which the *condottieri* (mercenary soldiers) fought. The greatest of all the mercenaries was Albrecht von Wallenstein, whose wealth and confidence was strengthened by marriage to a rich widow. Wallenstein had commanded a regiment of Walloon cavalry at the battle of the White Mountain, and had seized the opportunity to buy a number of confiscated noble estates for a fraction of their true value. In addition to his duchy of Friedland, he was soon master of a substantial military-industrial complex which produced all the armaments and equipment his armies needed.

A sixteenth-century Swiss miniature shows a witch-burning. Since misfortune was easily blamed on magic and witchcraft, witch-hunting was particularly virulent in times of crisis.

In December 1625 an alliance was signed at the Hague between England, Denmark, the United Provinces, and Frederick V of the Palatinate. The Danes promptly invaded Germany and Wallenstein offered the emperor 40,000 mercenaries free of charge, the emperor in return offering Wallenstein command of the imperial army. It was an excellent arrangement for both sides. The emperor got a first rate army led by a soldier of genius, while Wallenstein had a free hand to make war pay. And pay it did.

Wallenstein opened his campaign with a victory at the Dessau Bridge over the Elbe on 25 April 1626, and drove the Protestant bands into Hungary. On 27 August 1626 he joined forces with Tilly to defeat Christian IV of Denmark and his northern German allies at Lutter am Barenberg near Salzgitter. Imperial troops occupied Holstein, Mecklenburg, and Pomerania so that the Baltic coast, except for the besieged port of Stralsund, was denied to the Protestants. On 22 May 1629 the Danish king signed the Peace of Lübeck. His lost lands were returned to him in return for a promise to keep out of the German war.

The Habsburgs had wisely been magnanimous towards the Danes, fearing that the Swedes might otherwise be tempted to intervene in the war, but their victory allowed them to entertain dangerously ambitious schemes. Wallenstein was appointed 'General of the Oceanic and Baltic Seas' and planned to build a canal joining the North Sea and the Baltic. The Protestant and anti-Spanish burghers of the Hanseatic towns were appalled by the suggestion and sought allies in their struggle against the emperor. They did not have to wait for long.

In March 1629 Ferdinand II made the colossal blunder of issuing the Edict of Restitution, by which all ecclesiastical property which had been secularized by the Protestants was to be restored to the Catholic Church. Then in July 1629 the emperor seized the lands of King Christian IV of Denmark's allies, the dukes of Mecklenburg-Schwerin and Mecklenburg-Güstrow, lands which their families had owned for 800 years, and granted these lands to Wallenstein. The imperial knights were outraged that the emperor had raised a mercenary soldier and arms dealer to their estate and thus struck a blow at the foundations of their legitimacy. What was worse, the emperor had not simply rewarded a trusted servant, which the imperial knights might have accepted, but he had granted Wallenstein these duchies because it was the only way he could pay off his immense debt to him.

Both the Edict of Restitution and the elevation of Wallenstein were attacks on the rights and privileges of the estates, and provoked a sharp reaction in both Catholic and Protestant camps. The archbishop elector of Mainz announced that he was 'offended and disgusted' by the Wallenstein affair. Maximilian of Bavaria, recently appointed elector, refused to support the election of the emperor's son as king of the Romans at the Electoral Diet of Regensburg. In 1631 Maximilian signed the Treaty of Fontainebleau, a defensive alliance between France and Bavaria. Once again the solidarity of the princes had proved to be stronger than the solidarity of faith, and the emperor was obliged to face the consequences. The Edict of Restitution was suspended, the candidature of his son Ferdinand was withdrawn, and Wallenstein was dismissed from the imperial service. He withdrew to his Bohemian estates to plot his revenge on the emperor and princes.

The Defenestration of Prague, 23 May 1618, in which two imperial officials were thrown out of a window in the Hradschin Castle by Protestants demonstrating against their counter-reformatory measures. Although they fell forty-five feet, the two officials landed unharmed. Catholics claimed their salvation was due to the intervention of the Blessed Virgin Mary. The truth was more prosaic; they landed on a soft-dung heap.

THE SWEDES INTERVENE

On 6 July 1630, three days after the electors met in Regensburg, Gustavus Adolphus of Sweden, the greatest champion of the Protestant cause, invaded the island of Usedom. On 17 September 1631 the Protestants defeated the imperial army under Tilly at Breitenfeld near Leipzig. Of Tilly's 36,000 men, 12,000 were killed and 8,000 taken prisoner. He also lost his entire artillery. Gustavus Adolphus had lost only 3,000 men and shown that he was a superior general to the great Tilly. After years of disaster for the Protestants, the Catholics had now at last been soundly defeated. The Protestants were spurred on not only by the victory, but also by the singular brutality of the imperial forces. In May, after a lengthy siege, Tilly's mercenaries stormed the Protestant stronghold of Magdeburg, one of the largest and richest towns in Germany. The troops indulged in an orgy of murder, plunder and rape which the general was pleased to call the 'Magdeburg Wedding'. The town was then burnt to the ground.

Maximilian of Bavaria and Tilly now desperately tried to stop the Swedish king from entering Bavaria, and made a stand on the River Lech in April 1632. Gustavus' troops managed to seize an island in the river and from here they unleashed murderous artillery fire on the Bavarian forces. Tilly was mortally wounded, Maximilian withdrew to Ingolstadt, and on 17 May Gustavus Adolphus entered the capital Munich in triumph. He was accompanied by the Winter King, who now saw that the return of Bohemia and of his electoral seat were within his grasp.

After the defeat at Breitenfeld, the emperor had approached Wallenstein and begged him to return. Wallenstein demanded absolute power of command and insisted that the emperor should not interfere in the conduct of the war. The emperor gave way, making Wallenstein the most absolute commander until Napoleon. Wallenstein was about to prepare his winter quarters, when he received the news that Gustavus Adolphus had decided to march into Saxony in the hope of engaging him in battle before the campaigning season ended. Wallenstein decided to meet the challenge and, on 16 November 1632, he faced the Swedish king at Lützen, an otherwise insignificant spot between Leipzig and Naumburg. The result was a narrow victory for the Protestants, but it was won at great cost. Gustavus Adolphus was killed in the fighting and, after the imperial troops had stripped him of all his possessions, his body was left naked on the battlefield, riddled with bullets.

Lützen was also to be Wallenstein's last battle. He was constantly intriguing behind the emperor's back, making overtures to all the emperor's enemies including the Winter King, Saxony, France, and even Sweden. His ambitions knew no limits, his megalomania was pathological. The emperor could not trust a vassal who had run out of control, and ordered that he be taken, dead or alive. Wallenstein was murdered on 25 February 1634 at Eger Castle in Bohemia by an Irish captain Devereux, while trying to escape from the emperor's killers. The absolutist princes could no longer tolerate the threat that mercenaries posed to their legitimacy. The imperial armies were now commanded by the emperor's son Ferdinand, king of Bohemia and Hungary.

Sweden's affairs were in the capable hands of the chancellor, Axel Oxenstierna, a skilful statesman. He had united the German Protestants in the League of Heilbronn, concluded on 23 April 1633. Oxenstierna's aim was to create a series of German satellite states which would be the pliable instruments of Swedish policy. Such ambitions were not lost on the Protestant states, who had no intention of becoming subservient to the Swedes. Gustavus Adolphus was dead, his army had degenerated from zealous crusaders to brutal soldiers of fortune, and the German princes were determined to strike out on their own. When the Swedes were decisively defeated by Ferdinand and the imperial army at Nördlingen in November 1634, the Protestant princes decided that the time had come to begin negotiations with the emperor and bring the war to an end.

On 30 May 1635 the Peace of Prague was signed and accepted by most of the German states. The exceptions were: Württemberg, which was still smarting under the effects of the Edict of Restitution; Calvinist Hessen-Kassel, which thought it could do better in war than in peace; and a few north German states which were under the influence of the Dutch or the Swedes. The peace guaranteed the legitimate rights of the princes and their territories were restored, apart from those of the hapless Winter King. The Edict of Restitution was formally abrogated. The empire was once again an association designed to maintain the peace and uphold the law. The peace did not, however, accept Calvinism as a distinct confession. Despite this obvious weakness, the Peace of Prague was a genuine compromise between imperial authority and the rights of the estates, and was an expression of the German princes' determination to put an end to a senseless war. That the peace did not hold was not the fault of the Germans, but was largely the responsibility of Cardinal Richelieu, France's chief minister from 1624–42.

THE FRENCH PHASE OF THE THIRTY YEARS WAR

A few days before the peace was signed, France declared war on Spain. Sweden, Holland, Savoy, Parma, and the anti-Habsburg German states sided with the French. Most of the German states remained in an alliance with the emperor and tried to defend themselves against the invading foreigners. The peace had hardly been signed when the war entered a new and even more brutal phase in which foreign armies murdered, raped and plundered their way across Germany.

The Swedes defeated the imperial army at Wittstock in the north of Brandenburg in October 1636, and again in November 1642 at Breitenfeld. In February 1638 imperial troops under General Jan von Werth defeated the French at Rheinfelden, only to be soundly defeated three days later because he allowed his men to run amok. Von Werth got his revenge in November 1643 when he smashed the French at Tuttlingen. In March 1645 the Swedes defeated the imperial army at Jankau, to the south of Prague, and marched on Vienna. They were joined by

A highly stylized nineteenth-century representation of two soldiers from the Thirty Years War.

Tilly's mercenaries stormed Magdeburg on 20 May 1631 after a lengthy siege, and laid waste to the city in a frenzy of rape, murder and plunder. Tilly (1559–1632) was born in Brabant, educated by the Jesuits, and learnt the art of war under Parma. He was given command of the imperial army at the outbreak of the Thirty Years War, and defeated first the elector Palatine and then the king of Denmark, Christian IV. He was killed in battle shortly after the Swedish king Gustavus Adolphus' victory at Breitenfeld.

George I Rákóczi, prince of Transylvania, but the emperor Ferdinand III hastily promised Rákóczi religious freedom in Hungary and a generous grant of lands, and he abandoned the Swedes. Exhausted and short of supplies, they retreated.

Once again the empire had been saved, but its position was becoming increasingly weak. John George of Saxony made his peace with the Swedes at Kötzschenbroda in September 1645 and Frederick William of Brandenburg then distanced himself from the emperor. Meanwhile two great French generals, Condé and Turenne, were at the beginning of their spectacular careers, Turenne winning a costly battle against the imperial forces at Allerheim near Nördlingen on 3 August 1645. When the Swedish army appeared in the south, Maximilian of Bavaria felt obliged to sign an armistice at Ulm in March 1647. He was soon to fight again, but his army was smashed by Turenne and the Swedish general Karl Gustav Wrangel, and Bavaria was defenceless against the ravages of their marauding troops.

All the major parties involved in the war – the emperor, Richelieu, Oxenstierna and Olivares, the 'Spanish Richelieu' – wanted to bring the war to an end, but all wanted a peace that would take their interests fully into account. It was not until 19 August 1645 that the emperor was able to invite the estates to attend a peace conference. The Swedes and Danes established themselves in Osnabrück, and the Spanish and Dutch sent delegates to Münster to discuss the ending of their eighty-year war. The French delegation also went to Münster. With 37 foreign and 111 German delegates, the discussions were immensely complicated and lengthy. A major breakthrough came when Maximilian von Trauttmansdorff, the emperor's skilful ambassador who had been largely responsible for the successful conclusion of the Peace of Prague, reached an agreement with the French by conceding Alsace. This meant that the French now controlled a vital sector of the Spanish Road. On 30 January 1648, the Spanish therefore hastily concluded their peace with the Dutch, who were now fully independent of the empire.

Sweden was given western Pomerania with the mouth of the Oder as well as Bremen and Verden, and Brandenburg got Halberstadt, Kammin, Minden, Magdeburg, Mark, and Cleves. Other territorial arrangements had to be made to reward faithful allies on all sides, but they proved easier to settle than the question of the 'Amnesty', the date at which violations of the Peace of Augsburg (1555) could legally be recognized. Obviously the Protestants wanted to have the earliest date possible, the Catholics the latest. Eventually the year 1624 was accepted, much to the annoyance of the Catholic party, which lost the north German bishoprics that had by then become Protestant. On 24 October 1648 the Peace of Westphalia was finally signed amid jubilation throughout Germany.

THE EFFECTS OF THE WAR

The Thirty Years War did not just cause untold suffering, it also acted as a powerful stimulus to modernization and the creation of the absolutist state. Lawyers announced that in times of acute danger the prince was justified in collecting taxes to defend the life and property of his subjects, without the formal approval of the

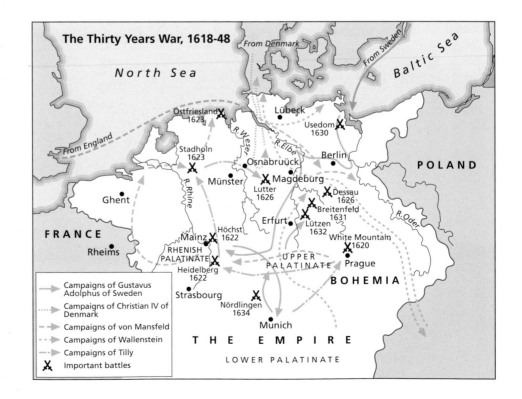

Simplicissimus

Hans Jakob Christoffel von Grimmelshausen's masterpiece, *Simplicissimus*, the 'adventures of an unusual vagrant by the name of Melchior Sternfels von Fuchshaim', was first published in five books in 1668 and was an instant success. Grimmelshausen responded to popular demand and wrote a sixth book, the *Continuatio* which was added to the second edition. The original Nuremberg edition was written largely in dialects and a Frankfurt publisher produced a more readable version of the book in standard German. Grimmelshausen adopted this revised edition as his own and added further sections to the book.

The story is set during the Thirty Years War, from about 1632–45. The young narrator, the son of a farmer in the Spessart, is driven away by plundering soldiers and spends two years with a hermit. On the hermit's death he is looked after by the commandant of Hanau until he is captured by marauding Croats. He makes his escape, works as a servant for a dragoon, becomes an officer in the imperial army, is taken prisoner, forced to marry, escapes to Paris, becomes a gigolo, earns his living as a quack doctor, goes to war again as a simple musketeer, sets out on pilgrimage, becomes a captain, wins a fortune and promptly loses it, settles down as a farmer, discovers that he was a foundling with an aristocratic title, travels about the world, returns home and ends his days as a hermit on an island.

The novel is a series of episodes and adventures which test the hero's resourcefulness and courage. They are vividly and humorously recounted, often bitingly satirical. The moral of the story is that man cannot discover his true humanity amid the 'madness' of the world, but only in tranquility and isolation. The novel goes beyond the picaresque tradition of Spain and Germany and points the way to the *Bildungsroman* — the novel which traces the inner development of the protagonist. The many episodes in the novel are thus representative of the hero's inner uncertainty. Whereas later *Bildungsromane* such as Wieland's *Agathon* and Goethe's *Wilhelm Meister* dealt with the problem of how the individual could live harmoniously in the world, Grimmelshausen, as a typical Baroque writer, felt that this was impossible. Man could only live in harmony with God if he turned his back on mankind and a depraved world.

Simplicissimus is not a historical novel about the Thirty Years War. A number of episodes from the war, some fantastic, others realistic, merely provide the background for much of the earlier part of the book, and the horrors of war are taken as striking examples of the wickedness of mankind. Grimmelshausen's historical reflections concentrate instead on the national question. He was fervently anti-French, despised French frippery, and was determined to get rid of the countless French words that had crept into the German language. His answer to the horrors of war was the revival of the universal Christian empire, which would include Turkey as a vassal state. The petty ambitions of the German princes were seen as a prime cause of present misery. Germany should therefore be based on a permanent alliance of the towns sending representatives to an all-German parliament.

His religious views were throughly ecumenical, and although he converted from Lutheranism to Catholicism, he had none of the blinkered fervour of a recent convert. As a man of his age he believed in witches, talismans, magic, and demons. His command of the German language, whether criminal slang, the convoluted speech of the court, or the German of Luther's Bible, raises him far above all contemporary writers.

Title engraving of the first edition of *The Adventurous German Simpleton*.

estates. Maximilian of Bavaria did not call on the estates during the entire war and announced that 'the imperatives of war silence the law'. Such were the war's horrors that it was agreed that princes should defend the state against its enemies and maintain domestic peace. This could best be done with a standing army rather than a horde of unreliable and ill-disciplined mercenary adventurers.

The more disciplined an army, the greater the authority of the officer corps. Now, even stupid and incompetent officers could perform their duties for the prince as cogs in a well-functioning machine. Since most of the officers in Germany were aristocrats, the standing of the aristocracy was enhanced. Service in the army reconciled the aristocracy to the absolutist state, and they were now prepared to serve the court, both in the bureaucracy and in the diplomatic service. Many of the aristocrats who were to set the tone of the forthcoming courtly age were ennobled in recognition of their services in the administration and the army. Few came from the ancient noble families.

The war had made it abundantly clear that politics and religion did not mix. The fatal combination of political ambition and religious fanaticism which had plunged the country into misery, demonstrated to both statesmen and clergy that the two had to be disentangled. Politics became secularized and religion was an essentially private concern. There were, however, frequent lapses back to earlier intolerance.

In the years between the Peace of Westphalia and the French Revolution, European states pursued their particular interests by means a complex system of alliances. Coalition wars were diplomatically and politically constrained so that, although armies were far larger and firepower far deadlier, they were far less destructive than the Thirty Years War. At the peace conferences, efforts were made to reach a rational new order in which differences were overcome and the best prospects for a lasting peace achieved. Religion was used as a propaganda weapon, but it was no longer a central issue.

The dream of a universal order had died with Charles V. Now a multiplicity of small states jockeyed for position. It was a situation which was easily exploited by the great powers who, in this golden age of diplomacy, intrigued with one another at the expense of the smaller states. Germany was now fully integrated into the European state system. France and Sweden were made guarantors of the new German order at the Peace of Westphalia. The Danish crown had territorial interests in Germany, and from 1714 the kings of England were electors of Hanover and dukes of Holstein and Oldenburg. The German states were free to make alliances with one another and with foreign powers. Germany was a battleground for the great powers, and the German states sought their support in the pursuit of their own interests.

In this new situation only the great powers really counted. Previously, small countries such as Burgundy in the fourteenth and fifteenth centuries with its excellent administration and fine army, or Holland with its wealth and maritime power in the late sixteenth and early seventeenth centuries, had been major players. Now extensive territory, a large population and considerable wealth were decisive. In the late seventeenth century only France, England, and Sweden really counted. Spain and Poland were finished as great powers, Holland was in rapid decline, and Germany was a power vacuum.

Wealth is the essential precondition of real power, and the German states were in a sorry plight in 1648. Agriculture had been neglected during the war so that a great deal of cultivated land had returned to the wild. The price of corn fell in Germany by about 50 per cent. Soldiers had slaughtered animals for food or confiscated those that could be used as draft animals. Mercenaries whose only profession was war continued to live off the land and had to be driven away or paid off. Disease and undernourishment caused a severe drop in the population in some areas, while others, such as Westphalia, Lower Saxony and the lower Rhine, Schleswig-Holstein, the North Sea coast, and the Habsburg lands remained virtually unaffected. After the war, the population rose slowly but steadily in most regions and a gradual recovery began.

This masterpiece of Gerard Terborch (c.1617–1681) records the solemn oath-taking which marks the conclusion of the Peace of Westphalia in the town hall of Münster in May 1648.

The vast majority of the small German states were incapable of creating an administration adequate to the needs of the modern state or of conducting an effective economic policy. They were simply too small and too poor to compete and often their modest resources were frittered away in ludicrous efforts to ape the courtly absolutism of Louis XIV, a widespread obsession that only benefited craftsmen in luxury trades like cabinet making. Only the larger states such as Brandenburg-Prussia were strong enough to implement policies which stimulated the economy. The elector ordered the construction between 1662 and 1668 of the Frederick William canal, which joined the Oder to the Spree, and gave government support to all manner of private industries including silk weaving, carpets and tapestries, soap, tobacco, and sugar. Many of these industries were in the hands of Huguenots who arrived in Prussia in 1683. Even Frederick William of Brandenburg, 'the Great Elector', was unable to achieve much in spite of all these efforts. Brandenburg-Prussia was too poor to provide the capital needed for major structural reform. He could not accept the revolutionary notions of his Dutch advisors, who argued that agriculture could not be improved without the abolition of serfdom and complete freedom of movement. Trade in Germany was hampered by countless customs barriers, and the great elector's suggestion of a conference of all the Elbe states to increase overseas trade came to nothing. Such particularism, which hurt a large state like Prussia, was disastrous to the smaller states. The absolutist state was based on a compromise between the prince and the aristocracy. This in turn meant a conservative and restorative social policy which acted as a brake on economic development.

Similar modest efforts to stimulate the economy were made in Saxony. When August the Strong of Saxony became king of Poland in 1697, the opportunities afforded by a larger market were exploited, and by the 1740s there was a vigorous rate of growth in the manufacturing industries. The agricultural sector was less healthy, and recovery from the effects of the Thirty Years War was painfully slow. The land had become depopulated and was left uncultivated. Farms were broken up into smallholdings or incorporated into the aristocratic estates. The shortage of labour drove up wages and landlords met the increases by exploiting their dependent peasants. Although formally there was no serfdom in Saxony, wage-earning peasants were obliged to perform so many additional duties and their legal rights were so diminished, that their position could scarcely be distinguished from that of the serfs.

Bavaria, the most modern and powerful of the German states in the early seventeenth century, had suffered terribly during the war. The population had been halved, and 900 towns and villages were devastated. As in Saxony, the aristocracy took advantage of the situation to increase their land-holdings. Recovery was slow and even as late as 1760 there were fewer farms in Bavaria than there had been in 1616. Efforts to encourage trade and industry within a mercantile system were hampered by an ambitious foreign policy, requiring a costly standing army.

The Habsburg lands, with the exception of Bohemia, had suffered far less from the effects of the war, but the emperors were too involved in dynastic difficulties, constitutional wrangles, and foreign wars to devote much effort to improving the economy. Much of the success of Austrian manufacturing was due to the initiative of foreigners, who came from the Netherlands, Italy, and England to seek their fortunes in a country which many saw as the land of the future. As in Brandenburg-Prussia and Bavaria, Austria's need of a substantial army meant that there was little money available for investment in long-term projects.

In this age of cabinet wars and diplomacy, economic and social policy was never given a high priority. The empire was beset by ambitious powers – Turkey, Sweden and France – which had to be kept at bay. In addition there was the struggle for power and later for hegemony within Germany which, from the time of the Diet of Regensburg in 1653–54, was to resolve into a rivalry between Brandenburg-Prussia and Austria. It took the catastrophe of the French revolutionary wars to force German princes and statesmen to admit that a sound economy and a more open society were the essential preconditions of political and military success.

Heidelberg castle, built in 1225, was the residence of electors palatine. Engraved in 1620 by Matthaeus Merian, it was destroyed between 1689 and 1693.

CHAPTER 6   # The Eighteenth Century

The division of Germany into hundreds of small states, each jealously protecting its economy, was a serious impediment to economic growth and modernization. But this curious structure had many positive achievements to its credit. The Treaty of Westphalia accepted the fact of the Reformation and granted equal rights to Catholics, Lutherans, and Calvinists throughout the empire. The principle that the ruler determined the religion of his subjects (*cujus regio, ejus religio*) was modified so that a change in the prince's religion did not mean that his subjects had to follow suit. Neither Protestants nor Catholics could be outvoted in a meeting of the Diet over matters of religion. A consensus, the *amicabilis compositio*, was reached after the two sides met separately. Religious parity was also achieved in all the major imperial institutions. Although still not entirely freed from the menace of religious intolerance and bigotry which had caused such untold suffering in the past, the German people enjoyed far greater religious freedom than most of their contemporaries.

CONSTITUTIONAL REFORMS

The Diet, which for decades had seldom met, was given a new lease of life. The peace treaty instructed the Diet to deal with all the constitutional issues which had not been settled in the Peace of Westphalia. The Diet which met in Regensburg on 30 June 1653 was in a sense a constitutional assembly, but it was unable to reach any conclusions and degenerated into a series of unseemly wrangles among the estates and between the estates and the emperor. In early 1654 the emperor Ferdinand III closed the Reichstag and it did not meet again until 1663 when his son and successor Leopold I was desperately in need of money to fight the Turks. This new Diet, the 'Perpetual Diet', met in Regensburg until the empire was dissolved in 1806. The estates were represented at the Perpetual Diet by delegates and, although it was powerless to prevent powers like Prussia and Austria from going to war, it provided a useful forum for the smaller states, neutralized their differences, and settled numerous conflicts. Regensburg was a place where deals could be made, alliances forged, and reactions tested.

Most of the legislative efforts of the Perpetual Diet were directed to questions which affected the entire empire – defence, the coinage, and economic policy. In 1731 the Diet passed a progressive piece of legislation which did much to end abuses in the guilds. In 1772 it forbade the exclusion of women from certain trades and put an end to the restrictions on the number of workers and apprentices a master craftsman could employ.

The high imperial court, the *Reichskammergericht*, was established by the princes in 1645. At first it met in Speyer, then it moved to Wetzlar in 1693 to escape the French, who were laying waste to the Palatinate. At the Peace of Westphalia it

Opposite: The grand staircase at the residence of the prince-bishop of Würzburg, designed by Balthasar Neumann (1687–1753) with frescos painted between 1750 and 1753 by Giovanni Battista Tiepolo (1696–1770). Neumann, the leading German architect of the period, was a military engineer in the service of the archbishop of Würzburg, but turned to architecture after a visit to Paris. He was subsequently appointed professor or architecture at Würzburg.

was agreed that Catholics and Protestants should have equal representation in the court. The estates were reluctant to grant the court enough money, so the back-log of cases was enormous. The suggestion that an appellant court be created was adopted in 1654, but it was a century before the funds were found to set the court up, and even then it was far from effective. Nevertheless, the court dealt with some 80,000 cases between 1554 and 1806 and it can safely be assumed that people did not spend time and money on such litigation unless it served a useful purpose.

The *Reichshofrat* was an alternative high court. It was an imperial court which sat in Vienna and was established by the emperor rather than the Diet. Although six Protestants sat on this court, all its members were appointed by the emperor and the Protestant princes protested that it was biased in favour of Catholics. Yet despite such complaints it was preferred to the *Reichskammergericht*, even by Protestants. It was a much more efficient court and reached judgment far quicker than the imperial court. It was less subject to squabbles between the estates and usually ruled in favour of the princes against their aggrieved subjects.

These courts, for all their shortcomings, provided the empire with a dual system of justice, one under the estates, the other under the emperor, which enabled serious conflicts to be settled by judicial means rather than violence. That these and the lesser courts of the German states performed their task relatively well is one reason why there was never a revolution in Germany. It was not because of the slavishly subordinate nature of the Germans that no Bastilles were stormed or princes decapitated, it was because most felt that recourse to the courts was an adequate guarantee of civil rights and that those in authority would make the necessary adjustments to overcome obvious injustices. There was no need for revolution from below where there was sufficient confidence in reform from above.

The Treaty of Westphalia confirmed the status of the imperial districts, the bodies intermediate between the small states and the empire. In areas where foreign powers were involved, or powerful German states pursued their own interests, they atrophied. When they were welcomed by small states such as Swabia and Franconia, they were an effective form of federal organization analogous to the United Provinces or the Swiss cantons, and were widely regarded as examples of republican virtue.

The Diet of Regensburg agreed that an imperial standing army, the *miles perpetuus*, should be created, the states being individually responsible for raising a contingent. The emperor got his army and the sovereignty of the states was further strengthened – the rights of the princes to tax their subjects in order to pay for their armies was sanctioned by imperial law. No litigation concerning military expenditure and taxation could reach the imperial courts. Frederick William of Brandenburg-Prussia, 'the Great Elector', managed to make the election of the emperor Leopold I dependent on his agreeing that the imperial courts should henceforth no longer consider any cases concerning taxation. The imperial districts were made responsible for mustering the troops for the imperial army.

Where the districts were not dominated by a powerful state, the federal system worked admirably. Where the district was dominated by a state such as Brandenburg-Prussia, the smaller states provided money and men for the army of their powerful neighbour. A clear distinction was now made between the 'armed' and the 'unarmed' states which greatly enhanced the relative strength of the former. Many a small state, such as Lippe or Paderborn, joined the ranks of the 'armed' states in order to enhance their prestige.

Absolutism in Germany was tempered by the rights of the empire and of the estates. The prince and his government could not ignore the rights of his subjects in matters of religion and of property since such rights were guaranteed by the imperial courts. Any fundamental political changes had to be approved by the estates. The Soldier King of Prussia, Frederick William I (1688–1740), announced in his characteristic mixture of German and French: *'Ich stabilire die Souveraineté wie einen Rocher von Bronce'* (I strengthen sovereignty like a bronze rock), but although he ruled a fully sovereign state, he was restrained by such external and internal factors and realized that it would be folly to challenge the position of the emperor.

In many of the Catholic states there was appalling religious intolerance. Between 1731 and 1732, 21,000 Protestants were expelled from Salzburg and fled to Prussia where they were put to work in the east repairing the damage done in the Great Northern War. This was a back-breaking effort as a result of which 25 per cent of the immigrants died within ten years. Prussia was the most religiously tolerant of all the German states largely because its population was so mixed, although the state did not relax its controlling influence over the Churches. Curiously enough most of the towns, later represented as havens of bourgeois tolerance and common sense, were singularly intolerant in matters of religion. This was as true of the predominantly Protestant Hanseatic towns as of the mixed towns in the south like Augsburg and Ravensburg where the parity provisions of the Peace of Westphalia did not produce tolerance and mutual respect but a hardening of the fronts and frequent outbreaks of violence.

BRANDENBURG-PRUSSIA

Prussia had certain peculiarities which distinguished it from other German states and which gave it its particular character. The conversion of the Lutheran elector Johann Sigismund to Calvinism in 1613 was exceedingly unpopular among his subjects, and he was obliged to acknowledge the rights of the Lutheran Church. There was thus no second Reformation in Prussia. The aristocracy which dominated the officer corps and the bureaucracy remained Lutheran. The court was Calvinist, as was much of the urban middle class. Tolerance was the only way to avoid a clash between the Calvinist minority and the Lutheran majority which had the solid support of the estates. The Great Elector, although devoutly Calvinist, realized the need for religious toleration, not because he believed in freedom of

Frederick William I's 'Tobacco Parliament' painted by George Lisiewski (1738–39). The Prussian king, known to contemporaries as '*le roi sergeant*' detested the extravagance of the Baroque court and was happiest in his all-male '*Tabakskollegium*'. Wearing uniform, he would smoke, drink beer and eat a simple meal with his civil servants, officers and invited guests, and discuss the matters of the day. This naive painting captures the dour simplicity and military strictness of 'the Soldier King's' court.

conscience, but for practical political reasons. Frederick II 'the Great' (1712–86) went further than any other German prince when he announced that 'if Turks and heathens come and want to populate the land then we shall build mosques and churches for them. Everyone must find salvation in their own way'. But this was not the toleration of an open-minded liberal. Religious freedom in Prussia was granted from above, not won from below as the result of a protracted struggle for individual freedom as it was in England or Holland.

Of all the Prussian Protestants perhaps the Pietists had the greatest influence. Pietism had begun at the time of the Thirty Years War as a reaction against the fanaticism and intolerance of the churches. It stressed inner piety, simplicity, and the direct relationship between the individual and God. The Pietists provided the perfect example of the much vaunted Prussian virtues of obedience, frugality, sense of duty, modesty, diligence, and social responsibility. They gave religious sanction to the aims of the Prussian absolutist state.

The great elector answered the revocation of the Edict of Nantes with the Edict of Potsdam in 1685 which welcomed the persecuted Huguenots to Prussia. Fifteen thousand accepted the invitation and made a tremendous contribution to the economy and to education. One-third of the founder members of the Academy of Sciences in Berlin, the brain-child of the Electress Sophie Charlotte and the great philosopher Leibniz, were of French origin. The French school in Berlin, founded in 1689 and known as the Collège Royal, was the finest in Prussia, and generations of the elite were educated there in the French tradition.

Frederick William I had little interest in the arts and sciences. It was Frederick the Great with his contempt for German culture and his admiration of the French who revived the Academy, appointing the French mathematician Maupertuis as president. D'Alembert, Condorcet and Diderot were made members of the academy. Voltaire stayed at the Prussian court in 1743 and again between 1750 and 1753. Prussian Huguenots played an important part in writing the great French encyclopedia and were encouraged in their endeavours by Frederick the Great, in spite of his serious reservations about their political views.

The east Elbian Junkers (aristocratic landowners), with their large estates worked by serfs, had profited from the rise in agricultural prices in the sixteenth century. They enjoyed the rights to police, administer the law, and make Church appointments on their estates. The great elector had forced the Brandenburg Diet to accept his *miles perpetuus* and thus no longer needed to get formal agreement to further taxation. An attempt to win a similar victory over the estates in East Prussia failed. The 'Long Diet' from 1661–63 and a second Diet between 1669 and 1672 refused to grant any further taxes. In 1662 Frederick William I marched with his army into East Prussia, and Hieronymus Roth, the leader of the Königsberg council, was flung into jail, where he remained for the rest of his life without a trial. In 1672 Colonel Christian Ludwig von Kalckstein, the leader of the noble opposition, was kidnapped while on a visit to Warsaw seeking support among the Polish aristocracy, and was tortured and executed. In 1674 taxes were forcibly collected in Königsberg and after 1704 taxes were collected in East Prussia without consulting the estates. The aristocracy had been robbed of its political rights.

In 1701 Frederick III, elector of Brandenburg, obtained permission from the Emperor Leopold to become 'King in Prussia' (Frederick I). The duchy of Prussia, soon to be known as East Prussia, was outside the boundaries of the empire so Frederick was a king in Prussia, and, still only an elector in the empire. Under Frederick I it seemed possible that Prussia might emulate French absolutism with its aristocratic and opulent court, but his miserly son, Frederick William I preferred the austerity of the barracks to the pomp of an imitation Versailles. The Soldier King financed his army by imposing a land tax on the aristocracy and by collecting money rather than demanding military service on the royal estates. Relations between the king and the aristocracy were still strained, and it was not until the reign of Frederick II that both sides recognized their common interests. The aristocracy needed the crown as a guarantee of their social status against the challenge of an upwardly mobile bourgeoisie. Frederick II needed the aristocracy

Sanssouci

Frederick II 'the Great' (1712–86) was a brilliant commander, a thoughtful writer, and a highly cultured man. His ambition was to be an enlightened all-rounder; a Voltaire or Leibniz who was also soldier and statesman. He said of the great elector (1620–88) that he gave the country all the necessary crafts, but he did not have the time to give it the pleasant arts. The spend-thrift Frederick I (1657–1713) had made of Prussia an Athens, Frederick William (1688–1740) made it a Sparta, Frederick wanted both. In Potsdam, he created the Athens of Sanssouci and a Sparta at the barracks.

As crown prince he had entertained friends and acquaintances at his country estate in Rheinsberg and he continued this tradition at the delightful Rococo palace of Sanssouci from 1745–1756, entertaining his guests in a small dining room. Voltaire was particularly struck by a large painting in this room for which Frederick had provided a sketch. It was an immensely priapic scene of satyrs and nymphs, embracing couples, cupids, whores and catamites that made the visitor think that 'the seven wise men of Greece were conversing in a brothel'.

Discussion was lively and free-ranging. Voltaire, with his biting wit, was a powerful influence on the young prince, forcing him to question all philosophical constructs. Conversation, entirely in French, was relaxed, and only God was spared from the biting wit of the king and his guests. Adolph von Menzel's splendid painting of 1850 shows Voltaire adressing a sceptical Frederick, while Maupertuis, the president of the Academy, stares defiantly at Voltaire. In this idealized scene the king is hardly the centre of attention, but this is far from the historical truth as no criticism of Frederick was tolerated. Lessing claimed that the only freedom enjoyed in Prussia was the right to talk any amount of nonsense about religion.

Other prominent guests included Francesco Algarotti, author of the enormously popular *Il Newtonismo per le Dame* ('Newton for the Ladies'), La Mettrie, the author of *L'homme machine*, who died of a surfeit of truffles, and Jean Baptiste d'Argens, a prolific denouncer of the evils of religion

By 1763 Frederick had become increasingly bitter, misanthropic and solitary, grimly attending to affairs of state. Many intellectuals preferred to admire the philosopher-king from afar and refused his invitations to come to Berlin. Frederick was unable to revive his soirées and Sanssouci became little more than a happy memory.

'Table Talk at Sanssouci' (1850) by Adolph von Menzel. Voltaire is seated third from the left, Frederick the Great is fifth from the left.

to provide a reliable officer corps. In his Political Testament of 1752 he stressed that one of his main aims was to preserve the aristocracy. To this end no bourgeois was to be allowed to buy the estates of an aristocrat. Unlike his father, Frederick II ceased to buy up the lands of the nobility and ennobled very few bourgeois. He left the nobility a free hand in their estates, and when they hit hard times granted generous loans to tide them over.

The Prussian elite was disciplined, obedient, and efficient and thus embodied the best of military virtues, but it was haughtily aristocratic. It held a snobbish contempt for the middle-class world of trade and commerce, even though aristocrats ran their estates as commercial enterprises, exported agricultural produce, built breweries and distilled schnapps. The Junker on his estates was the paternalist lord of a virtually self-governing community in which the social gulf between lord and peasant was unbridgeable. It was an efficient system, but it purposefully blocked the path to political and social modernization and rejected bourgeois and liberal values. The vast mass of the population were excluded from any form of participation in the affairs of state.

Unlike most of the German states in the eighteenth century whose economies were distorted by the demand for luxury goods, Prussia emphasized agriculture, foreign trade, and manufacture. Artisans, craftsmen, jewellers, and bankers all profited from the extravagance of the Baroque courts and the capitals of many a German state prospered under the *ancien régime*, but a state could never aspire to be a great power without solid economic backing. On his accession to the throne, Frederick William I promptly ordered the arrest of Frau Liebermann, Berlin's leading jeweller and banker, to whom his father was heavily indebted, and imposed a regime of almost pathological austerity upon the court.

Recruitment to the Prussian army was based on the canton system of 1733. The country was divided up into a series of districts each of which provided the manpower: 5,000 men for an infantry regiment, 1,800 for a cavalry regiment. All the young men in a canton were enrolled on the regimental lists, swore an oath of allegiance to the king and were issued with a pass. The urban bourgeoisie and property-owners were usually exempted from military service, so that the bulk of the soldiers were peasants. The officers were mostly Junkers. Henceforth the Prussian aristocracy was forbidden to serve in foreign armies and their children were forced to attend the cadet school in Berlin from the age of twelve. Many of these children were taken to Berlin under police escort.

The social relationships between landowner and serf were thus reproduced in the army. Frederick William I wrote in his political testament that his successor should 'employ the aristocracy and counts in the army and make their children into cadets, so that the entire aristocracy will be brought up from childhood to know no other master except God and the king in Prussia'. The military system provided Frederick the Great with an army of 80,000 men in 1740, when his rival Austria only had 110,000 men in arms, even though Austria had more than twice the number of inhabitants. The military system also put the social order in quarantine: the peasants were placed under a double serfdom, the aristocracy made into a privileged elite that enjoyed the king's favour.

On the one hand, Prussia was a modern state with an efficient and reasonably honest bureaucracy, a healthy economy, an exemplary code of laws and a fine army, but it was socially ossified with little possibility for liberal democratic forces to develop. It was an authoritarian, bureaucratic and paternalistic state. The peasantry were oppressed, not so much by poverty or exploitation, but as the result of a historically conditioned servile mentality which made it impossible for them to articulate their needs, frustrations, and emancipatory aspirations.

The situation in the towns was quite different. The bourgeoisie were largely exempted from military service and were free to make their fortunes or serve in the highest echelons of the civil service. But their social mobility was strictly limited and they were unable to buy their way into the ranks of the aristocracy as they were in England or France. Frederick II forbade the sale of aristocratic estates to wealthy bourgeois, although this prohibition was often evaded. The social gap between the classes was widened by the emphasis on the exclusivity of the aristocracy in the army and the administration. The bourgeoisie in Prussia got rich, but they were painfully reminded of their social inferiority and their lack of political power.

GERMAN SOCIETY IN THE EIGHTEENTH CENTURY

During the eighteenth century there was a sharp increase in the birth rate; women got married much younger, thus lengthening their legally and religiously sanctioned period of fecundity. Although in most families a child was born every two and a half years, usually only two survived into adulthood. Upwards of one-third of newborn children died, and in many areas 70 per cent died under the age of fourteen. The fact that there were no major outbreaks of the plague in this period seems due more to good luck than enlightened public hygiene policy. The towns were deplorably filthy and passers-by found the piles of human faeces outside the royal palace in Berlin most offensive. Smallpox was rampant and was a major cause of death. Respiratory diseases, particularly tuberculosis and typhus, were common causes of death, and high infant mortality was due to common infectious diseases as well as a high percentage of still births.

In spite of social ostracism and, in many places, public floggings of unmarried mothers, the number of illegitimate births was extremely high. At the end of the century in Protestant Berlin about 10 per cent of births were illegitimate, in Catholic Munich about 20 per cent. In rural areas, although there was more sympathy for such conduct, only about one birth in sixteen was illegitimate. As restrictions on marriage were relaxed under the influence of Enlightenment thought, the number of illegitimate births dropped significantly.

In the eighteenth century, the nobility accounted for about 1 per cent of the total population. The vast majority of the nobility owed their titles to their local prince

The courts

After the Treaty of Westphalia there were 250 princedoms in Germany which sent representatives to the Diet. All of these maintained more or less elaborate courts. In addition there were the estates of the imperial knights, some of whom were rich enough to hold court. Similarly the bishops and abbots, who owed their positions to dynastic clout rather than their piety or religious zeal, lived in great splendour, and did not deny themselves female company — considered to be an essential component of secular court life.

These courts all had a similar organization. In addition to the traditional councillors, Catholic courts had a court confessor, Protestant states a court preacher. Doctors, artists, architects, gardeners, musicians, theatre directors, horse trainers, historians, soldiers, game-keepers, servants, and pages were attached to the court and given grandiose titles such as *Hochkapellmeister*, which did not disguise the fact that they were usually poorly paid lackeys. Princes' consorts also maintained their own smaller courts, as did their children, with ladies-in-waiting, tutors, and instructors.

All court activity centred around the prince. When he travelled, most of the court travelled with him. Elaborate court ceremony served to enhance the status of the prince and to discipline the courtiers. It was both a representation and a cementing of the social order. Ceremony determined social values, set the fashion, and established behavioural norms. The extravagant ritual of the court provided employment for local artisans and craftsmen, leading to the development of luxury industries. These luxury industries were often highly profitable and were encouraged by enterprising princes. Frederick the Great, although notoriously tight-fisted in his later years, complained that his father's miserly behaviour had forced Johann Friedrich Böttger, the founder of Meissen porcelain, to move to Dresden.

By the later eighteenth century the lavish ceremonial, pompous military parades, back-biting intrigues, and frivolous behaviour of the courts had become topics of censure amongst the critical writers and commentators of the day. Many courts were undoubtedly extravagantly wasteful but some, such as Mannheim and Weimar, were great cultural centres, and all sponsored the architects, artists and landscape-gardeners who produced the masterpieces of the Baroque and Rococo. Courts were seen as an exciting and dramatic world where people could realize their full potential, and even a critical mind like Leibniz felt that they served a useful purpose by offering positions to people who would otherwise be penniless.

'The arrival of Archduke Maximilian at the Residential Palace', painted in 1780 by J. Franz Rousseau.

A view of Dresden by Antoinio de Dipi Joli (1700–77). August the Strong of Saxony and King of Poland rebuilt his capital at Dresden, and held court there in the manner of Louis XIV. His enthusiasm for magnificent architecture, the opera and for his Meissen porcelain factory made Dresden a great cultural and artistic centre, but ruined Saxony's finances.

rather than to the emperor. In some areas, particularly in the south-west, most of the aristocracy owed their titles directly to the emperor. The imperial aristocracy were represented in the Diet, the imperial princes and counts each having a single vote. In order to protect these rights and privileges the aristocracy would only marry within their own ranks and were thus far more aloof and exclusive than their English counterparts. Since they were unable to marry wealthy commoners, they were often also considerably poorer.

The clergy was still a privileged estate and the Catholic electors and prince bishops all came from the nobility, many of whom were imperial knights. Despite the reforms agreed at the Council of Trent, most of them were pluralists, few had any theological training, and some had not even been ordained. They were worldly princes who left spiritual affairs to a suffragan (a subordinate bishop). The sons of bourgeois and peasants could, if they had received the proper theological training, become minor bishops and abbots or even serve on some of the cathedral chapters. One-third of the seats of the Cologne chapter, for example, were reserved for commoners with a doctorate in theology. Most of the lower clergy came from bourgeois and artisanal families.

The Protestant clergy were solidly bourgeois and, as married men with large families, they set an example of solid family life which had a profound effect on the development of a specifically middle-class mentality. The Protestant clergy served the state by recognizing the prince as the '*summus episcopus*' (head bishop), by reading the princes' edicts from the pulpit, and by preaching obedience to those in authority. Protestants stressed subordination to civil authority, Catholics were more sceptical. The political consequences of these approaches were considerable.

Poverty was a major problem in late eighteenth-century Germany and it has been estimated that 20–25 per cent of the population lived below the poverty line. Protestants shook their heads at the news that 25 per cent of the inhabitants of the ecclesiastical states lived in abject poverty, but overlooked the fact that 30 per cent of the population of Berlin at the end of the Seven Years War were recipients of poor relief. Not all of these beggars came from the lowest social classes. Noblemen down on their luck, unemployed officers, and bankrupt bourgeois tramped the roads of Germany along with the thousands of paupers of less exalted station.

Urban life in the late eighteenth century was increasingly stultified and it needed the impact of the French and industrial revolutions for there to be a fundamental change. The patrician families monopolized political power. The guilds enjoyed excessive privileges which acted as a brake on economic growth. Even in Hamburg, the most liberal of the German cities, where a proud middle-class refused to allow the aristocracy to own property, the citizenry was divided into nine different classes, each with diminishing legal rights. The sumptuary laws, which ordained the appropriate clothing for the different social stations, were still on the statute books although increasingly ignored. Following the lead of the courts, the frivolous fashions of the Rococo and the obsession with French fashions overcame sartorial barriers.

The ruins of the Church of the Cross (*Kreuzkirche*) in Dresden by Bernardo Bellotto (1765). The church was badly damaged by Prussian artillery in 1760 and the tower collapsed in 1765. Bellotto (1721–80) was the nephew of Canaletto, the most popular topographical painter of the day.

The eighteenth century was in many ways the golden age of the landowning aristocracy, provided that the opportunities offered were not wasted by greed and profligacy. This was the age of modern estate management, but also of the rake and the speculator. Apart from eastern and north-eastern Germany, cash rents and leases had in many instances replaced labour service and payments in kind. East of the Elbe enclosures, which increased greatly as a result of the disruption of agriculture during the Thirty Years War, enlarged the estates of the Junkers and condemned many smallholders to serfdom. Hereditary serfdom was, as Frederick II remarked, virtually indistinguishable from slavery. Not only was the legal position of the East-Elbian serfs far worse than that of the peasantry in the west and south, they were also disadvantaged economically. There was widespread poverty and deprivation among the western peasants, but they were still freer and usually more prosperous than their fellows in France or in the east. This is a further reason why the French revolution had relatively little impact in Germany.

Conditions were so bad in the East that there were frequent local revolts by the peasantry in Silesia, Brandenburg, and East Prussia. Efforts by reforming administrators, such as Ernst William von Schlabrendorff in Silesia, either triggered off revolts caused by rising expectations or were frustrated by the local aristocracy. Frederick II's efforts to protect the peasantry also failed because of resistance by the local courts and the suspicions of the peasants themselves, who felt they were being tricked. He had far greater success on his own estates, where he reduced the labour service from five to three days a week and created 50,000 hereditary farms where peasants owned the land rather than having a mere right to its use.

Much of the royal demesne was leased out, mostly to bourgeois agricultural entrepreneurs. Officials were instructed to ensure that high returns for leases were not achieved at the peasantry's expense, but most were highly qualified and aggressive businessmen, and many made considerable fortunes buying up aristocratic estates, even though this was officially forbidden. Most royal lease-holders had sufficient capital and expertise to modernize their farms and were not restricted by the hidebound conventions and legal restrictions of the aristocratic estates. They were a modernizing factor in a traditional aristocratic society.

Many Junker estates were seriously endebted. Although the value of estates rose dramatically in the last three decades of the eighteenth century, and the price of agricultural produce rose appreciably faster than the price of manufactured goods, the burden of debt grew still faster. This was caused largely by ill-considered speculation in property. Frederick II granted credits to help aristocratic landowners to modernize their estates, but more often than not they used the money for further speculation, running up huge mortgages. The old system could not be reformed, it could only be altered fundamentally, but it took the crushing defeat of Prussia by France in 1806 to convince the Prussian aristocracy that such restructuring was essential.

In the years before the French revolution, the burden of feudal obligations was reduced in most of the German states. Margrave Charles Frederick of Baden lessened the labour service on his estates in 1773 and again in 1786, and in 1783 he abolished serfdom. Yet even in Baden the peasantry were still subjected to labour service and there were limitations on their freedom of movement. In 1785 the peasantry were permitted to buy themselves free from these feudal obligations but very few were able to do so. The same was true in Bavaria in 1779, where hardly any peasants on the royal demesne could afford the compensation payments which enabled them to become freeholders.

The situation was hardly better in the trades. Apprenticeships lasted for two to six years followed by two to five years as a journeyman. The candidate then completed his 'masterpiece' and had to pay a considerable sum in order to sit for his examination. In some instances the apprentice had to own property of a certain value in order to be admitted to a guild. Few had sufficient funds to meet these requirements, almost the only way for a journeyman to become a master-craftsman was to marry his master's widow. It is for this reason that in many places up to one-third of married men had wives who were considerably older than themselves. Apprentices and journeymen were often badly treated and there were a number of strikes and riots in protest against such abuses. The army was called in to suppress the tailors' strike in Breslau in 1793, leaving twenty-seven dead. Imperial edicts regulating apprenticeships and the guilds were generally ignored.

There were three principal modes of production in late eighteenth-century Germany: in an artisan's workshop; tendering work to home-based labourers; and in manufactories. Textiles and clothing were largely produced by tendering. Manufactories were sizable pre-industrial enterprises that were free from supervision by the guilds. They were owned and organized by an individual capitalist, or managed on behalf of the state. The workers were wage-earners who owned no part of the means of production. Factories are distinguished from manufactories by the use of machinery – the first German factory was a cotton mill opened near Düsseldorf in 1784 where English machinery was used. Only 7 per cent of German workers were employed in just over 1,000 manufactories in 1800. Given that many states actively encouraged manufacture as part of their mercantile policy, this is not a very impressive number. The fastest rate of growth was in the Rhineland where towns like Krefeld and Duisburg were important manufacturing centres and Solingen steel already had a European reputation. Industry flourished in a free atmosphere where adventurous entrepreneurs were not restrained by burdensome government regulation and absolutist control.

In spite of all these problems only Italy had such a multiplicity of important urban centres. There were the court cities such as Munich and Dresden, or Bonn where the archbishops and elector of Cologne held his court, the great cathedral towns like Mainz, the old imperial cities like Nuremberg, wealthy bourgeois centres like Hamburg, and university towns like Göttingen. As in Italy this rich

Mozart as a guest of the Viennese Free Masons' lodge, painted by an anonymous artist in 1790. Whereas Haydn was a liveried servant of Prince Eszterhazy and conscious of his lack of freedom, once Mozart left the service of the archbishop of Salzburg he was obliged to earn his living as a freelance composer. Nevertheless, he was still dependent on his mostly aristocratic sponsors. Beethoven was the first composer who did not have to write for specific commissions and was treated as an independent artist by his patrons.

urban life was a result of political decentralization and particularism. The empire had no capital like London or Paris. The emperor was crowned in Frankfurt and usually lived in Vienna. Since 1663 the Diet met in Regensburg, the imperial court was in Wetzlar and the chancellor lived in Mainz. Many contemporaries bemoaned the lack of a capital city, but Germany had a large number of vibrant urban centres in which a remarkable culture was nourished and where a self-confident middle class gradually developed.

MUSIC AND LITERATURE

When Maria Theresa ascended the throne, Vienna began to decline as a great musical centre. The empress had little patience for elaborate court ceremonial, and the expenses of war forced her to economize. She thus refused to give the young Mozart a position and warned her son, the Archduke Ferdinand, not to appoint him saying: 'I cannot think why you have to employ a composer or any such useless people ... these people wander around like beggars, and anyway he is part of a large family'. Between 1743 and 1778 Mannheim, under the Elector Karl Theodor of the Palatinate, was the great musical centre of Germany. He maintained a large orchestra, an opera company, a ballet where as many as one hundred dancers appeared on stage, and employed two music directors, one for French and one for Italian opera. The English musicologist Charles Burney, who did not have a very high opinion of German music, reported that the Mannheim orchestra was a brilliant collection of soloists and composers, but that it was an army of generals, better suited to draw up plans for a campaign than to fight a battle. Johann Wenzel Anton Stamitz, a virtuoso violinist, was the founder of the Mannheim school.

The composer Franz Joseph Haydn (1732–1809). This portrait was painted by Thomas Hardy while Haydn was in London in 1792.

Johann Sebastian Bach

Johann Sebastian Bach was born in Eisenach in Thuringia on 21 March 1685, the son of the local bandmaster. At the age of seventeen he obtained a lowly position as 'lackey musician' in Weimar and shortly afterwards was made organist at an insignificant church where he neglected his duties and quarrelled with his choir and musicians. In 1707 he moved to Mühlhausen in Thuringia, where he argued with the pietist minister, who wanted only the simplest of music. His big opportunity came in the following year when he was offered the post of court organist at Weimar. The duke was highly appreciative of his abilities, and it was here that he composed some of his finest organ works including the preludes and fugues, toccatas and fugues, fantasies and fugues, and the inventive and introspective chorale preludes.

Bach, who was not appointed *Kappellmeister* at Weimar, became anxious to leave, and accepted a position offered by Prince Leopold of Cöthen. Duke Wilhelm Ernst of Weimar sent him to jail for four weeks for breach of contract and then dismissed him. He was happy in his new appointment and there followed a period of increased creative output, marred by the sudden death of his wife, who left him four surviving children. In the following year, 1721, he married the twenty-year-old Anna Magdalena with whom he had thirteen children, of whom six survived.

Most of Bach's orchestral works were composed for the musicians at Cöthen, including the *Brandenburg Concertos*, so called because he presented the score to the marqrave of Brandenburg who admired his compositions. He also wrote the bulk of his harpsichord and chamber music at Cöthen, the greatest masterpiece being Book I of the *Well-Tempered Keyboard*. As at Weimar, Bach combined the flair of the Italian school, particularly Vivaldi, the striking rhythmic invention of the French, with the more complex and elaborately contrapuntal German style.

A striking portait of Johann Sebastian Bach, attributed to Johann Ernst Rensch the elder, painted c.1715.

In 1722 Bach was appointed Kantor at St Thomas' School in Leipzig, a prestigious but onerous appointment. In his first year there, Bach wrote a complete set of about sixty cantatas for the church year. He appears to have written a total of five such cycles, although most have been lost. Bach was also active as a teacher, travelled extensively, spent a lot of time playing *Hausmusik* with friends, organized concerts, and still had energy to spare to argue with his employers.

A towering masterpiece of the Leipzig period was the *Saint Matthew Passion,* composed in 1727, in which all the musical discoveries he had made in his more private pieces were combined in a work of exceptional richness and emotional depth. *The Goldberg Variations* for keyboard, written in 1741, were a kind of musical testament. They are a set of thirty virtuoso variations in all manner of musical forms linked together by the same bass pattern. *The Musical Offering*, written for Frederick the Great in the same year, is also a brilliant collection of different forms. *The Art of the Fugue*, written in the 1740s, was his memorial to a form of which he was the past-master. His last great work, a Catholic mass, was never intended for public performance. Bach, despite being seen by many of his contemporaries as old-fashioned, nevertheless provides a summary and apotheosis of the Baroque in a series of unsurpassed masterpieces.

Among the leading figures were his two sons, Anton and Carl, as well as Franz Xavier Richter, Ignaz Holzbauer, Anton Filtz, Carlo Toeschi, and Christian Cannabich. The greatest contribution of the Mannheim school was to establish the norms of a modern orchestra, its instrumentation and its characteristic sound, in place of an ad hoc collection of musicians. The first violin conducted the orchestra, usually using his bow, rather than leading from a harpsichord. The Mannheim composers also developed the sonata form and created the outline of the classical symphony. The Mannheim style was eclectic and musicians came from all over Europe, each making an individual contribution to create a new musical language.

Berlin was also an important musical centre, for Frederick II was an accomplished flautist and competent composer. Johann Joachim Quantz composed 300 flute concertos for the king to play, and Franz Benda, Christian Friedrich Carl Fasch, and Bach's son Carl Philipp Emanuel were also resident composers. The 'Berlin School', composed largely according to Frederick II's taste, was conservative, melodious and Italianate. The king also sponsored lavish productions of Italian opera in the Berlin opera house which opened in 1742, but the expenses of his wars forced him to economize and eventually it was forced to close for eight years from 1756. Frederick II's conservative taste and shortage of cash tempted many composers to leave Berlin for less stuffy and better paid appointments. C.P.E. Bach, whom Frederick had employed merely as a harpsichordist and who was paid less than an Italian singer, went to Hamburg as a replacement for Telemann in 1767.

Friedrich von Schiller (1759–1805), in the uniform of the Württemberg military academy where he studied law and medicine. He is shown reading from his first play *The Robbers*, written at the age of twenty-two, a revolutionary attack on society of such lasting power that the Nazis felt it prudent to ban the play. For Schiller, theatre was a kind of court of law where 'the mighty of this world hear what they never, or seldom, hear – the truth.

Music was not confined to the courts and churches. Public concerts were held in Hamburg from 1722, in Frankfurt from 1723 and in Leipzig from 1743. The famous Gewandhaus concerts in Leipzig began in 1781. Composers were thus sponsored by courts, wealthy individuals, and also by concert promoters. From the 1780s Vienna was indisputably the music capital of the world, with Haydn and Mozart producing a series of unparalleled masterpieces. The classical Viennese style was self-consciously international. Haydn could justly claim that 'my language is understood throughout the world' and Mozart wrote. 'it would be an everlasting disgrace for Germany if we Germans seriously began to think like Germans, act like Germans, talk like Germans, and even sing like Germans!!!' He was, nevertheless, given to violent bouts of xenophobia. It was the lasting achievement of the Viennese classical composers that they indeed spoke to the whole world, not only across national borders but also across classes.

German literature came of age in the second half of the eighteenth century, a period of quite extraordinary richness. The models were English, particularly Shakespeare and Laurence Sterne, as well as the critical bourgeois works of the French Enlightenment. Many of the important works contain elements of political and social satire such as Lessing's *Minna von Barnhelm* (1767) and *Emilia Galotti* (1772) or Schiller's *Kabale und Liebe* (1784), but they deal with themes of lasting interest in a literary and philosophical language of enduring fascination. Lessing's *Nathan der Weise* (1779) is an impassioned plea for religious toleration and freedom from prejudice and a classic expression of the German Enlightenment's concept of humanity.

The influence of Shakespeare and of the English concept of 'sentiment' is plainly apparent in another leading literary movement of the time: the 'Storm and Stress' (*Sturm und Drang*) to which the young Goethe and Schiller belonged, along with Herder and Jakob Michael Reinhold Lenz. It was a protest movement of young writers, most of them in their twenties, who were in revolt against their stuffily 'enlightened' elders. They were self-appointed geniuses and outsiders, most of whom were to end their lives with dramatic suicides or as poverty-stricken pariahs. They rejected the schoolmasterly pedantry of the Enlightenment philosophers and the restrictive norms of behaviour dictated by bourgeois conformism. These middle-class precursors of the hippies emphasized feelings, sensations, and the power of nature. The young Goethe saw this ideal personified in the proud rebel *Prometheus* (1773). Goethe produced the archetypal 'Storm and Stress' figure in *Leiden des jungen Werther* (The Sufferings of Young Werther). Soon sensitive young men throughout Germany and beyond dressed in Werther's blue tails and yellow waistcoat, fell unhappily in love and ended their tormented lives with a pistol. Lessing and the Enlightenment figures were appalled at this display of self-indulgent subjectivity and emotional hypertrophy, and condemned its lamentable social effects. In doing so they missed much of the brilliant sociological analysis, its telling criticism both of aristocratic and bourgeois society, and its impassioned

Faust

The ancient tale of a man who made a pact with the devil dates back to the Middle Ages. By the beginning of the sixteenth century he is given the name Doctor Faustus, a scholar whose hunger for knowledge was such that he sold his soul to the Evil One. It was a story which both Catholics and Protestants used to attack the pantheistic curiosity of the likes of Parecelsus, an alchemist and physician who was one of the foremost medical researchers of his age. To the Enlightenment, Faust was an absurd creature, a mixture of crackpot and charlatan. He first became a hero to the 'Storm and Stress' writers of the late eighteenth century, who saw him as a Promethean hero who defied convention and social restraints. Goethe converted this caricature, which had been used in so many polemics, into a universal figure.

Faust fascinated Goethe throughout his creative life. The first sketches, the *Urfaust*, were written between 1772 and 1775. In 1790 he published *Faust, ein Fragment*, a reworking of the original material. Part One of *Faust* was written between 1797 and 1806, and the second part completed in 1831 shortly before his last birthday. Goethe's Faust is a man searching to overcome the contradictions between the self and the world, ideal and reality, art and life, good and evil. Because he never ceases to search he is finally saved and Mephistopheles loses his wager with God. Mephistopheles is no longer God's equal, fighting an even battle for his soul. He is helpless against the power of love, against creative genius, and against free ethical decision. Yet Goethe's character is still 'Faustian' in that he is imperfect. All his plans, how-ever laudable and grandiose, have within them fatal flaws.

Part One met with general critical acclaim, although some churchmen found the hero's character somewhat reprehensible, and Madame de Staël, with her typically French belief that the classical unities had to be preserved, found the form questionable. Part Two was almost universally condemned. Rationalists felt that Goethe was dabbling in mystical gibberish, Catholics accused him of blasphemy, Protestants claimed that he was a materialist, and Romantics condemned the work as full of scientific hubris. No one bothered to examine the literary qualities of the work. Young Germans like Heine praised Part One as 'progressive', but felt that Part Two with its final redemption scene was hopelessly 'reactionary', although it had nothing to do with the Christian concept of redemption. Heine felt that Faust was too unpolitical and tried to turn it into a tract for social reform.

With the foundation of the Reich in 1871, a frantic search began for a truly 'German' hero. Faust had already been coopted for this improbable role by nationalists who saw him as the embodiment of the 'German spirit'. This ideological misuse of Goethe's masterpiece reached new depths with Oswald Spengler's efforts to convert it into a pagan, Romantic, nationalistic, and imperialist myth, with Faust as the personification of Western man. This reached its final form when Doctor Faust, the Promethean hero, was transformed into a model for the ranks of the Nazi storm-troopers. Like all great masterpieces, *Faust* is open to a myriad of interpretations and can easily be misused. In a typically arrogant but nevertheless truthful remark, Goethe described his work as a mystery that would continue to fascinate later generations.

Detail of 'Scenes from Faust' by Carl Vogel von Vogelstein (1788–1868).

claim for the rights of the individual. It is precisely these aspects of the book that assure its place among the great literary works of the time.

The great writers soon went beyond Storm and Stress. Schiller examined historical subjects and saw art as a realm of freedom which transcended reality, a realm in which alone morality could develop. But Schiller was too much of a historian not to keep his feet on the ground and was an outspoken critic of the petty absolutists and a powerful advocate of freedom of speech. The dialectical tensions between nature and reason, knowledge and faith, and the individual and society, could no longer be seen as demanding choices, and attempts to surpass these contradictions were now the order of the day, including such masterpieces as Kant's *Critique of Pure Reason* (1781) and Goethe's *Wilhelm Meister's Apprenticeship* (1795) the greatest *Bildungsroman*, an exploration of the education and development of the individual. In *Iphigenie auf Tauris* (1787) Goethe paints the picture of an idealized reconciliation between the needs of the individual and the imperatives of society through personal sacrifice. Although Goethe was of a more conservative disposition than Schiller, he too returned frequently to the theme of the individual in revolt against a restrictive society. In *Faust*, Goethe examined a series of fundamental issues such as the relationship between good and evil, God and the devil, understanding and error, reality and myth, and guilt and forgiveness. *Faust* is the greatest masterpiece in the German language.

The Romantics such as Novalis, Arnim, Brentano, Eichendorff, and Tieck, who wrote between the late eighteenth century and the 1830s, were not youthful rebels like the Storm and Stress writers, even though they were influenced by them. They emphasized the power and beauty of nature, the romance of the German medieval past, and were strongly swayed by nationalist sentiment. E.T.A. Hoffmann and Jean Paul were close to Romantics, but strongly influenced by the eccentric humour and innovatory technique of Laurence Sterne. Heinrich von Kleist and Friedrich Hölderlin, two of the outstanding writers of the younger generation, were also too individualistic and complex to be placed under any simple heading.

THE WARS OF FREDERICK THE GREAT

On 20 October 1740 the Emperor Charles VI died and Maria Theresa succeeded to all the Habsburg lands without internal difficulty. The Pragmatic Sanction, which secured the succession through the female line, and which had been negotiated with the estates was thus successful. The question remained as to whether the European powers would honour their pledges to uphold the Pragmatic Sanction. Frederick II of Prussia, who had succeeded to the throne on 31 May, invaded the wealthy Austrian province of Silesia on 16 December on the basis of a somewhat dubious claim to the succession.

The Prussian army defeated the Austrians at the battle of Mollwitz on 10 April 1741 and Frederick II won an instant reputation as a daring young general. In fact he had left the battlefield thinking that all was lost when the Austrian cavalry put

Immanuel Kant (1724–1804). This woodcut by J.L. Raab shows the philsopher in old age. Kant's profound dissatisfaction with the empiricism of Locke and Hume and the rationalism of Descartes resulted in what he termed the 'Copernican revoluion in philosophy'. He insisted that the ordering principle of reason existed in the mind of the subject, not in the object of contemplation. Without the individual human there could be no thought, and without thought there could be no objects, no world. This is the fundamental position of German idealism.

the Prussians to flight. A determined Prussian counter-attack by the infantry led by Field-Marshal Kurt Christoph von Schwerin determined the outcome of the battle. Frederick II now looked around for support and, in the Treaty of Breslau of 4 June 1741, he allied with France, Spain, Bavaria, Saxony, Poland, Sweden, Naples, Cologne, and the Palatinate, and the War of Austrian Succession began.

The Bavarian Wittelsbachers saw a golden opportunity to deal their Habsburg rivals a crushing blow. The Franco-Bavarian army marched into Austria and Vienna was threatened. Then it turned north into Bohemia to join with August III's Saxon and Polish forces and seized Prague. The Bavarian elector Karl Albrecht was crowned king of Bohemia and in January 1742 the electors unanimously appointed him king of Rome and thus the future emperor. In the following month he was crowned emperor as Charles VII, the first non-Habsburg emperor since 1438. His triumph was short-lived, for the Austrian army promptly marched into Munich and occupied the Bavarian capital.

Since the Bavarians depended entirely on the French and Prussian armies the Austrians were determined to split the anti-Habsburg alliance. At Breslau, in June 1742, Frederick II's conquest of Silesia was accepted, and the Wettins of Saxony and Poland made their peace with the Austrians, becoming faithful allies for years to come. However, the peace with Prussia was not to last for long. The Austrians, supported by the English and the Dutch in the 'Pragmatic Army', recaptured Prague and prepared for a decisive engagement with the French. Frederick II signed alliances with the Bavarians and the French and in the summer of 1744 marched into Bohemia, taking Prague and advancing towards Budweis and Tabor. A counter-attack by the Austrians forced Frederick to retreat and the Prussians soon found themselves dangerously isolated. The Warsaw Quadruple Alliance was concluded between Austria, England, Holland, and Saxony in January 1745 and Bavaria left the anti-Habsburg front in April. Charles VII managed to win back his Bavarian lands but died shortly after his arrival in Munich. Bavaria had proven far too weak to provide an alternative to a Habsburg-dominated empire and there was never a chance of Germany becoming unified under Bavaria.

On 4 October 1745 Maria Theresa's husband was crowned emperor as Francis I, but the celebrations were overshadowed by a series of defeats at the hands of the Prussians. On 4 June they had defeated the Austrians at Hohenfriedberg in Silesia, on 30 September at Soor in Bohemia and on 23 November at Hennersdorf. In December Frederick II entered Dresden, and the second Silesian War was ended on Christmas Day 1745 with the Peace of Dresden, a triumph for Frederick II by which he was granted further territory, a huge indemnity, and a guarantee for Silesia which was accepted by England and Holland.

Frederick II returned to Berlin in triumph as Frederick the Great. With the failure of the Bavarian bid for power there was now no question that the fate of Germany was to be decided by the outcome of the dualism between Prussia and Austria. In 1740 Prussia had one-sixth of the area of Austria and one-third of the population and yet had virtually single-handedly stolen a prosperous province from its great rival and confirmed its status as a European power.

On 16 January 1756 Prussia and England signed the Convention of Westminster which upheld the territorial status quo in Germany and thus sanctioned Frederick the Great's seizure of Silesia. Maria Theresa was determined to win this province back from the 'evil man of Sanssouci', and her chancellor, Kaunitz completed his *renversement des alliances* by signing a treaty with France in May, 1756. Frederick II had made a major blunder, for he assumed that the traditional animosities between Bourbon and Habsburg would ensure that relations between Paris and Berlin would remain cordial, even though England, Prussia's new ally, was at war with the French in North America.

Frederick II, surrounded by powerful enemies and without an effective ally, decided to fight what he was pleased to call a preventive war. The Prussians had some easy successes against Saxony which they invaded in September 1756, but they were soon faced with an overwhelming alliance of Austria, France, Russia, Sweden, and the majority of the German princes. The Swedes occupied Pomerania, the Russians East Prussia, Silesia was lost, and an Austrian army briefly occupied Berlin. Two remarkable victories saved Prussia. On 5 November 1757 a French and imperial army was defeated at Rossbach, even though the Prussians were outnumbered two to one. In December an Austrian and imperial army, also double the size of the Prussians, was defeated at Leuthen.

Rossbach and Leuthen gave the Prussians only a breathing space, and soon they suffered a further series of defeats which culminated in the battle of Kunersdorf in 1759. This victory by the Austrians and Russians was not followed up, the lost opportunity described by Frederick the Great as the 'miracle of the house of Brandenburg'. In fact all the belligerents were exhausted. In December 1762 the English ratified the Treaty of Fontainebleau with France, and abandoned Prussia.

When the Empress Elizabeth of Russia died on 5 January 1762, she was succeeded by Peter III, a great admirer of the Prussian king who immediately ended the war and signed an alliance. Peter was deposed by his wife and probably murdered in July, but although Catherine II revoked the alliance she did not resume hostilities. Sweden also withdrew from the war and Frederick II was soon able to attack Silesia and Saxony with an army of 210,000 men.

By now all the remaining belligerents were tired of war, and peace negotiations made rapid progress, concluding at the Peace of Paris on 10 February and the Peace of Hubertusburg on 15 February 1763. Prussia emerged from the Seven Years War if not triumphant then at least intact. In spite of the overwhelming odds against him, Frederick II had managed to hang on to Silesia. As many soldiers lost their lives in the Seven Years War as in the Thirty Years War: 500,000 died, 180,000 of them Prussians. The economy was ruined, the currency was debased, and inflation was rampant. Frederick immediately set about stabilizing the currency, reforming the administration and encouraging economic growth. His efforts were successful.

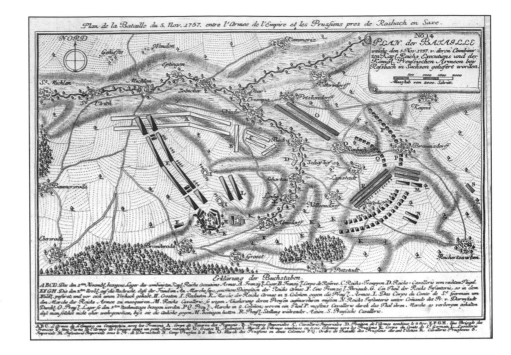

A contemporary plan of the battle of Rossbach, 5 November 1757, which was one of Frederick the Great's finest victories in the Seven Years War. He defeated a French army under Soubise which was supported by imperial forces.

Both Prussia and Austria needed the support of an ally after 1763, and this could only be Russia. England turned its back on continental policies and concentrated on its new empire. France was allied with Austria; Maria Theresa's daughter Marie Antoinette had been married to the Dauphin in 1770, and from 1774 he reigned as Louis XVI. In 1763–64 Frederick the Great supported the candidacy of Stanislaus II Poniatowski, one of the tsarinas's discarded lovers, for the Polish throne. This calculated offence to both Vienna and Paris was followed by a defensive treaty between Prussia and Russia. Catherine and Frederick had hoped that Stanislaus Poniatowski would be a man of straw, but he made a determined effort to reform Poland, an effort the Russians were bent on frustrating. Russia's designs on Poland were of great concern to the Austrians, so the young Joseph II, Maria Theresa's successor and a great admirer of Frederick the Great, set about improving relations with Prussia.

By 1772 Russia, Austria, and Prussia agreed to settle their differences at the expense of Poland, which was divided up among them, with Austria getting the largest share, and a rump state being left to Stanislaus Poniatowski. In 1777 the Prussian-Russian alliance was renewed. On New Year's Eve Maximilian III Joseph, the elector of Bavaria, died without a son. The Bavarian claimant, Karl Theodor of the Palatinate, fearing trouble from Prussia, suggested that Austria should take Bavaria in exchange for the Austrian Netherlands, a proposal which was enthusiastically welcomed in Vienna. Frederick the Great stirred up resistance in the German states against the emperor. At the same time he worked out a complicated series of territorial exchanges with Joseph II which they dared not put into effect for fear of reaction among the German states. In July 1777 Frederick the

Great invaded Bohemia posing as the champion of the states' rights against a
tyrannical emperor, a hypocritical pose which won him considerable popularity,
and the War of the Bavarian Succession began.

The struggle for Bavaria was fought with no great enthusiasm on either side,
hence its contemptuous soubriquet 'The Potato War'. Russia and France acted as
intermediaries and in May 1779 the Peace of Teschen was concluded, restoring the
status quo, and guaranteeing Karl Theodor's succession in Bavaria. The most
important result of the war was that Russia was made a guarantor of the imperial
consitutution.

THE IMPACT OF THE FRENCH REVOLUTION

At first Prussia tried to exploit the opportunity offered by the French Revolution to
weaken Austria, and supported the Jacobins in the Austrian Netherlands. The
situation changed with the death of the emperor Joseph II in 1790, followed by the
accession of his brother Leopold II. The new emperor was determined to end the
war with Turkey and ready to renounce all territorial claims. In the Convention of
Reichenbach of 27 July 1790 Prussia undertook to mediate between Austria and
Turkey and ceased to support the Jacobins in Liège.

On 27 August 1791 Prussia and Austria signed the Pillnitz Declaration which
demanded that Louis XVI's sovereign rights should be respected and envisaged
intervention in France if all the European powers agreed. On 7 February 1792 the
two states signed an alliance. The Pillnitz Declaration was no more than an empty
gesture, since the European powers would never agree to intervene in France; it did

The Prussian envoy Baron von
Plotho kicks the imperial high
court advocate Dr Aprill
downstairs in Regensburg on
14 October 1757. Baron von
Plotho was Prussian delegate
to the Reichstag and also
organized an effective network of spies from his base
in Regensburg. When Dr
Aprill brought him a note
threatening to outlaw Prussia
from the empire, von Plotho
responded by throwing him
downstairs in an incident
which soon became part of
Prussian mythology.

nothing but provide useful propaganda material for the party in France which favoured war. The Austro-Prussian alliance did not settle the fundamental differences between the two states. On 1 January 1792 the peaceful emperor died and was succeeded by his arch-reactionary son, Francis II. On 20 April France declared war on Austria and Prussia.

The coalition army was under the incompetent command of Charles William Ferdinand, Duke of Brunswick-Lüneburg. He marched into the Champagne having issued a manifesto in Koblenz in which he promised to flatten Paris if a single hair of the king's head were harmed. On 20 September 1792 his army met the revolutionary army under Dumouriez at Valmy. The Germans, suffering from supply difficulties and widespread sickness, were subjected to several hours of artillery fire and then retreated. Goethe, who was present on the battlefield claimed thirty years later to have told the soldiers: 'Here today a new epoch in world history begins, and you can say that you were there'.

After the victory at Valmy French troops under General Custine occupied Speyer, Worms, and Mainz, and marched into the Austrian Netherlands, but the Prussians and Austrians were still far more concerned about eastern Europe than about the threat from revolutionary France. On 23 January 1793 Prussia agreed to Catherine II's proposal for the second partition of Poland whereby Prussia gained Danzig, Thorn, and Posen. The Austrians were infuriated that they had not been consulted and were determined to get their revenge on Prussia.

In spite of these fundamental differences between Prussia and Austria, the empire declared war on France on 22 March 1793. The Prussian contingent was increased, thanks to a subsidy from England, but Austria and Prussia never coordinated their strategies and both were more concerned about the future of Poland than they were about the threat from Jacobin France. After some initial success in which much of the territory that had been lost was regained, the coalition armies were pushed back. The Prussians signed the Peace of Basel in April 1795 in which they withdrew from the war and the French recognized northern Germany as a neutral zone. Prussia was to be compensated for the losses it had sustained on the left bank of the Rhine with territories, mostly ecclesiastical, on the right bank. This promise was never kept. Prussia's flagrant breach of the imperial constitution and its betrayal of the loudly trumpeted solidarity of Pillnitz were widely criticized.

After a series of defeats at the hands of Napoleon in northern Italy and with their homeland under attack, the Austrians were obliged to sign the humiliating Peace of Campoformio on 17 October 1797. Austria lost all its territory to the left of the Rhine and in Italy as far as the Adige, receiving Venice as a compensation. As in the case of Prussia, Austria was compensated with territory to the right of the Rhine. The emperor had flagrantly breached the constitution of the empire and sold out its main supporters, the Church and the petty princes. It was now only a matter of time before the empire came to an end.

At the Congress of Rastatt which began on 9 December 1797, the French negotiated with a peace delegation from the empire which included many of the imperial estates. These discussions were exceedingly tricky because the compensation agreements made with Prussia and Austria remained secret and the estates wished to preserve the integrity of the empire. The French demanded all territory on the left bank of the Rhine, all the bridges over the river and the destruction of all fortresses. In response to mounting French demands, the English, Austrians, and Russians formed the Second Coalition and France replied by declaring war on Austria on 1 March 1799. French troops promptly crossed the Rhine. On 28 April 1799 Hungarian hussars murdered two of the French delegates to the Congress of Rastatt, bringing the negotiations to an abrupt end.

The Austrians were soundly defeated at Marengo and Hohenlinden and, on 9 February 1801 were obliged to sign the Peace of Lunéville. France received all territory left of the Rhine; Austria lost much of its remaining territory in Italy, but kept Venice, Istria, and Dalmatia. Napoleon now began to redraw the map of Germany in earnest and the empire was finally doomed.

In October 1801 the Diet recommended the formation of a Deputation to work out the details of the territorial compensation outlined in the Treaty of Lunéville. The French and Russians compensation plan was accepted by the Deputation in a slightly modified form in November 1802. The future of Germany was thus determined by France and Russia, and the princes paid handsome bribes in order to get a favourable transfer of property. The Imperial Deputation was little more than a rubber stamp for the French and the Russians.

The aim of French policy was to weaken Austria and to divide the empire up into a number of stronger states. To this end the French negotiated separate treaties with Prussia, Bavaria, and Württemberg. The Imperial Deputation's conclusions, the *Reichsdeputationshauptschluss* of 25 February 1803, abolished the ecclesiastical principalities with the exception of the prince bishop of Mainz who remained chancellor of the empire, and the lands of the Hoch-und Deutschmeister and Maltese orders (military-religious orders with their own territories). The Catholic Church was no longer the imperial Church. Countless small states vanished, including all the free cities with the exception of Bremen, Hamburg, Lübeck, Frankfurt, Nuremberg, and Augsburg. In the process, 3,161,000 Germans changed their states. Baden, Hessen-Kassel, Württemberg, and Salzburg were made into electorates but were never to exercise their rights. The bishoprics and cathedral chapters were no longer aristocratic preserves for after secularization they did not offer such great material rewards. The effects of the secularization on the peasantry were very mixed. Some peasants became independent farmers, some were reduced to poverty, while others went on much as before as tenants of a new landlord.

Shortly after the *Reichsdeputationshauptschluss*, France and England went to war again. The French then violated the peace treaty with the empire by attacking Hanover. On 11 April 1805 Russia made an alliance with England and declared war. On 9 August Austria joined the coalition. Prussia remained neutral, even though Napoleon had flagrantly violated the neutrality of northern Germany. Bavaria, Baden, and Württemberg sided with the French against the emperor, an unconstitutional act which clearly showed that the empire no longer had much substance. The battle of Austerlitz on 2 December 1805 was one of Napoleon's greatest triumphs and forced the Austrians to sign the humiliating peace of Pressburg. Bavaria and Württemberg not only became independent kingdoms but also made substantial territorial gains, as did Baden. The southern German states used their sovereignty to annex the estates of the imperial knights and the free cities.

On 12 July 1806 Napoleon formally created the Confederation of the Rhine. Sixteen states, among them Bavaria, Württemberg, and Baden, left the empire to form a confederation under the protection of the French emperor. Napoleon also created a new kingdom of Westphalia, with Kassel as its capital, for his brother Jérôme, and the duchy of Berg for his brother-in-law, Murat. The Confederation of the Rhine never became a viable 'third Germany' with its own identity and loyalties. This was largely because the French were increasingly seen as an occupying power and the burden of providing soldiers for Napoleon's armies was onerous and deeply resented.

Prussia still remained neutral. In July 1806 Russia guaranteed the integrity of Prussia, and Prussia promised not to provide Napoleon with any troops to attack Russia. When England and France began to negotiate the future of Hanover the Prussians mobilized their army. With extraordinary foolishness Prussia then demanded that Napoleon withdraw all his troops from southern Germany, restore the territory taken by Murat, and permit the formation of a North German Confederation under Prussia. Napoleon did not even bother to answer this

The Canonade at Valmy, 20 September 1792, in which the French revolutionary army routed coalition forces.

After defeating Prussia at the twin battles of Jena and Auerstadt Napoleon and his general staff entered Berlin through the Brandenburg Gate on 27 October 1806. Painting by Charles Meynier (1807).

ultimatum and on 9 October Prussia declared war. Five days later the Prussian army was crushingly defeated at the twin battles of Jena and Auerstedt. On 27 October Napoleon held a victory parade in Berlin. The Prussian king fled to Memel with his government. In Berlin the governor, Frederick William von der Schulenburg, handed over the arsenal to the French and made the famous proclamation 'A citizen's main responsibility is to stay calm' (*Ruhe ist die erste Bürgerpflicht*).

CHAPTER 7 | # Reform, Restoration, and Reaction

Although the Prussian army had been soundly defeated and Berlin occupied in 1806, Prussia was still formally at war with France. In the Convention of Bartenstein the Prussians and Russians agreed to continue the struggle against Napoleon, but on 14 June 1807 Napoleon defeated the Russians at the battle of Friedland and the Russians sued for peace. The situation had thus become quite hopeless for the Prussians and they consequently signed the Peace of Tilsit on 9 July 1807.

Prussia almost ceased to exist at Tilsit, and it was only the energetic pleading of the tsar that saved Frederick William III's throne. Prussia was left as a rump eastern state comprising Brandenburg, East Prussia, and Silesia and with only 4.5 million of its former 10 million inhabitants. Prussia was occupied by 150,000 French soldiers and had to pay for their upkeep as well as 154.5 million francs in reparations. The French demand was reduced to 120 million francs, but even this sum was too much for the Prussians, so they were finally called upon to make monthly contributions of 4 million marks. The Prussian army was reduced to 42,000 men, 16,000 of whom were to be put at France's disposal in the event of renewed hostilities with Austria.

THE REFORM OF THE GERMAN STATES

Napoleon imagined that the introduction of the *Code Napoléon* and a modern constitution would be enough to win over the Germans. This proved a serious mistake. Westphalia, under his brother Jérôme, was a typical example of a state run by a corrupt military oligarchy: it was ruthlessly plundered by the French and reduced to near bankruptcy. Jérôme may have started out with some reforming intentions, but his practice of giving handsome rewards to his followers soon brought this to nothing. Westphalia, a state which was supposed to be a model for others to emulate, was soon the scene of widespread social unrest. On the other hand, the Napoleonic period was not quite the disaster for western and southern Germany that many historians have imagined. In fact, reforms were made in Bavaria, Baden, and Württemberg. All three states had absorbed a large amount of territory and thus needed to create a degree of uniformity. In Austria attempts were made to push through some reforms between 1805 and 1809, but these efforts by Count Stadion were constantly frustrated by the court and by the estates who resented his attempts to centralize government and to create a modern ministerial system. In Prussia reform was a matter of life or death. If the state were not fundamentally reformed, it would never be able to regain its status as a major power and would be condemned to remain a third-rate petty kingdom.

In many of the German states the French Revolution gave a further impetus to a reforming movement that had already begun, although its aims were confused and often contradictory. In both Westphalia and Bavaria a representative body was created on paper, but in Bavaria it never met and in Westphalia it met only twice. In both instances the electorate was minute, made up only of the very wealthy. The electoral system was immensely complex and indirect, and the 'National Representation' neither lived up to its name, nor exercised any real power, even on paper. In Westphalia the National Representation was permitted to 'assister au repas' (join at the table) of the royal couple. In a farcical imitation of the Versailles of Louis XIV, the representatives merely watched with growling stomachs while King Jérôme and his queen ate.

French pressure, the end of the empire, and the *Reichsdeputationshauptschluss* (final decision of the imperial deputation), which redrew the map of Germany, gave the reformers a golden opportunity. When Napoleon demanded that the *Code Napoléon* be introduced in Bavaria, Montgelas was able to use French threats to convince the estates to accept his proposed reforms. The Bavarian criminal code of 1811 was the most progressive in Germany and contained the fundamental principle of modern jurisprudence – *nulla poena sine lege* (no punishment without a law). Bavarian reforms included the creation of a new ministry with five principal departments, and the separation of the judiciary from the administration. The tax privileges of the estates were ended, and entrance into the state bureaucracy was no longer by purchase but was based on qualifications. In 1809 Protestants were given the same rights as Catholics. In 1813 Jews were granted full freedom to worship, although they still suffered certain legal restrictions. The Bavarian constitution of 1808 guaranteed individual liberty and property rights and referred to the people as 'citizens', a remarkably liberal term. Bavaria was still an absolutist state, but public opinion could not totally be ignored. Many of the old privileges of the estates had now been abolished and the way was cleared for later liberal reforms.

In 1805 Duke Frederick Augustus II of Württemberg abolished the old constitution based on the estates and, with the support of Napoleon, created a unified state out of his newly won territories, over which he was crowned King Frederick Augustus I in 1806. He granted religious equality to all Christians, further weakening the privileged Protestant clergy which had played such an important role in the former estates. Frederick I was an absolutist monarch whose reforms also paved the way to a modern constitutional state.

In Baden the margrave Charles Frederick was an enlightened reformer who ruled from 1746 until 1811 and who was greatly admired both by Frederick the Great and by Napoleon. Yet in spite of many progressive structural reforms, the state got into serious debt as a result of Baden's expansionist policy during the revolutionary wars. Emmerich Joseph Baron von Dalberg was called upon to reform the finances and introduced an income tax, issued government bonds on a commercial basis, and placed the banks under strict supervision and control.

Caspar David Friedrich

The greatest of the German Romantic painters was born in Greifswald in 1774. Friedrich was not interested in reproducing nature, some of his finest landscapes are purely imaginary. He used the sketches he made from nature as a vocabulary for his highly personal pictorial language. Most of his paintings expressed complex emotions, signified hidden meanings, and acted as metaphors for his private obsessions. He saw all of nature, including the human soul, as an expression of the godly, as part of the *Weltgeist* ('world spirit'). Art, philosophy, literature, and science were all part of a higher unity. Thus almost all his paintings show figures, usually with their backs turned, set in dramatic landscapes. Humans are as much a part of nature as the trees and rocks around them.

In many of his paintings human figures are placed in the foreground, usually painted in dark shades, gazing at the distant horizon. By 1810 Friedrich felt that, in the awesome presence of nature, humans were of no account and could only contemplate its glories in pantheistic humility.

Friedrich suffered from bouts of depression and was shattered by the news of Prussia's defeat in 1806. He sought solace in frequent trips from his home in Greifswald to Neubrandenburg and the island of Rügen, but his paintings became increasingly melancholic and gloomy; sunlit meadows gave way to misty pine forests and foreboding sunsets.

His studio was spartan: the walls were undecorated monochrome, the floors bare; even the window that

looked out over the Elbe was partially shuttered. This was a completely private space from which the mundane world had been rigorously excluded. Although by 1806 he was widely appreciated and financially secure, he continued to live an ascetic, solitary life, devoting all his efforts to his art.

Friedrich appeared to be a confirmed bachelor, but in 1818 he married an extremely young woman, Caroline Bommer. From then on, the wanderer of the early paintings had a fashionably dressed companion and wore a three-cornered hat symbolic of German nationalism. The paintings are often lighter in colour, but are still infused with unease and longing.

After a period of frantic work Friedrich fell into a depression in 1824 and for two years painted only in watercolours. In 1835 he suffered a stroke and never again painted in oils. In 1837 he declined further and sketched only owls and gravestones. He went insane and died in Dresden on 7 May 1840.

Caspar David Friedrich, 'The Chalk Cliffs of Rügen' (after 1818).

Baden, Bavaria, and Württemberg were the first German states to organize the national debt according to clearly defined legal principles.

In Prussia there had also been substantial reforming progress before 1806. Frederick the Great's grossly unfair system of indirect taxation, the *Regie*, which he had copied from France, was abolished on his death in 1786. Two years later freedom of conscience was written into the law. The new civil code was finally introduced in 1794. In 1799 half a million serfs on the royal demesne were set free. The qualifications for judges and civil servants were made more demanding.

Baron Karl vom und zum Stein became first minister in Prussia in 1807, the successor to Karl August Count Hardenberg. Stein held ideas which were a mixture of conservative and liberal elements. As an imperial knight he was a proudly individualistic aristocrat who saw the rights of the estates as guarantees against

absolutist abuse of individual rights. His proposed reforms of the towns and communes were progressive in that they foreshadowed the town and local councils which were to become a characteristic of nineteenth-century liberal Europe, but at the same time the reforms were based on a revival of earlier freedoms that had been pushed aside by the absolutist state. His predecessor, Karl August Count Hardenberg, also sprang from ancient aristocratic stock, and like Stein was not a Prussian. Both Stein and Hardenberg wished to mobilize the latent forces of the nation for an essentially conservative cause. They intended to reform the administration, both centrally and locally, put the finances on a sound footing, improve agriculture and industry, reform education and the law, and build an army that could liberate the country.

In 1807 Stein undertook a series of fundamental reforms with breathtaking speed. On 9 October 1807 Frederick William III issued a decree liberating the serfs with effect from 11 November 1810. Not only were the serfs liberated, but aristocratic estates could now be freely bought and sold and entry to the professions was no longer dictated by social standing. The major problem was that of compensation to the landowners for lost services, the subject of two further decrees in 1811 and 1816. These left the poorer peasants landless and exacted heavy compensation payments from those who were better placed. It has been

A view of Cologne cathedral by Samuel Prout (1783–1852). Germany's largest Gothic cathedral remained unfinished for centuries. In September 1842 Frederick William IV of Prussia laid the foundation stone for the completion in an elaborate ceremony.

Detail of a portrait of the
philosopher, Georg Friedrich
Hegel (1770-1831), by Jakob
Schlesinger. Whereas previous
philosophers had insisted
that subject and object were
distinct entities, Hegel suggested that truth resided in
an awareness of the unity
of such contradictions.
History is a dialectical
process whereby the spirit
gains knowledge and struggles towards the truth. 'Philosophy,' he wrote, 'is its own
time captured in thought'.

estimated that the landowners received twelve billion marks in compensation payments and 2.5 million acres of peasant land, so that the free peasants became either landless labourers or hopelessly indebted. Stein's intention of creating a strong class of yeomen farmers on the British model was frustrated by aristocratic resistance.

In the long run, the real winners were the middle-class. The small peasant holdings had no economic future; because of poor soil and relatively low productivity, only large-scale production was viable. Even if the peasant holdings had been protected, most would almost certainly not have survived the agricultural crisis –the result of the disruption of agriculture and exports caused by the revolutionary and Napoleonic wars, coupled with a rapidly rising population. The Junker landowners were short of capital and sold out to wealthy bourgeois. In the course of the nineteenth century two-thirds of the aristocratic estates in the east were sold to these despised 'tradesmen'.

Stein's reforms of city government became law on 19 November 1808. Those who met modest property qualifications were granted political rights, with the exception of soldiers, Jews, Mennonites (an anabaptist sect founded in 1536), and the under-aged. A town council was appointed by means of a two-tiered electoral system. Stein was unable to extend this limited form of self-government to the country districts; self-government in rural areas was the subject of decrees in 1825 and 1828.

Stein reformed the cabinet so that there were five distinct ministries, forerunners of modern government departments. The ministers for home and foreign affairs, for finance, education, and the army ran their own ministries without interference from the king's personal cabinet advisors, and had the right of access to the king. The state was thereby centralized, and the administration largely freed from the tiresome whims of the monarch and his close advisors. These reforms came into effect on 24 November 1808, the day of Stein's dismissal when the French learnt of his plot for national resistance.

Hardenberg, who succeeded him, established the principle of ministerial responsibility for legislation; ministerial counter-signatures were now required on royal decrees. In 1810 and 1811 a series of edicts were published concerning trading regulations and business taxes which destroyed the monopoly hold of the guilds over certain trades and which established the principle of freedom of trades (*Gewerbefreiheit*). The trades were now supervised by the state, not by the guilds, and control was far less strict. These changes were designed to encourage economic growth and thus to increase the state's revenues, tax inequalities between town and countryside having been abolished. The attempt to end certain tax privileges of the aristocracy was fiercely and effectively resisted; it was tried in 1818, again unsuccessfully, and was only partly successful in 1861.

Similar reforms of the trades were introduced in Westphalia and parts of western Germany at around the same time, but Saxony did not reform until 1861,

Württemberg and Baden 1862 and Bavaria 1868. However, these states, for all their economic backwardness, were politically far more liberal than Prussia. The social effects of economic freedom were painful, creating a large class of landless labourers and unemployed artisans who depressed wages and swelled the growing mass of paupers. It was a long time before the upheaval began to generate the increased prosperity of the industrial age.

The most remarkable of the Prussian reforms was that of the army. The aim of the reformers was to create a people in arms on the French model, a people prepared to defend their property and their liberty. This implied that they should have liberty and property to defend, that they should not be subjected to brutal discipline and mindless drill, and that the officer corps should no longer be an aristocratic preserve, but should be open to the talented. In 1810 Scharnhorst founded the War Academy, where staff officers were to be trained under the supervision of Carl von Clausewitz, author of the classic treatise *On War*. The reformers seized the opportunity offered by the forced reduction of the army to dismiss a large number of aged and incompetent officers. Only two generals, Blücher and Tauentzien, remained on active duty. The army reformers were mostly extremely liberal in their political views, for they knew that the army could not be infused with national pride and a fighting spirit unless its personnel were free men. It is thus hardly surprising that many of them resigned their commissions in the period of reaction after 1815.

Educational reform was largely the work of Wilhelm von Humboldt, a man who had never been to school, who was made responsible for education in 1809. His humanistic ideal was that each individual should develop his own talents according to his own abilities and that the state should provide the necessary setting for this to be possible. In his view the state was obliged to educate the people, not so that the state should be strengthened, but as a moral obligation. Humboldt's neo-classical humanism was no doubt fraught with all manner of contradictions, but his practical achievements were considerable. Thanks to his efforts the University of Berlin was founded in 1810. At the new university the humanities were particularly emphasized, for Humboldt wanted to educate free men with an inter-disciplinary curriculum rather than to produce narrow specialists or professionals. For him, the pursuit of pure knowledge was the paramount goal of education. As the rector of Berlin University, Fichte, said in his inaugural address: 'The true life-giving breath of the university ... the heavenly ether is without doubt academic freedom'.

Humboldt also reformed the school system, creating two levels: the preparatory school (*Elementarschule*) and the grammar school (*Gymnasium*). The grammar schools, like the university, emphasized the humanities, particularly Latin and Greek. They replaced the 400 Latin schools in which pupils learnt by rote and were mercilessly beaten. These new schools were self-consciously elite institutions whose teachers had to have university degrees. In 1812 a school- leaving certificate

(*Arbitur*) was made the precondition for entry to university. These educational reforms did much to create a highly educated and often liberal bourgeois elite. Although the reforms were far from democratic and the poor were necessarily excluded from the benefits of a more open system, they did much to break down the old social barriers based on the estates, and they anticipated the bourgeois nineteenth century. It took a considerable time before this new spirit had an effect on elementary schools (*Volksschule*) which had been created by Frederick the Great and in which retired Prussian NCOs flogged a rudimentary education into hapless children. New teacher training colleges were established to instruct the next generation of teachers in the new pedagogy.

Part of the problem of the Prussian reforms was that they were, at least in part, the result of an unpleasant necessity. As the king stated in his foundation decree for Berlin University, Prussia had to make up for the military power it had lost with intellectual power. Once that military power was restored, the reforms tended to go by the board. The old order could not be propped up indefinitely and the reformers had accurately assessed the spirit of the times, but the success of the old elites in hanging on to power in Prussia, long after its objective basis had vanished, was to have unfortunate consequences.

THE WARS OF LIBERATION

By 1812 France was in serious economic difficulties. The French had blockaded Europe in an attempt to stop imports from and exports to Britain, but the blockade was every bit as harmful to France as it was to Britain. Most of the French ports were ruined. The wealthier bourgeoisie who had been among Napoleon's strongest supporters were beginning to grumble. A defiant Russia continued to trade with Britain, and British goods began to seep into western Europe. Napoleon assembled an army of 700,000 men, of whom 30,000 were Austrians and 20,000 Prussians, and began his ill-fated trek to Moscow. The army plundered Germany for provisions, creating widespread hunger.

Napoleon's retreat from Moscow in October 1812 and the collapse of his army tempted his reluctant allies to abandon his cause. On 30 December General Yorck von Wartenburg, the commander of the Prussian contingent in the Grande Armée, signed the Convention of Tauroggen with the Russian general Diebitsch. Although the general did not have the permission of his king, the Prussian army in Russia was now neutral. Hardenberg obtained the king's permission to renounce the convention of Tauroggen and negotiated with the French, but at the same time kept the lines open to Russia and Austria.

On 27 February 1813 the Prussians and Russians concluded the Treaty of Kalisch. The Russians, who had been advised on German affairs by Stein since June 1812, agreed that Prussia should return to the frontiers of 1806 with the exception of the Grand Duchy of Warsaw, compensation for which would be found in northern Germany. Russia undertook to provide 150,000 men, Prussia 80,000. On

By introducing universal military service, the Prussians mobilized an army of 280,000 men, but Napoleon was still able to defeat the alliance at Grossgörschen and Bautzen. During peace negotiations in the summer of 1813, the British, Swedish, and Austrians joined the coalition. His army decimated after the Russian campaign, the economy in ruins, and fighting a two-front war against a united and determined coalition, Napoleon went from defeat to defeat. On 16 October 1813 the battle of Leipzig began, the largest battle fought to date; it ended after four days in disaster for Napoleon, but with heavy allied losses. Napoleon refused to negotiate a compromise peace. Having concluded a twenty-year quadruple alliance at Chaumont on 9 March 1814, the allies occupied Paris. Napoleon was given the

17 March, the day after Prussia declared war on France, Frederick William III issued a remarkable appeal 'To My People' in which he called for sacrifices from all classes 'if we do not wish to cease to be Prussians and Germans'. Its appeal to German nationalism shows how profound was the effect of the French revolution, even though he still spoke as a monarch to his subjects.

Battle between the French and Austrians at Edelsberg Bridge near Vienna 1809.

island of Elba as a sovereign monarchy and allowed to keep his title of emperor, but it did not disguise the fact that he was a prisoner-of-war.

On 1 March 1815 Napoleon landed unexpectedly in the south of France, hoping that he would find wide popular support and that the coalition would fall apart. Neither gamble paid off. He patched together an army and won a number of battles, but he could not possibly win the campaign. On 18 June 1815 he was defeated by Wellington at Waterloo, a battle in which the Prussians under Blücher and Gneisenau played a critical role. Napoleon retreated to Paris and on 22 June resigned. His hundred days were over.

THE GERMAN FEDERATION

At the Congress of Vienna (1814–15), the peace conference at the end of the Napoleonic wars, the British, who had played by far the most important part in Napoleon's defeat, were determined that Prussia should be strengthened and extended to the Rhine, forming a strong defence against renewed French ambitions in northern Europe. However, the British did not want to see the Prussians so powerful that they might threaten to dominate Germany. This seemed highly likely since Russia supported Prussia's claim to Saxony, as compensation for Prussia agreeing that the Grand Duchy of Warsaw should go to Russia. The 'Saxon question' worried the Austrians and, together with the British and the French, they formed a secret alliance to frustrate the plan. The 'Saxon question' thus gave the French foreign minister, Talleyrand, the opportunity he needed to end France's isolation and become a partner in the discussions. In the end Prussia received two-fifths of Saxony.

The Austrian foreign minister, Metternich, had no desire to restore the petty German states, but wished to create a German Federation under Austrian leadership which would result in a balance of power between Prussia and Austria and the smaller German states. Hardenberg was broadly in agreement with Metternich, but wanted Prussia to have a greater say in the Federation, particularly in northern and western Germany.

The German Federation consisted of thirty-four states and four cities, Bremen, Frankfurt am Main, Hamburg, and Lübeck. The aim of the Federation was 'the preservation of Germany's peace at home and abroad, and the independence and inviolability of the individual German states'. A federal Diet (*Bundestag*) was to meet in Frankfurt under Austrian presidency, attended by delegates from the states. Austria and Prussia, even when they were supported by the four kingdoms of Saxony, Bavaria, Hanover, and Württemberg, could be outvoted in both the 'Inner Council' or in a plenary session of the Bundestag. The confederation was thus not an Austro-Prussian condominium as it is sometimes represented. The sovereignty of the individual states was restricted in that federal law was binding and they could not enter alliances which threatened the Federation or individual member states. Article 13 of the federal act declared that all member-states were to have constitutions, but Prussia and Austria ignored this provision until the revolutionary year of 1848. Nevertheless, article 13 was an encouragement to German liberals, and there was considerable constitutional advance in the south German states in the years after the Congress of Vienna.

Germany was still a federation of princes and, as the duke of Wellington said to Stein, it could only continue to exist as long as the federal institutions were upheld by Austria and Prussia and supported by public opinion. Otherwise Germany was nothing more than a common language and a common culture. Many hoped that the German spirit which existed in the common struggle of the German states against the French, would find adequate political expression after the war; they were to be disappointed.

Austria dominated the German Federation, but also controlled Italy, kept Russia at a distance, and maintained a watchful eye on France. Austria, in 1840 a country with 6,400,000 Germans, 14,820,000 Slavs, 5,305,000 Hungarians, 4,548,000 Italians, and 1,567,000 Romanians along with numerous smaller ethnic groups, was not capable of mastering this situation. The state had gone bankrupt in 1811 and never got its finances in order, being burdened with a large foreign debt, an inadequate capital market and an antiquated economy. In 1820 the Russian embassy in Vienna reported that Austria's finances were wretched and that the state only kept going by borrowing increasingly large sums of money. In such a situation war would be a catastrophe for the country.

Prussia's great strength was its reformed and efficient administration. Hardenberg continued his reforms from the Congress of Vienna until his death in 1822, strengthening the ministries and the Council of State (*Staatsrat*) and thus ensuring that there could be no return to the monarchical absolutism of the pre-revolutionary period. This government by a liberal bureaucracy dominated by the aristocracy became increasingly less liberal after the reductions in the size of the civil service in the austerity measures after 1825. Hardenberg's reforms did not go far enough for many liberals, and he followed Metternich's reactionary policies against students and would-be revolutionaries. The dominant position of the aristocracy in the Prussian army was drastically to hinder the development of a bourgeois-liberal political culture in Prussia. The great political decisions in nineteenth-century Germany were to be made by blood and iron, as Bismarck pointed out with cruel realism, and the army was further strengthened. An industrial society developed which served an autocratic, aristocratic, bureaucratized state, but it did not enjoy the political rights and freedoms for which the liberal reformers had struggled.

Liberal constitutional reforms – a degree of representational government, a written constitution, and guarantees of freedom of speech – were carried out in a number of the German states at this time. Saxony-Weimar introduced a liberal constitution in 1816, Baden and Bavaria both followed suit in 1818, Württemberg in 1819 and Hessen-Darmstadt in 1820. A degree of representative

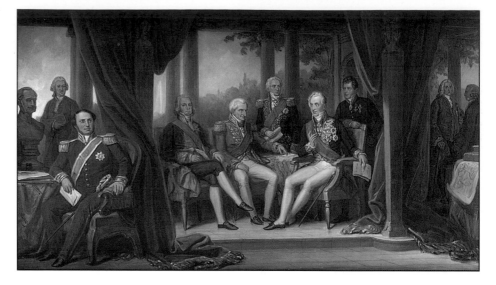

A meeting of important statesmen at the time of the Congress of Vienna. The central figures from left to right are Talleyrand, Montgelas, Hardenberg, Metternich and von Gentz. Painting by Engelberg Seibertz (1813–1905) for a fresco in the conference room of the Maximilianeum in Munich.

government was thereby achieved which made these states among the most progressive in Europe.

Local government, which, despite frequent corruption, had enjoyed certain freedoms in the age of absolutism, was seldom in a position strong enough to resist the centralizing tendencies of the bureaucracy. In a series of lost battles over local privileges, the rights of the guilds, and the mounting poverty, local governments saw their scope for action shrink.

One extraordinary residue from the age of feudalism, and a major hindrance to national integration, was that article 14 of the federal act guaranteed the particular rights of some eighty aristocratic families which had ruled independent states in the old empire. Their estates were thus virtually states within states, and remained feudal enclaves within a modernizing constitutional framework. In some instances this was not quite as disastrous as might have been feared. Under the Fürstenbergs in Donaueschingen, for example, the economy and culture flourished. If some of these lofty aristocrats were arch-reactionaries, like Prince Wilhelm Ludwig von Sayn-Wittgenstein, others like Prince Karl von Leiningen were liberals.

THE RESPONSE TO RADICAL NATIONALISM

Some hoped that the Bundestag would become a genuine national forum. Others had vague liberal dreams for the future of Germany. Among students in the fraternities (*Burschenschaften*), the memory of 1813 was still vivid, and the excitement of the wars of liberation was a marked contrast to the tedious daily grind in lecture hall and library. Some radical students, particularly in Giessen and Jena, called for revolutionary activism. Their leader was a hot-headed arm-chair terrorist, Karl Follen, who taught law at Giessen. On 23 March 1819 one of Follen's assiduous followers, Karl Ludwig Sand, murdered the popular writer and Russian informant, August von Kotzebue, in Mannheim. Frederick William III, who was

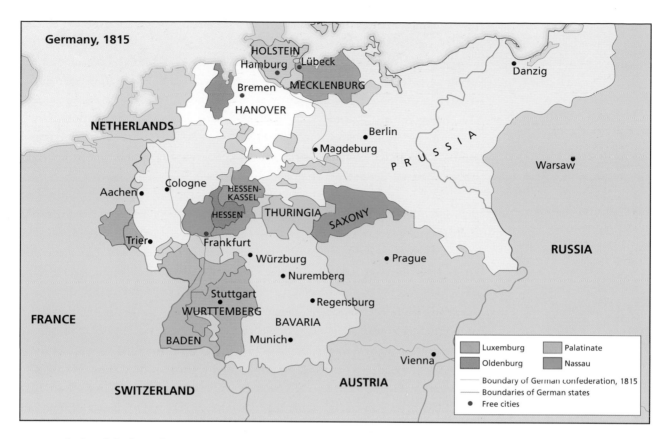

extremely fearful of revolution, was convinced that this was part of a widespread conspiracy rather than a single dramatically unhinged exception to the resolutely peaceful German nationalist movement, and he took firm counter-measures. Sand was executed publicly on 20 May 1820 as a warning to any fanatics considering emulating his example. His heroic poise on the scaffold merely confirmed his status as a liberal idol, and a monument to his memory was erected in 1869. His executioner made a pretty penny by converting the wood from the scaffold into a shrine, where devout patriots could pay homage to this youthful national martyr.

The Austrian emperor and Metternich were in Rome when Kotzebue was murdered, and they did not return to Austria for months. On 1 August 1819 Metternich met Frederick William III at Teplitz, a spa in Bohemia, where he persuaded the king to agree to close supervision of all German universities, press censorship, and an end to constitutional reform. Shortly afterwards ministers from the larger German states met in Karlsbad; Metternich managed to push the resulting 'Karlsbad Decrees' through the Bundestag in a flagrantly unconstitutional manner, and they were published on 20 September 1819. Metternich now believed that it was all or nothing – revolution or reaction. He also believed that without a reactionary course Austria would have to withdraw from the Federation. Through the Karlsbad decrees Metternich secured Austrian domination of the Federation, but this in turn created insoluble problems for Austria. Not the least of these was a powerful faction in Vienna which felt that the empire should come first and that the Federation was at best of secondary importance.

Under the terms of the Karlsbad decrees a federal representative was appointed to supervise each university. All teachers suspected of holding subversive views were to be dismissed. The fraternities were disbanded, academic freedom denied, and the universities brought under federal control. Although the situation in each state was different and professors who had been dismissed from one university were often offered a chair in another, the general atmosphere in the German universities was depressing, anxious, and dull.

All printed matter of less than 320 pages was subjected to pre-censorship. The longer works could be censored after publication if they contained 'breathtaking theories and infectious madness'. An Investigation Commission was established in Mainz to track down revolutionaries. Since it discovered few such dangerous spirits, it is often represented as a somewhat comical institution, but in fact its very existence did much to increase the atmosphere of fear and suspicion which crippled the intellectual life of Germany in these years.

The federal constitution of 1815 required each of the German states to introduce a constitution. Although the framers of the federal constitution intended this to mean some form of representative government, the wording of the clause was vague enough for it to be interpreted in many different ways, and some argued that the restoration of the old provincial Diets was enough to meet this requirement. In the Final Act of Vienna, the last piece of legislation dealing with the threat of revolution, it was required that all such constitutions should uphold the monarchical principle. This was something of a compromise which did not go as far as Metternich and other reactionaries would have liked, and which permitted the liberal south German constitutions to remain unchanged. The Final Act marked the end of any hopes that the federal constitution might develop along liberal lines, or that the constitutional process could continue in the individual states. The German Federation became uniquely a system of repression. New constitutional mechanisms were used to defeat the spirit of the new, and the old regime used constitutional institutions to destroy constitutionalism.

THE *ZOLLVEREIN*

Although the bourgeoisie were frustrated in respect of their constitutional aspirations, in the economic sphere they were far more successful. Their aim was to create a German common market protected by a relatively high customs duty. Industry would thrive behind a protective tariff until it had reached the point where it could confidently face the competition from Britain. The higher tariff also appealed to those, like Austria, who were opposed to the idea of free trade. The first steps towards the creation of a common tariff were taken in Prussia. In 1818 all tariff barriers between the Prussian provinces were abolished, making Prussia a free trade area. This was coupled with high transit duties which were enforced by

Das Lichten eines Hochwaldes.

'Felling the Forest'; a contemporary caricature celebrating the inauguration of the customs union (*Zollverein*) on 1 January 1834, when eighteen states formed, under Prussian auspices, a free trade area.

an efficient customs service. Not only was the Prussian tariff a result of liberal economic thought, it was also designed to further Prussia's interests in Germany. As the Prussian minister of finance, Friedrich Christian von Motz, wrote it was: 'an independent policy for German unification, independent from the Federation and if necessary against the Federation'.

Most of the German states regarded the Prussian tariff as an act of blatant self-interest, made worse by the widespread hunger in Germany where the new tariff increased the price of imported food. In 1819 a group of industrialists and merchants formed the 'German Association for Trade and Commerce' (*Deutsche Handels-und Gewerbeverein*) to formulate a German policy to stimulate trade and commerce at a time of serious economic dislocation.

The Prussians continued to expand their customs area by bringing a number of neighbouring states into their system and then, in February 1828, concluding a customs treaty with Hessen-Darmstadt which gave them a foothold over the River Main. A treaty was negotiated with the Bavarian-Württemberg customs union in 1832–33. Metternich, who was keenly aware of the political consequences of the Prussian customs union, had tried to persuade Bavaria not to join, but his negotiating team had refused to budge on such issues as transit duties, traffic on the Danube, and Austria's protective tariffs. The resulting German customs union (*Zollverein*) came into effect on 1 January 1834. A number of states promptly joined, including Saxony, the Thuringian states, Frankfurt and, in spite of pressure from the French, Baden. A common market of twenty-five million Germans was now under the skilful and flexible leadership of the Prussian bureaucracy.

The Wartburg Festival

The fraternity of university students (*Burschenschaften*), which was founded in Jena in 1815, was the most influential of the organizations calling for constitutional reform, national unity and freedom. These nationalist groups were of concern to the authorities who felt that politics was the business of governments, not of the associations of free citizens which pre-figured political parties. The *Burschenschaften* particularly attracted students from Protestant universities in southern Germany. The students chose as their colours the black, red, and gold of the crack free corps regiment, the Lützow Scouts (*Lützower Jäger*), who had fought with great distinction in the Napoleonic wars. These colours were soon adopted by all liberal nationalists and in 1848 were adopted for the national flag. Of the 8,000 German students in 1815, beween 1,000 and 1,500 joined the movement, a rather disappointing result for the organizers.

The Wartburg Festival was held in October 1817 in celebration of the fourth centenary of the Reformation and fourth anniversary of the 'Battle of the Nations' at Leipzig. The liberally inclined Grand Duke Carl August von Sachsen-Weimar-Eisenach gave his permission for the festival to take place on a hill opposite the castle where Luther had resided. It was attended by 500 students from at least thirteen universities, the main contingent of 168 coming from Jena.

On the first evening of festival a radical minority built a bonfire and a number of books considered to be 'un-German' and reactionary were thrown into the flames. Among the works burnt were the *Code Napoléon* — a hated reminder of foreign domination — and the Prussian police laws. A Prussian lancer's corset, a wig, and a corporal's swagger-stick were also put in the fire, as symbolic of repression, the old regime, and militarism. Calls for liberal reforms and national unity were a matter of grave concern to the authorities; the police were unleashed and a number of arrests were made.

The fraternities continued in secret and became more radical as a result of repression in most states. In 1819 the fraternities were banned; when they were revived after 1848 they became politically conservative.

A procession makes its way to the Wartburg Festival on 18 October 1817.

Industrialization made modest progress during this period, but it was not until the second half of the century that the rate of growth became spectacularly rapid. As late as 1846–47 less than 3 per cent of the working population in the *Zollverein* were classified as factory workers. The decisive stimulus for industrial expansion was the building of the railways. The first major effort was the seventy-nine-mile stretch from Linz to Budweis built between 1827 and 1832, but this was a horse-drawn railway. In England, the Stockton to Darlington railway had been opened in 1825 for Stephenson's locomotive, but the first steam-driven railway in Germany, from Nuremberg to Fürth, was not opened until 1837. There followed a frantic and un-coordinated period of railway building in which private companies snapped up profitable lines and governments tried, with varying degrees of success, to bring some kind of order into the chaos. An Austrian delegate to the Frankfurt parliament who wished to go back to Vienna was obliged to take the Rhine steamer to Dusseldorf, the train to Berlin, and from there home.

Railway-building had an enormous social and economic impact. Transport costs were reduced by as much as 80 per cent, leading to a far greater degree of mobility. Frederick William III had asked why anyone should wish to get to Potsdam half an hour sooner, and complained that now the meanest of his subjects could travel as fast as he. These slightly absurd remarks highlight the fact that railways led to a certain democratization of transportation, just as mass air travel has done in our own day. Even more important was the stimulus given to the iron and steel industry and to machine-building. Germany was able gradually to master the art of producing straight rails and dependable locomotives, and the rolling mills and workshops were soon working to capacity.

GERMAN SOCIETY

Compared with the minutely graded society of the eighteenth century, the society of Biedermeier Germany was egalitarian in outward appearance. This was noticeable in dress; sumptuary ordinances were long since past, and aristocratic and bourgeois men dressed in uniform black, or in a dark and sober colour. Old social distinctions remained behind this facade of equality and simplicity. In 1840 about 60 per cent of industrialists came from working-class or petit-bourgeois backgrounds. In Silesia and Bohemia aristocrats became prosperous entrepreneurs, but many aristocrats, particularly in East Elbia, held 'trade' in snobbish disgust. Some, on the other hand, were tempted by industrial wealth to marry beneath themselves, while wealthy businessmen were often ennobled. The levelling tendencies of industrial capitalism were counteracted by the restorative policies of this reactionary period, and capitalism led necessarily to new forms of inequality.

The emperor Ferdinand's Northern Railway from Brünn to Raigern was opened on 17 November 1837. Railway-building began in Germany in 1835 when the stretch from Nuremberg to Fürth was completed. Germany soon had the most extensive railway network on the continent of Europe and railway-building created a vast appetite for machinery, iron, steel, coal, and metals and thus acted as a spur to the industrial revolution in Germany.

The Biedermeier idyll was most clearly expressed in the importance ascribed to family virtues. The emphasis was on privacy, on the separation from the world of work and struggle. The family was seen as a safe haven from the stress of the outside world, a focus of private hopes and dreams, an institution which gave life its true meaning. It was now clearly understood that the choice of a partner should be dictated by mutual attraction and respect, and that hopes were focussed on the children to carry on the family tradition. The family thus provided a reassuring substitute for religious faith, which was dwindling under the impact of eighteenth-century rationalism.

Crass social distinctions could not be hidden behind the refined and levelling simplicity of the age, and were expressions of wide disparities in wealth. Even within the working-class these distinctions were extreme. In a calico printing works in Chemnitz the relationship between the highest and lowest weekly wage was 13:1. In such a situation it is almost impossible to make meaningful calculations of average wages or living standards. It is certain that poverty was widespread and that in the 1840s it became even more acute, in part because artisans, particularly in the textile industry, were unable to compete with industrial production. Between 20 and 30 per cent of the population were in receipt of some form of charity, and the majority led lives that made a mockery of the somewhat smug idyll of the modest Biedermeier family.

The German Jewish community had won significant rights and freedoms since the late eighteenth century, but the fact that they gained the most from enlightened reforms was due to the sorry fact that for centuries they had been persecuted, exploited, isolated, and subject to special regulations. In a secular bourgeois society there was no room for discrimination against religious minorities. The emancipation of the Jews was an integral part of the emancipation of society from an antiquated semi-feudal system based on the estates. That it was never complete is evidence of the incomplete nature of the reforms.

Practising Jews formed a mere 1.1 per cent of the population of the German empire in 1816, and only 1.2 per cent of the same area in 1871. During this half century the Jewish community ceased to be divided between a handful of very rich families and a vast majority of desperately poor people and became, by and large, solidly bourgeois. Efforts were made by both the state authorities and the Jewish community to encourage Jews to take up agriculture and become artisans, but this met with limited success. Having been excluded from such trades for centuries they preferred to remain in their traditional professions as merchants and bankers, and tended to profit from the remarkable industrial expansion. They were particularly successful in banking: by 1882 one-fifth of all those working in banks and in the stock exchange were Jewish. By contrast the number of Jewish pedlars declined to less than 2 per cent by the end of the century.

Excluded from the officer corps, a traditional means of social advancement, Jews were keenly aware of the advantages of a university education. By the 1880s

Rahel von Varnhagen

Rahel Levin was born in Berlin in 1771, the daughter of a rich but uncultured Jewish merchant. She was an extremely intelligent, open-minded, and inquisitive young woman whose tutors gave her an excellent grounding in French and mathematics. She studied Voltaire, Rousseau, Fichte, Kant, and her beloved Goethe.

She was ashamed of her family background and regarded her Jewishness as a dreadful misfortune. When two engagements to aristocrats were broken off, she became convinced that, being neither good-looking nor of a good family, she would never find a husband. She converted to Christianity, and changed her first name to Friederike. Finally, at the age of forty-three, she married the twenty-nine-year-old diplomat and writer Karl August Varnhagen von Ense, a man of distinctly liberal views.

Their marriage was exceptionally happy. When she had been married for a year she wrote to a friend: 'My great joy is that I don't even notice that I am married! In everything, big and small, I am free to live and feel as I will. I can tell Varnhagen everything and be completely truthful, and that fills him with happiness and joy. I make him happy too, I alone.' She rejected the conventional role of a wife as obedient and submissive and insisted that wives be the free and equal partners of their husbands. Her view was that marriage had to be based on mutual love and understanding, and should not be merely a financial arrangement or means of advancement. She emphasized the importance of personal growth, believing it came only through interaction with other people, especially loved ones.

Rahel Levin began her salon before her marriage in her modest attic apartment. She regularly held open house, without formal invitations, and people from all walks of life came to discuss literature, art, and philosophy in an informal manner. Her ancient housekeeper poured tea for the guests and no other refreshments were served. This austerity was a marked contrast to the aristocratic salons of Paris where magnificent receptions were given. In spite of her frugality, the salon was attended by Hohenzollern princes and aristocrats, such as Prince Radziwill and Count Dohna, and statesmen such as Friedrich Gentz mingled with civil servants, army officers, professors, and stars from Berlin's theatre and opera. She played host to many of the great writers of the day: Friedrich Schlegel, Clemens von Brentano, Tieck, Chamisso, La Motte Fouqué, Jean Paul, Heine, and Ludwig Börne. Other distinguished guests included the Humboldt brothers, Schleiermacher, and the sculptor Johann Gottfried Schadow.

Rahel Levin was one of a number of Jewish hostesses. Other prominent salons were held by Henriette Herz, Dorothea Mendelssohn, Sarah Levy, and Amalie Beer, of whom only the last two remained of the Jewish faith. These hostesses were successful not because German-Jews were emancipated and integrated, quite the contrary. It was precisely because they were outsiders that they could provide the neutral ground on which people from different stations in life could meet as equals.

A tea party at Rahel von Varnhagen's, woodcut by E. M. Simon.

The Biedermeier family idyll saw the family as a comfortable refuge from the stresses and pressures of the outside world. Wilhelm Friedrich Erich and his family are depicted in this spirit in an anonymous painting of 1828.

Opposite: Nuremberg by Samuel Prout (1783–1852). This prosperous medieval city was a major financial centre as well as home to some of Germany's finest artists and craftsmen, of whom Albrecht Dürer is the most renowned. The first German railway was built in 1835 between Nuremberg and Fürth, evidence of the city's wealth and the skill of its engineers.

some 10 per cent of Prussian students were practising Jews, who went on to play a prominent and distinguished role as doctors, lawyers, and artists, but it was not until 1859 that a Jew first became a professor in Göttingen nor until 1860 that a Jew was first appointed a judge in Hamburg .

A deep-rooted antipathy towards the Jews still remained and was in many cases strengthened by such developments. To a traditional distrust and suspicion was added a bitter envy of their success. Jews made an enormous contribution to German life, and the German Jewish community was prominent in the reform movement within Judaism. German was the lingua franca of nineteenth-century Judaism. This too was not without problems. Orthodox Jews feared that social assimilation would lead to a watering-down of their religion and compromise their traditional way of life. Yet for all these difficulties, the interaction between Germans and Jews in the nineteenth century was fruitful to both sides. Nothing indicated the terrible disaster that lay ahead.

The great strength of German scholarship in the first half of the nineteenth century was in philosophy and the humanities; the sciences were somewhat neglected. This situation was to be dramatically reversed in the second half of the century. The land of 'Poets and Thinkers' was host to some very curious ideas. Schelling and the 'natural philosophers' took Newton to task for his empiricism, and insisted that nature could only be understood by intuition and contemplation. Physicians, like Feuchtersleben in Vienna and Ringseis in Munich, denounced 'materialist' medicine and called for a new approach that combined prayer, the

laying on of hands, and meditation along with slightly more modern therapeutic practices. The proponents of empirical scientific investigation had a singularly hard struggle against these priestly doctors and poetic contemplators of the marvels of nature.

The outstanding German scientist of the age was Justus Liebig. He was discovered by Alexander von Humboldt as a twenty-one-year-old student of Gay-Lussac in Paris. Humboldt immediately secured a chair for the young scientist in Giessen, where he built the first modern laboratory in a German university. Liebig was one of the most inventive scientists of the age. With his work on chemical fertilizers he was the founder of agricultural chemistry. He discovered chloroform and chloral and played a key role in the discovery of the benzol radical. He invented a number of scientific appliances, of which the best known is Liebig's condenser. On a more mundane level he gave the world Liebig's meat extract. In his works on organic chemistry he showed that he was also a great systematizer and methodological innovator.

Much of the important literary work of this period was in the field of literary theory. Philosophical speculation took the place of creative writing. Friedrich Schlegel's *History of Old and New Literature* tried to place literature in a world historical setting and attempted to reconcile medieval Christian idealism with the exigencies of the modern world. The Hegelian, Georg Gottfried Gervinus, in his *History of the Poetic National Literature of the Germans* argued that the task of literature was to help create the German nation.

The great tradition of Romantic lyrical poetry was carried on by Joseph von Eichendorff, Eduard Mörike, and Annette von Droste-Hülsdorff. Heinrich Heine and Ludwig Börne were the outstanding representatives of 'Young Germany', a group of politically engaged writers who were to fall foul of the censors in 1835 and who were then forced into exile. The immediate cause for this repression was the publication in 1835 of Karl Gutzkow's novel *Wally the Sceptic* which attacked the churches and advocated the emancipation of women and free love.

SIGNS OF CHANGE

In July 1830 revolution broke out in Paris, and Charles X lost his throne and was succeeded by Louis Philippe, 'the bourgeois king'. The Belgians rose up against the Dutch and created an independent country with a progressive constitution. There were similar uprisings in Italy and in Poland. In northern Germany, with the notable exception of Prussia, many states made constitutional concessions similar to those that had already been made in the south.

In Brunswick the duke's carriage was stoned, and his palace besieged. He had lost the support of much of the bourgeoisie, the aristocracy and the officer corps, and he abdicated in favour of his popular brother. The masses set fire to the palace without the authorities intervening, Prince William succeeded with the support of the English crown, and a new constitution was promulgated in September 1831.

In Saxony dissatisfaction with the reactionary regime of the aged King Anton and his chief minister Hans Georg von Carlowitz was widespread, and the king prudently appointed his nephew co-regent after a series of riots and demonstrations throughout the kingdom. A new and more liberal government was appointed which instituted modest reforms, and a new constitution was introduced on the south German model in September 1831. In the following year feudal obligations were abolished.

In Hanover riots in 1830 resulted in modest constitutional reforms. These were annulled in 1837 when the personal union with Britain was ended, and the new King Ernst August began his ferociously reactionary reign. In electoral Hesse the mob threatened Elector William II that, unless he called a representative assembly, there would be a civil war. The elector stalled and there was widespread violence throughout the state. He called upon the Bundestag to intervene to restore law and order, at the same time summoning a constitutional Diet in Kassel which presented the new constitution in January 1831. William II refused to cooperate with the new Landtag and was forced to abdicate in favour of his son Frederick William.

Austria, Prussia and the Federation stood aside in 1830 and let events take their course. This was in large part due to the fact that Austria and Prussia's attention was focused elsewhere, particularly on Italy and Poland, and the Federation would not act unless on the orders of the two powers. Developments in the north were a tremendous stimulus to the south German liberals, who formed a number of national associations, published several new newspapers and journals, and did all they could to mobilize public opinion.

The centre of activity was the Bavarian Palatinate where the Patriotic Association in Support of the Free Press (*Vaterlandsverein zur Unterstützung der freien Presse*) was formed at Zweibrücken in 1832. The association called for a free press as the necessary precondition of the unification of Germany and of a democratic Europe. It organized a mass meeting at Hambach on 27 May 1832 to celebrate 'Germany's rebirth'. Some 20,000–30,000 people attended the meeting, waving the black, red and yellow flag of German liberalism and the white eagle of Poland, and listening to rousing patriotic speeches. The Hambach Festival was a unique event, a massive demonstration of people from all over Germany in favour of national unity solidly based on democratic principles. The movement failed for two main reasons. The nationalists were hopelessly divided between moderates and radicals, and the authorities suppressed the movement with the utmost severity. Prompted by Metternich, Bavaria declared a state of emergency and sent an ancient field-marshal into the Palatinate to round up the radicals and remove the trees of liberty which had provocatively been planted throughout the region. The nationalist leaders were either arrested or fled into exile.

One month after the Hambach Festival the Bundestag passed the 'Six Articles' which drastically limited the rights of the Diets and established a Control Commission to ensure that the parliamentarians obeyed the new law. Many of the

Heinrich Heine (1797–1856) first attracted attention with his *Gedichte* ('Poems') published in 1822. These were followed by two early master-pieces *Das Buch der Lieder* ('The Book of Songs') and *Reisebilder* ('Travel Pictures') which were a critical and commercial success. He travelled to Paris in 1830 and remained there for the rest of his life. In his *History of Religion and Philosophy in Germany* (1834) he introduced the French to the revolutionary implications of the philosophies of Kant and Hegel. Heine has been seen as a glowing patriot and a cynical traitor, as a principled republican and a paid lackey. He had the courage to stand alone, and in most instances history has proved him right.

states objected vigorously to the principle that federal law was above state law and to the formation of yet another federal police agency. The Central Office for Political Investigations was founded in response to an attack by a group of Heidelberg students on the main guard house in Frankfurt. This dramatic gesture did not trigger off a general revolt as the students had hoped. The masses were apathetic, and the rebels were rounded up by a battalion of soldiers who lost six men in the encounter; one student was killed.

The constitutional states were powerless against Austria and Prussia, and Metternich forced through further repressive legislation at the Ministerial Conference of Vienna between January and May of 1834. In 1836, 204 students were arrested in Prussia; 39 were condemned to death and four were ordered to be broken at the wheel. The death sentences were eventually commuted to prison sentences, many of them for life. When Frederick William IV ascended the throne in 1840, they were all pardoned.

Prussia had the liberals completely under control, but had increasing difficulty with Catholics, particularly in the western provinces. According to Tridentine practice, the children of marriages between Catholics and Protestants had to be brought up as Catholics. In 1803 the Prussian government ordered that the children of mixed marriages should be brought up in the religion of the father, at least in the provinces east of the Elbe. This ruling was extended to all of Prussia in 1825. Although the Vatican was anxious to reach a compromise on this issue, intransigence on both sides led to conflict. In November 1837 the archbishop of Cologne was arrested for insisting that his conscience forbade him to follow the instructions of the king in every instance. Other bishops in the east, in Posen, Ermland, Kulm, and Breslau, were also jailed for defying the Prussian law on mixed marriages. In 1840 the new Prussian king, Frederick William IV, brought the conflict to an end by making major concessions to the Catholic Church. The Prussian state had suffered a serious defeat, but it was one which neither the Austrians nor the south German constitutional states were able to use to their advantage. For the Austrians the Prussian radicals were altogether too radical, for the liberals the Catholics were too conservative.

In 1837 the British King William IV died and was succeeded by Queen Victoria. Since the Hanoverian throne passed through the male line, William IV's brother, the sixty-six-year-old duke of Cumberland, became King Ernst August. The new king promptly annulled the constitution of 1833, having secured the support of Austria and Prussia. Seven professors at the university of Göttingen protested, among them the historians Dahlmann and Gervinus as well as Jakob Grimm, one of the brothers of fairy-tale fame. The 'Göttingen Seven' were exiled. These events were debated in the Bundestag, but only Bavaria, Saxony, Württemberg, Baden, and the Saxon duchies voted to uphold the constitution of 1833. By condoning an illegal act by a member-state, the Federation lost all credibility. The Göttingen Seven travelled throughout Germany denouncing the regime in Hanover and

Struwwelpeter

Heinrich Hoffmann, the author of *Struwwelpeter*, a collection of vividly illustrated children's stories told in verse, was born in Frankfurt in 1809. He studied medicine in Heidelberg and Halle, then returned to Frankfurt where he worked as a general practitioner and in a free clinic. Between 1844 and 1851 he taught anatomy and in 1851 he was given a position in an institute for the insane and epileptics in Frankfurt. Between 1859 and 1864 he built a model psychiatric hospital outside the city which was run along exceptionally progressive lines. Were he not the author of one of the most famous of children's books he would be remembered as a pioneer in the treatment of the mentally ill.

In 1844 Hoffmann searched for a picture book to give his three-year-old son for Christmas. He was unable to find anything suitable and therefore set about making the book himself. He realized that small children were more impressed by pictures than by words, and he found the high moral tone of contemporary children's books absurd and offensive. He described contemporary children's books as 'altogether too enlightened and rational, falsely naive, unchildlike, untruthful, artificial'. His pictures are exaggerated and droll, with no pretence to realism, and appeal to a child's imaginative fantasy. The book was designed for a child's use. Drawn on thick paper and loosely bound, it could withstand some rough treatment, its pages could be easily turned. The first edition of 1,500 copies was sold out within a few weeks and it has subsequently sold more than twenty-five million copies.

The eponymous hero of the book was modelled on an advertisement for a patent recipe for baldness which showed what might happen if a child got hold of a bottle. Struwwelpeter is a self-confident anarchist, confidently standing on a pedestal, who flatly refuses to cut his nails or comb his hair. In the original edition he appeared anonymously at the back of the book, but he became such a popular figure that he was placed on the front cover of the third edition of 1846, and given the name 'Untidy Peter'.

The story of 'Little Pauline' who set herself on fire with a match is based on a true story. 'Lucifers' first appeared in 1829 and caused a number of accidents. The other stories in the book teach children from the ages to three to six not to mistreat animals, mock people of different race, suck their thumbs, play with their food, or lean back in their chairs.

Hoffmann observed the anorexic, the hyper-active and the permanently inattentive in his professional career and published a scientific book on the subject in 1859. He also painted pictures for his little patients and found them to be useful therapeutic tools. Hoffmann the amateur painter and versifier, Hoffmann the delightfully gentle and amusing family man, and Hoffmann the progressive psychiatrist combine in *Struwwelpeter* to produce a work of genius.

Illustrations from an 1845 English edition of *Struwwelpeter*.

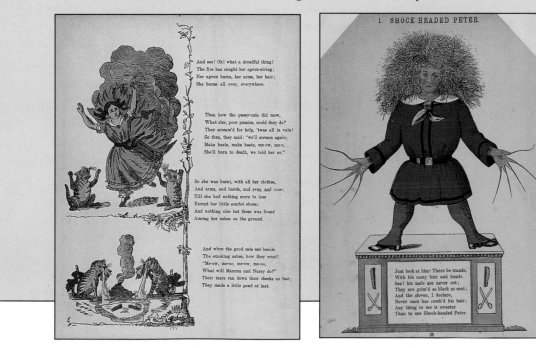

pouring scorn on the failed Federation. Dahlmann wrote that belief in a peaceful development of the constitutional process in Germany was destroyed by this decision of the Bundestag.

Strident and aggressive German nationalism was expressed in popular poems such as Hoffmann von Fallersleben's *Deutschlandlied*, later to become the national anthem. This new nationalism was directed outside, with fulminations against the 'Romanism' of France and the 'Slavism' of Russia. Political differences among nationalists were overcome by hatred of a common enemy, and cosmopolitan liberalism was replaced by a chauvinistic nationalism with ugly racist overtones.

The year 1840 was also a turning point in that Frederick William IV came to the throne of Prussia. He was a highly intelligent but indecisive man, filled with curiously Romantic notions of the Christian Germanic ideals of the Middle Ages, and a belief that German nationalism had a place in this strange Gothic revival. He had an astonishing ability to make electrifying utterances which on closer examination were either highly ambiguous or meaningless. For all his bizarre shortcomings he was an infinitely superior monarch to Ferdinand I of Austria, who succeeded to the throne in 1835. Ferdinand was a cretinous epileptic whose mentor, the Archduke Ludwig, was a man of the utmost insignificance.

Frederick William IV's reign began with a series of liberal gestures which gave great encouragement to the reformers. The struggle with the Catholic Church ended and numerous political prisoners were pardoned. The king countered the demands for constitutional reform, which were encouraged by these measures, by making gnomic and evasive utterances or by throwing the more radical proponents of constitutional liberties in jail. In 1842 he permitted representatives of the provincial estates to meet in Berlin to advise the government. This did not satisfy the reformers, and was altogether too much for the conservatives, to say nothing of Russia and Austria. Tsar Nicholas I and Metternich warned the king not to make any concessions to the liberals.

Frederick William IV wanted to reconcile throne and altar and thought in German national rather than narrowly Prussian terms. A dramatic expression of these ideas was the festival organized in September 1842 to celebrate the beginning of the completion phase of Cologne cathedral, where building had ceased in 1559. The principal speakers were Frederick William IV and the Archduke John of Austria, who travelled to Cologne in the company of Metternich. The king referred to the event as a symbol of the unity of Germany. The archduke said: 'As long as Prussia and Austria and the rest of Germany, wherever German is spoken, are united, we shall be as solid as the stone of our mountains'. This was reported in the press as: 'No longer Prussia and Austria, but one Germany, as solid as our mountains'. Thanks to this faulty report of the speech, the Archduke John was later appointed 'Reich Administrator' by the Frankfurt parliament.

In an attempt to overcome the state's financial difficulties Frederick William IV assembled the United Diet in Berlin in 1847. It was made up of the 612 members of the provincial Diets. Its members were mostly aristocratic landowners, many of whom were liberals who wanted constitutional reform. One of the main items for discussion was a thirty million-taler loan to build the eastern railway from Berlin to Königsberg. The United Diet refused to grant these credits unless the constitutional question was discussed, whereupon the king closed the Diet and ordered work on the railway to stop.

The political crisis in Bavaria had a more romantic cause. The sixty-year-old Ludwig I, who had always had an eye for the girls, was much smitten by a young Irish dancer from Limerick whose stage name was Lola Montez. Her antics caused much distress in devout Catholic circles and the reactionary government resigned when the king wished to give his pompadour the title of countess of Landsfeld. The new ministry was noticeably more liberal, but opposition to the king's scandalous behaviour grew. When the young countess recruited a bodyguard of liberal students, these protests reached fever-pitch. Regretfully, the king felt obliged to part from Lola who left Munich and, after a further successful career as a courtesan, died a penitent in Astoria, Long Island, at the age of forty-three.

In Hanover Ernst August continued to resist the demands of both houses of the Diet for constitutional reform. In Hessen the new elector, Frederick William I, confronted the estates. In Saxony liberal and radical voices grew louder in the Landtag, as they did in Baden, Württemberg, and Hessen-Darmstadt. Even in the Bundestag a more liberal spirit was noticeable. Lively debates over the publication of its procedures and over censorship sprang some surprises. Prussia favoured freedom of the press and secured a majority against Austria for a more lenient censorship law. There were numerous proposals for reform of the Federation along more liberal lines, among them a memorandum from Queen Victoria's husband, Prince Albert of Coburg.

The Prussian foreign minister, Joseph Maria von Radowitz, proposed that the Federation have a common code of law, foster close economic and technical cooperation between the German states, and reform its army. He suggested that if Austria did not agree to these proposals then Prussia should go it alone by appealing to the Bundestag or negotiating with individual states. Radowitz insisted that Prussia was the true German state which stood or fell with Germany, whereas Austria, with its huge multi-national empire, was only partially concerned with German affairs.

Frederick William was sympathetic to Radowitz's ideas, but he would not entertain a Germany without Austria. 'Germany without Triest, the Tyrol, and the wonderful Archduchy,' he exclaimed, 'would be worse than a face without a nose.' Even Metternich was prepared to discuss the proposal, and called for a meeting on federal reform to be held in Dresden on 25 March. But by that time the revolution had spread to Germany and Metternich was out of a job.

Social conditions were appalling in these years. Mass unemployment, poverty, and hunger plagued many areas of Germany. A series of bad harvests from 1845 led

The old town hall in Berlin was built between 1260 and 1270, but was torn down in 1866. This painting by Wilhelm Brücke shows the town hall in 1840.

to food riots in Berlin, Vienna, Stuttgart and Ulm. In Upper Silesia 80,000 cases of typhus were reported. A worldwide recession caused high unemployment and numerous bankruptcies. But by the time the revolution of 1848 began, the economy was already on the upswing and real incomes were rising sharply. Economic causes thus combined with the political uncertainty to create an explosive situation, but later improvements in the economy helped to dampen revolutionary enthusiasm.

The Silesian weavers

Germany was smitten with a series of disasters in the mid 1840s. From 1843–47 there was a widespread famine caused by potato disease and the failure of the grain harvest. The famine reached its worst level in 1847 and in Silesia alone 80,000 people contracted typhus as a result of starvation and some 16,000 died of the disease. In 1847 there were more than a hundred riots in Germany, excluding the Habsburg lands, the most dramatic of which was the 'Potato Revolution' in Berlin in April.

An extensive report by the liberal medical professor, Rudolf von Virchow, on conditions in Silesia caused a sensation. Famine and poverty were effectively used by the left to question the legitimacy of existing governments and, combined with the political upheavals, created an explosive situation.

Hunger fuelled working-class unrest. Real wages dropped by more than 45 per cent between 1844 and 1847. The worst hit group were the Silesian linen weavers. In Prussia only 2,628 cotton looms were mechanically operated by 1847, and there were still 116,832 old-fashioned handlooms. The ratio was much the same for wool and linen. German textile manufacturers were unable to compete with the British, and even higher *Zollverein* (German customs union) tariffs brought little relief. Small-scale production and low productivity meant high costs so that exports declined.

Whereas output in wool and cotton increased and German manufacturers were gradually able to meet the challenge of British, French, and Belgian imports, the linen industry stagnated and declined. The industry was organized on semi-feudal lines, and the equipment was hopelessly outmoded. In 1844 the combination of poverty, famine, and political unrest resulted in a desperate revolt. The weavers stormed the factories, smashed machinery, burnt the account books in which their debts were recorded and demonstrated outside the houses of the factory owners. The army was called in and within three days quiet was restored.

The tragic plight of the Silesian weavers outraged contemporaries and excited the imagination of artists like Heine, Gerhart Hauptmann, and Käthe Kollwitz. The weavers were the innocent victims of the industrial revolution. Their misery was due to the backwardness of the German linen industry, which could only be overcome by replacing the handloom by a mechanical loom and thus taking away their livelihood. Some were able to retrain and benefited from the exceptional increase in real wages between 1848 and 1850. Most of those who survived disease and famine joined the growing ranks of paupers, and confirmed Karl Marx in his belief that the pauperization of the masses was the necessary consequence of industrial capitalism.

'The Silesian weavers', oil painting (1844) by Carl Wilhelm Hubner (1814–79).

<table>
<tr><td>CHAPTER 8</td><td></td></tr>
</table>

CHAPTER 8   *The Unification of Germany*

On 24 February 1848 barricades were built in Paris, Louis Philippe fled the country, and France once again became a republic. In January revolutionary outbursts had occurred in Italy. On 3 March in Hungary the radical liberal nationalist Kossuth called for the constitutional reform of the Habsburg monarchy. These events were bound to have an effect in Germany, where the reform movement had been gathering momentum. As early as 12 February Friedrich Bassermann, a liberal publisher, had given an impassioned speech in the Baden parliament calling for a federal Germany similar to the United States of America. In Baden, Württemberg, and Hessen there were urgent demands for freedom of the press, constitutional reform, trial by jury, and for an all-German parliament.

1848: THE REVOLUTIONARY YEAR

The German revolutionary movement was diffuse and confused. In the state capitals the crowds demanded the resignation of existing governments. Artisans and craftsmen indulged in Luddite violence against factories and machines, peasants demanded the abolition of feudal obligations, and country houses were plundered and burnt. Arsenals were stormed and the people armed. Sober lawyers drew up blueprints for constitutional reform while radicals dreamt of Utopia. On 5 March fifty-one reformers, mainly from southern and western Germany, met in Heidelberg. They included radical republicans like Hecker and Struve and monarchists like Heinrich von Gagern, the leading liberal in Hessen, who wanted to revive the empire with the Prussian king of Prussia as emperor. The liberals outweighed the radicals and it was agreed that a 'pre-parliament' should meet in Frankfurt. A committee of seven men was appointed to select the 574 delegates.

The Bundestag had made an appeal for moderation on 1 March, and on 9 March recognized the liberal black, red and gold flag as the federal colours. On the following day a committee was formed consisting of seventeen moderate liberals who were to make proposals for constitutional reform. They began their deliberations at the end of the month. Meanwhile Heinrich von Gagern, who was fearful that the radicals might get the upper hand, negotiated with Bavaria, Baden, Württemberg, Nassau, and the two Hessens in the hope that reform of the Federation would come from the existing governments via the Bundestag, rather than from a potentially radical parliament. All these efforts failed, principally due to the resistance of Bavaria.

In many of the states reactionary governments were dismissed and replaced by moderate liberals in the hope that the radicals would be kept at bay. Gagern was appointed principal minister in Hessen-Darmstadt. New moderate governments were created in Baden, Württemberg, Hanover, Saxony, and in most of the smaller states. In Bavaria Ludwig I felt obliged to abdicate on 20 March, and his son

Maximilian II appointed a reforming government under the conservative but federalist Count Bray-Steinburg. Elsewhere the change was violent. On 13 March street-fighting in Vienna resulted in sixty deaths and the Austrian chancellor Metternich fled the country, but the new government of Count Kolowrat was made up of representatives of the old order. Fresh demonstrations on 15 May obliged the emperor to leave Vienna and the radicals formed a Committee of Public Safety. The two sides were now clearly on a collision course.

There were demonstrations throughout Prussia, and Prince William, the king's brother, prepared to take military action. The presence of large numbers of soldiers in Berlin only served to make the situation more volatile. When Metternich was forced to flee, Frederick William IV decided to make a conciliatory gesture and on 18 March he announced that censorship would be abolished, that the United Diet would reconvene, and that Germany should have a constitution. A large crowd assembled outside the royal palace in Berlin. Some were there to thank the king, others to encourage him to go further along the path to reform, others to demand that the troops should be withdrawn from the capital. General von Prittwitz ordered the soldiers to disperse the crowd. Shots were fired, barricades were built, and at least 230 people were killed in the fighting. The army was unable to clear the barricades and on 19 March the king ordered the troops to leave Berlin. Frederick William IV attended the funeral of those who had died in the fighting, and then took part in a ceremony handing over arms to the revolutionary citizens' militia. On 21 March he rode around Berlin, swathed in the black, red, and gold colours of the revolution and announced: 'I wear colours which are not mine, but I do not want a throne, I do not want to rule, I want Germany's freedom, Germany's unity, I want order, I swear to God!'. On the same day he issued a proclamation which contained the famous and characteristically opaque utterance: 'Henceforth Prussia merges into Germany'. No one could quite make out what all this meant, but it seemed as if the people had won a decisive victory.

A new Prussian ministry was formed under Ludolf Camphausen and David Hansemann, prominent representatives of the moderate liberalism of the Rhineland; the former was a wealthy banker, the latter a textile manufacturer. The United Diet met again and voted for a democratic election of a national assembly. On 1 May elections were held throughout Prussia both for the National Assembly and the Frankfurt parliament.

The Camphausen-Hansemann government was anxious to maintain the authority of the crown and to ensure that the economic well-being of the state was not threatened by radical political demands. A compromise might have been possible between the financial and industrial bourgeoisie and the old order had it not been for the existence of a powerful reactionary clique around Prince William, Otto von Bismarck, and the king's adjutant, Leopold von Gerlach. For the moment this group was relatively weak. Prince William had fled to London, Bismarck was isolated with his extreme views, and Gerlach had yet to stiffen the king. A new

A scene on the barricades on the Alexanderplatz in Berlin, March 1848. At least 230 people were killed in street-fighting in Berlin, and eventually Frederick William IV was forced to order the troops to leave the city.

newspaper, the *Neue Preussische Zeitung*, soon known as the *Kreuzzeitung* on account of the iron cross on the title page, spread the ultra-conservative gospel. The soldiers in Potsdam waited impatiently for the chance to recapture Berlin.

The radicals formed a minority in the pre-parliament, and Friedrich Hecker, the revolutionary from Baden, walked out of the assembly with some forty delegates when his republican ideas were rejected. Hecker went to south Baden, where he enjoyed some popular support, and called for an armed uprising on behalf of the republic. His ill-disciplined mob advanced on Freiburg, but was defeated by troops from Baden and Hessen; by the end of April this ill-fated adventure was over.

The date and method of election to the Frankfurt parliament was left to the individual states, so there were considerable differences in the sizes of the electorates and in the electoral systems, and the guidelines laid down by the pre-parliament were open to very different interpretations. By 18 May 350 delegates had been elected, enough for a quorum, and the parliament formally opened at the

Paul's Church in Frankfurt. At the suggestion of Heinrich von Gagern, who was elected speaker of the Frankfurt parliament, the Archduke John was made Reich administrator, the chief executive. He appointed Queen Victoria's half-brother Prince Leiningen minister-president, the Austrian Anton von Schmerling was made minister of the interior, and the Prussian General von Peucker minister of war. The Bundestag was thus pushed aside and Germany had a new government.

It was soon questionable whether the government had any real authority. General von Peucker ordered the army in each of the German states to hold parades and to offer three cheers for the archduke. This was not enough for the radicals in Frankfurt who wanted the troops to swear an oath of allegiance to the Reich administrator, but it went far too far for the Austrians and Prussians who flatly refused to carry out the order. Hanover announced that the weather was not good enough to hold a parade. Bavarian troops cheered the archduke, but also their own king and the German people. Most other states dutifully carried out von Peucker's wishes with their minute armies.

The Frankfurt government was equally unsuccessful in gaining the diplomatic recognition of the great powers. Neither tsarist Russia nor republican France had any desire to see a united Germany. The British were somewhat more sympathetic but the prime minister, Lord Palmerston, hesitated to extend diplomatic re-cognition to a regime that did not yet have an air of permanence. A number of European states did recognize the new German government, including Sweden, the Netherlands, Belgium, and Switzerland; the United States also encouraged this new experiment in federal government by granting diplomatic recognition. However, none of this could make up for the refusal of the great powers to accept the new regime, nor could it conceal the fact that it was completely impotent. The federal government had no executive power, no money, no military support, no constitution, and parliament was hopelessly divided on all key issues.

The spring and summer of 1848 was a period of frantic political activity with no tangible progress. In Prussia there were 50 conservative associations, 300 liberal constitutional organizations and 250 democratic groups. The best organized were the Catholics: their Pious Association of Religious Freedom demanded that the rights of the Church should be written into the constitution. More than 90 per cent of the petitions sent to the Paul's Church came from Catholics. In October the first all-German Catholic congress was held in Mainz, the largest and most influential extra-parliamentary meeting held during the revolutionary year.

A daguerreotype (c.1850) of the brothers Grimm. Jakob (1785–1863) is standing, Wilhelm (1786–1859) is seated. The brothers were famous collectors of German folk tales. Jakob was also a delegate to the Frankfurt parliament of 1848.

Prussian landowners organized the 'Junker Parliament' which elected a fifty-man committee to lobby the Prussian national assembly. In Frankfurt artisans and craftsmen formed the reactionary General Craftsmen's and Trades' Congress (*Allgemeine Handwerker-und Gewerbekongress*) which denounced liberal free-trading policies and demanded that the guilds should be restored to protect their interests against the inroads of industrial capitalism. The liberals and radicals were still seriously divided, in spite of some efforts to organize on a national basis, and an unbridgeable gap between anti-capitalist radicals and anti-capitalist Catholics permanently weakenened the forces critical of industrial society.

It was perhaps characteristically German that matters of principle were felt to be of greater moment than the solution of immediate political problems. Thus the Frankfurt parliament was able to agree on a modest catalogue of fundamental rights about which they debated at inordinate length. They did not include social issues and firmly upheld bourgeois property rights. Even more contentious was the national question. Polish nationalists denied the right of German delegates to speak on behalf of the people of Posen. The question of Poland was debated between 24 and 27 July. The one Pole in the Frankfurt parliament, the theologian Jan Janiszewski, made an impassioned plea for equal rights for Poles and Germans. Although his speech was favourably received it had no effect on the final outcome of the debate. Posen was declared to be an integral part of the German Federation.

The six Italian delegates from South Tyrol proposed that the Trentino and Rovereto should cease to be part of the Federation. In the subsequent debate there were some appalling examples of the intolerant, brutal, and racist nationalism of the right and centre. Jakob Grimm spoke of the 'un-German' men who had proposed the motion. The historian, Friedrich von Raumer, spoke of the scientific fact that there were victorious and vanquished nations, that right belonged to the former and the delegates were entranced when he ended with the words: 'Germany would rather perish than surrender and hand over part of the fatherland'.

In Bohemia and Moravia the Czechs, under the leadership of Franz Palacky, had successfully boycotted the elections to the Frankfurt parliament and convened a Slav congress in Prague. The Frankfurt parliamentarians were appalled at these developments, one delegate describing Bohemia as 'a wedge driven into the German oak in order to split it'. A motion declaring Bohemia and Moravia to be parts of the Federation was passed with an overwhelming majority, many on the left voting in favour on the grounds that Germans brought progressive civilization to these backward areas.

According to the Treaty of Ripen of 1460 the two duchies of Schleswig and Holstein were to be joined together in perpetuity. The Danes now wished to incorporate Schleswig into the Danish state. In order to uphold the claims of the Federation, Prussian, Hanoverian, and other German troops under the command of the Prussian General Wrangel marched against the Danes. Due to pressure from Britain, France, and Russia and thanks to Swedish intermediaries, an armistice was

There were no political parties represented in the Frankfurt Parliament in 1848. Like-minded reformers met in the local inns and beer halls after which their factions were named. Throughout Germany political banquets were held at which, as Bismarck remarked, there were many resolutions and majority votes, but precious little was achieved.

signed between the two sides at Malmö on 26 August 1848. By the terms of the agreement, German troops would withdraw from Schleswig-Holstein, and the nationalist provisional government established at Kiel would be dissolved. The federal government proposed that the treaty of Malmö should be ratified, but the motion was defeated by 238 votes to 221, the left voting solidly against what they believed was a betrayal of the German national cause. The Leiningen government resigned over the issue. The treaty was finally ratified by a majority of one vote; many centre delegates, who were anxious that the new government should have a working majority, changed their position.

The ratification vote was held on 16 September 1848. On the following day a massive demonstration was held in Frankfurt against the 'traitors' in the Paul's Church, whereupon the new minister-president, Schmerling, called in Prussian and Austrian troops who were stationed in nearby Mainz. Barricades were promptly built in Frankfurt and an attempt was made to storm the Paul's Church. In the ensuing street battle eighty people were killed. The political centre of gravity now moved to the right; all those who regarded the left as red republicans, bloodthirsty revolutionaries, and irresponsible anarchists saw their fondest prejudices confirmed. It was plainly evident that the Frankfurt parliament, now protected by Austrian and Prussian troops, could only continue its deliberations as long as Austria and Prussia were prepared to tolerate it. The counter-revolution in these two countries sealed its fate.

In Prussia the mildly radical National Assembly faced the king and his reactionary advisors. Gradually the left began to split apart as delegates sought to find a compromise with the court party. In November a conservative government was appointed under Count Frederick of Brandenburg and on 5 December Frederick William IV dismissed the National Assembly and proclaimed a new constitution.

An unfair caricature of Frederick William IV of Prussia depicts him calling for the use of artillery against the revolutionaries in 1848. In fact, he handed over arms to a revolutionary citizens' militia.

The Frankfurt parliament insisted that if Austria were to be included in the Federation, a clear distinction had to be made between the German and non-German parts of the empire. The Habsburg empire had thus to be divided, a suggestion which was unacceptable to the new, eighteen-year-old emperor, Francis Joseph. The Frankfurt parliament then agreed that the imperial crown should be offered to the king of Prussia. On 2 April 1849 a parliamentary delegation went to Berlin but was turned down flat by Frederick William IV. A passionate believer in the divine origin of sovereignty, he could not accept 'the crown from the gutter' and described an imperial crown offered by a parliamentary majority as 'the iron collar of slavery'. The Prussian king not only put an end to any hope of German unity, he denied that the Frankfurt parliament had any legitimacy. On 14 May the Prussian government demanded of the Archduke John that he disband the Frankfurt parliament and all the Prussian delegates were ordered to resign.

Prussia was merely following the Austrian lead. On 5 April the Austrian minister-president, Schwarzenberg, had ordered all the Austrian delegates to resign. These events made the debates over the German constitution, which had been concluded on 28 March with the acceptance of a federation, utterly pointless, and the extreme left grew correspondingly restless. Barricades went up in Dresden. There were violent clashes in parts of Prussia, and units of the territorial army (*Landwehr*) joined the rebels. In Iserlohn 100 died as a result of a clash between the Landwehr and the regular army. In Württemberg the pressure on the king was so great that he felt obliged to accept the federal constitution. In the Palatinate guerillas took up arms, and in Baden the army mutinied. This 'May Movement' was confined to the predominantly rural, petit-bourgeois area of the Palatinate, and did not spill over into the industrial regions of the Rhineland, Thuringia, and Saxony.

The Frankfurt parliament slowly dissolved. On 4 May 1849 Heinrich von Gagern, still clinging to the illusion that it was possible to build a consensus, called for new elections, but the Archduke John refused to take this unrealistic step. A few days later Gagern followed his monarch's instructions and resigned from the parliament along with sixty other representatives of the centre. They left Frankfurt with a clear conscience, announcing that the constitution was ready and needed only a head of state to put it into effect. The left were equally bereft of a sense of reality. They believed that the elections would be held on 15 July and that a hard core of dedicated democrats would complete the glorious task of creating a united and democratic Germany, if necessary by force of arms.

Most of the centre and right having left the Paul's Church, the majority was now on the left. Archduke John appointed a government under General Prince Sayn-Wittgenstein which was promptly defeated in a vote of confidence by 191 to 12, with 44 abstentions. The government remained in office and a number of delegates who had voted for the motion of no-confidence now left Frankfurt in disgust. The hard core left that remained was unable to link up with the May Movement to form a revolutionary power, and a majority voted to move the parliament to Stuttgart to escape from the Prussian and Austrian troops stationed in Frankfurt and Mainz.

Below left: Landscape near Ischl by Ferdinand Waldmüller (1793–1865).
Below right: 'A visit to the Artist's House', c.1855 by Moritz von Schwind (1804–71).

They may also have established contact with the revolutionaries in Württemberg and Baden. While some delegates remained in Frankfurt, the majority went to Stuttgart where they were soon chased away by the Württemberg army, the people showing no particular enthusiasm for their cause.

Prussian troops restored order in the provinces, crushed the rebellion in Saxony, and marched into the Palatinate, where they defeated the ill-disciplined rebels under the command of the Polish General Sznayde. Prince William, later to become the first emperor, returned from London and earned the nickname 'the Grapeshot Prince' for his energetic pursuit of revolutionaries. Another Polish officer, Anton von Mieroslawski, was a somewhat more effective leader of the irregular forces in Baden, but the struggle was unequal and he soon had to capitulate. There followed a series of court martials and numerous executions. Eighty thousand people left Baden, most of them going to the United States. Between 1849 and 1854 some 1,100,000 Germans emigrated.

The Prussian army having crushed the revolution, Frederick William IV was sympathetic to the plan of the Prussian foreign minister, General Joseph Maria von Radowitz, for a little German solution – Germany without Austria under Prussian hegemony, but nevertheless closely linked to Austria. It was a solution which the reactionary advisors found unacceptable in that it contained unpleasant liberal and nationalist elements. It was also unacceptable to the Austrians. Radowitz then negotiated the 'Alliance of the Three Kings' with Saxony and Hanover, which created a federal Diet in Erfurt, envisaging that a new constitution would be worked out between the Diet and the governments. Some 150 liberals, among them Gagern, Bassermann, and Jakob Grimm met in Gotha at the end of July 1849 and agreed that this was an acceptable compromise. The 'Gothaers' betrayed the liberal democratic principles of the federal constitution of 28 March, and accepted in its place a reactionary federation under a counter-revolutionary Prussia. They justified their pro-Prussian stance by reference to the Prussian constitution of December 1848 which created a House of Representatives (*Abgeordnetenkammer*). One-third of the members of this house were elected by the 4.7 per cent of the population who paid the highest taxes; the next third by the 12.6 per cent in the next tax bracket; the remaining third by the remaining 82.7 per cent. The system, which lasted until 1918, was designed to ensure a conservative majority.

The left was appalled by these developments and boycotted the elections to the Erfurt parliament. Conservatives were hardly more enthusiastic. Of the twenty-six states in the Erfurt Union only twelve accepted the new constitution. Given the determined opposition of Austria and of a pro-Austrian Bavaria, the Erfurt scheme had no chance of success. The Austrian minister-president, Schwarzenberg, insisted that the Erfurt parliament was contrary to federal law and threatened military intervention. On 21 February 1850 Hanover left the Erfurt Union and joined with Bavaria, Saxony, and Württemberg to form the Alliance of the Four Kings, which supported Austria's plans for a greater German Federation to include the non-German territories of the Habsburg monarchy and a token parliament. The liberals were now faced with Hobson's choice: either a little Germany with modest liberal concessions under a Prussia where reactionary forces were predominating; or a greater Germany which ignored the nationality principle by including the non-German Habsburg lands, and which was totally without liberalism.

It has often been argued that the failure of the 1848 revolution in Germany was due to the spinelessness of German liberals and democrats. However, the failure of the revolution was not due to the peculiarities of the German national character, but to a complex set of reasons. Conservative forces were still overwhelmingly strong. The revolutionaries had contradictory political, economic, and social aims and no clear plan of action; they were overtaken by events, and were unable to find a satisfactory solution to the national problem.

The German bourgeoisie had already made substantial advances and inroads into the old elitist system and so could no longer pose as the champions of a radically new order. The proletariat, which Karl Marx saw as the revolutionary class, was far too rudimentary to play a significant role. The petite bourgeoisie had the most advanced political ideas, but economically they were defending the status quo against the remorseless advance of industrial capitalism. Faced with radicalism from below, the bourgeoisie sought the protection of the conservatives, and many an artisan and craftsman also made common cause with conservatives who shared their fear of bourgeois economic power.

The legacy of 1848 was unfortunate. The pointless resolutions and majority votes of the 'professors' parliament' were taken as examples of the futility of parliamentary democracy. The radicals were painted as violent and mindless dreamers with nothing positive to offer. The virtues and realism of the old order were contrasted with the impotent idealism of the liberals.

THE AFTERMATH OF THE REVOLUTION OF 1848

Events in Hessen brought the conflict between the Erfurt Union and the Austrian-dominated Bundestag to a head. In September 1850 the elector proclaimed martial law, but the army, judiciary, and civil service refused to obey. The Bundestag voted for armed intervention in Hessen, and Austrian and Bavarian troops were sent to aid the elector. The elector then withdrew from the Erfurt Union. Prussia, feeling that the hostile troops placed between Berlin and the Rhineland provinces were a threat to its security and an insult to its prestige, decided also to send troops into Hessen. Austria had the full support of the tsar, and Prussia being in a weak military position was obliged to negotiate. On 28 November, at Olmütz in Moravia, the Prussians agreed to end the conflict and come to terms. The Erfurt Union was dissolved and Prussia rejoined the revived Bundestag.

While there was much talk of the 'humiliation of Olmütz', the Austrians had in fact gained very little. The fundamental question of hegemony in Germany had not been resolved, and Austria had lost an opportunity to crush Prussia that was never to recur. The Bavarian foreign minister, von der Pfordten, said with great prescience: 'The struggle for hegemony in Germany has been decided and Austria has lost'. At the Dresden conference of ministers, from January to May 1851, Prussia was not able to win parity with Austria, but succeeded in frustrating Austria's attempts to include the entire empire in the Federation and to strengthen the federal executive.

The failure of the revolution of 1848 meant that the process of industrialization did not lead to any fundamental change in the social structure. Indeed the aristocracy were able to strengthen their position. They retained police powers over their estates in Prussia which were not modified until 1872 and again in 1892. The percentage of aristocrats in the higher ranks of the army increased. They were particularly favoured in the civil service because they were considered politically reliable. The bourgeoisie abandoned its political ambitions and concentrated on making money and the pursuit of professional careers. The years between 1846 and 1873 were ones of spectacular economic growth which brought the middle-classes great wealth.

It was not until the Crimean War that Prussia was able to regain some of the ground it had lost in 1850. Austria had a number of reasons for opposing Russia. The Austrian foreign minister, Count Buol-Schauenstein, wished to preserve the status quo, prop up Turkey to restrain Russian ambitions, and possibly make some territorial gains in the Balkans. At first it was hoped that this could be achieved by armed neutrality, but on 2 December 1854 Austria signed an alliance with Britain and France, occupied the Danubian principalities which had been abandoned by Russia, and moved a sizable army to the Russian frontier.

Railways offered a safe investment with a hope for high speculative gains. Investment in railway stocks had a positive effect in livening the stock markets and the capital market. Railway building further helped industry, providing the critical marginal demand which, for under-capitalized companies with low profit margins, was essential for their survival

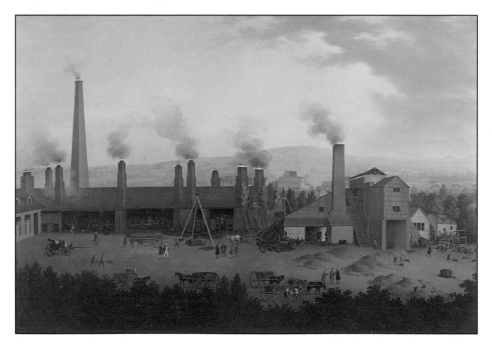

Bismarck, the head of the Prussian delegation in Frankfurt, firmly resisted Austrian attempts to dominate the Federation. He reacted to the Austrian proposal that half of the federal army should be mobilized in support of their anti-Russian policy by proposing that Prussia should form an anti-Austrian front among those German states which wished to remain neutral. He was able to secure a majority in the Bundestag which opposed the Austrian mobilization scheme. Russia was outraged at Austria's behaviour, and Austria had joined the allied camp too late to profit from their victory. Prussia earned the gratitude of Russia without alienating the British or the French, and triumphed over Austria in the Federation.

In the period immediately after the Crimean War the initiative in the Federation was seized by the middle states. Supported by Austria and therefore only reluctantly accepted by Prussia, a federal commercial law was introduced, and the exchange rates between the north German thaler and the south German gulden were fixed. Reform efforts by Saxony's minister-president Beust, which included a proposal for a federal court, provoked endless bickering between Bismarck and the Austrian envoy in the Bundestag, Rechberg. Austria backed these proposals in the hope of winning support among the middle states against Prussia. Prussia opposed them in order to frustrate these Austrian designs.

Unter den Linden, Berlin's main boulevard, is viewed from the royal palace (*Stadtschloss*), by Wilhelm Brücke (1800–70). Decorated with statues of the Hohenzollern kings, Unter den Linden went through the city to the Brandenburg Gate. It was destroyed in the war and could not be revived to its former splendour in a divided city.

By 1857 Frederick William IV, who had often behaved in a somewhat strange manner, had become so mentally disturbed that he was unable to continue in office, and his affairs were conducted by his brother, Prince William, who was formally made prince regent in 1858. Much to people's surprise 'the Grapeshot Prince' dismissed the unpopular reactionary government of Otto von Manteuffel and appointed a liberal conservative administration under Prince Karl Anton von Hohenzollern, the head of the Catholic branch of the Prussian royal family.

Prince William hoped that by making some token gesture to the liberals he would be able to continue with much the same policies without provoking strong opposition. After eight years of reactionary government, the change of administration was enough to raise liberal hopes, and the Landtag elections returned an overwhelming liberal majority. Prince William's new government was anxious to appease Austria, whereas in Frankfurt Bismarck hoped to use the crisis in Italy – the defeat of Austria in 1858 by an alliance of France and Piedmont-Sardinia, which paved the way to Italy's unification – to humiliate Prussia's rival. He proposed that the opportunity offered by Austria's war with France should be seized and that the Prussian army should march south 'with frontier posts in their knapsacks'. Public opinion was strongly against such a policy. A victory for Italian nationalism was seen as a defeat for the German cause, removing the Austrians from northern Italy.

Austria hoped to win the military support of the Federation against Piedmont and France. The Prussian foreign minister, Schleinitz, wanted to wait until Austria was weak enough to be obliged to make concessions in the Federation in return for military support. An Austrian envoy offered Alsace and Lorraine to Prussia as a reward for their support. The Prussians demanded the supreme command over the federal forces and equality with Austria in the Bundestag. These schemes came to nothing as the Austrians suffered crushing defeats at Magenta and Solferino, and the emperor Francis Joseph immediately ordered the opening of peace talks with France's Napoleon III.

Many Germans blamed Prussia for Austria's defeat. Prussia, it was argued, had betrayed the national cause. Austria's defeat was a defeat for Germany, a shameful humiliation of the Germanic race. The wave of nationalist feeling in 1859 was more conservative than ever before, even in democratic circles. The liberals and democrats learnt from the defeats of the 1848 revolution that their only chance of success was to work with the governments, not against them. Liberalism had become timid, cautious, and was ever anxious not to provoke a return to the reactionary policies of an Otto von Manteuffel. The liberals were fearful of forming a mass party and would not even seriously consider political alternatives to the existing state. They did not aspire to power and wanted little beyond some control over the budget and a few legal guarantees. The liberal labour leader, Hermann Schulze-Delitzsch, refused to stand for election to the Prussian Landtag on the grounds that it might embarrass the new administration. Even Ferdinand Lassalle and his General German Workers' Association (ADAV), formed in 1863, believed that society could be changed within the existing state and through the monarchy. Only a handful of radicals mocked this singular lack of courage and conviction.

BISMARCK AND THE PRUSSIAN CONSTITUTIONAL CRISIS

Prince William had spent all his life in the army and was determined that it should be reformed. His minister of war, Albrecht von Roon, presented the House of Representatives with a comprehensive plan which proposed to end the independent role of the Landwehr, to increase the time of service from two years to three, and from three years to four in the cavalry. The sizes of the yearly intakes were also to be greatly increased. These reforms were designed to create thirty-nine new infantry regiments and ten new cavalry regiments, and required a 25 per cent increase in revenue.

These proposals were unacceptable to the liberals, who did not want to see any strengthening of the Prussian military state. They had a great sentimental attachment to the Landwehr, a territorial army beloved of the patriots of 1813 and which had proved not altogether reliable during the revolution of 1848. William I, who had become king in 1861, reacted angrily to this opposition, dismissed the conservative liberal government, and replaced it with a reactionary administration. This move only increased the support for the liberals in the Landtag, and the budget appropriations were once again refused. Roon and his friends then made the final desperate suggestion that Bismarck, who was the Prussian ambassador in Paris, should be appointed to head a government which would solve the constitutional crisis.

The Prussian government was domestically paralyzed by the constitutional struggle over the army reform, but in Germany considerable economic progress was made. The Cobden Treaty of 1860 between Britain and France had created a west European free trade zone which Napoleon III hoped the *Zollverein* would join. Free-trading Prussia saw this as the golden opportunity to exclude protectionist Austria. In addition the German National Association (*Deutsche Nationalverein*), which had been formed in 1859 by bourgeois liberals interested in creating a smaller Germany under Prussian leadership, was growing rapidly in both size and influence. On 29 March 1862 Prussia concluded the trade treaty with France. Even at the height of the constitutional crisis, the Prussian House of Representatives ratified the treaty by a vote of 264 against the 12 votes of the Catholic faction. In a further insult to Austria, Prussia formally recognized Victor Emmanuel as King of Italy, thus accepting a revolutionary nationalist regime against the claims of legitimacy and international law.

William I received Bismarck in the Babelsberg castle outside Berlin on 22 September 1862. He was extremely sceptical about this appointment, but Bismarck won him over by promising to serve him as a feudal vassal would serve his lord. In return the king gave him a free hand to do what he thought best. In his speech to

Wilhelm Brücke's view of Berlin shows Unter den Linden, with the New Guardroom (*Neue Wache*) and the Armoury (*Zeughaus*). On the left is Prince Henry's palace, on the right the entrance to the opera house. Berlin was Germany's largest city, the capital of Prussia and soon to be the national capital. It was the centre of government, with a vibrant cultural and social life, thriving industry, all the social disparities and problems of a modern city, and its own distinct and infectious spirit.

the budget commission of the Landtag on 30 September, Bismarck offered a compromise and presented the chairman with an olive branch he had picked in the south of France. But at the same time he insisted that Prussia had to remain strong if it were to pursue the forceful German policy so dear to the liberal majority. He also trotted out the notion, popular in conservative circles, that there was a 'hole in the constitution'. According to this ingenious theory, since the constitution did not say what should be done in the event of a deadlock between the government and the Landtag, the government could do whatever it saw fit in order to carry out its duties. His speech also contained the famous words: 'The great questions of our day are not decided by speeches and majority votes, which was the great mistake of 1848 and 1849, but by blood and iron'. Mention of blood and iron caused a most unfavourable reaction throughout Germany, right across the political spectrum from conservatives to radical democrats. Here was a reactionary and a Prussian militarist of almost grotesque proportions.

In 1863 Russian Poland was once again in revolt. Bismarck promised the tsar his full support in the Alvensleben Convention of 8 February, a move which alienated the French government which was sympathetic to Polish nationalism. This move also enraged the German liberals. While they had no sympathy for the aspirations of the Poles living in Germany or close to the border, whom they regarded as

Wagner

Wagner was born in Leipzig in 1813 and received much of his early musical training at the St Thomas's School where Bach had once taught. Having written two unsuccessful operas, he was appointed conductor in Riga. In 1839 he went to Paris where he worked on *Rienzi*, successfully performed in 1842. Three months later *The Flying Dutchman* opened, a more compact and dramatic work on one of Wagner's favourite themes: redemption by love. This opera was also well received and won him the position of royal *Kapellmeister* to the Saxon court in Dresden. He wrote *Tannhäuser* in 1845 and *Lohengrin* in 1847, but his career was interrupted when he was forced to flee during the upheavals of 1849, having made a brief appearance on the barricades.

The 1850s he spent mostly in Switzerland, where he began his epic *The Ring of the Nibelungen.* At the same time he wrote *Tristan and Isolde*, the most intensely erotic of all operas and a celebration of his passion for Mathilde Wesdonck, the wife of his generous patron. Since his publisher would not accept the mammoth 'Ring' he began *The Mastersingers of Nuremberg* to earn some money. Here Wagner abandoned his Young German idealism and adopted an unattractive nationalism and xenophobia, although this contradictory work still has great charm and humanity.

In 1864 Wagner was invited by King Ludwig of Bavaria to move to Munich. He promptly seduced Cosima von Bülow, Liszt's daughter and the court conductor's wife, marrying her in 1870. Wagner continued with the Ring cycle for which Ludwig built a special opera house in Bayreuth. The first performance was in 1876 and it was instantly recognized as a masterpiece. Wagner's final opera, *Parsifal*, was first performed in 1882. He died in Venice in 1883.

In his mature operas he abandoned traditional melody and used *Leitmotiven*, themes which represent particular characters or emotions. He made extensive use of chromaticism and at times forsook key altogether, using unresolved chords to create a troubled, yearning atmosphere. Wagner wrote prolifically and prolixly. His repulsive anti-Semitic tract, *Jewishness and Music,* was a sacred text to Cosima, and became part of the National Socialist canon. But Wagner was a composer of supreme genius. Tchaikovsky wrote of *The Ring*: 'Whatever one might think of Wagner's titanic work, no one can deny the monumental nature of the task he set himself, and which he has fulfilled; nor the heroic inner strength needed to complete the task. It is truly one of the greatest artistic endeavours which the human mind has ever conceived.'

Richard Wagner at home in his Villa Wahnfried at Bayreuth.

inferior creatures, the liberals romanticized those Poles who were struggling against tsarist absolutism. More than ever before, Bismarck was seen as a totally unacceptable reactionary.

The year 1863 is also a significant date in that Ferdinand Lassalle was appointed president of the newly formed General German Workers' Association (ADAV), and thus became the founder of Social Democracy. The new party called for an independent workers' party committed to universal suffrage and to cooperative labour. In 1866 August Bebel and Wilhelm Liebknecht, more or less orthodox disciples of Karl Marx, founded the Saxon People's Party, which combined Socialists with more radical liberals. At a meeting in Eisenach in 1869 the party was renamed the Social Democratic Workers' Party (SDAP). It had a broadly Marxist programme and proclaimed, like the Lassalleans, that 'the emancipation of the working class must be won by the working class itself'. In 1875 the Lassalleans and the Eisenachers combined at a conference in Gotha to form the Socialist Workers' Party of Germany, which was later named the Social Democratic Party of Germany (SPD). Its programme combined Marxist and Social Democratic elements and appeared to its opponents to be alarmingly radical, and even revolutionary.

THE STRUGGLE FOR HEGEMONY

The Austrians tried to counter Bismarck's increasingly aggressive Germany policy by proposing far-reaching federal reforms. The details of their proposals remained a closely guarded secret which was to be revealed at a meeting of the German princes chaired by the Austrian emperor. Francis Joseph travelled to Gastein where William I was taking the waters, personally to invite him to the conference, which was scheduled to start a fortnight later. Bismarck, who was with the king in Gastein, tried to persuade him to refuse the invitation, but William hesitated. Only when an Austrian adjutant visited William I immediately after his meeting with Francis Joseph, and virtually demanded an immediate answer, was the king so insulted that he agreed with Bismarck. Bismarck now countered the Austrian move by calling for direct elections throughout Germany for a national parliament. The fierce reactionary of February seemed by August to have donned the mantle of the liberals of 1848.

In spite of Prussia's refusal to attend, the meeting of heads of state in Frankfurt went ahead as planned. The Bundestag was decorated with the black, red, and gold flag which had not been seen since 1851. Nationalist hopes ran high, the emperor was given a rapturous reception by the people, and the conference began with great pomp on 18 August. The emperor's opening address was followed by a long silence, broken by the duke of Mecklenburg-Schwerin, who suggested that a further invitation should be sent to William I, now relaxing in Baden Baden after the strains of his cure. King John of Saxony, the shrewdest and most experienced of the German princes, travelled to Baden Baden and begged on behalf of 'thirty heads of state with a king as their messenger' that William I should go to Frankfurt. Once again Bismarck persuaded his reluctant monarch not to go. It was a long struggle between king and minister which left both exhausted. The king had a nervous collapse, Bismarck unwound by smashing glasses in his bedroom.

Prussia's refusal to attend spelt the end of the conference. None of the German princes could consider a federal Germany that excluded Prussia. Austria realized that the dream of a greater Germany under Austrian hegemony could not be achieved. The only possible solution to the German problem was for Austria to cooperate with Prussia. This meant in effect that the dream of a greater Germany was over.

Bismarck had skilfully avoided being outmanoeuvred by Austria and it was now his turn to outmanoeuvre Austria. The crisis in Schleswig-Holstein provided him with the perfect opportunity. When the new king of Denmark, Christian IX, proclaimed a constitution in December 1863 which stated that Schleswig, the majority of whose population was German, was an integral part of Denmark, the German Federation protested at this breach of international law, and Prussian and Austrian troops marched against Denmark in February 1864, enthusiastically supported by the vast majority of Germans of whatever political hue. The Danes were quickly defeated, and Jutland and Alsen were occupied. During the summer a conference was held in London at which the Federation and the Austrians supported the claims of the duke of Augustenburg to the duchies of Schleswig and Holstein. Bismarck, who from the outset intended to annexe the duchies, successfully managed to block this plan, and the conference ended inconclusively. In October 1864 peace was signed in Vienna, and the Danish king handed over Schleswig, Holstein, and Lauenburg to Austria and Prussia. The duchies were now an uneasy condominium in which the Austrians for political, military and geographical reasons were the junior partners. A number of schemes to solve the resulting dilemma were proposed and rejected. Finally, on 14 August 1865 at the Convention of Gastein, Schleswig was given to Prussia, Holstein to Austria, and Austria sold Lauenburg to Prussia for 2.5 million thalers.

By the summer of 1865 Bismarck was determined to go to war with Austria, in alliance with Italy. His own political position was weak. The constitutional crisis which had brought him to power was still unresolved. Anti-Prussian sentiment was rife in Germany, and the duke of Augustenburg was still immensely popular. War was a desperate gamble which might solve all these problems. William I wished to avoid a breach with Austria and was horrified at the idea of an alliance with Italy, which he regarded as an illegitimate and revolutionary state. He therefore ordered Bismarck to try to reach a compromise with Austria. Bismarck simply ignored these instructions and devoted his energies to winning foreign political support for his anti-Austrian course.

On 8 April 1866 an alliance was signed with Italy in Berlin. Italy agreed that, should Prussia go to war with Austria within the next three months, it would immediately attack Austria. Bismarck thus virtually committed Prussia to go to war by July. On 9 April, the day after Bismarck had signed the secret treaty with Italy, Prussia proposed the election of a national assembly by universal suffrage to discuss the future of the Federation. Bismarck was thus appealing directly to the smaller German states and to the liberals. The attempt was a failure. The *National Verein* warned that such a reactionary minister could not possibly create a liberal Germany. Bismarck was not impressed and remarked: 'One does not shoot with public opinion, but with powder and lead.'

With tensions mounting in Germany and the news that the Italians were preparing for war, the Austrians mobilized first their southern and then their northern forces. The Italians urged the Prussians to mobilize, and they obliged in early May. Austria now appealed to the Bundestag to settle the Schleswig-Holstein question and called a meeting of the Holstein Diet. Prussia complained that this was a breach of the Treaty of Gastein and sent troops into Holstein. Austria called for the mobilization of the federal army against Prussia, and a narrow majority voted in favour of the motion.

Prussia faced what at first seemed a formidable coalition of Austria, Bavaria, Württemberg, Baden, Saxony, Hanover, Electoral Hessen, Hessen-Darmstadt, and most of the small central and south German states. But the Austrians failed to coordinate the efforts of their allies. The Prussians moved swiftly against Hanover and Hessen and were soon in possession of Frankfurt. The Prussian chief of staff, von Moltke, sought to fight a decisive battle in Bohemia. The Prussians marched in three armies which joined together in northern Bohemia. The Austrians under Benedek failed to stop the Prussian advance from Dresden and now found themselves trapped near the fortress at Königgrätz. Benedek urged the emperor to

French prisoners captured during the Franco-Prussian War are held in a German prisoner of war camp at Wahner Heide near Cologne. Losses on both sides in the Franco-Prussian war were extremely heavy. The bulk of the French army was encircled at the Battle of Sedan on 2 September 1870 and the Germans took 104,000 prisoners of war, among them the seriously ill Emperor Napoleon III.

seek peace, but Francis Joseph refused. On a rainy 3 July the third Prussian army arrived on the field to help win a decisive victory in which 44,000 Austrians were killed, wounded, or taken prisoner. Prussian losses were 9,200 men. The Prussians now marched on towards Vienna.

In northern Italy the Austrians had better luck, defeating the army at Custozza and the navy at Lissa. All now depended on the attitude of the French, to whom Francis Joseph had appealed on the day of Königgrätz to act as intermediaries. There followed weeks of highly complicated negotiations in which Bismarck pitted his wits against the wily Napoleon III. The compromise which was reached was acceptable to Bismarck. Germany would be divided into three parts: a North German Federation under Prussia would include the newly annexed territories of Schleswig-Holstein, Hanover, electoral Hessen, Nassau, and Frankfurt; a southern German Federation was proposed for Bavaria, Württemberg, Baden, and Hessen-Darmstadt but was rejected by Prussia which preferred to negotiate with separate states and strengthen the ties of the Zollverein; and Austria was now separate and distinct from the rest of Germany. At the peace conference, Saxony was included in the North German Federation with full guarantees of its territorial integrity and sovereignty.

THE FRANCO-PRUSSIAN WAR

As early as August 1866 Bismarck negotiated military conventions with Bavaria, Württemberg, and Baden. Early in the following year a similar treaty was signed with Hessen-Darmstadt. Bismarck had good reason to press for these treaties since at the end of July Napoleon III suddenly demanded a return to the frontiers of 1814 which included Luxembourg, parts of French-speaking Belgium, the Rhineland Palatinate and Rhine Hessen, including Mainz, as compensation for his benevolent disposition towards the North German Federation. The crisis soon blew over, but Bismarck and Moltke were already thinking in terms of a war with France in which Prussia would be supported by the south German states, possibly even by Austria.

The *Zollverein*, and thus Prussian influence in Germany, was further strengthened by the creation of a customs parliament (*Zollparlament*) in which all the member states of the *Zollverein* were represented. Elections were by universal and equal manhood suffrage so that populous Prussia dominated the parliament. Its field of competence included customs, transport, and trade regulation.

Anti-Prussian sentiment was still strong in the south, fuelled by a fear of Prussian domination and Catholic conflict with Protestant Prussia. There were increasing calls for protection against overbearing Prussian industrial might. Elections for the customs parliament were held around New Year, 1867–68, and resulted in a resounding victory for the southern particularists. In Württemberg the popular mood was summed up in a slogan which claimed that all Prussia had to offer was: 'Pay taxes, shut your trap, and become a soldier!' In Catholic Bavaria greater Germans warned of the dangers from the 'Protestant military power' to the north. Yet in spite of these setbacks Prussia was able to get most of the important legislation through the customs parliament, and for all the opposition of southern industrialists and farmers, most shared in the growing prosperity and saw concrete advantages in maintaining links with Prussia. Delbrück, Bismarck's 'chief of general staff for economics', managed to counter south German opposition by negotiating a free trade agreement with Austria in 1868 which denied the south German states the support of their still powerful anti-Prussian neighbour. This treaty was ratified by the customs parliament without too much difficulty.

Only by very skilful diplomacy was it possible to bring the southern German states into the Prussian fold. The defensive alliances with the south German states, the key to Prussian policy, were widely unpopular. In Baden they could be forced through only by emergency decree, and everywhere the increased taxation needed to improve the army was deeply resented, leading to the formation of anti-Prussian, greater-German parties.

Meanwhile, relations between Prussia and France grew steadily worse. Napoleon III had failed to get the massive territorial compensation he felt was his due for his neutrality in 1866. Both sides armed, the Prussians thanks to the 'iron budget' by which the liberals abandoned their right to question military expenditure. The British foreign secretary, Lord Clarendon, called this frantic arms race 'a disgrace to our age and civilization'. Most observers were convinced that war between France and the North German Federation was inevitable, and many thought it desirable. For France war offered the possibility of directing internal political tensions outwards and uniting the nation against a common enemy. For Bismarck war with France was his one chance to complete the process of little German unification on Prussian terms.

In the spring of 1870 the Spanish parliament offered the throne to a member of the house of Hohenzollern-Sigmaringen, a Catholic branch of the Prussian ruling family. The French felt threatened with encirclement by a hostile Prussia. In May the anti-Prussian right in France won a great victory in a plebiscite, and a new foreign minister was appointed; Gramont was a determined opponent of the little German solution. On 21 June the prince of Hohenzollern-Sigmaringen accepted the candidature and this was formally announced on 3 July. In a provocative speech in the chamber of deputies, Gramont openly threatened Prussia with war if this attempt to revive the empire of Charles V was not instantly stopped. On 12 July the prince withdrew his candidature. The French then made an appalling mistake. They had scored a victory over Prussia and the candidature had been withdrawn, but now they wanted to humiliate Prussia to the point of risking a war in which they were without allies or support. They demanded that Prussia should agree never to support any future revival of the Hohenzollern candidature. Napoleon III announced in a newspaper interview that a renewal of the Hohenzollern candidature would mean that France would go to war. Bismarck, confident that neither Britain nor Russia would become involved in a dispute over the Spanish throne, prepared for war. Gramont instructed Benedetti, the French ambassador in Berlin, to visit William I at Bad Ems and request a promise that he would never support or renew the candidature. Benedetti travelled to Bad Ems on 13 July and on the same day Napoleon III and his council of ministers agreed that France would go to war if the guarantee was not forthcoming. Benedetti's behaviour was altogether too much for the Prussian king, who politely but firmly scorned this blatant attempt to humiliate him. A telegram describing these events arrived in Berlin on the same day. Legend has it that Bismarck rewrote and edited the telegram in order to provoke a crisis, but in fact the published version of the telegram was not substantially altered. France had already decided for war before the publication. On 14 July the French army mobilized and on 19 July France formally declared war, having rejected Britain's offer to mediate. In the south German states there was widespread support for Prussia, and they honoured the defensive treaties and went to war in defence of Germany against an aggressive France.

After a series of engagements with a high butcher's bill on both sides, the French army was besieged in Metz and crushed in the battle of Sedan on 2 September. Napoleon III was among the more than 100,000 prisoners taken at Sedan. Yet in spite of these victories the war continued. Léon Gambetta, a bohemian radical, electrifying orator, and ardent republican called for a war of national defence. The Prussians lay siege to Paris and had to contend with a nerve-wracking guerrilla war. The conservative republican, Thiers, made peace with the Prussians on 26 February 1871, but Paris was still under siege, and the radical Commune was proclaimed on 18 March. The troops of the Third Republic now took over the siege, under the watchful eyes of the Germans, and crushed the Commune with exceptional savagery. The war was over and the uneasy Republic had to put up with German occupying troops until 1873.

In October 1870 Bismarck began negotiations with the four south German states over the formation of a new German Federation. By 25 November all four agreed on a German empire with the king of Prussia as its emperor. The treaties were then ratified by the respective parliaments so that the foundation of the new state 'from above' was given a degree of legitimacy 'from below'. The empire was formally constituted on 1 January 1871 in a singularly unspectacular manner. On 18 January 1871 the Grand Duke Frederick I of Baden proclaimed William I German emperor in the Hall of Mirrors in the Palace of Versailles.

Under the new constitution the south German states were virtually annexed by the North German Federation. They received a few more seats in the upper house, the Bundesrat, but Prussia had enough seats to be sure of blocking any constitutional changes. There were twenty-five states in the new federal state, four kingdoms, six grand duchies, five duchies, seven principalities and three free cities. The states had some residual rights. The kingdoms of Prussia, Bavaria, Saxony, and Württemberg each had their own armies which formed a German army under the emperor's supreme command only in time of war. The kingdoms also had the right to levy their own taxes on wines and spirits, and Bavaria and Württemberg had their own postal systems. The emperor's sovereignty resided in the rather mundane fact that he was hereditary chairman of the Bundesrat, but he had considerable powers. He could call and dismiss the Bundesrat and the lower house (Reichstag) and he appointed the chancellor and the secretaries of state.

There was remarkably little enthusiasm for the elections for the first Reichstag. Only 51 per cent of the electorate voted and the decision was indecisive. The National Liberals with 125 of the 382 seats were the big winners. Along with thirty Old Liberals and forty-six Progressives they could form a majority. Bismarck's supporters among the Free Conservatives won a mere thirty-seven seats; the Conservatives who were more critical of the chancellor received fifty-seven seats. The Catholic Centre party won sixty-three seats. The first meeting was held in the royal palace in Berlin. The kaiser sat on the throne of Henry III, which had been brought from Goslar for the occasion, and gave the Reichstag its marching orders in a speech prepared by Bismarck. He was surrounded by princes and generals in gala uniform so that the dreary parliamentarians appeared to be no more than insignificant bystanders.

Most Germans, inspired by the stunning victories of von Moltke's army, welcomed the new empire euphorically. Businessmen grew rich, soldiers basked in the glory of their victorious campaigns, intellectuals were fired by nationalist fervour. But others had their doubts. Prussian conservatives feared that their

German troops parade down the Champs Elysées in Paris on 1 March 1871 to celebrate the victory over France in the Franco-Prussian War of 1870–71.

beloved country would henceforth be a mere province in a country ruled by universal suffrage and dominated by a greedy and coarse bourgeoisie. Some south German Catholics resented the disproportionate power of the Protestant north.

The German empire was an authoritarian state and its parliament, although elected by universal manhood suffrage, had limited powers. The power of the monarchy was untouched, the nobility retained their privileged position, and the army was further strengthened. Bismarck's revolution from above had manipulated liberalism and nationalism to protect the traditional elites and to frustrate the democratic forces. Germany was politically, economically, and militarily immensely powerful, but it was seriously flawed. A modern bourgeois and capitalist society existed within the framework of an archaic and autocratic state. The tensions and contradictions within the empire were soon to lead to military defeat, social upheaval, and political bankruptcy.

The German headquarters in Versailles in 1870 are painted (1900) by Anton von Werner. *From left to right:* Blumenthal, Crown Prince Frederick, Verdy du Vernois, William I, Moltke, Roon and Bismarck.

CHAPTER 9   *The German Empire*

One of the first major problems facing the new empire was the question of the relationship between the state and the Catholic Church. During the election campaign the Centre Party had suggested that German troops should be sent to Rome to protect the pope, French troops having left in September 1870. The Prussian government supported the pope as a conservative force in the modern world and offered him a safe haven should he be obliged to go into exile, but the Catholic Church was often an uneasy element within the modern secular state.

The Prussian-German empire was strongly flavoured with Protestantism. Most Catholics had made their peace with the little German Reich but, much to Bismarck's distress, they strongly supported the rights of the member states. By contrast, Polish Catholics and their co-religionists in Alsace and Lorraine were antagonistic towards the empire. The situation was further complicated by the fact that the German Catholic Church was divided between the 'Old Catholics' who refused to accept the decisions of the Vatican Council of 1869–70 including the new dogma of papal infallibility, and those who remained faithful to the teachings of the Church.

The struggle against the Catholic Church, the *Kulturkampf*, was fought in the individual states, not in the Reich. The 'Pulpit Paragraph', which passed through the Reichstag in 1871, made political agitation in sermons illegal, and remained in force until 1953. The Prussian May Laws of 1873 put religious schools under strict state control. In other Prussian measures, which were copied in many of the other states, civil marriage was made compulsory, the Jesuit order was banned, the state was given a say in Church appointments, and state payments to the Church were stopped. The Vatican ordered the German bishops to ignore these measures; the state responded by arresting and exiling a number of prominent clerics.

Bismarck had to make various concessions to the liberals in order to maintain their support in his struggle against the Catholic Church. He had to agree to certain changes in criminal and commercial law and control of the press, that went rather too far for his taste. Persecution of the Church only served to strengthen the Centre Party, and was opposed by most conservatives, who objected to the limitations on the influence of landowners over local schools and saw the attack on the Church as an example of Godless liberalism. By 1875 Bismarck had begun to realize that the *Kulturkampf* had been a serious mistake.

THE FOUNDATION OF THE REICH

Bismarck wished to avoid a repetition of the Prussian constitutional crisis by proposing an '*Äternat*' (everlasting law) which would mean that the Reichstag would relinquish its control over the military budget. Since this amounted to 90 per cent of the budget, the liberals were determined to stop this measure. They demanded the creation of a federal ministry of war with a minister responsible to the Reichstag. Bismarck threatened to dissolve the Reichstag and announced that he would resign if the crisis was not ended. The liberals, as usual, began to get cold feet and sought a compromise. The result was the 'Septennat' by which the demands of the military were to be met for the next seven years.

The foundation of the Reich was followed by a period of frantic economic activity until 1873. Then industry was faced with a crisis of over-production, and the money market with over-speculation. In May 1873 the Vienna stock exchange collapsed, German investors became increasingly nervous, and banks ran into serious difficulties. There was competition from cheap foreign grain imports, much of it coming from North America. Agrarians and industrialists began to agitate for protective tariffs and an end to liberal free-trading policies. In November 1873 industrialists in the Rhineland and Westphalia formed the Association of German Steel and Iron Industrialists (*Verein deutscher Stahl- und Eisenindustrieller*) which became a nationwide lobby calling for increased railway-building, no further tariff cuts, and a reduction in the price of coke. They were supported by the appropriately titled 'Long-Name Association' (*Verein zur Wahrung der gemeinsamen wirt-*

schaftlichen Interessen in Rheinland und Westfalen – Association for the Protection of the Economic Interests of the Rhineland and Westphalia). The master strategist behind this movement was Henry Axel Bueck, secretary-general of the Long-Name Association who, in 1876, became secretary of the Central Association of German Industrialists (*Zentralverband Deutscher Industriellen*), a radical group of protectionists. Bueck, who owned an estate in the east, formed a protectionist alliance between the 'smoke-stack barons' in industry and the 'cabbage junkers' on the land. He was the first to see that public opinion could be manipulated and members of parliament be influenced on behalf of sectional interests. He was thus the founding father of the anti-democratic pluralism of interest groups which was characteristic of imperial Germany. The Navy and Army Leagues, the Colonial League, and the Pan-Germans agitated outside the framework of parliament, diverting political energy from the strengthening and extension of parliamentary democracy and civil liberties.

In 1875 Bismarck also suffered his first major foreign policy setback. In response to a vote in the French chamber of deputies in favour of a substantial increase in the army, the semi-official Berlin newspaper *Die Post* published an article under the provocative headline 'Is War in Sight?' The Prussian general staff viewed such a prospect with equanimity, but Bismarck merely wanted to humiliate France

Prince Bismarck 'the Iron Chancellor', portrayed in uniform by Franz von Lenbach (1836–1904). This is one of Lenbach's many portraits of the chancellor that combine technical brilliance with profound psychological insight. Bismarck was born in Schonhausen in Brandenburg in 1815. He was an ultra-royalist member of the Prussian parliament in 1848. In 1851 he became Prussian envoy to the Bundestag in Frankfurt. In 1862 he was appointed minister-president of Prussia. In 1871 he became chancellor of the New German empire and was made a prince. He resigned in 1890 and died in 1898.

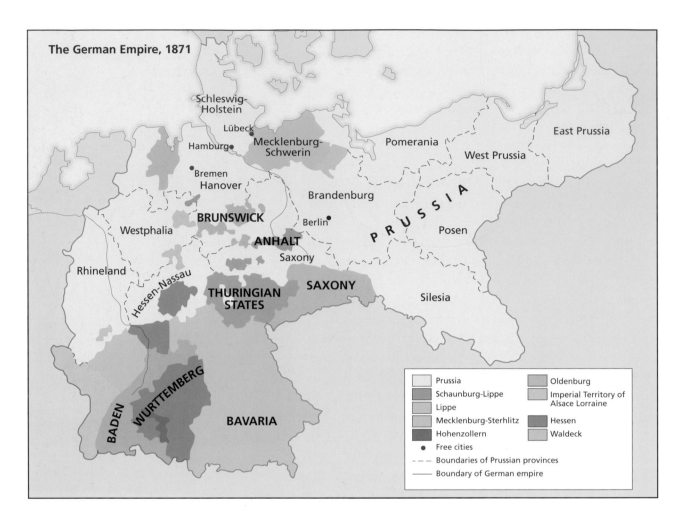

diplomatically. This was a serious miscalculation. The French foreign minister, the Duc de Decazes, skilfully set about winning support, and the Austrians, although still loyal to Berlin, joined France in urging the British to act as intermediaries. Bismarck was left isolated, the governments in London, St Petersburg, Rome, and Paris forced him to back down. Bismarck's foreign policy had now reached a turning point. Germany clearly could not seek to dominate Europe, it had to be content with what it had and respect the interests of the other powers. Bismarck commented on the War in Sight crisis: 'A strong Germany wishes to be left in peace and to develop peacefully', for this to be possible Germany had to maintain a strong army since 'one does not attack someone whose dagger is loose in the sheath'.

In the summer of 1875 Bosnia and Herzegovina rose up against the Ottoman Empire. Serbia, Montenegro, and Bulgaria soon followed suit. The Turks crushed these rebellions with great savagery, but in 1877 Russia declared war on the Ottomans and forced Romania to assist in the campaign to drive the Turks from Europe. Peace was concluded at San Stefano in March 1878, and a greater Bulgaria was created which stretched to the Aegean.

The proclamation of William as emperor

In 1870 Chancellor Otto Bismarck persuaded the south German states to accept the constitution of the North German Confederation, and a series of treaties to that effect were signed in November. The southern states were allowed to reserve certain rights and a constitutional debate was thereby avoided. The constitution of the German Reich went into effect on 1 January 1871. The new constitution of 16 April 1871 merely formalized the residual rights of the states and apportioned representation in the upper house, the Bundesrat.

The king of Prussia was proclaimed as emperor in Versailles on 18 January 1871 — a day of particular significance because it had been the coronation day of the first Prussian king, Frederick I. The Sun King's palace was a military headquarters, and most of the German princes were in uniform for the coronation. Anton von Werner's painting (*below*) captures the martial aspects of the event. The German empire had been founded by blood and iron as the result of a victory over France — it was thus neither a peaceful nor a democratic process, and this was reflected in the ceremony. The kaiser was proclaimed by the princes, as medieval kings had been.

William I had serious reservations about becoming 'German Emperor'. He wanted to be called 'Emperor of Germany' and was outraged when Bismarck argued that the title would be unacceptable to the princes. On the eve of the proclamation William said: 'Tomorrow is the unhappiest day in my life. We will bury the Prussian monarchy and you, Prince Bismarck, are responsible!'

The princes were also far from enthusiastic, fearing that liberals might thrive in the new Reich. Ludwig II of Bavaria had to be handsomely bribed from Bismarck's 'Guelph Fund' — the money that had been seized from Hanover in 1866. Ludwig's brother Prince Otto was present at the ceremony and reported: 'I cannot tell you how incredibly sad and pained I felt during this scene... Everything was so cold, proud, glittering, showy, boastful, heartless, and empty.'

The proclamation of King William I as emperor in the Hall of Mirrors, Versailles, by Anton von Werner.

In the midst of these events Bismarck composed a lengthy memorandum at Bad Kissingen in which he agreed with the French journalist who had said that he suffered from '*le cauchemar des coalitions*' (the nightmare of coalitions). He hoped Britain would become deeply involved in Egypt, after Disraeli's purchase of the Suez canal shares, and that Russia would be engaged in the Black Sea. Both powers would be locked in rivalry, making it impossible for them to join together in an anti-German coalition. The rivalry between Russia and Austria in the Balkans meant that Russia needed Germany's support, while Anglo-French colonial rivalry meant that Britain could also be brought on board. His ideal was that 'all the powers with the exception of France need us, and as far as possible will be stopped from forming coalitions against us as a result of their relations one with another'.

The Russian victory over the Ottoman empire was highly alarming to both Britain and Austria, and both powers made it clear that they were considering war. The Russians, knowing that they would lose such a conflict, began negotiations in London in which they agreed to give up much of what they had won at San Stefano. These terms were to be ratified at an international conference in Berlin which opened on 13 June 1878, presided over by Bismarck. Many of the Russian conquests were restored to Turkey, the administration of Bosnia and Herzegovina was left to Austria, and a grateful sultan offered Britain Cyprus.

The reaction of the Pan-Slavs was harsh, and the watchful Russian censors allowed countless attacks on the chancellor to appear in the Russian press. Bismarck was once again haunted by the *cauchemar des coalitions*, the worst nightmare of all being a possible alliance between Russia, Austria, and France. In a fit of near panic Bismarck proposed first a customs union with Austria then, when it was refused, a defensive treaty. William I was appalled at this break with the pro-Russian tradition of Prussian foreign policy and warned that it could lead to an alliance between tsarist Russia and republican France. He stressed the weakness of an Austria that would never be able to set its house in order, and pointed out that Britain's attitude to Germany was uncertain.

Bismarck brushed aside these shrewd objections, arguing that he proposed a purely defensive alliance which could well be more of an attraction than a threat to Russia. The danger of Pan-Slavism would be checked, the line to Russia would soon be opened again, Austria could no longer contemplate an alliance with France, and Britain, he insisted, would be favourably disposed towards the Dual Alliance between Austria and Germany concluded on 7 October 1879. There were two fatal errors in this assessment. Russia and Austria had diametrically opposed interests in the Balkans, and the British showed no

Caricature of the League of the Three Emperors. Bismarck is seen manipulating Tsar Alexander III, Francis Joseph of Austria-Hungary and the German emperor William I. In fact, Bismarck's attempts to placate the Russians were unsuccessful.

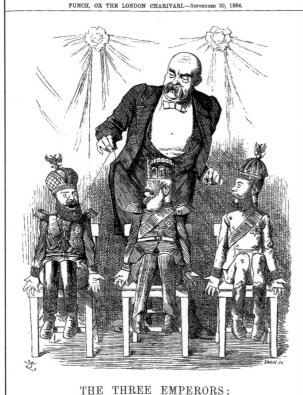

PUNCH, OR THE LONDON CHARIVARI.—September 20, 1884.

THE THREE EMPERORS;

OR, THE VENTRILOQUIST OF VARZIN!

enthusiasm whatsoever for the Dual Alliance. Germany and Russia were soon locked in a bitter tariff battle, and the general staffs of both powers continued their planning for a preventive war.

The Dual Alliance was an agreement that Germany and Austria would stand together in the event of an attack by Russia. Should France attack Germany, Austria would remain neutral and would only go to war if Russia attacked. Bismarck was quick to see that this defensive alliance could easily be turned into an offensive alliance if either Germany or Austria provoked the *casus belli*. In numerous memoranda he warned of this danger, but he came to realize that if Austria was in danger of defeat, even in a war which it had begun, Germany would have to go to its defence. Austria had to remain a great power if the balance of power in Europe was to be maintained.

Bismarck had hardly signed the Dual Alliance when he began to look for other options in what was later to be idealized as the 'game with five balls'. In March 1881 the tsar was assassinated and Russia plunged into a political crisis as the hunt began for terrorists and anarchists who enjoyed the sympathy of much of the bourgeoisie and intelligentsia. The Russian foreign minister Giers was pro-German, and negotiations to revive the Three Emperors' League, between Austria-Hungary, Russia, and Germany, were swiftly concluded on 18 July 1881. The three powers agreed to remain benevolently neutral in the event of a war with a fourth power, even if that war had been started by one of the signatories. Bismarck thus secured Russian neutrality in the event of a war with France. But the agreement was soon in ruins as a result of the Bulgarian crisis.

The crisis, which began in 1885, faced Germany with a two-front war. The war between Serbia and Bulgaria threatened to involve both Russia and Austria, their respective allies. Russian troops were moved up to the frontier and began a series of aggressive manoeuvres. Meanwhile in France the minister of war, Boulanger, began to clamour for revenge against Germany, and the chamber of deputies agreed a sizable increase in military expenditure. The Germans knew of the staff talks between the Russians and French and of the export of French weapons to Russia. Germany was painfully aware of its vulnerability as a middle European power.

Bismarck countered the French threat by expanding the army; this acted as an effective deterrent. Russia proved to be a more difficult problem. In 1885 increased German tariffs reduced the import of Russian wheat and rye by 50 per cent. In early 1887 the Russian government forbade foreigners to own land in the western provinces, resulting in the expropriation of numerous Germans. The Germans countered with the 'Lombard Ban' which prohibited advances against Russian securities. The Russians then moved their money from Berlin to Paris, granting the French government a loan of 100 million francs to help finance the army increases. In December 1887 the German tariffs on rye and wheat were again increased.

In the midst of this crisis Bismarck managed to negotiate the Reinsurance Treaty with Russia which was signed on 18 June 1887. The Russians promised to remain neutral in the event of a war between Germany and France. In spite of the Dual Alliance the eventuality of a war between Austria and Russia was not mentioned. Bismarck also expressed his sympathy for Russian ambitions in the Bosphorus and Dardanelles, for he was convinced that this would bring Russia into conflict with Britain to Germany's advantage. The Reinsurance Treaty, regarded by Bismarckians as a perfect example of his diplomatic genius, was a hopelessly contradictory and temporary measure designed to meet an immediate crisis.

Bismarck was convinced that for there to be lasting European stability Britain had to be brought into the Dual Alliance. In 1889 he proposed a military alliance to Lord Salisbury, but this was turned down flat. Britain could settle colonial questions with Germany but had no interest in being tied to an unpredictable state in the middle of Europe between the two basically hostile powers of Russia and France. Bismarck's hope that rivalry between Russia and Britain might oblige the British to reconsider and make a commitment to the Dual Alliance proved vain. Bismarck's policy for European security was thus based on wishful thinking. The five balls could not be kept in the air and Germany was to lose its freedom of action.

The kaiser grants Chancellor Bismarck an audience. Lithograph after a painting by Konrad Siemenroth (1854–1915). Although Bismarck was a devoted monarchist his relationship with William I was often tempestuous. He would use every histrionic device and form of blackmail to get his way. In a number of instances William's reservations about his Chancellor's politics were proven justified.

BISMARCK'S DOMESTIC POLICY

Not only were the foundations of Bismarck's foreign policy laid in 1878–79 with the Dual Alliance, these years also mark a fundamental change in domestic politics which has often been described as the Reich's 'second foundation'. In 1874 a simple-minded journeyman cooper took a pot-shot at Bismarck in Bad Kissingen. The youth confessed that he sympathized with the Centre Party, and Bismarck seized the opportunity to introduce a bill in the Reichstag strictly controlling all associations and clubs. The bill was rejected and replaced by a loosely worded amendment to the criminal code, known by its opponents as the 'rubber paragraphs', restricting the freedoms of the press and of association. Eduard Lasker, the brilliant and principled liberal opponent of the chancellor, led the opposition to the new bill, and once again it was rejected. Bismarck now appealed to public opinion, already made uncertain by the onset of a major recession, painting a horrific picture of liberals and Socialists determined to overthrow the state, backed by a majority in an irresponsible Reichstag. By such means his defeats in the Reichstag were turned into a political victory.

In the elections of 1877 Lasker and his left liberals lost their key position in the Reichstag, and the centre of gravity moved to the right. Some conservatives were now calling for protective tariffs against foreign grain, right-wing liberals for protective tariffs for industry. For Bismarck there was a further advantage in increasing tariffs which went beyond the possible formation of a centre-right majority in the Reichstag. Tariffs were indirect taxes which were paid to the Reich. A substantial increase in indirect taxation might mean that the government would no longer have to go cap in hand to the states for the 'matricular payments', subsidies paid by the states to the federal government.

On 11 May 1878 a deranged carpenter tried to shoot the kaiser as he drove along Unter den Linden in Berlin. Bismarck announced, without a shred of evidence, that the would-be assassin was associated with the Social Democratic Party (SPD), a party made up of Marxists, Lassalleans, and sundry idealists which had held its founding conference in Gotha in 1875. He now demanded an anti-Socialist law and denounced all who opposed the suggestion as sympathetic to regicide. On behalf of the right liberals, the National Liberal member Bennigsen correctly argued that the proposed law amounted to a 'war against the Reichstag', and again Bismarck was denied a parliamentary majority.

Yet another madman came to Bismarck's rescue. On 2 June 1878 one Dr Nobiling, an unemployed scholar, aimed his shotgun at the kaiser and wounded an eighteen-year-old officer. Bismarck saw this new assassination attempt as a golden opportunity to dissolve the Reichstag, bring in the anti-Socialist laws, destroy the liberals and get a majority for his tariff reform. In the Bundesrat, Baden voiced its objection to the dissolution of the Reichstag. Bismarck insisted that he needed to have unanimity and threatened to resign or to overthrow the constitution by coup d'état. The Bundesrat complied, and the elections of 30 July 1878 returned 106 conservatives and 125 liberals, the Centre Party thus determining the majority. The SPD won nine seats to its previous twelve.

'The rolling-mill' by Adolph von Menzel (1815–1905). A striking industrial painting by a virtuoso artist who is best remembered for his representations of fashionable life and historical scenes.

Everything now depended on the attitude of the Centre Party. It detested the SPD for its atheism and materialism, but memories of the *Kulturkampf* were too vivid for it to be enthusiastic about emergency laws. As a result the anti-Socialist laws were more symbolic than effective. The party was banned, meetings were forbidden, and Socialists were denied a publican's license; but SPD candidates could still be elected to the Reichstag. Socialist members continued to launch their tirades against the system, and party conferences were held in Switzerland where papers were published and distributed throughout Germany.

It proved only marginally easier for Bismarck to get a majority for the protective tariffs. A powerful interest group, the Free Economic Association (*Frei Wirtschaftliche Vereinigung*), had 204 members among the Reichstag deputies, but powerful groups opposed the tariffs. Most Prussian landowners felt that their export markets would hold up and that the threat of cheap grain from Russia and North America was exaggerated. Furthermore they feared that higher tariffs would only help the industrialists, whom they detested as vulgar parvenus who soiled their hands with trade. Free conservatives wanted a drastic reduction of direct taxes to compensate for the increase in indirect ones. The Centre Party, always concerned about states' rights, was worried that the increased revenues going to the Reich would leave the states without any budgetary powers. Left liberals and Socialists knew that increased indirect taxes would further hurt the poor, who were already suffering from the effects of the depression.

The Centre Party was won over by assurances that the *Kulturkampf* would be toned down or even ended, and by the acceptance of an ingenious formula known as the Franckenstein Clause whereby any income in excess of 130 million marks going to the Reich from customs duties would be divided up among the states, who would then return the necessary funds through the matricular contributions. The budgetary rights of the states were thus preserved.

The tariffs were remarkably low and were not yet protective: 10 to 15 per cent on industrial goods, less for agricultural produce. It was not until 1885 and 1887, after enormous efforts by Bismarck, that they were raised to protective levels. The tariff increases of 1879 were nevertheless enormously important in that they marked the beginnings of the alliance between agriculture and industry, between rye and iron, which was to be the cornerstone of Wilhelmine politics. The break with the liberals who remained faithful to their creed was final and irrevocable. The free-trading ministers all resigned, including the ministers of finance and agriculture as well as Falk, the minister of education who master-minded the *Kulturkampf*. The Centre Party, with its ability to tip the scales, was now in a powerful position, but the brief golden age of the Reichstag had passed. Politics was now a matter of interest groups, lobbyists, and cheap compromises.

If the anti-Socialist laws were the stick, social insurance was the carrot. Germany lagged far behind England in legislation controlling labour conditions, and France's social security system was far more advanced. Bismarck hoped that a pension scheme would turn the working class into loyal and conservative *rentiers*. State socialism was, in Bismarck's view, the best antidote to social democracy. The first measure to pass the Reichstag was the health insurance bill of 1883 which provided sickness benefits from the third day of a sickness for a maximum of thirteen weeks. Accident insurance was introduced in 1884 after three years of debate. Benefits amounted to two-thirds of average earnings and began in the fourteenth week when sickness benefits ceased. It was a no fault insurance, administered by cooperative associations of employers (*Berufsgenossenschaften*). In 1889 the Disability and Old Age Pension Act became law. The pensions were very modest, by 1914 averaging 152 marks per year. The average annual industrial wage in 1913 was 1,083 marks.

None of these schemes was universal or generous, and they were therefore resented by workers and employers alike. The legislation did nothing to stop the growth of social democracy, since social control rather than emancipation from hardship was its guiding principle. Nevertheless Bismarck's social legislation was far superior to similar measures in France or Britain, and did provide a basis for further reform.

COLONIAL POLICY

In 1881 Bismarck announced: 'There will be no colonial policy as long as I am chancellor', even though in the previous year he had tried to bale out a German firm whose business in the South Seas had gone far into the red. Yet in 1884–85 Germany established colonies in South-West Africa, East Africa, Togo and Cameroon, New Guinea, the Bismarck Archipelago, the Solomons, and the Marshalls. The motives behind Bismarck's imperialism were many and varied. In part it was a response to problems created by the great depression. Colonies were expensive, tiresome, and potential sources of irritation, but it was assumed that they would provide markets for German goods, assure supplies of raw materials, and afford openings to markets in Africa and the Pacific.

Bismarck was also keenly aware that colonialism could divert attention away from Germany's exposed position in central Europe, and also divert the attention of disgruntled Germans away from domestic politics by exciting their imagination with a vision of an overseas mission. Through colonialism the country might be bound together again as it had been in 1871. Bismarck used colonialism in the election campaign of 1884 to discredit his critics for their lack of vision and patriotism, and to undermine the position of the crown prince, whose liberal and pro-British views could be countered by anti-British jibes.

Almost all these calculations proved to be false. Germany's position in central Europe was weakened by colonies that could not be defended without building a vast fleet, which in turn would lead to far more serious complications. Economically the colonies were a disappointment. Only 0.1 per cent of the value of German exports went to the colonies and only 0.1 per cent of total imports came

A German colonial administrator in tropical uniform with a cigar and walking-stick surrounded by his boys c.1905. Germany's colonial adventures in the late nineteenth century proved to be a drain on the Reich's resources, and Bismarck preferred to concentrate on European politics.

from them. By 1905 only 2 per cent of Germany's foreign investments were in the colonies, which were inhabited by a mere 6,000 Germans, most of them civil servants and soldiers. A few arms-dealers, schnapps distillers and manufacturers of cheap cloth made some money, but the expense to the Reich was very high. By the end of his chancellorship Bismarck was disillusioned with imperialism, and the exchange with Britain of Zanzibar for Helgoland in 1890 indicated his desire to concentrate on European affairs.

WILLIAM II 'THE KAISER'

William I died in the spring of 1888 at the age of ninety-one and was succeeded by his son, Frederick William, who reigned for a mere ninety-nine days as Frederick III. The new kaiser was a liberal, a great admirer of the British constitution, and was married to Queen Victoria's eldest daughter. Cancer of the throat relieved Bismarck from the fear of a 'German Gladstone ministry', but with Frederick III were buried the hopes for a liberal Germany and an accommodation with Britain which would secure Germany's precarious position. Nietzsche described his death as a great and decisive misfortune for Germany.

Frederick III's son, William II, was also a great and decisive misfortune for his country. Described by his English uncle, King Edward VII, as 'the most brilliant failure in history', William II was highly talented but superficial, a neurotic braggart and romantic dreamer, a militaristic poseur, passionate slaughterer of wild animals, and father of seven children. He was happiest in the exclusive circle of his homosexual and transvestite intimates. His loathing of England was dictated by a feeling of inferiority and by his hatred of his English mother whom he placed under house arrest as soon as his father died. This contradictory, blustering, and insecure figure embodied all the contradictions of the Germany of his day.

William II was twenty-nine when he succeeded to the throne and he had already made it plain that he wished to escape from under the shadow of a chancellor who was forty-four years his senior. He told his cronies: 'I'll let the old boy potter along for another six months, then I'll rule myself.' The major conflict between kaiser and chancellor was over social policy. William II wished to be known as the 'social kaiser' who won the working class away from the Socialists and secured their loyalty by his concern for their welfare. His ideas were confused and ill-considered borrowings from the court preacher, Stoecker, who felt that social reform, Protestantism, and a healthy dose of anti-Semitism were enough to seduce the working-class. William II thus opposed Bismarck's request that the anti-Socialist laws be renewed and stiffened, and urged a conciliatory approach to the great miners' strike of 1889. He argued that the Germans, unlike the British, 'had ignored their workers, squeezed them like lemons and let them rot on the muck heap' and proposed an international conference to discuss working conditions. Bismarck said that this was cheap toadying to the lowest classes and an absurd attempt to make everybody happy. In order to keep William II from intriguing with his colleagues, Bismarck reminded the kaiser of a cabinet decree of 1852 which said that ministers could have an audience with the king only after they had received permission from the minister-president. To this William II replied publicly: 'I shall destroy anyone who stands in my way!'

The Reichstag elections on 20 February 1890 resulted in a defeat for Bismarck's cartel of liberals and conservatives and the chancellor now proposed to overthrow the constitution and rule without the Reichstag, if necessary by a coup d'état. Bismarck was defeated by the universal suffrage he had introduced, and by the Prussian king whose powers he had enhanced. He had no support for such drastic measures among politicians, generals, civil servants, or businessmen, and handed in his resignation on 18 March 1890. The young kaiser gladly accepted it.

Most people were relieved that the pilot had been dropped and applauded the kaiser when he announced: 'The course remains the same, full steam ahead!' Once it was clear that the course was not quite the same, and as dissatisfaction with the government grew, Bismarck became an almost mythical figure. It was widely believed that under 'the Iron Chancellor' things had been much better, an article of faith on the right that was reinforced by the publication of the old man's memoirs, a literary masterpiece as well as a devastating and mendacious critique of his successors. Protestant Germany was soon peppered with bombastic Bismarck memorials, totemic tributes to a man who had put Germany on the path to national glory. It was not long before that path ended in disaster.

Kaiser William II poses in full dress uniform for a photograph taken in about 1900. William II personfied the least attractive aspects of the Germany of his day. Convinced that his was a world-historical mission, he consistently overestimated his considerable abilities. He lacked a sense of proportion and combined bombastic arrogance with a nagging sense of inferiority. He was to lead his country to disaster.

The new chancellor, Lieutenant General Leo von Caprivi, was an outstanding soldier, but had only limited political experience, gained as head of the admiralty. He was a moderate who disliked imperialism, felt that a large fleet would be suicidal, and aimed to alleviate social conflicts and tensions. He intended to bring in further social legislation, reduce the price of food, encourage industrial exports, and stem the yearly drain of 100,000 emigrants – talented and conscientious people who contributed so much to the economies and cultures of the United States and Canada. He was disliked by the conservative agrarians for his attempt to reach a trade agreement with Russia whereby German industrial goods would be exchanged for Russian corn; they referred to him as the 'chancellor without an acre or a blade of grass' (*ohne Ahr und Halm*). Imperialists objected to the Helgoland-Zanzibar treaty with Britain and responded by founding the Pan-German League, the most strident of the interest groups in imperial Germany. Caprivi attempted to achieve a moderate consensus at home including the SPD, to increase exports of industrial goods, and to improve relations with Russia and reach an agreement with England. He failed because of the fickleness of the kaiser, the power of the right-wing interest groups, and the impossibility of integrating the Social Democratic Party into the political life of the empire. In 1895 the kaiser described the SDP as 'a gang of people who do not deserve to be called Germans'.

Caprivi did not have the freedom of manoeuvre to liberate Germany from the *cauchemar des coalitions*. Russia and France began military talks in 1892 and in the following year signed a trade agreement. The Russians then announced that any country that did not afford them most favoured nation status would face additional tariffs of 20 to 30 per cent. The Bundesrat responded to this defiant gesture by increasing the tariff on Russian goods by 50 per cent. The Russians responded in kind and virtually closed their ports to German ships by astronomic increases in harbour dues. Trade between the two countries came to a virtual stand-still. The Russian fleet visited Toulon in 1893 and shortly afterwards the military convention was ratified.

Since Germany was Russia's most valuable trading partner, this situation caused an intolerable strain on the Russian economy. Negotiations to end the tariff war began in 1893 and were completed the following year when each side offered the other most favoured nation status. The trade war was over, but Russia's military convention with France was still in force. Caprivi faced further barrages from the conservatives and the Farmers' League (*Bund der Landwirte*), for ruining agriculture which was said to be the backbone of the nation, the source of true Prussian values. At the court, intrigues were mounted against the chancellor whose position became hopelessly weak.

In 1892 the Prussian minister of education, Zedlitz-Trützschler, had proposed an educational reform which would give the churches considerable influence over the schools. Caprivi's aim was to win over the Centre Party in the Reichstag by this concession and placate the kaiser, who insisted that the schools should emphasize traditional values so as to counter pernicious modern philosophies like socialism. Prussian liberals condemned the proposed legislation as a serious threat to academic freedom, the proposal was withdrawn and the minister resigned. Caprivi also resigned as Prussian minister-president and the office was given to an ultra-conservative, Botho von Eulenburg. The separation of the offices of Prussian minister-president and Reich chancellor, which had happened once briefly under Bismarck, was fatal.

Two years later the Prussian government suffered another major setback. Botho von Eulenburg proposed an 'Anti-Revolution Bill' (*Umsturzvorlage*) in the Bundesrat, an absurd move, as there was no possibility of obtaining a majority for such a measure in the Reichstag. The kaiser contemplated a coup d'état. Both Eulenburg and Caprivi resigned. The chancellor wanted an opening to the left and social harmony, rather than confrontation as proposed by Eulenburg and the Prussian minister of finance, Miquel, who was patching together a right-wing coalition under the slogan 'concentration politics' (*Sammlungspolitik*). The bill was the object of the first debate in the new Reichstag building which was opened in December 1894. It was defeated. The crisis only served to harden the fronts. On the one side stood the authoritarian state and its supporters among the conservatives and right liberals, engaged in a frantic witch-hunt against Socialists and left liberals, who were seen as Godless revolutionaries and enemies of the state. On the other side there were those who remained true to democratic principles and who wished to make Germany into a properly functioning parliamentary democracy.

The anti-revolution bill was a clear demonstration that William II had abandoned his idea of becoming the 'social kaiser'. He was now committed to the ideas of the reactionary steel baron Carl Ferdinand von Stumm-Halberg, and believed in industrial paternalism, the industrialist as 'master in his own house' who looked after the material and spiritual needs of his workers much like the traditional Junker on his estate. Strikes amounted to treason, and anything that remotely resembled socialism had to be extirpated. The new chancellor, Prince Chlodwig zu Hohenlohe-Schillingsfürst, admitted in his first address to the Reichstag that he had no programme. In fact this ancient Catholic of impeccable pedigree was the front man for 'King' Stumm.

In 1895 the Prussian ministry of education learnt that the young physicist Martin Arons, who was teaching at Berlin University, was a member of the SPD and spent some of his considerable fortune in supporting a Socialist monthly journal. The ministry demanded that he be dismissed. The great economist Gustav Schmoller replied on behalf of the university that there was no legal grounds for such a blatant attack on academic freedom. The government then pushed through the 'Lex Arons' which gave it the right to dismiss the likes of Dr Arons. There followed two years of struggle between the ministry and the university which finally ended with the dismissal of Arons and a triumph for the anti-Socialists and anti-Semites.

The 'Lex Heinze', an attempt to strengthen the censorship laws, failed in the Reichstag in 1900 thanks to the determined opposition of the liberals and Social Democrats. The distinguished military historian, Hans Delbrück, concluded that liberal Germany needed the Socialists. A party which still talked of revolution and the dictatorship of the proletariat was the strongest upholder of liberal freedoms against bigoted Catholics and Pecksniffian conservatives.

Miquel's *Sammlungspolitik* was based on an uneasy coalition of agrarians and industrialists, held together by a common fear of socialism and a determination to keep the liberals and the Centre Party in their place. It masqueraded as a non-political movement in defence of 'national labour' in the loyal service of the 'personal regiment' of William II. The fragility of this coalition was exposed when the conservatives rejected a proposal to build a canal joining the Rhine, Weser, and Elbe. The agrarians argued that this would increase the flow of cheap foreign grain, benefit industry, and thus attract workers away from agriculture to the industrial centres. Although the kaiser was a passionate canal enthusiast, the conservatives and the Farmers' League ensured that the measure was defeated in 1899 and again in 1901. In 1904 a compromise was reached which gave the agrarians the assurances that the state would control the towing fees in their interest and that the canal was not to go as far as the Elbe. The Centre Party's consent to this measure was won by lifting the ban on the Jesuits. In return the Centre agreed to waive the Franckenstein clause to help the Reich out of its financial misery.

Agrarians and industrialists also disagreed about 'world politics' (*Weltpolitik*), the raucous new phase of German imperialism. Bernhard von Bülow, a vain, ambitious, and smooth diplomat who was appointed secretary of state for foreign affairs in 1897, announced in the Reichstag: 'The days when the Germans left the land to one of their neighbours and the sea to the other, keeping only the sky for themselves and when pure theory reigned are now over... We do not wish to put anyone in the shade, but we also demand our place in the sun.' Bülow's first place in the sun was China. Germany took a valuable coaling station, and built the Chinese an excellent German brewery, and the powers were not concerned. His next move was to propose the 'Baghdad Railway', which was to run from Berlin to Baghdad. This would give Germany a powerful strategic position in the Ottoman empire, and opened up the prospect of developing Mesopotamia and continuing the railway line to the oilfields and to the Persian Gulf at Basra. The railway made slow progress, largely due to financial problems and was far from completion by the time World War I began.

Bismarck realized that good relations with Britain were the key to Germany's security. The half-English William II with his neurotic hatred of the British was quite incapable of exploiting the possibilities offered as Britain gradually emerged from splendid isolation. In January 1896 the kaiser sent President Krüger a telegram congratulating him on his defence of the Boer republic against Dr Jameson's raid. British feathers were ruffled by this clumsy diplomatic move, and

The Berlin stock exchange in the Burgstrasse, a building designed by Friedrich Hitzig (1859–64). The shortage of capital in Germany was largely blamed on the poor performance of the Berlin stock exchange. This was in turn blamed on the excessive regulations and stamp duties necessitated by the Stock Exchange Act of 1896. This much-criticized legislation was characteristically described by the kaiser as 'idiotic'. Investors found that more lucrative opportunities were available outside Germany.

suspicions about the motives behind the opening of the Kiel canal in the previous year, which allowed German warships to pass from the Baltic Sea to the North Sea, were further fuelled.

THE CULTURE OF THE WILHELMINE EMPIRE

Although the Wilhelmine empire was brash, vulgar, and aggressive, its intellectual and cultural life was enormously rich. This was born of the tension between an uncritical confidence in technical progress and a deep-rooted bourgeois fear that things would soon go drastically wrong. Karl Marx, Sigmund Freud, and Albert Einstein delivered shattering challenges to accepted truths. In the visual arts abstractionists challenged the realists like Adolf Menzel, whose virtuoso historical paintings of Frederick the Great and of William I's court delighted a wide public.

In architecture the functional rationalism of Peter Behrens, Alfred Messel, and Ludwig Hoffmann triumphed and established the rules of the modernist grammar. They warded off the art nouveau attack, for this soon proved to be a purely decorative style, even though its self-conscious decadence brought it wide and lasting popularity. Expressionist architecture, such as Erich Mendelsohn's Einstein tower in Berlin, was dismissed as elitist, pessimistic, and oddly old-fashioned. The new architecture was technological, practical, free from spurious decoration, and expressed a bold confidence in the benefits of social engineering.

Brahms was the last of the great classical composers. He was born in Hamburg in 1833 and in 1862 moved to Vienna, where he died in 1897. He was hailed by Schumann as a genius when he was twenty, but it was not until his *German Requiem* was first performed in 1869 that he enjoyed popular success. Musically he was a conservative and was sharply critical of the 'new music' of Liszt and Wagner. Among his many works, his four symphonies, four concerti, chamber music, and songs remain essential parts of the classical repertoire. The Wagnerians themselves came under attack from 1909 when Schönberg published his *Three Pieces for Piano*, and the 'New Viennese School' began their experiments with atonality which were to revolutionize music.

Literature remained realistic, but its tone had changed. Theodor Fontane in masterpieces such as *Effie Briest* and *The Stechlin* had criticized Prussian society, but remained deeply attached to it, believing it fully capable of reform. Thomas Mann did not share this optimism and painted unforgettable portraits of a society in irredeemable decline. Gerhart Hauptmann's social critical dramas scandalized bourgeois Germany, brought him the Nobel prize in 1912, and made him the poet laureate of the Weimar Republic.

Friedrich Nietzsche's apocalyptic vision of the age, expressed in a language of intoxicating power and brilliance, went far beyond the weary pessimism and anxious speculations of his contemporaries. He challenged the 'millennia of lies', attacked the assumptions on which all previous philosophy was based, dismissed rationalism, religion, democracy, and even normal human decency. As his syphilitic mind became increasingly unhinged, he called for a new race of heroes, of 'blond beasts' who, freed from all the inhibiting rubbish of the past, would build a new world on the ruins of the old. He left an appalling legacy of irrationalism and elistism, and his heirs were to wreak still further damage.

By contrast, Max Weber, the founder of modern sociology, was a rigorous rationalist. He argued that the social sciences could never be used to support value judgments: 'An emipirical science can teach no one what he should do, but only what he can do, and in certain cases what he wants to do.' Weber hoped to keep politics out of scientific investigation, to achieve the highest possible degree of objectivity. Science, Weber argued, was supported by the 'ethics of responsibility' (*Verantwortungsethik*) which led to compromise and understanding, whereas politics subscribed to 'dispositional ethics' (*Gesinnungsethik*) which were divisive and confrontational. The fundamental values which Weber, an enthusiastic nationalist and imperialist, upheld in all his scientific work were his understanding of the needs of the German nation state and his firm belief in the virtues of bourgeois society.

THE NAVAL BUILDING PROGRAMME AND PREVENTIVE WAR

In 1898 Admiral Tirpitz was appointed head of the Admiralty (*Reichsmarineamt*) shortly after Bülow was made secretary of state for foreign affairs. Tirpitz was a close confidant of the kaiser and shared his mania for a huge fleet which would be able to destroy the Royal Navy and make Germany a world power. Like his monarch, Tirpitz suffered from a lack of proportion and an excess of hubris. He had the organizational genius, the technical skill, the self-confident determination, and the demagogic flair needed to push through his programme. Tirpitz argued that his massive ship-building programme would solve domestic political difficulties by whipping up enthusiasm for the fleet as a whole generation of little boys were forced into sailor suits. He announced that the social order would be put in quarantine and that he had found the antidote to 'educated and uneducated Social Democrats'. The fleet was thus aimed both against England and the Reichstag.

Tirpitz's first naval bill of 1898 called for the building of two squadrons of battleships. He mounted an extraordinary propaganda campaign to whip up public opinion in favour of ship-building. Learned professors travelled the length and breadth of the country preaching the new gospel. Journalists wrote thousands of fiery articles, lecturers entranced village audiences with their epidiascopes, and naval officers soberly warned of the need for coastal defence. Enthusiasm for the fleet was widespread. Ship-builders and industrialists saw the opportunity for vast profits, merchants longed to teach their British rivals a lesson, imperialists dreamt of further colonies, patriots wanted to stand up to the British brutes who had herded the noble Boers into concentration camps, and the Social Democrats welcomed the increased opportunities for employment and higher wages.

Grand Admiral Alfred von Tirpitz (1849–1930), the founder of the German high seas fleet.

Tirpitz's plan was a mortally dangerous gamble whose stakes were world power or annihilation. The future would be decided in a vast naval battle somewhere between Helgoland and the mouth of the Thames. It was a strategy which gave the politicians no room for manoeuvre. Bülow, who was appointed chancellor in 1900, was the perfect amanuensis to an emperor who now sought legitimation through naval building and breast-beating imperialism rather than worthy but dull social programmes. He came from the impoverished lower aristocracy and, like so many German politicians then and now, saw politics as a means to achieve wealth and status. He was an ambitious and unctuous courtier, the 'minister of fine appearances'. After his fall from grace he told himself: 'You had the choice between two routes: a modest life, consul-general in Cairo or Sofia, envoy in Athens or The Hague, under-secretary of state, finally with luck a few years as ambassador, then retirement as Mr von Bülow, with precious little money, to spend the autumn of my life in Bonn or Venice; or minister, prince, tycoon, Villa Malta, an historic figure. The last is not possible without disputes, enemies, and battles.'

Bülow's support in the Reichstag, which he could manipulate but not lead, lay in the Miquel right-wing block. In 1901 he appeased the agrarians by withdrawing the second canal bill and by dropping a number of ministers who no longer enjoyed their confidence, including Miquel who was felt to be too close to industry. His tariff increase in the following year was far too small for the agrarians, but far too much for the Social Democrats, who made substantial gains in the elections of 1903 by denouncing the agrarians for forcing up the price of food and thus lowering real wages. The new tariff was 0.50 marks per 100 kilos of grain rather than the 7.50 marks the agrarians had demanded. The Farmers' League denounced the government; such was their disgust that some conservatives were prepared to join the Social Democrats in opposition.

The naval bill of 1900 called for two further squadrons of battleships. The British were alarmed and hardly placated by Tirpitz's 'risk theory' whereby the aim was to build a fleet that was so large that no other navy would run the risk of confronting it. British naval enthusiasts were eager to take up the challenge and the naval race was on, reaching a new phase in 1905, when the British built the *Dreadnought*, a huge vessel that made Tirpitz's battleships obsolete. The Germans were now in a difficult situation. The Kiel Canal was too narrow for these monsters, the shipyards of Wilhelmshaven too small, and the Reich did not have the money to compete with the British at this level.

In 1905 the advocates of preventive war in the Prussian general staff argued that the moment had come. Russia had been humiliated in the war with Japan and was in the middle of a revolution. There was still no substance in the Franco-British *Entente Cordiale* because of the weakness of both countries: the British had not yet recovered from the Boer War, the French were preoccupied with colonial affairs. The non-military members of the government, however, were more cautious; they wished to exploit the situation to secure a diplomatic triumph over the young *Entente*. William II's advisors urged him to go to Morocco in order to demonstrate German interests in a country which, although nominally a sovereign state, had fallen clearly into the French sphere of influence. The French foreign minister, Théophile Delcassé, the architect of the *Entente Cordiale* and the force behind French imperialist policy in Morocco, offered the Germans trade concessions, but

Von Tirpitz mounted a massive propaganda campaign to generate public enthusiasm for his battleship-building programme. This poster is for an exhibition on the Kurfürstendamm in Berlin in 1910 in which model ships, propelled by men concealed inside them, manoeuvred in a large pool.

this was not enough. In order to fuel the crisis, the Germans demanded an international conference on Morocco. The French president Rouvier dismissed Delcassé in order to placate the Germans, and offered further trade concessions, but the Germans insisted on a conference, which was to meet in Algeçiras. The conference was a lengthy and rather pointless affair which left the Germans isolated, the French confirmed in their position in Morocco and further strenghtened the *Entente*.

After this disastrous failure William II tried another tack, meeting the tsar at Björko in the hope of winning him over to an anti-British position. Willy and Nicky got on splendidly and agreed to help one another in the event that one was attacked in Europe, and they imagined that they would be able to persuade the French to join in. It was an absurd proposal that the Russians soon repudiated. Bülow, the architect of this inept scheme, offered his resignation, but the kaiser refused. In spite of the setbacks of the *Dreadnought* programme, the Morocco debacle and the disappointment of Björko, the German elites could not tolerate a retreat by negotiation and disarmament which would cause a loss of face. They could only hope that the coalition which encircled them would fall apart, and meanwhile prepare for preventive war.

In 1906 the Centre Party joined the Social Democrats in the Reichstag to defeat a bill for an additional twenty-nine million marks for Germany's murderous war against the Hereros, a rebellious tribe in the German colony of South-West Africa. This was a shattering defeat for Bülow and for *Weltpolitik*, but the ensuing 'Hottentot Elections' of January 1907 were a triumph for the 'Bülow Bloc', a revival of Bismarck's cartel of conservatives and right-wing liberals; the Social Democrats lost half their seats.

Although Bülow thus secured a comfortable majority for his *Weltpolitik*, there was no money left in the till to finance it. The expenses of the naval building programme, the army increases of 1893, 1899, and 1905, and colonial wars in China and Africa left the Reich with an annual deficit of 200 million marks. Attempts to overcome this deficit with estate duties alienated the conservatives, while increased indirect taxes angered the left. Rising costs, mainly for rearmament, caused the annual deficit to reach 500 million marks and by 1908 the Reich owed 4,000 million marks. The vast majority of the Reichstag were opposed to further increases in estate duties and indirect taxes, and the conservatives announced that they were leaving the Bülow Bloc.

On 28 October 1908 the London *Daily Telegraph* published some typically unfortunate remarks made by William II to a British colonel, Stuart Wortley. The kaiser said that the English were as 'mad as March hares' in harbouring suspicions about Germany. The Germans had refused to join in a continental coalition against Britain at the time of the Boer War, and the kaiser had advised Queen Victoria how to beat the Boers and Lord Roberts had followed his advice. The German fleet was simply designed to protect the merchant marine. This blustering nonsense, which

The kaiser's manoeuvres, 1884. The Prussian army held full-scale manoeuvres annually to test the abilities and leadership skills of the general staff officers. The army was the finest in the world, but its obsessive concern with political reliability and social exclusiveness meant that it was too small to fulfil the ambitious tasks it set itself.

had been vetted by both Bülow and the foreign office, annoyed the British and the Germans equally and led to a rift between Bülow and the kaiser. Having lost the support of the conservatives and the Centre for his finance bill, and no longer enjoying the kaiser's confidence, Bülow felt obliged to resign. On 26 June 1909 the kaiser was pleased to accept this request.

The new chancellor, Theobald von Bethmann Hollweg, was a somewhat colourless bureaucrat who lacked the forcefulness to push through the finance reform, and his much vaunted 'politics of the diagonal', an attempt to find a consensus, did not disguise the fact that there was little room for compromise. In foreign affairs his main aim was to ensure that the British remained neutral in the continental war which he felt was inevitable. When an avenue of limes was planted on his estate at Hohenfinow on the Oder, he commented that it was a waste of effort since in a few years time it would be in Russian hands. Such pessimism was in marked contrast to the heady rhetoric of Bülow.

In 1911 the French sent troops to Morocco to support the sultan against rebel forces. The German foreign office demanded compensation for this breach of the Algeçiras agreement and suggested that Mannesmann, a large mining company who had their eyes on the mineral deposits of southern Morocco, should be given a free hand. To back up the German claim the gunboat *Panther* was sent to Agadir. The British government, appalled at this clumsy show of strength, warned the Germans not to push their claims to part of Morocco, but they refused to back down. The Berlin stock exchange grew increasingly nervous. A way out was finally found. Germany was given a piece of the Congo and gave up some of Togo, while Morocco remained in the French sphere of influence. Europe had gone to the brink of war in 1911 over an insignificant sandy waste. German nationalists were outraged that Germany had backed down, the kaiser was accused of timidity, and Bethmann fell even lower in their esteem.

The AEG factory in Berlin in 1904. The electrical industry began in Germany in the 1860s and soon firms such as AEG and Siemens were to be world leaders. Success in the electrical and chemical industries of the 'second industrial revolution' contributed to making Germany Europe's leading industrial nation.

Uneasiness over the foreign political situation and the effects of a recession which began in 1911, resulted in a triumph for the Social Democrats and Progressives in the elections of January 1912. The Socialists more than doubled their number of seats and were now the larger faction in the Reichstag.

In February 1912 the British war minister, Lord Haldane, visited Berlin and suggested that were the Germans to cut back their naval building programme, the British would remain neutral if Germany were attacked. This was unacceptable to the Germans. Although they could not afford to build many more ships, they considered the British proposal an insult to their national pride. Although British suspicions of Germany were increased and the logic of German policy was leading to preventive war, relations between the two countries outside Europe improved. In 1913 agreement was reached over the future of the Portuguese colonies should that country be unable to pay their massive debts. Problems over the Baghdad railway and Turkish oil concessions were solved, and a treaty giving Germany and Britain virtual control over Turkey, with Germany as the senior partner, would have been ratified but for the war.

In 1912 Serbia and Bulgaria, soon to be joined by Greece and Montenegro, began to drive the Turks out of Europe. The alliance was enthusiastically supported by Russia, but Austria-Hungary was fearful that the Serbs intended to establish a naval base on the Adriatic, and thus become an even greater threat to the Dual Monarchy. Bethmann warned the Russians that they were playing with fire. The British government let it be known that they would not tolerate a German attack on France. Europe pulled back from the brink when a solution for Austria-Hungary's

München, 6. Oktober 1914

19. Jahrgang Nr. 27

SIMPLICISSIMUS

Liebhaberausgabe

Alle Rechte vorbehalten

Begründet von Albert Langen und Th. Th. Heine

Abonnement halbjährlich 15 Mark

Copyright 1914 by Simplicissimus-Verlag G. m. b. H. & Co., München

Deutsche Wacht in Kiautschau

(Zeichnung von O. Gulbransson)

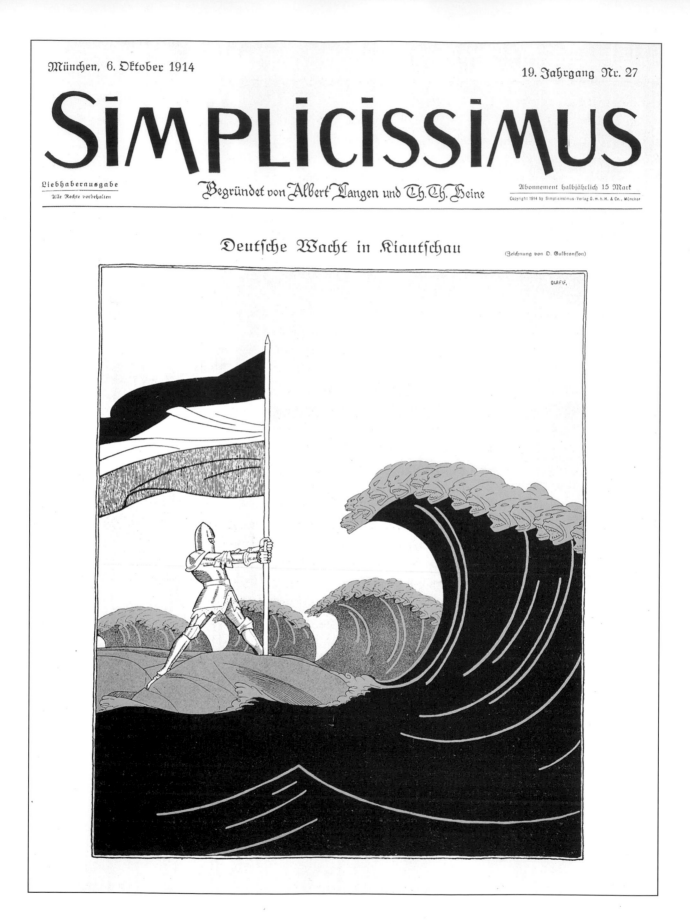

fears was found. An independent Albania was created which blocked the Serbian advance to the sea.

On 28 June 1914 the Archduke Franz Ferdinand was assassinated in Sarajevo, the capital of Bosnia-Herzegovina, two provinces which had been annexed by Austria-Hungary in 1908. In Austria the predominant feeling was that the assassination of the heir to the throne by a member of the Serbian secret society, the Black Hand, which was known to have close links to both the Serbian and Russian governments, was the golden opportunity to strike at Serbia. On 5 and 6 June the German government issued the 'blank cheque' to the Austrian envoy. Austria was given an assurance of full German support whatever happened in the Balkans, a disastrous departure from Bismarck's diplomacy.

Bethmann hoped that the Austrians would carry out a swift surgical strike against Serbia which would not give the Russians time to intervene, but the Austrians were far too slow. The virtually unacceptable ultimatum to Serbia was not sent until 23 July. The younger von Moltke, the chief of general staff, was taking the waters in Karlsbad and did not return to Berlin until 25 July, by which time the Russians had partially mobilized in support of Serbia. He was now convinced that war was inevitable and felt that the situation for Germany was propitious. The minister of war, Falkenhayn, who also returned to Berlin on 25 July, pressed for war. Confirmation that the Russians had mobilized did not reach Moltke until 7 a.m. on 31 July, but he had already decided to mobilize and thus plunge Europe into war. The kaiser and Bethmann wanted to take up the British offer to negotiate, but German troops were already in Belgium and could not be halted without jeopardizing the Schlieffen Plan (in which, in its modified form, the bulk of the German army would march through Belgium, wheel south before Paris, and encircle the French army as it moved back from the frontier to defend the capital). Germany's forward strategy and Bethmann's 'leap in the dark' resulted in a European and world war. The misery caused by this unimaginable and senseless slaughter was to call in question the moral and cultural basis of European civilization, and provoke a profound spiritual crisis from which Europe has still not fully recovered.

Opposite: A caricature of October 1914 by Olaf Gulbransson (1873–1958), the Norwegian artist who was a leading contributor to the satirical magazine '*Simplicissimus*' captures the beleaguered mood of Germany on the brink of World War I.

CHAPTER 10   *The Weimar Republic*

By August 1914 Belgium had been overrun and German divisions had reached the outskirts of Paris. However, they were soon pulled back to help extricate their northern forces from the brilliant French counter-attack on the Marne. Both armies now began the 'race for the sea' in an attempt to outflank one another. After a dead heat, two lines of trenches were dug from the channel coast to the Swiss border and four years of static warfare began. Falkenhayn, who replaced Moltke as chief of the general staff, tried to regain the strategic initiative by punching a hole through the *Entente* lines at Ypres, but the attempt was a failure which cost 80,000 German lives. The attack on the village of Langemarck by youthful volunteers singing the national anthem ended in a mass slaughter which provided the nationalist right with a powerful myth, but demonstrated to the high command that infantry attacks on machine gun emplacements were a prohibitive waste of manpower. For a while the only viable strategy on the western front was a war of attrition in which the *Entente* wasted its resources in costly attacks.

In East Prussia relatively weak German forces were surprised by the Russian army's swift mobilization and rapid advance. Hindenburg, brought out of retirement to command the forces in East Prussia, and his second-in-command Ludendorff, were sent to stabilize the situation and won a great victory at Tannenberg in a classic battle of encirclement. The Russians lost 50,000 men and 92,000 prisoners against German losses of 10,000. The Russians then lost a further 70,000 men and 45,000 prisoners in the winter campaign in Masuria. Although Tannenberg was celebrated as a great victory and Hindenburg became seen as a guarantor of success, the battle was not decisive and the campaign in the East continued for another three years, ending only with the collapse of the tsarist empire.

Germany was united as never before in the heady days of August 1914 when the troops went into battle happily convinced of the righteousness of their cause and confident of an early victory. Only a handful of revolutionary socialists and principled pacifists opposed the war. The political parties and the civil administration were pushed aside by the Army Supreme Command (OHL) and the commanding generals in the corps' districts, who were given dictatorial powers under a law which came into effect at the beginning of the war. The generals believed that victory and the achievement of their over-ambitious war aims – frontier changes in the West, living space in the East, and extensive annexations in the Baltic – would silence the demand for democratic reforms. The less likely military victory looked, the more excessive the war aims became, and by 1917 a left-of-centre coalition had begun to form in the Reichstag which called for an end to the war and for far-reaching reforms.

In August 1916 Hindenburg and Ludendorff were appointed to the high command, Falkenhayn's ingenious strategy having failed in the Verdun campaign.

German steel helmets are destroyed according to the armistice agreement of 1918.

They immediately set about bringing the country under even tighter military control by means of the Hindenburg Programme and the Law on Patriotic Service (*Vaterländische Hilfsdienst*). The kaiser had virtually abdicated as 'Supreme Warlord' by allowing the chief of his general staff to make all the important decisions. Civilians, from the chancellor down, all saluted the demi-gods in uniform. Germany was now a military regime, some would claim a military dictatorship; the remnants of the constitution acted, in Ludendorff's words, as a 'lightning conductor' – the civilians took the blame for the failures of the military rulers.

In 1917, risking American involvement, the Germans tried one more desperate gamble, an unrestricted submarine offensive. Although the Germans had few submarines, they calculated that Britain would be starved of transatlantic supplies and within months be forced to sue for peace. This proved to be the decisive year, with the United States' entry into the war and the Bolshevik revolution. Far from using the common threat of Bolshevism as a possible basis for peace negotiations, the OHL insisted on carving out a vast empire in the east, taking over control of the Baltic States, the Ukraine, and the Caucasus, and tying down large numbers of troops that could have been much better employed on the western front.

In March 1918 the Germans began their final offensive 'Operation Michael', a carefully prepared and skilfully executed attack on the junction of the French and British fronts between Amiens and Rheims. The initial results were spectacular, but the Germans lacked the reserves and supplies to exploit their deep penetration. The *Entente*'s counter-offensive began in mid-July, but the German lines held until 8 August, a black day for the German army, when the *Entente* broke through at the Somme with massed tank units, and the Germans fled in panic. At his headquarters Ludendorff suffered a nervous collapse; it was obvious that the war was lost and on 29 September he and Hindenburg advised the politicians to seek an armistice.

Cover design by Lina von Schauroth for *The Great War: Documents, Dispatches and Reports* from the *Frankfurter Zeitung*. German soldiers in field grey uniform and steel helmets move along a communications trench. This is a typical example of the unsentimental and unheroic art of the best German propaganda in the later stages of the war.

There followed a series of skilful moves by the political and military elites to shift the blame for a lost war onto the Reichstag majority in order to discredit parliamentary democracy and contrive their return to power. On 29 October the navy in Kiel mutinied rather than embark on a suicide mission. On 7 November the Bavarian monarchy was toppled. On 8 November the revolution spread to Cologne and Brunswick. Throughout Germany Workers' and Soldiers' Councils formed menacing imitations of the Russian Soviets. For the *Entente* to agree to an armistice the kaiser had to go, and since the army would fight no longer an armistice had to be signed immediately. Hindenburg did not have the courage to tell his kaiser this bitter truth so delegated the unpleasant task to Ludendorff's successor, General Groener. On 8 November Groener told the kaiser: 'The army no longer stands behind Your Majesty!' and early on 10 November William II left for exile in Holland, leaving Germany without an emperor and Prussia without a king. Few but the Prussian officer corps regretted his abdication, for he had symbolized the arrogant, aggressive and hubristic policies that had led Germany to disaster.

THE FOUNDATION OF THE WEIMAR REPUBLIC

Prince Max von Baden, a decent but feeble interim chancellor, handed over the reins to Ebert, the leader of the SPD. It was an unconstitutional move by the prince, a revolutionary act which the Socialist Ebert at first refused on account of its dubious legality. He was prompted by the more realistic Scheidemann, a prominent Social Democrat, who remarked: 'Oh, come on – just say yes!' and a provisional government was formed of three majority and three independent Socialists. On 11 November Erzberger, a civilian and Centre Party Reichstag deputy, signed the armistice in a railway carriage in the forest of Compiègne. Walther Rathenau's biting comment on these events was soon to be confirmed: 'We Germans call a general strike by a defeated army a revolution.'

The news that Germany had capitulated came as a shattering blow to the vast majority of the people. Apart from a few square kilometers in Alsace, the front was still miles away from the frontiers of the Reich and the OHL had revealed nothing about the seriousness of the situation. This was to prove a fatal legacy to the Weimar Republic: it was a regime born of a defeat few could accept. Matters were made worse by Hindenburg and Ludendorff refusing to accept responsibility for the disastrous outcome of their March offensive, and by their insistence that civilians should conduct the armistice negotiations. The OHL was determined to discredit the democratic parties, as Ludendorff emphasized in an address to his fellow officers on 1 October 1918: 'I have asked His Majesty to bring into government the gentlemen whom we have principally to thank for this pretty pass. It is *they* who must now enter the ministries and sign the peace, *they* who must now taste the soup we have been served!'

It was something of a miracle that Germany survived World War I as a nation, albeit with some drastic frontier adjustments. The French were determined that

Bismarck's Reich should be destroyed and hoped that the left bank of the Rhine would be France's new frontier. Germany was saved largely because the British and Americans wished to preserve it as a bulwark against Russian Communism. However, there was never any danger that Germany would go the way of Russia; what appeared to some a revolution was in fact merely the collapse of the old state. The vast majority of the German left were Social Democrats who wished to take the democratic route to socialism and who abhorred the brutal dictatorship of Lenin's Bolsheviks.

Germany's radical left lacked the ruthlessness of true revolutionaries. Their plan was to call elections in the factories and barracks of Berlin and to elect delegates for a Soviet to meet at the Busch Circus, which would then overthrow Ebert's provisional government (the Council of People's Representatives). This plan was frustrated by Otto Wels, Berlin's SPD boss, who hastily organized SPD-dominated soldiers' councils to hold the balance of power.

On the evening of 10 November 1918 General Groener telephoned Ebert and assured him that the army would give him full support if he joined the struggle against Bolshevism. Ebert accepted without hesitation. He detested Bolshevism, German troops were still fighting against Bolsheviks and Poles in the East, and he wanted to ensure the German army's orderly demobilization. The army was assured that authority of the officer corps would not be challenged by the soldiers' councils or be subject to political control.

Relations between the SPD and Independent Social Democrats (USPD) on the Council of Peoples' Representatives became increasingly strained. A break occurred over the handling of the Peoples' Marine Division, a band of ostensibly leftist marines who were to guard the chancellory. In the event, these greedy mercenaries helped themselves to art treasures and held Otto Wels hostage for their

Rosa Luxemburg (1871–1919) giving a public address during a meeting of the Socialist International at Stuttgart in 1907. Luxemburg was one of the leaders of the left-wing organization, the Spartacus League, which became the Communist Party of Germany on New Year's Eve, 1918, and participated in a revolutionary uprising on 5 January 1919. The revolt was rapidly crushed and Luxemburg and Liebknecht, outstanding leaders of the radical left, were murdered by anti-Bolshevik troops on 15 January.

demands. On 24 December regular troops loyal to the regime bombarded the palace and a negotiated settlement was reached whereby the marines disbanded and the troops were withdrawn from Berlin. The USPD members of Ebert's government who resigned in protest were replaced by three SPD members, leaving it unprotected. It could have been overthrown were it not for the scruples of the left-wing Ernst Däumig, who argued that the German people would never forgive the radicals if they overthrew the regime on Christmas Eve.

Having missed this golden opportunity, the extreme left around Karl Liebknecht's radical Socialist group the Spartacus League, reconstituted itself as the Communist Party of Germany (KPD) on New Year's Eve. On 5 January 1919 the government dismissed Berlin's police president, Emil Eichhorn, a USPD supporter who given to dramatic outbursts of revolutionary rhetoric. This dismissal triggered off a spontaneous armed revolt which was hesitatingly supported by the leadership of the KPD, radical trades unions, and Berlin's central committee of the USPD.

Although the government had fled from Berlin on 5 January the uprising had little chance of success. On 11 January Gustav Noske, recently appointed to the Council of Peoples' Representatives, entered Berlin with his anti-Bolshevik troops and after two days of intense street fighting the uprising was crushed. On 15 January the outstanding leaders of the radical left, Karl Liebknecht and Rosa Luxemburg, were killed by Noske's troops. The victory over the revolution was complete, but the legacy was dangerous. Noske had used the Free Corps, mercenary bands of ultra-conservatives who were delighted to kill Communists, but also sought the overthrow of Ebert's government. Many SPD supporters felt that Noske had been too harsh in his treatment of the insurgents, and argued that by using the Free Corps he had let a dangerous genie out of the bottle.

Elections were held on 19 January 1919 by universal suffrage for those over twenty, and by proportional representation. The KPD boycotted the election, but nineteen parties fielded candidates. The SPD obtained 37 per cent of the vote but failed to gain the absolute majority for which they had hoped, while the USPD won only 7.6 per cent and ceased to play any further significant role, its members gradually returning to the SPD or joining the KPD. Together with the Centre Party and the German Democratic Party (DDP), the SPD had 76 per cent of the vote showing that the vast majority of Germans wanted a liberal, democratic, republican government. The SPD's ambitious plans for the nationalization of heavy industry, mining, and banking soon had to be shelved. The country was starving, malnutrition killed 250,000 people, and by the end of 1918 average daily calorific intake was only 1,000. Industry was running back to peacetime production levels, battling against chronic shortages of raw materials. In such a situation only a few blind ideologues called for major nationalization.

The first priority was to restore law and order. There were armed uprisings by radical factions not only in Berlin but also in Brunswick, Eisenach, Erfurt, Gotha, Halle, Leipzig, and the North Sea ports. In Munich an anarchist republic had been proclaimed. There were numerous strikes, with that of the railwaymen causing further shortages. In southern and western Germany separatists were winning support, and all Germans waited anxiously for the outcome of the peace conference at Versailles.

THE TREATY OF VERSAILLES

The Germans knew that the peace terms would be extremely harsh, but the final text of the treaty presented to their delegation on 7 May 1919 exceeded their worst fears. Germany was to lose 14 per cent of its territory and 10 per cent of its population, along with half its iron ore and a quarter of its coal deposits. Germany's colonial empire was to be dissolved and all its foreign investments and patents lost. Even more alarming were the demands for reparations, to include 60 per cent of the country's coal production for ten years, 90 per cent of its merchant navy, most of its modern railway locomotives and rolling stock, half its dairy cattle, and one quarter of its chemical and pharmaceutical products. Its army was limited to 100,000 men, its navy to 15,000, and its armed forces were not to have tanks, airplanes, submarines, or poison gas.

The foreign minister, Count Brockdorff-Rantzau, returned to Berlin and urged the government to reject the treaty. President Ebert, backed by three DDP and three SDP ministers – Scheidemann, Landsberg and Bauer – agreed. The Centre Party, led by Matthias Erzberger, along with Noske, Wissell, Schmidt and David for the SDP, argued that the government had no alternative but to accept. The High Command drew up plans for a defensive campaign behind the Elbe and an offensive against

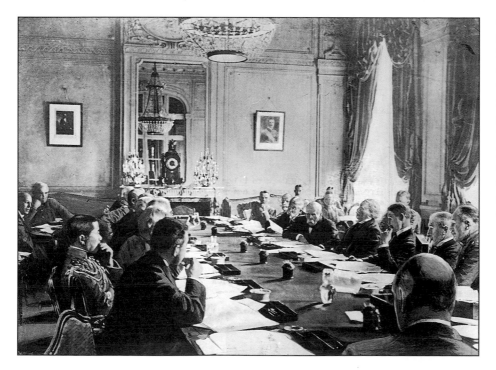

Clemenceau, Lloyd George and Wilson at the Versailles Peace Conference, 1919: Clemenceau is on the right with the walrus moustache, next to Lloyd George who gazes at the ceiling, while Wilson is to his left is in a pensive mood. Serious differences between the three statesmen put an end to dreams of a new world order.

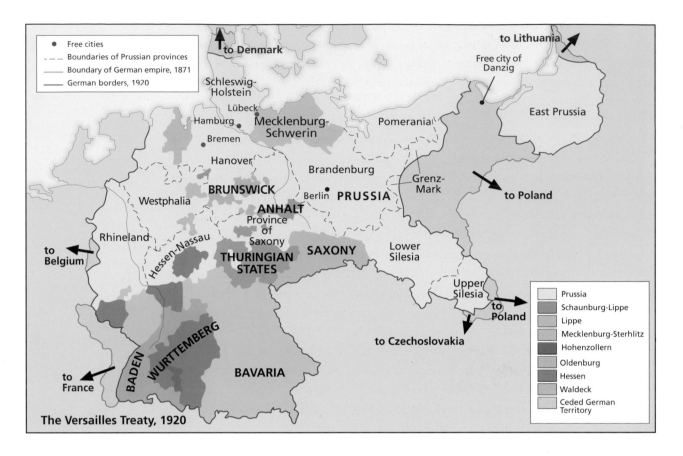

The Versailles Treaty, 1920

Poland. 'Operation Spring Sunshine' confidently predicted that within a week Warsaw would be in German hands. In the eastern provinces of the Reich plans were laid for a separate state where German identity would be preserved and nurtured for recovery of the lost territories. These extraordinary Prussian particularist ideas were favourably received by the government in Berlin and there was much romantic talk about the role of Prussia in freeing Germany from the Napoleonic yoke.

The decisive voice against such nonsense was General Groener, Ludendorff's successor. He had little sympathy with Prussian nationalism and insisted that only if Germany remained united could it win back what it had lost. The Social Democratic and Centre factions now supported acceptance of the treaty and Scheidemann resigned as chancellor, having persistently argued against. A new minority government, tacitly supported by the DDP, was formed under Gustav Bauer. On 22 June 1919 the text of the treaty was debated in the Reichstag: 237 voted for acceptance, 138 against with 5 abstentions, with support for acceptance coming from all parties. On 28 June the German delegation signed the treaty.

The treaty was bitterly resented by Germans of all political persuasions. This was not so much because of the territorial losses or reparations, as the high moral tone affected by the *Entente*, an attitude which all felt to be the height of hypocrisy.

The demand that the kaiser should be extradited and tried as a war criminal was felt particularly insulting. The German colonies were seized under the pretext that German colonial rule had been incompetent and immoral. The 'war guilt lie' of paragraph 231 was especially resented and its translation deliberately distorted to be even more offensive. All Germans rejected the treaty and were determined to see it revised, yet it was not severe enough to stop the revisionists from having their way. Few Germans realized that the treaty could not be made to stick, and most despaired of the future.

In nationalistic, aristocratic and conservative circles this despair soon turned to anger against Friedrich Ebert's government. At first many reactionary organizations had been prepared to accept a democratic regime as the best assurance against Bolshevism, but increasingly their condemnation of it became violent. Waverers joined the anti-democratic camp when, on 18 November, Field Marshal von Hindenburg appeared before the parliamentary commission investigating the causes of Germany's defeat and solemnly announced that 'an English general' was perfectly correct in saying that 'the German army had been stabbed in the back'. Hindenburg lent enormous prestige to the notion that the democratic forces in Germany were traitors and criminals. The republicans had no leaders of the stature of a Bismarck or an Adenauer, men who might have reconciled the people to the new regime. They were dull bureaucrats, party hacks, and opportunists. Most of the republic's supporters were 'rational republicans' (*Venunftrepublikaner*), men who, like Gustav Stresemann, disliked the 'revolution' but saw no alternative to the parliamentary regime. The republic was thus hated by many, and merely tolerated by its supporters.

THE CRISIS YEARS 1920–23

On 12 March 1920 the army minister, Gustav Noske, was informed that Lieutenant General von Lüttwitz, commanding officer in East and Central Germany, and Captain Hermann Ehrhardt's disbanded volunteer Marine Brigade II were going to mount a putsch during the night. The army refused to defend the government. The *de facto* chief of the general staff, von Seeckt, is purported to have said, 'The Reichswehr does not shoot at the Reichswehr!' The government fled to Dresden, and then, still fearful, on to Stuttgart.

Lüttwitz seized Berlin where Ludendorff attended the victory parade. Wolfgang Kapp, the political leader of the putsch, who had not been told by Lüttwitz and Ehrhardt of their plans, was caught by surprise and moved into the chancellory, but the staff refused his orders. The federal and Prussian ministries continued to function as if Kapp did not exist and the Reichsbank refused to finance him. The suggestion that soldiers should storm the bank was rejected out of hand – officers, after all, were not bank robbers. Even the officers in the army ministry refused to accept orders from Kapp or Lüttwitz, while Seeckt prudently reported sick. Senior officers in the provinces and the majority of anti-republicans soon realized that the putsch was a failure and that Kapp was utterly powerless. On 14 March the *Entente* announced their intention to impose a blockade if Kapp remained.

There is a persistent myth that the Kapp-Lüttwitz putsch was defeated by a general strike and that the organized working class saved the republic. In fact the republic was saved by conservative bureaucrats who refused to cooperate with such an ill-prepared adventurer. On 13 March the government's press officer published a call for a general strike which bore the names of the president and Social Democratic ministers, even though they had not approved the move. The strike, such as it was, began on Monday 15 March, but only seriously affected the working-class districts of Berlin. It was quickly radicalized, with calls for revolution, and soon became more of a menace to Gustav Bauer's government than to Wolfgang Kapp; there was general relief when it ended. Kapp's adventure was over and he flew to Sweden on 17 March, while Lüttwitz fled to Hungary.

The radical left now threatened to topple the government. In the Ruhr a red army was formed of some 50,000 men from all parties and was belatedly supported by the Communists, reluctant to be associated with assorted anarchists, Social

A long queue forms outside a Berlin soup kitchen in the early 1920s. Post-war shortages and economic disruption caused widespread malnutrition and starvation.

Democrats, and Catholic trades unionists. The Reichswehr was unable to master the situation and the government resorted to Free Corps thugs who had previously supported Kapp. The fighting continued until mid April and cost 3,000 lives. The Reichswehr leadership which had refused to support Kapp was now called upon to fight strikers answering a call by the SDP. Noske resigned, his efforts to ally the SPD and the Reichswehr a failure.

The elections of June 1920 resulted in a disastrous defeat for the SPD and the Democrats. The Weimar Coalition was reduced from 66 to 43 per cent of the Reichstag seats. The extreme left – the Communists and USPD – had 20 per cent and the extreme right – the German National People's Party (DNVP) and German People's Party (DVP) – 28 per cent. A centre-right government was formed under elderly centrist Constantin Fehrenbach. The Coalition parties which stood unequivocally for democracy were never again to obtain a majority. In Prussia the situation was far more encouraging. A new Social Democratic government was formed under Otto Braun and Carl Severing, tough realists who had proved their mettle during the Kapp putsch, and who immediately purged the administration and police of elements with questionable loyalty to the constitution. Prussia, once known for bone-headed reaction, was now a stronghold of republican virtue.

On 29 January 1921 the Allies presented their bill for reparations. German officials had estimated that it would be 30,000 million gold marks, payable over thirty years. The Allies, urged on by greedy and vengeful electorates in France and Belgium, demanded 226,000 million marks, plus 12 per cent of German exports. Annual payments were to increase from 2,000 million to 6,000 million marks.

The Fehrenbach government refused the Allied ultimatum and French troops occupied Düsseldorf, Duisburg, and Ruhrort. Fehrenbach resigned rather than sign an agreement. With the Americans and British urging the French to reduce their demands, it was agreed to set the debt at 132,000 million marks with annual payments of 6 per cent interest plus reduction of principal amounting to 2,000 million gold marks. Also, 26 per cent of the value of German exports was to go into a reparations account. If the Germans failed to agree within one week the Allies threatened to occupy the Ruhr and requisition its entire production. The new centrist chancellor Joseph Wirth had no alternative but to sign.

The government felt that it was politically unfeasible to increase taxes in order to pay the reparations and therefore borrowed heavily from the banks, increasing the government debt and fuelling the already alarming inflation. The Allies' refusal to be paid in devalued marks or in kind and their insistence on gold and hard currency soon exhausted the Reichsbank's reserves, while protectionist policies in Britain and France made it impossible for Germany to increase its exports. The Reichsbank resorted to printing money to buy foreign exchange, resulting in uncontrolled inflation.

In April 1922 Germany and the Soviet Union were invited to a conference in Genoa to discuss reparations and other European economic problems. The two pariah nations had already formed a close partnership cemented by a common detestation of Western imperialism and of liberal democracy. Their trade relations were close and expanding and two years earlier the German military had opened tank and flying schools in Russia, with Reichswehr and Red Army officers working together on manoeuvres. In April 1922 they signed a treaty at Rapallo, granting one another most favoured nation status. But this was hardly the diplomatic revolution it was felt to be by the Allies. Nor did it mark a resounding defeat of the Versailles system. Far more important was the fact that the English prime minister Lloyd George failed to persuade the French to moderate their demands on Germany.

In November 1922 Wirth was overthrown. The SPD, anxious to win back the USPD, could no longer afford a coalition with the DVP, the party of heavy industry. The SPD also had serious misgivings about the treaty of Rapallo which had been negotiated behind its back. Wirth's economic policy was sharply attacked by the left for slavishly following the prescriptions of the Reichsbank. When an attempt to form a broad coalition under Konrad Adenauer, the mayor of Cologne, failed due to the SPD/DVP split, a minority government was formed under Wilhelm Cuno, a prominent businessman without any political experience. Cuno had hardly been appointed when, on 9 January 1923, the reparations commission, against the wishes of the British delegation, sent five French divisions and a team of experts into the Ruhr to discover why Germany was failing to meet its payments.

Most Germans regarded the French action as invasion and united to resist the foe. The government called for a general strike or 'passive resistance'. The French responded by imposing martial law in the Ruhr. Although the industrial action was so effective that the Lorraine steel industry had to close for lack of coal and France faced a serious economic crisis, the German government could only pay the cost of its closed Ruhr by using the printing press. By April, German inflation was out of control. In the Ruhr there began a guerilla war whose unlikely hero was Leo Schlageter, a fascist terrorist whose praises were hymned by both the radical right and the Communists. With the Prussian government taking a firm stand against violence and forcing Cuno to dissociate from the extremists, the chancellor appeared on the brink of a nervous breakdown. On 13 August he was replaced by Gustav Stresemann, founder and leader of the DVP, who headed a broad coalition government in which the SPD played a prominent role.

Stresemann realized that the country could not afford to continue the 'struggle for the Ruhr' and on 26 September he announced the end of the passive resistance. This earned him the undying hatred of the right, with Ludendorff branding him a pacifist, freemason and 'artificial Jew'. The left joined in condemnation of a man who had betrayed the national cause, and when he threatened to abolish their hard-won eight-hour day, they withdrew their support for the coalition, forcing his resignation on 3 October. Three days later he was back in office heading a government with greatly reduced Social Democratic representation, but this was an obviously temporary administration.

Learning that the struggle for the Ruhr had been abandoned, on 26 September the Bavarian government, without consulting Berlin, proclaimed a state of emergency. The Reich responded by declaring a state of emergency throughout Germany. Two weeks later the Social Democratic governments in Saxony and Thuringia appointed some Communist ministers, insisting that this was a defensive move against the dangers of fascism and military dictatorship – in other words against rightist Bavarian extremism. Bavaria promptly broke off diplomatic relations with Saxony and Thuringia – a curious move made possible because the old imperial system of exchanging envoys among the states survived the collapse of the monarchies.

The Bavarian crisis deepened when the Reichswehr minister, Gessler, ordered the local army commander General von Lossow to ban the National Socialist daily newspaper, *Völkischer Beobachter*, which had launched an attack on President Ebert and on Gessler. Von Lossow ignored this order, Gessler dismissed him, but the Bavarian minister von Kahr simply appointed him commander of a Bavarian army. The Reich now had to respond to an act of high treason, but the Reichswehr, as at the time of the Kapp putsch, would not move.

The Communist Party provided the Reichswehr with an excuse to act when the new ministers in Saxony and Thuringia made inflammatory speeches against Bavarian fascists and the military dictatorship of the Reichswehr. Stresemann ordered the governments of Saxony and Thuringia to dismiss the Communists and when they refused he sent in the Reichswehr; the governments were deposed. Thus he answered the Bavarians who claimed that the Berlin government was soft on Communism and also blocked the way to Berlin should von Kahr, or another extremist such as Adolf Hitler, decide to emulate Mussolini's 'March on Rome'.

The SPD left the coalition and Stresemann lost his majority in the Reichstag, but von Kahr could no longer complain that the Reich was controlled by Marxists. On 8 November 1923 von Kahr called a meeting in the Bürgerbräukeller in Munich to discuss the situation. The meeting was rudely interrupted by Adolf Hitler who announced that the 'national revolution' had taken place and that he had appointed a provisional government including von Lossow, the Bavarian police chief Seisser, and General Ludendorff.

Adolf Hitler was born in 1889, the fourth child of an Austrian customs official. He left school early, and led a bohemian existence in Vienna as a painter and unskilled labourer. During the war he reached the rank of corporal in a German infantry regiment and won the Iron Cross, first class. In 1919, he had joined the German Workers' Party (DAP) – a group supported by the Thule Society of well placed anti-Semites and extreme nationalists who hoped to gain influence over the working class. Hitler's reputation as an orator had attracted huge crowds to DAP meetings and he worked tirelessly to strengthen the party's organization. In 1920 the party's name was changed to the National Socialist German Workers' Party (NSDAP), and in 1921 Hitler became its chairman. The party's programme was a

Hitler's abortive coup in Munich 9 November 1923. A swastika flag flies over the city hall, as storm troopers ride past. The brief coup came to an abrupt end when the storm troopers were fired on by the Munich police force.

mixture of anti-Semitism, simplistic economic theory, and pseudo-socialist rhetoric. Stresemann responded to Hitler's putsch by granting plenipotentiary powers to von Seeckt who ordered the Reichswehr to oppose Hitler. Lossow obeyed, realizing that Hitler was merely bluffing. Hitler's absurd march through Munich on 9 November was ended by a brief salvo from the Munich police; he was arrested and spent a brief time in prison where he began work on *Mein Kampf*.

Stresemann had mastered the situation in the Ruhr and Bavaria and had stabilized the mark, but the left could not forgive him for his actions in Saxony and Thuringia, while the right felt he had betrayed the national cause. On 23 October 1923 he took the unusual step of calling a vote of confidence; he lost by 231 votes to 151 with 7 abstentions. President Ebert presciently remarked to the SPD leader that for the next ten years they would suffer the consequences of their stupidity in voting Stresemann out of office.

THE FULFILMENT YEARS 1924–30

Stresemann was no longer chancellor, but he served in a number of different governments as foreign secretary until his death in 1929. He realized that the Versailles treaty could only be revised if Germany showed a certain willingness to fulfil its obligations. He knew that Alsace and Lorraine were lost for ever, but hoped to negotiate the return of Eupen and Malmedy from Belgium and to have an early plebiscite in the Saar. In the East he was determined to regain Danzig, the corridor between Germany and East Prussia, and as much territory as possible. German nationalists condemned Stresemann, failing to recognize his pragmatic understanding of possible German restoration.

In January 1924 an Anglo-American committee, chaired by American banker Charles G. Dawes, arrived in Berlin to study German reparations. The resulting Dawes Plan suggested that Germany should receive a loan of 800 million gold marks to stimulate the economy and that annual payments should be reduced to 1,000 million marks for the first five years, rising to 2,500 million. As a guarantee that these payments would be made, the Allies would have a degree of control over the national railways and the Reichsbank, and part of German industry would be mortgaged. The Dawes Plan still left Germany with a heavy burden of debt and the total sum was still not defined, but at least the Allies had accepted the principle that reparations should be based on Germany's ability to pay. The next step in Stresemann's fulfilment policy was taken in February 1925 when he proposed a security treaty with France and Belgium. The French were deeply suspicious of German motives and did not reply for four months. Finally a conference was held at Locarno to discuss Stresemann's proposal.

The negotiations were carried out in a relaxed atmosphere, largely made possible by French foreign minister Aristide Briand's flexible approach. Germany, France, and Belgium agreed not to change their frontiers by force and Germany freely accepted the demilitarization of the Rhineland. Britain and Italy guaranteed this 'Rhineland Pact'. Germany guaranteed that any frontier disputes with France, Belgium, Czechoslovakia, and Poland were to be settled by international arbitration. France signed treaties with Poland and Czechoslovakia promising support in the event of German attack.

Locarno seemed to mark the real end of the war and the beginning of a new era of peace and cooperation. Stresemann, Briand, and the British foreign secretary Austen Chamberlain were awarded the Nobel peace prize in recognition of this achievement. One power did not join in the general jubilation; the Soviet Union was convinced that Locarno was aimed against it, and indeed France had sought the right to march troops through Germany in the event of war with the Soviets. Stresemann had rejected this suggestion and in order to allay Soviet fears signed a friendship treaty on 26 April 1926. With these new cordial relations with the western powers and a reinsurance treaty with the Soviet Union, Stresemann was now in a strong position to begin a peaceful revision of the eastern frontier. In September 1926, after a dramatic speech by Briand and amid scenes of jubilation, Germany took its seat in the council of the League of Nations in Geneva.

In spite of the Dawes Plan, Germany still found it impossible to meet the yearly reparations bill. The situation was made all the the more precarious by the heavy burden of public debt on the municipalities, particularly Cologne. The Americans invested heavily in short-term loans to cover these debts and no-one foresaw the coming world depression. A conference chaired by American Owen D. Young was held from January to June 1929 again to discuss reparations. The French, British,

A propaganda poster for the German Democratic Party addressed 'To those who want to carry the country to freedom'. A German patriot carries the country up steps marked 'Kapp Putsch', 'London Ultimatum', 'Murder of Rathenau', 'Collapse of the Currency and Occupation of the Ruhr', and 'Reparations Scheme' while being pelted by a Communist and a Nazi. The party portrays itself as one of decent Germans trying to overcome all the difficulties of the day while being attacked by extremists on left and right.

and Belgians insisted that their debts to the United States be covered by payments from Germany. After some acrimony, the Young Plan was finally agreed. For the next fifty-nine years Germany was to make annual payments of about 750 million gold marks rising to 2,000 million and then steadily reducing as the debt was amortized. Most of the Dawes restrictions on Germany's economic sovereignty were abolished and the French and Belgians agreed to an early vacation of the Rhineland. It was a major triumph for Stresemann, but it was to be his last. On 3 October 1929 he died of a heart attack, worn out by his efforts to win support at home for his subtle attempts to restore his country's greatness.

At home the Stresemann years were stable but far from prosperous. The middle class lost their savings in the crash of 1923, civil servants had their incomes reduced, and 25 per cent of state employees lost their jobs in the austerity programme of 1923–24. The disgruntled middle class was a rich recruiting ground for the National Socialists after 1929. Export industries did relatively well, in part because industrial wages remained low. Unemployment rose sharply in the winters of 1926–27 and 1927–28. Yet in spite of these difficulties these were for many the 'golden twenties'. Europe was at peace, the rebellious young were bent on enjoying life, travel became more affordable, and there was a general feeling that the world was entering a new, more peaceful age.

Culturally too this was a golden period. The 1920s were the years of the Bauhaus, of dada's anarchic attacks on traditional art and literature, of twelve-tone music, of major new writers including Thomas Mann, Bertolt Brecht, Hermann Hesse, Erich Kästner, Ernst Jünger and Erich Maria Remarque. German cinema was second to none and theatre and cabaret were politically engaged and excitingly experimental. Yet the much vaunted 'Weimar culture', crushed under the jackboots of the SA and spread abroad by talented exiles, is something of a misnomer. Virtually all the important artistic movements which were developed during the Weimar Republic had in fact already been firmly established in the Wilhelmine period.

The cultural life of Weimar was elitist but claimed to reach out to the masses; it was deeply bourgeois but affected a bohemian contempt for bourgeois decadence and narrow-mindedness. Intellectuals claimed that bourgeois values had been destroyed in the mud of Flanders, but few were certain what should replace them. In such a moral vacuum, the crude certainties of an Adolf Hitler or a Joseph Stalin could provide an attractive security of purpose. The creed of instinct, feeling, and passion was powerfully packaged in the philosophy of Martin Heidegger whose nihilist existentialism had an irresistible appeal for students and lent National Socialism an intellectual respectability. Others, such as Thomas Mann, Ernst Troeltsch and the influential Max Weber, upheld the great tradition of rational thought against the mounting tide of irrationalism and anarchism from both left and right. They were the 'rational republicans' who supported the republic as offering the best possible chance of resolving Germany's problems, as being the

The Bauhaus

The Bauhaus was an art school sponsored by the socialist government of Thuringia and was opened in 1919 with the architect Walter Gropius as director. The emphasis was on handicrafts and an end to what Gropius called the 'arrogant class distinction' between artists and craftsmen. Although local reactionaries complained that the school was a hive of Communist Jews, in the early years it was a collection of bohemians who espoused vegetarianism, eastern religions, communal living, pacifism, and the occult. Their leader was an Austrian, Johannes Itten, but Gropius had no sympathy for Itten's mysticism and backward-looking devotion to arts and crafts, and in 1923 László Moholy-Nagy was appointed his replacement. He was a devotee of the art and technology movement and played an important part in developing the characteristic Bauhaus style.

There was little that was original about this style. Gropius was influenced strongly by Le Corbusier and Van Doesburg and by two journals which preached the new aesthetic – *L'Esprit Nouveau* and *De Stijl*. The Bauhaus exhibition of 1923 was held under the banner 'Art and Technology – a New Unity'. Mies van der Rohe exhibited a model of a glass skyscraper, and Marcel Breuer exhibited some chairs still regarded as classics of modern design.

The new right-wing government closed the school in 1925. Gropius promptly opened a new school in Dessau whose mayor felt it would put the city on the cultural map. At Dessau art and technology triumphed over the less mechanical artistic notions of Kandinsky and Klee, who left. Moholy-Nagy announced that photography meant the end of painting and resigned, complaining that the Bauhaus had become a mere technical school. Gropius resigned in 1928 and pursued an active career as an architect and designer of Adler cars. Meyer took over and announced 'building is just organization'. Theatre was dropped from the curriculum. The concentration was now on design rather than art.

In January 1932 the Dessau town council closed down the Bauhaus, the SPD members of council abstaining during the crucial vote. Mies van der Rohe moved the school to an empty factory in Berlin where the Nazis closed it again in April 1933.

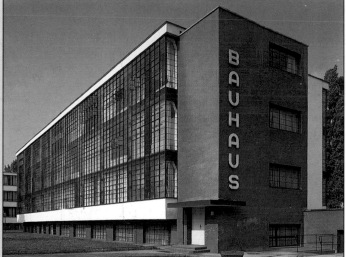

'The Staircase in the Bauhaus' (1932) by Oskar Schlemmer (1888–1942). *Above:* The State Bauhaus School, built in 1925, designed by Walter Gropius (1883–1969).

lesser evil. This was hardly an inspiring vision, and provoked the mockery of the great satirists of the day like Kurt Tucholsky and Carl von Ossietzky.

President Ebert suffered vicious attacks from the satirists' pens because of his support for the republic they despised. He showed courage and wisdom in appointing centrist governments, and was sharply critical of his own party's refusal to compromise responsibly. Like Stresemann he died young, in February 1925, exhausted by a series of attacks on his honour and patriotism. With little support, he fought 173 libel cases to defend his name; even his own party considered expelling him.

No candidate was able to win the necessary absolute majority in the first round of the presidential elections. The left therefore agreed to support the Centre Party's candidate, the ex-chancellor Wilhelm Marx, a dull but highly competent administrator. The right urged the candidature of Field Marshal Hindenburg, a man whose reputation remained untarnished and a link with a glorious and heroic past. Hindenburg had no interest in politics and took considerable persuasion to enter the contest. He won a narrow victory only because the centrist Bavarian Peoples' Party supported him rather than Marx. The republicans' chances were further weakened by the folly of the Communists, whose candidate Ernst Thälmann polled 6.3 per cent of the vote, enough to have given Marx victory.

Hindenburg served the republic to the best of his limited abilities and never breached the constraints imposed by the constitution. He was surrounded by men of dubious intent – aristocratic landowners, nationalistic officers, and anti-republican paramilitarists – and his three closest advisors were his son Oskar, an intriguer of modest talent, Otto Meissner, the opportunist head of the president's office, and Colonel Kurt von Schleicher, a trusted political fixer from the Reichswehr ministry. Their influence grew steadily from 1930 with the president's increasing senility.

The elections of May 1928 were a setback for the nationalists and left the Social Democrats with almost one-third of the Reichstag seats. The National Socialists were reduced from fourteen seats to twelve. It was to be the last chance for the Weimar coalition. The new chancellor was the Social Democrat Hermann Müller, a colourless but effective bureaucrat typical of the German political class. He was detested by the right for being a signatory to the Versailles treaty and dubbed 'Versailles Müller'.

Müller's greatest difficulty was his own party. In 1927, as permitted under Versailles, a new battle cruiser had been commissioned. The Communists had mounted a vigorous campaign against this decision during the election and the Social Democrats had demanded housing and food for hungry children rather than a useless naval vessel. Müller realized that if the coalition was to survive the government would have to build the cruiser, but the Social Democratic faction was united in opposition to the project. Thus observers were treated to the absurd spectacle of Social Democratic ministers voting against their own government.

Supported by the right, the government won the vote and the coalition was saved, but parliamentary democracy had suffered a severe setback. The Centrist DVP withdrew from the coalition when its renewed demand for more ministerial posts was denied. Stresemann, seriously ill and deep in negotiations with the Young Commission, now had to expend much time and energy persuading the DVP to reconsider its decision.

Strikes in the Ruhr were ended by arbitration, skilfully conducted by the Social Democratic minister of the interior Carl Severing, but both the employers and labour were left dissatisfied. Unemployment was rising and the influx of foreign capital dwindling. The mark came under heavy attack and was saved only by the the Bank of England's intervention. On 1 May 1929 a Communist uprising in Berlin resulted in nineteen deaths. Radicalized farmers from Schleswig-Holstein in the Countrymen's Movement (*Landvolkbewegung*) staged bombings in northern Germany. Political violence increased as radicals from left and right grew ever more strident in their denunciations of the republic.

Amid this turmoil the right mounted a campaign against the Young Plan, but only 14 per cent voted for the anti-Young plebiscite. For the National Socialists this was a triumph because they were now able to join forces with the DNVP and appear as respectable members of the right rather than extremists. The DNVP, under the leadership of press baron Alfred Hugenberg, had become increasingly radical and outspoken in its attacks on parliamentary democracy, resulting in the resignation of a number of moderate conservatives. But although a major political force, the DNVP was still virtually without a voice.

An even more serious development was the right turn of the Centre Party under its new leader Ludwig Kaas, a priest who detested the SPD and sought an accommodation with the DNVP. Without the support of the Centre Party the Weimar coalition could not survive. Stresemann's successor as leader of the DVP, Ernst Scholz, was a committed 'anti-Marxist' determined to end his party's association with the SPD. Many Social Democrats, on the other hand, were complaining that their membership of the coalition was a betrayal of socialist principles and a shameful compromise. They argued that the party should regain its integrity in uncompromising opposition.

The great coalition was therefore becoming a pathetic collection of disgruntled and quarrelsome ideologues, blind to the weaknesses of parliamentary democracy, and ignorant of the threat posed by the extremists. That it collapsed was ultimately the fault of the SPD. Faced with a budgetary deficit of 1,500 million marks and unemployment rising from 1.8 to 2.8 million in one year from January 1929, the DVP proposed a reduction in unemployment benefits. The SPD insisted instead that employers' premiums be raised from 3.5 to 4 per cent. Despite opposition from the left and the trades unions, a compromise was reached whereby the higher premiums would be phased in gradually. In March 1930 Müller, seriously ill and soon to die, was forced to resign.

Election poster for the German Democratic Party, May 1928. The slogan reads: 'Women Think About It! Increased Rents, Unemployment, Lack of Housing, Customs Duties, Inflation, Higher Taxation. No More Right-Wing Governments. Vote German Democratic Party List'. The economic misery of ordinary people is blamed on the policies of successive right-wing governments.

THE COLLAPSE OF THE WEIMAR REPUBLIC

Hindenburg can hardly be blamed for not attempting to establish a new majority coalition, parliamentary democracy having so miserably failed. Following the advice of von Schleicher who wanted an independent, anti-parliamentary, anti-Marxist regime, he called upon the Centrist leader Heinrich Brüning to form a new government.

The SPD, KPD, and National Socialists greeted the government with a vote of no-confidence, defeated thanks to the support of the DNVP. Brüning warned that if he did not find a parliamentary majority for his austerity measures he would be obliged to use 'unusual means', by which he meant the emergency presidential powers set out in paragraph 48 of the constitution. When he proposed tax increases and benefit reductions, which he justified by falling prices, the SPD, KPD, and the Hugenberg wing of the DNVP combined to defeat him. Hindenburg then used his emergency powers to pass these measures, but the SPD proposed a successful motion against the use of paragraph 48, whereupon Hindenburg dissolved the Reichstag. There was now no Reichstag to vote against the use of paragraph 48.

In September 1930 there followed a violent and disturbing election campaign. The SPD complained about the misuse of emergency powers, while the government parties blamed the present misery on the profligacy of the socialists and trades unions. With most politicians colourless bureaucrats, only the radicals appealed to the disillusioned electorate. The Communists thundered on against the imperialism of the Versailles Treaty and the Young Plan, about the inequalities of the tax system and the evils of capitalism. The Nazis promised an end to the self-interest and squabbling of the discredited parties, describing an attractive new order of classlessness and national unity. Above all they promised leadership, and in Adolf Hitler they had a spellbinding orator and an organizational genius. He mounted a brilliant campaign.

When the votes were counted the National Socialists were the big winners. Even Hitler was amazed at the results, with 18.3 per cent of the popular vote and their seats increased from 12 to 107. Although the Centre Party hung on to most of its support, the bourgeois parties which backed Brüning lost heavily. The anti-democratic National Socialists, Communists, and DNVP, with 255 of the 577 seats could thus block all of Brüning's attempts to change the constitution and restore the monarchy or pass an emergency bill, since such measures needed a two-thirds vote. But at least they did not have a majority, and the Weimar Republic was not yet doomed.

The National Socialist triumph caused deep concern both at home and abroad and there was widespread fear that Germany was heading for a civil war. Otto Braun spoke for many when he told the United Press that what was needed was a 'big coalition of sensible groups'. He managed to convince his party that they had to support Brüning and accept the use of article 48, otherwise the president would

The Threepenny Opera

In 1928 Ernst-Josef Aufricht took over direction of the Theater am Schiff-bauerdamm in Berlin and was looking for a play to open the new season. The Marxist playwright and poet Bertolt Brecht suggested John Gay's *Beggars Opera*. Aufricht was enthusiastic. Brecht began to write some additional songs which were set to music by Kurt Weill. Caspar Neher designed the sets and Ernst Engel directed. The result was *Die Dreigroschenoper* ('The Three-penny Opera') – the smash hit of the German theatre in the inter-war years.

The success of the work was due not only to Weill's brilliant score which included masterpieces like 'Mack the Knife', and Brecht's witty and biting lyrics, but also to the fact that the audience identified with the musical's message. Left, right, and centre had no difficulty in accepting the analogy between politicians and gangsters. Brecht had not yet become a fully-fledged Communist, but he was already bent on destroying the republic. Socialist political correctness is merci-fully compromised in *The Threepenny Opera* by its sparkling humour and ironic twists, qualities that are sadly lacking in most of Brecht's later work.

Although Brecht took the story from John Gay and added stylistic elements from François Villon and Rudyard Kipling, it is still a highly original text. It tells the story of a gangster Macheath ('Mack the Knife'), who falls in love with Polly Peachum and marries her. His father-in-law organizes London's beggars and provides them with costumes, his motto being: 'My business is to awaken pity'. Peachum thinks that his daughter is far too good for a rogue like Macheath and wants to see him hanged. Mrs Peachum does a deal with Whorehouse Jenny, who betrays Macheath to the police. Macheath escapes but cannot resist another visit to the brothel and is again betrayed by Jenny. This time he ends on the scaffold, lacking the money to bribe his gaolers. At the last moment he is saved by a royal pardon on the king's coronation day and is given a peerage, a castle and a hand-some annuity.

Brecht's aim was to deliver a lecture on the evils and hypocrisies of bour-geois society, but to do so in a light-hearted and comical manner. However like so much cabaret, *The Threepenny Opera* failed in its didactic intent. The comfortable bourgeois in the audience were richly amused. 'First comes the nosh, then comes morals' sings Macheath, and applause came from the stalls. Brecht was deeply disap-pointed that his script had so little impact and completely re-wrote the story, but the new screenplay was not adopted when the opera was filmed. Weill left for America in 1933, where he composed a number of superb musicals, and wrote one of the great-est masterpieces of popular music – *September Song*. Henceforth Brecht collaborated with Hans Eisler, an orthodox Communist who lacked the sparkle, irony, and wit that made Weill a composer of genius.

A scene from a production of *The Threepenny Opera* at the Royal Court Theatre in 1956.

either call fresh elections and almost certainly provide further triumph for the Nazis, or form a new government and include the parties of the extreme right.

Brüning believed that the Nazis could be tamed. If they were given the odd ministerial position in Prussia, or even in the Reich, they might well become respectable and responsible,and abandon their wild rhetoric and thoughtless violence. The chancellor met Hitler in October 1930, but the conversation was unsatisfactory. Hitler treated Brüning to a party political tirade and left him with the impression that any further negotiations were impossible. This impression was heightened when the Reichstag opened. Nazi thugs marched through Berlin smashing the windows of Jewish shops while in the chamber the Nazis demanded the rejection of the Treaty of Versailles, the nationalization of the banks, and the expropriation of finance capitalists and Jews. The Nazis and other right-wing parties, enthusiastically supported by the Communists, proposed a series of no-confidence votes in the chancellor. These were all defeated and his proposals for emergency powers were sent to committee.

Brüning hoped to stimulate exports with a strong dose of deflation, building up foreign reserves for reparations and increasing industrial employment. He further hoped to convince the Allies that in the prevailing circumstances their demands were unreasonable and should be cancelled. He felt that if he could end reparations, the radical right would lose much of its appeal. There were two major difficulties: first, to convince the Allies of Germany's good faith he had to try apparently to satisfy the Young Plan, making himself vulnerable to rightist attack; second, the economic crisis was far more serious than anyone had believed. By the end of 1930 German unemployment had reached five million, which was proportionally the highest level in the world, and it was still rising. Salaries in the public sector were cut by 23 per cent, unemployment and welfare benefits were slashed, and taxation was increased sharply. Brüning hoped these draconian measures would convince the Allies that Germany had reached the absolute limits of its ability to pay.

Brüning suffered a severe setback when his scheme for a customs union with Austria was denounced by the French as a treaty violation. The French withdrew their funds from Austria, precipitating the collapse in May 1931 of a major bank, the Creditanstalt. In the following month President Hoover proposed a moratorium on reparations payments, but this was too late to save the German economy. In July, after the collapse of the Danat, one of Germany's largest, all banks were closed and placed under government control. Later, in January 1932 a conference was held in Lausanne to discuss German reparations, but before the conference met Brüning foolishly revealed his aim to end all such payments. The French ambassador, André François-Poncet, was outraged. The French were now determined not to let Germany off the hook, but Brüning's chances of negotiating an end to reparations were still good, as were the prospects for a satisfactory outcome to the disarmament talks in Geneva.

At home, widespread misery and helplessness were worsened by Brüning's austerity programme. Germany was now hovering on the brink of civil war, with the radical right poised to deliver the death blow to what was left of republican freedoms. In October 1931 the anti-republican right put on a massive show of strength at Bad Harzburg. Uniformed Nazis marched alongside Free Corps veterans as Hitler rubbed shoulders with prominent soldiers, industrialists, and businessmen, among them Seeckt, Lüttwitz, and Hugenberg. But he made it plain he was his own man. The Social Democrats responded by creating the Iron Front, an organization of toothless paramilitaries given to impressively choreographed displays of republican strength. Hindenburg had his first meeting with Hitler on the eve of the Bad Harzburg rally and was not impressed. The president, whose portrait appeared on the postage stamps, announced with heavy wit that he might make him post minister so that he could lick his backside.

In the presidential elections of 1932 Hindenburg was victorious, but not impressively so, and he was disgusted that his support came from the centre and the left. Hitler won 36.8 per cent of the popular vote in the second round. Hindenburg showed little gratitude to Brüning for his campaigning, and his entourage urged him to drop a chancellor too dependent on SPD goodwill. Otto Braun's Prussian government, the last remnant of the Weimar coalition, was determined to crush the National Socialists, and asked Brüning to ban the party's paramilitaries. In April 1932 Brüning and his interior minister General Groener, reluctantly conceded when Braun threatened to ban these uniformed bands in Prussia. Brüning now appeared to be in Otto Braun's pocket.

Hindenburg and his advisors, Schleicher and Meissner, saw their chance to topple Brüning when the chancellor ordered an end to 'Eastern Assistance' (*Osthilfe*), a programme of low interest loans to eastern landowners who were facing financial difficulties. It was an expensive, politically motivated programme designed to help the Junkers, and could no longer be justified. In future only potentially profitable estates were to be assisted; the hopelessly indebted would be divided up into smallholdings for the peasantry. To Hindenburg's Junker cronies this was 'agrarian bolshevism', a direct assault on the Prussian way of life, and they urged the president to dismiss Brüning. The chancellor had little support. Elections in Prussia resulted in the defeat of Otto Braun's Social Democrats, and the Weimar parties in Germany's largest state now had only one seat more than the National Socialists. Otto Braun resigned but continued with a caretaker government. Hindenburg dropped Brüning and on 1 June 1932 appointed Franz von Papen successor.

Papen was an obscure Centre Party backbencher who called for a right-wing coalition government to include the National Socialists. He had consistently opposed the SPD in the Prussian Landtag. Papen was a man of modest ability but considerable charm who had served in the same regiment as Oskar von Hindenburg, a point very much in his favour, and Hindenburg took to him

Paul Ludwig von Hindenburg (1847–1934). He was the famous victor of the Battle of Tannenberg in 1914, when Russian troops were routed by the Germans. He became chief of the general staff from 1916–18, and in 1925 he became the candidate of the right-wing for president. He served as president of the republic from 1925–34, appointing Hitler as chancellor in 1933.

Above left: 'Debauchery', a scene in a Berlin night club by George Grosz (1893–1959), which reveals Grosz's simplistic expressions of disgust at the moral depravity of the Weimar Republic
Above right: 'Wartime Invalids Playing Cards' (1920) by Otto Dix (1891–1969); a typical example of the politically correct art of the Weimar Republic

immediately. Papen's cabinet consisted largely of aristocratic landowners and he announced that he intended to create a 'New State' based on the obscure ideas of Othmar Spann and Edgar J. Jung in which 'true estates' would replace class and 'organic leadership' replace democracy. Welfare benefits were to be drastically cut, Christianity would give Germany the strength to combat 'cultural Bolshevism' and face its foreign enemies, while 'national' forces were to be fostered. For the Weimar parties the circumstances of Papen's appointment and the vagueness of his programme were intolerable. Prudently he resigned from the party before being ousted, the Centre now considering him worse than Hitler. Amid violence akin to civil war, new elections were called.

Papen's first fatal step towards creating his 'New State' was to topple the government of Prussia. Acting on a rumour that Otto Braun's Social Democrats had made an alliance with the Communists to combat National Socialism, and using the violence in Hamburg as an excuse, Papen appointed a Reich commissar for Prussia in place of the legitimate government and declared a state of emergency in Berlin and Brandenburg on 20 July.

The end of the Prussian state was an illegal move, a putsch which destroyed the last bastion of German democracy. The republican parties stood helplessly by. The labour movement would not risk calling a general strike, fearing that few would answer. The episode was soon forgotten in the election, when the National Socialists were again the big winners; with 230 seats they were now the largest faction in the Reichstag. The next largest, the SPD, had only 133, the KPD had an impressive 89, and the Centre Party with its Bavarian branch had 97. The election was a triumph for the anti-democrats, but a disaster for Papen and Schleicher. The Nazis were now far too strong to accept orders from the agrarians, industrialists, and bankers behind Papen's government. Papen offered Hitler two ministerial posts, but Hitler told Hindenburg that he would accept nothing less that the chancellorship. Papen could not work with the new Reichstag so dissolved it, but not before it had passed a no-confidence vote of 512 to 42 – the worst result for any chancellor in German history.

Political violence and strikes grew steadily more widespread. Fifty people were killed in the fortnight after the elections. In the Berlin transport strike of November 1932 National Socialists, Communists and university students worked closely together. The new election held amid this chaos was a setback for the National Socialists who lost two million votes, while the Communists made substantial gains. It looked as if Papen could now go ahead and realize his plans for his 'New State', but Hindenburg took his oath to the constitution seriously and would not contemplate overthrowing the parliamentary regime. Hindenburg ordered Papen to negotiate with the parties, but both the SPD and the Centre Party refused. Some members of the DNVP, DVP, and Bavarian Peoples' Party (BVP) backed the chancellor, but they accounted for only13.4 per cent of the seats. Papen therefore resigned, but continued to head a caretaker administration in the hope that Hindenburg would change his mind.

Hindenburg negotiated with the parties to try to form a majority government. He told Hitler that he would consider appointing him chancellor if he could find a Reichstag majority. Hitler could not; the right and its backers wanted Papen. Hitler then wanted to form a presidial government ruling by emergency decree, as Brüning and Papen had done, but Hindenburg refused on the grounds that this would lead to one-party dictatorship. As no-one was able to form a viable

Much of the painting during the Weimar Republic was politically motivated and tended to rely on stereotypical icons of reaction, militarism, capitalism and moral depravity. Max Beckmann (1884–1950) was able to capture the profound malaise of the times in a powerful imagery which never stooped to caricature and which transcended the specific issues of the day. 'The Femina Bar' was painted in 1936.

parliamentary government, Papen was confident that Hindenburg would reappoint him. At this juncture Schleicher circulated a study by the Reichswehr claiming that Germany was heading for a civil war which the army and police would be unable to control. Hindenburg was greatly alarmed and told Papen that much to his regret he had decided to appoint Schleicher in his stead. Local elections at the beginning of December were a disaster for the National Socialists. In Thuringia their vote was 40 per cent less than in the summer. The economic signs were encouraging and many commentators predicted that, having peaked, Hitler and National Socialism were now on their way out.

The new chancellor had a reputation as a reactionary general and an unprincipled opportunist, but in fact he was something of a dreamer and ideologue. He believed in the possibility of a third way between socialism and capitalism in which Prussian conservatives could cooperate with responsible workers against greedy capitalists and fanatical Marxists. His somewhat confused ideas were close to those of Gregor Strasser, the chief organizer of the Nazi Party, who remained a faithful anti-capitalist and felt Hitler's involvement with industrialists and bankers a betrayal. Schleicher hoped to split the Nazi Party by appointing Strasser vice-chancellor. On the night of 8–9 December Strasser agonized whether to challenge Hitler, while Hitler, facing the loss of his party's control, contemplated suicide. Finally, Strasser's nerves failed him and he slipped away from Berlin. Hitler quickly smashed Strasser's power base in the party and unity was restored.

Schleicher still hoped to win over the Strasser wing of the Nazi Party and join forces with the moderate labour movement. To this end he proposed an imaginative welfare programme, social legislation and deficit financing designed to stimulate economic activity. Many trades unionists welcomed Schleicher's initiative, but the SPD leadership was so demoralized and unimaginative, all they could propose was another no-confidence vote, while the unions were persuaded to decline Schleicher's offer. Otto Braun was almost alone in realizing that the real danger lay in National Socialism. He offered his support to Schleicher if he would restore the *status quo ante* in Prussia, dissolve the Reichstag, postpone elections until the spring, and concentrate on combating the Nazis. Schleicher doubted whether Hindenburg would agree to a dissolution, felt that Braun had little support in his own party, and still hoped to woo Strasser.

Meanwhile, Strasser had regained his nerves and Hindenburg was ready to appoint him vice-chancellor, when Hitler mounted a savage attack on his disloyal minion. Finding himself without support, Strasser retired to private life as a dispensing chemist. Schleicher's failure to form a viable government gave Papen his opportunity for revenge. The industrialists and bankers still supported Papen, whose reflationary policies they had welcomed, and they were highly alarmed by Schleicher, whom they saw as a socialist in uniform. Papen argued that if Hitler were made chancellor the government would have a viable majority in the

Reichstag, and Hitler could be controlled and manipulated by the more moderate conservative forces. On 4 January 1933 Papen discussed these plans with Hitler and it was agreed that Papen should be Hitler's vice-chancellor, and that the DNVP be given a number of ministerial positions in the new government.

The only obstacle to Hitler's appointment was Hindenburg's dislike of the 'Bohemian corporal'. The decisive factor in his change of mind was the attitude of the agrarians who, aggrieved at Schleicher's complaints about their misuse of the *Osthilfe*, were calling for Schleicher's replacement by Hitler. Hindenburg was also persuaded by General von Blomberg, the army commander in East Prussia, and his chief of staff von Reichenau, that the Reichswehr would welcome Hitler as chancellor. The president imagined that Blomberg was speaking for the entire army. In fact he and von Reichenau were the only senior officers who supported the National Socialists. Hindenburg's remaining reservations were removed when Hitler agreed that Papen should be vice-chancellor and commissar for Prussia, and that Blomberg should be Reichswehr minister. Hindenburg imagined that his beloved Prussia and the army would thus not fall into the hands of the vulgar, radical National Socialists. Wild rumours that Schleicher and the generals were plotting a coup gave Hindenburg the final push, and on 30 January 1933 he called upon Hitler to form a government.

The right was delighted with the appointment. The only National Socialists in the cabinet were Hitler and Frick who, although minister of the interior, had no jurisdiction over Prussia. Papen confidently told a friend that they had 'employed' Mr Hitler and that within two months they would have him completely at their command. On the left there was resignation and helplessness. One improbable observer saw the situation with complete clarity. General Ludendorff wrote to his former superior officer Field Marshal von Hindenburg: 'By appointing Hitler chancellor you have handed over our sacred German fatherland to one of the biggest demagogues of all time. I solemnly prophesy that this wretched man will plunge our country into the depths and will bring unimaginable suffering to our nation. Future generations will curse you in your grave for this action'.

CHAPTER 11 | *National Socialist Germany*

Initially, Hitler was anxious to appear a traditional statesman. He worked closely with the established bureaucracy in the chancellory and the foreign office. The right was convinced that it had him under control, while the left insisted he was merely a puppet of the industrialists and land-owners. Both illusions sprang from the assumption that Hitler's appointment as chancellor was the end of a process. In fact it was the beginning of one, the breathtakingly rapid establishment of a fascist dictatorship. Hitler and his party had no experience of government and had used parliamentary bodies only as platforms for their propaganda, but they had an anarchic energy and an insatiable thirst for power which might well have led to self-destruction had it not been contained and controlled by a superb bureaucracy and military machine. Their task was made easier by the 1930 failure of parliamentary democracy.

THE ESTABLISHMENT OF THE NAZI STATE

On 1 February 1933 Hindenburg agreed to Hitler's request to dissolve the Reichstag. This enabled him to rule by presidential decrees for seven weeks and to conduct an election campaign from a position of exceptional power. The 'Decree for the Protection of the German People', which Hindenburg signed into law on 4 February, gave the government the power to silence any of the opposition parties by claiming that they were 'spreading obvious untruths' or 'endangering the vital interests of the state'. Hindenburg agreed to Papen's demand for the dissolution of the Prussian Landtag and all local governments, effectively a second coup d'état. On 22 February the Nazi Party's paramilitary organizations – the SA and SS, Hitler's personal bodyguard – were employed as auxiliary police in Prussia to combat the leftist threat, a move also approved by Papen. Göring now began his systematic purge of the Prussian bureaucracy and police force, and started replacing loyal republicans with ultra-conservatives and National Socialists.

The military, who had many reservations about the Nazis, were easily won over by Hitler. On 3 February he had attended a dinner for senior commanders and assured them that the army would remain outside politics, that he intended to rearm and introduce universal military service, and that his main aim was to eradicate Marxism. Many overheard his remarks about 'radically Germanizing' the East, to win *Lebensraum* (literally 'living space').

Göring and Schacht found it equally easy to convince twenty-five leading industrialists led by Krupp, chairman of the Reich Association of German Industry (RDI), to provide the Nazi Party with a handsome election fund. The end of parliamentary democracy was welcomed as a necessary precondition for the struggle against the Marxist unions and the achievement of national unity and strength. Three million marks seemed a modest price to pay for the realization of this programme. Throughout the election campaign there were bans on the left-wing and democratic press, which were lifted only after appeals to the supreme court. SA and SS teams attacked Social Democratic and Communist meetings and the police searched party offices for incriminating evidence. One thing was lacking – clear evidence that the Communists were contemplating an uprising. The opportunity came at 9.0 p.m. on the evening of 27 February when a fire was discovered in the Reichstag which soon destroyed the building. At 9.27 the

Adolf Hitler (1889–1945) in National Socialist party uniform by an unknown artist. Hitler, the petit bourgeois, had a typically Philistine taste in art and chose to be portrayed in the conventional pose of a Great Man. Though he always appeared in public in uniform he wore civilian clothes whenever he was in private, especially in his favourite Bavarian retreat.

police arrested a Dutch journeyman mason, Marinus van der Lubbe; he was a Communist sympathizer.

A fierce debate began as to the cause of the fire, a debate which has yet to be settled. Was it orchestrated by the Nazis to give them the excuse they needed, or did van der Lubbe act alone? Certainly there is no evidence that the Communists had planned it. During the night of the fire Göring ordered the arrest of all leading Communists, including members of the Reichstag. Party offices and the Communist press were closed down. The Social Democratic press was banned for the remaining two weeks of the election campaign. On the following day Hindenburg signed the 'Presidential Decree for the Protection of the People and the State' which permitted arbitrary arrest and the suspension of all civil liberties. The decree also gave the Reich government power to limit the sovereignty of the federal states, a vital step in the establishment of the Nazi dictatorship. Indeed, the decree was the dictatorship's fundamental law and remained in force until the bitter end; that it was unconstitutional hardly mattered. The supreme court in Leipzig, by ruling that there had been no Communist conspiracy, removed the legal basis of the decree, but by then it was too late.

The elections took place on 5 March 1933 and were disappointing for the National Socialists. Despite the terror, the silencing of the left, and a brilliant campaign, they won only 43.9 per cent of the vote. However, since the Communist deputies, with 12.2 per cent, were all arrested, the Nazis had no need of a coalition partner in the Reichstag and the DNVP was quickly excluded.

The centralization of power, known as 'coordination' (*Gleichschaltung*) began on the day of the election, when the Hamburg senate was forced out of office and replaced by National Socialists on the pretext that it could no longer guarantee law and order. One by one the German states were brought under the direct control of Berlin. Only in Bavaria was there any serious opposition to these unconstitutional moves, but the government of Dr Heinrich Held, having at first resisted the SA threats, was forced to accept the Nazi General von Epp as a commissar responsible for law and order. On 16 March, Held resigned.

The head of the SS, Heinrich Himmler, began his remarkable career in law-enforcement with the appointment of von Epp. Himmler became police chief of Munich and then took control of the political police in Bavaria. He was still a relatively obscure figure, overshadowed by his more brilliant and sinister lieutenant, Reinhold Heydrich. Ernst Röhm and his thugs in the SA played a far more prominent role in these early months, beating up politicians, flinging opponents into hastily improvised prisons and torture camps, and terrorizing the population. SA troops destroyed Jewish shops, stole their merchandise and incarcerated or killed their owners. In many places prominent SA men became police chiefs and continued their purge under a mantle of legitimacy.

The SA also began an assault on the capitalist system, to the considerable alarm of Hitler's new allies in industry and banking. An SA unit marched into the

Frankfurt stock exchange and demanded the resignation of the board of directors. The SA attacked the Socialist cooperative stores and demanded positions on the boards of directors of banks and industrial concerns. Hitler refused to listen to Papen's complaints about these anarchic outbursts, but was also beginning to feel that the revolution had to be institutionalized, that the spontaneous violence of the SA had to be ordered and bureaucratized. The opening of the first concentration camp at Dachau near Munich, under the supervision of Himmler and Heydrich, was the first step in this direction.

In order to placate those who were alarmed at the violence of the SA and the rhetoric of Nazi fanatics, an elaborate festival of national revival was organized on 21 March, the day that the Reichstag was re-opened in Potsdam. The date was symbolic; it was not only the first day of spring, but also the day on which Bismarck had opened the first German Reichstag in 1871. The ceremony was held in the Garrison Church in Potsdam by the grave of Frederick the Great. Hindenburg appeared in a field-marshal's uniform, Hitler in an immaculate morning coat. The cynically staged performance was enormously popular. Hitler's obeisance before Hindenburg was seen as proof that the revolutionary fervour of National Socialism would be restrained by traditional Prussian values and that the anarchy of the SA would be curbed by the legendary efficiency of Prussian bureaucracy.

The Reichstag met for one purpose only, to put an end to the last vestiges of parliamentary rule. A two-thirds majority was needed to pass the Enabling Act which interior minister Frick had prepared, and this was easily achieved, as the parties believed it was aimed only against the Communists. The SPD alone voted against the motion, giving the impression that there was a broad consensus for Hitler's dictatorial ambitions. Those who pointed out that the Enabling Act was flagrantly unconstitutional were soon to be in prison or exile.

With the Enabling Act the political parties became irrelevant. The Communist Party was never formally banned, but it had already been destroyed. The Social Democratic trades unions, which had earlier distanced themselves from the SPD and had sought an accommodation with the Nazis, were banned on 2 May 1933. On 10 May Göring ordered the seizure of all SPD assets and on 22 June the party was outlawed. The DNVP and the Stahlhelm came under increasing attack, and a number of members were arrested on bogus charges of Marxist sympathy. Hugenberg caused a scandal during the economic conference in London in June by demanding German colonies and Eastern expansion; it was now easy for Hitler to dismiss him. The remaining members of the DNVP and the Stahlhelm were absorbed into the Nazi Party and the SA.

On 28 March the Catholic bishops, meeting in Fulda, had pledged their loyalty to the new regime. Anxious to conclude a concordat, the Vatican had denounced political Catholicism. The Centre Party was thus abandoned by the Church and left powerless, having voted for the Enabling Act. On 5 July the party saw no alternative to self-dissolution. The concordat was concluded three days later and

Storm troopers picket a
Jewish store during the anti-
Jewish campaign of 1 April
1933. The slogan reads:
'Germans Defend Yourselves!
Do Not Buy from Jews!'

silenced the Catholic Church as a possible centre of opposition to the regime. On
14 July the Nazi Party was proclaimed the only legal political party in Germany.

In the early weeks of the regime there were vicious anti-Semitic outbursts in
which SA thugs played a prominent role, but it was not until 1 April that the Nazis
organized a systematic boycott of Jewish shops in Germany. Reactions were mixed:
some were curious; others sympathized with Jewish shopkeepers whom they had
patronized for years; many ignored the warning that 'Germans should not buy from
Jews'. There was little enthusiasm for the action amongst ordinary people.

On 7 April 1933 the 'Law for the Reconstruction of the Professional Civil
Service' was enacted under which Jews and members of opposition parties were
dismissed from public employment. Within a year 4,000 lawyers, 3,000 doctors,
2,000 civil servants and a large number of university professors, artists, musicians,
and actors lost their livelihoods simply because they were Jewish. Only those who
had served in the war were spared, through the personal intervention of President
Hindenburg. Although most German Jewish organizations failed to realize the
seriousness of the situation and advised Jews to remain in the country, some 37,000
emigrated in the first year of the Third Reich.

In the 'Action against the Un-German Spirit' of 10 May, university towns lit bonfires into which were thrown the works of such prominent authors as Heinrich Heine, Sigmund Freud, Erich Maria Remarque, Heinrich Mann, and Erich Kästner. Meanwhile Goebbels, as minister of propaganda, took full control of the radio, which until then had been only partially state-owned. The national and provincial press were also placed under strict supervision, and a large number of newspapers closed.

Gleichschaltung affected every walk of life. Professional organizations of doctors, lawyers, and farmers were all brought under Party control. Henceforth there were only National Socialist beekeepers' associations and National Socialist cycle clubs. Even the village skittles teams were supervised by the Party. As a result, Germany's vigorous and varied club life withered, and people stayed at home or visited the local pub, becoming increasingly watchful for police informants.

The breakneck speed of these changes began to worry Hitler, who told a group of leading Party functionaries on 6 July that the revolution was over and that the period of consolidation of power had begun. 'The Party,' he said 'is now the state'. The mass party and the SA radicals had played an invaluable role in bringing Hitler to power, but now they were beginning to threaten his government. Ernst Röhm feared that the revolution was losing its dynamic and 'falling asleep'. In the summer of 1933 he proclaimed: 'It is high time that the national revolution should become the National Socialist Revolution', and at mass meetings called for a programme to drive out the reactionaries from the military, the bureaucracy, and from industry. He was determined that the Reichswehr, which Hitler had spared from the process of *Gleichschaltung*, should be purged. 'The grey rock of the Reichswehr,' he announced, 'will disappear beneath the brown wave of the SA.' Hitler could not tolerate such a suggestion. He needed the Reichswehr professionals to supervise rearmament and provide military expertise. The street-fighting men of the SA might be fired with political zeal, but they had none of the skills needed to fight a modern war. The Reichswehr was alarmed by Röhm's ambitions and suggested that the SA should form a territorial force under army control. Hitler knew this was unacceptable to Röhm, could not break his pact with the Reichswehr, so had no alternative but to get rid of the SA boss.

The army was perfectly willing to make some concessions to the National Socialists. In February 1934 the swastika was adopted as an official military emblem and the traditionally anti-Semitic officer corps purged its ranks of Jews. In the same month Hitler told Röhm and the army minister Blomberg that the SA

Hitler addresses an immense crowd at Tempelhof airfield, Berlin, on 1 May 1934. The organizers claimed that the crowd numbered two million. Hitler, in spite of his unattractive accent and lack of mastery of the German language, was an extraordinarily effective orator who took great pains in the preparation of his speeches and paid minute attention to every detail of timing, gestures and inflection. Even his opponents testified to his uncanny ability to sway a crowd.

should restrict its activities to political indoctrination and pre-military training, that the Reichswehr would remain independent, and that the revolution was over. Röhm was furious with Hitler, whom he described to his cronies as 'an ignorant corporal', and swore that he would ignore the agreement he had made. Pressure from the SA rank and file to resist Party atrophy and the 'reactionaries' was mounting, and Röhm's criticisms were becoming increasingly strident.

Röhm, the second most powerful man in the Reich, had powerful enemies. Göring, Goebbels, and Hess were jealous of his position and were determined to topple him. Himmler and Heydrich resented the fact that the SS played second fiddle to the SA. And the Reichswehr was determined to frustrate his ambitions. Criticism not only of the SA but also of Hitler's regime was now coming from conservative circles. On 17 June, Papen delivered a speech at Marburg attacking the regime's 'unnatural totalitarian aspirations' and arguing that the 'German revolution' was an excuse for 'selfishness, lack of character, untruthfulness, ungentlemanly behaviour and arrogance'. He called for a return to traditional conservative values and insisted that the independence of the judiciary should not be compromised.

Goebbels censored Papen's speech, so it was not reported by press or radio. Its author Edgar Jung was arrested on 26 June. Papen offered his resignation, but Hitler refused. Although there was no evidence that the SA was planning a coup, on 30 June many prominent critics of the regime were murdered and many scores settled. Hitler personally arrested Röhm who was still in bed in a boarding house in Bad Wiessee. One of Röhm's lieutenants was caught in bed with a boy, so Hitler could pose as a champion of public decency, although Röhm's notorious homosexual exploits had not troubled him before. In the next few hours some 100 people were murdered, including Schleicher and his wife, the former Bavarian minister-president von Kahr, and a completely innocent music critic Dr Wilhelm Schmidt, who had the misfortune to be confused with the SA leader Ludwig Schmitt. Hitler hesitated before ordering his friend Röhm's execution, but told the commandant of Dachau concentration camp to kill him the next day.

Although the state had degenerated to the level of a criminal organization there was widespread enthusiasm for these murders. The Reichswehr was delighted that a tiresome rival had been silenced and ordinary Germans were relieved that the radicals and fanatics had been disciplined. There was widespread admiration for Hitler's decisive action and the myth of the Führer was further enhanced. The advance of the SS went almost unnoticed, and with Hitler making them independent of the SA, they were soon to prove far more dangerous rivals to the Reichswehr than the SA had ever been.

THE CONSOLIDATION OF THE NAZI DICTATORSHIP

On 2 August 1934 Hindenburg died and was buried with great pomp at Tannenberg, the site of his greatest victory. In a flagrantly unconstitutional move

Hitler promptly combined the offices of chancellor and president. Blomberg responded by calling upon the army to make an oath of allegiance to Hitler, rather than to the constitution as had previously been the practice. This caused many officers pangs of conscience, and some began to contemplate active resistance.

Outwardly, the Nazi regime seemed highly centralized and ruthlessly efficient, with Hitler in full command. But although he was an absolute dictator, it was never possible for him to control all aspects of government. His social-Darwinian belief that the best would succeed led to his creation of a series of competing government bodies and special commissions. The strong leaders, such as Schacht (the minister of economics), Frick (the interior minister), Speer (later to become armaments minister), and even Himmler, who tried to introduce some order, were all frustrated; there was always scope for ambitious radicals. In June a senior Party official had written to Frick: 'Legally the state governors (*Reichsstatthalter*) are subordinate to you as minister of the interior. Adolf Hitler is governor of Prussia. He has delegated his powers to minister-president Göring. You are also Prussian minister of the interior. As Reich minister of the interior Adolf Hitler and the Prussian minister-president are legally subordinate to you. Since you are the same person as the Prussian minister of the interior you are subordinate to the Prussian minister-president and to yourself as Reich minister of the interior. I am not a legal scholar, but I am sure that such a situation has never occurred before.' Such chaos meant that National Socialism never lost its activist dynamic by becoming bureaucratized. If parts of the Nazi movement degenerated into routine place-seeking and corruption, others became increasingly radical and violent. Both strains came together in the 'Final Solution' in which meticulous bureaucy and murderous extremism combined with horrific results.

Hitler detested desk-bound specialists and was fond of repeating his conviction that one brilliant idea was worth more than a whole life of conscientious paper-shuffling. The 'leadership principle' (*Führerprinzip*) justified the appointment of special plenipotentiaries to cut through red tape and get things done: Dr Fritz Todt was given the task of building the autobahns; Heinrich Himmler's SS was placed directly under Hitler and cut across the fields of competence of countless established institutions. This administrative Blitzkrieg led to some great achievements in the early years of the regime, but by 1942 the all-powerful Bormann was complaining that far too much energy was wasted on interdepartmental rivalry and the struggle for power.

Hitler's position as the 'Führer', standing far above the political rivalries and struggles of his underlings, was enhanced by a series of remarkable successes in foreign policy and economics and, in the early stages of the war, on the battlefield. By contrast, the Nazi Party became increasingly unpopular. Local Party officials, known contemptuously as 'golden pheasants' because of their braid, were loathed as self-satisfied, idle, and corrupt. During the war they were seen as cowards whose positions exempted them from military service. Hitler was largely immune to such

The 1936 Olympic Games

The Berlin Olympics of 1936 were a propaganda triumph for the Nazis. In 1933 the regime had made every possible effort to host the forthcoming games and was determined to use them to show the new Germany to the world in the best possible light. Violence, discrimination, and racial hatred were to be scrupulously concealed behind the facade of a chic, cosmopolitan, and fun-loving Berlin. Germany was to be shown as a healthy, hard-working, prosperous, and contented society with a superb welfare state. The games were meticulously organized, lavishly presented, and generously hosted. National Socialism took a back seat, political slogans were removed, the ubiquitous swastika sparingly used. Jews enjoyed a temporary respite from their persecutors.

The magnificently staged opening ceremony was also a political triumph. Although Hitler had occupied the Rhineland only a few months before, the French team marched around the arena giving the Hitler salute. Kings, presidents, politicians, and princes came to Berlin to see Adolf Hitler, the saviour of a great nation, rather than to enjoy the sport. The high and mighty of the Third Reich gave magnificent receptions for distinguished foreign guests. Goebbels hosted an Italian evening for 1,000 on the Pfaueninsel. Göring went one better by building an entire miniature village in eighteenth-century style in the garden of his ministry, and spent hours on the back of an unfortunate pony driving a roundabout. In the evening he held a banquet in the Berlin opera house which was entirely redecorated in cream-coloured silk for the occasion. Ribbentrop celebrated his appointment as German ambassador to Britain by pouring vast quantities of champagne down the throats of his 700 guests under a huge marquee in the garden of his villa in Dahlem.

These parties made the Nazi elite socially respectable. They mingled with members of the aristocracy, bankers and industrialists, film stars, athletes, and nouveaux riches. André François-Poncet, the French ambassador whose memoirs provide a fascinating account of these years in Berlin, remarked that it was impossible to believe that such suave and charming hosts could also be murderers, torturers, and warmongers. Hitler appeared in the Olympic arena as a man of peace and international understanding while at the same time he had ordered the armed services and industry to be ready for war within four years.

The games were a triumph for Nazi Germany. Their team lay in first place, winning thirty-three gold, twenty-six silver and thirty bronze medals, with the USA in second place. The greatest surprise at the games was England's victory over Canada in the ice-hockey finals. The greatest shock was that the hero of the day was Jesse Owens, who won three gold medals, with a new world record in the 100-metres and olympic records in the 200-metres and the long jump, as well as being a member of the winning relay team. He was a superb athlete and a delightful personality, but as an African-American he was unacceptable to Nazi racists. Hitler refused to compromise his principles by shaking hands with this outstanding representative of a race which he considered subhuman.

Victors in gymnastics at the XI Olympic Games in Berlin, 1–16 August 1936: 1 Schwarzmann (Germany), 2 Mack (Switzerland), 3 Frey (Germany).

criticism: 'If only the Führer knew' was a common lament, and the worse things were, the greater his role as focus of the nation's hopes and dreams became.

There was no clear distinction between the Party and the state. Many leading figures held both Party and state offices, among them Goebbels, Himmler, Hess, Rust, and Darré. The Gauleiters, who were Party officials, often also held government office as Reich governors (*Reichsstadthälter*) or minister-presidents. The SS, seen as the perfect expression of National Socialism, combined aspects of state and Party to a degree which transcended both. Himmler and his ambitious and murderous underling Heydrich, wrenched the political police in Bavaria free from any legal and administrative constraints, and turned it into a perfect instrument of terror, backed up by the uniformed SS and the concentration camps. In Prussia Göring had converted the old political police into the Secret State Police, known by the acronym Gestapo (*Geheime Staatspolizei*), but as yet it was not quite as free from constraint as its Bavarian equivalent.

On 17 June 1936 Himmler was appointed police chief of the whole of Germany. Policing, which had hitherto been a matter for the individual states, was now centralized under the head of the SS, a party political organization. Himmler was theoretically a state secretary for police affairs under the minister of the interior, but Frick knew only too well that, as chief of the SS, Himmler was answerable only to the Führer. Himmler declared that the police had no intention of enforcing the law, but that its task was to 'reflect the reality of the National Socialist Führer state' and to 'carry out the wishes of the leadership'.

At first the police force was divided into two main branches – the Order Police (*Ordnungspolizei*) responsible for routine police work, and the Security Police (*Sicherheitspolizei*) made up of the Criminal Police (*Kripo*) and the Gestapo. In 1939 the Security Police was combined with the Security Service (*Sicherheitsdienst* – SD), the Party's spy service, to form the Reich Security Main Office (RSHA) under Heydrich. In 1937 Himmler announced that there were five main divisions of the SS: the General SS were part-timers who underwent military training; the Auxilliary Troops (*Verfügungstruppe*) were a territorial army reserve and auxiliary police force which in 1938 formed the basis of the Waffen-SS; the Death's Head Units ran the concentration camps and, in Himmler's words, 'eradicated crime and racially inferior trash'; the Security Service was the 'ideological information agency' of the Party and state; and the Racial and Settlement Main Office was to ensure that the German race was purified and provided with *Lebensraum*.

Not all policemen were in the SS, and many did not meet the rigorous, if bizarre, racial and physical criteria for membership. The SS were concerned to create a new racial order, extirpate the evil works of Jewish-Bolshevik 'subhumans', and build a curious atavistic society that was based on the traditions and superstitions of a distant Germanic past. After the appalling outbursts of violence against Jews by the SA in the early weeks of the regime and the banning of Jews from public employment in April 1933, anti-Semitism became slightly more moderate. Despite

Uniformed paramilitary organizations were a characteristic of Weimar politics. Both the Communist Party and the Social Democrats had similar organizations. The SA was the militant uniformed wing of the Nazi party until 1934 but was later to be eclipsed by the SS which, in the early years, had simply provided Hitler with his bodyguards.

calls for a more active policy, little happened except the banning of Jews from the armed services in May 1935. Suddenly, in September 1935 Hitler, who was in Nuremberg for the Party rally, demanded a 'law on the Jews'. A draft was hastily drawn up in the middle of the night by the exhausted staff of the interior ministry who had no idea what was expected of them. Hitler approved the draft at 2.30 a.m.

The Nuremberg Laws forbade marriages between Jews and 'citizens of German or similar blood'. Jews could not employ 'Aryan' domestic servants. They could not display the German national flag and could not enjoy the full privileges of citizenship. The law did not specify who was considered to be Jewish, thus giving a wide scope for interpretation to the more vicious anti-Semites, but those affected were reassured by the promise that this would be the final piece of anti-Jewish legislation. Although the Nazis insisted that Jews were a race, the definition of a Jew was someone who had at least three grandparents who were practising Jews. A 'half-Jew' was considered to be Jewish if he practised Judaism. Ultimately, Jewishness was defined in religious rather than racial terms, although some racial fanatics were to spare some orthodox Jews on the grounds that they were not 'racially' Jewish.

The Nazis paid particular attention to youth, insisting that he who controlled youth controlled the future. Boys joined the Young Folk (*Jungvolk* – JV) from the age of ten to fourteen and then donned the uniform of the Hitler Youth (*Hitler Jugend* – HJ). From the outset the emphasis was on military discipline, sense of community, vocational training, sport, and political indoctrination. The youngest members of the Jungvolk learnt their catechism: 'Our Leader Adolf Hitler was born in Braunau on 20 April 1889. His father was a customs officer, his mother a housewife...' Yet in spite of massive efforts to force German youth into the HJ, only 60 per cent of those eligible were members as late as 1936. The parallel organizations for girls were the Young Girls (*Jungmädel*) and the League of German Girls (*Bund Deutsche Mädchen* – BDM) in which girls were trained for their future roles as wives, mothers, and housewives. Both HJ and BDM members were frequently excused school to attend courses and functions. Deaf to teachers' complaints, the authorities placed 'character', 'willpower', and 'racial spirit' far above 'cold intellect' and a 'mechanical world-view'.

Initially, these youth organizations had much of the anti-bourgeois radicalism, elitism, and emotional anti-intellectualism of the youth movements in Wilhelmine Germany, but soon they degenerated into vast bureaucratic training camps for soldiers, housewives, and Party officials. Many young people became disenchanted with National Socialist regimentation and many teachers omitted the new ideology from their history and literature classes. Education remained traditionally conservative rather than National Socialist. Ambitious attempts to create a 'new aristocracy' of racially pure, physically strong, and ideologically motivated youth in Nazi- and SS-run schools failed to have much effect. Germany was soon at war and the pupils in these institutions were among the first to be called for auxiliary work with the military, with evacuees, and later, with refugees.

NAZI ECONOMIC POLICY

The popularity of the National Socialist regime was due to its notable economic successes and foreign policy triumphs. On 1 February 1933 Hitler delivered a radio address in which he promised to abolish unemployment within four years. This seemed an improbable boast, but he was true to his word. By 1936 not only had unemployment been overcome, at a time when unemployment in the USA still ran at 20 per cent, but in some areas there were even serious labour shortages.

The Nazis continued with the Keynesian policies of the Papen and Schleicher governments, but did so with extraordinary determination. In the first two years 5,000 million marks were spent on improving the infrastructure, on subsidies for private housing, and on greatly increased armaments orders. The most dramatic and highly publicized of these programmes was the building of the autobahn network. This was done to create work and for propaganda purposes, not for strategic reasons as is often claimed. The generals preferred to move their troops by train, and had no say in where these highways were to be built.

Working women who married were given a credit of 1,000 marks if they gave up their job; 378,000 women had taken advantage of this offer by the beginning of 1935, creating the same number of jobs and injecting millions of marks into the consumer goods market.

Deficit spending on this level was soon to create serious problems, particularly when armaments began to take the lion's share of the budget. In 1933 arms accounted for 4 per cent of public spending, by 1936 it was 39 per cent, and by 1938, 50 per cent. Government income was insufficient to meet this huge increase; in 1938 it spent 30,000 million marks with a revenue of only 17,700 million. Krupp, Siemens, Gutehoffnungshütte, and Rheinmetall, four of Germany's most powerful industrial enterprises, formed the *Metallurgische Forschungsgemeinschaft* (Mefo) in 1933 with the modest capital of 1 million marks, and Schacht, president of the Reichsbank, introduced bills of exchange known as Mefo Bills in order to finance the deficit. Companies with armaments contracts could draw bills on Mefo, bills which were discounted by the Reichsbank and soon became a virtual second currency. The dangers of runaway inflation grew very real, so the Reichsbank stopped issuing Mefo bills in the spring of 1938.

Henceforth armaments were paid for by granting tax credits and by forcing banks and insurance companies to lend the government huge sums which the regime hoped to repay after a successful war of conquest. Arms orders on this scale disrupted foreign trade. As early as 1934 Schacht had introduced his 'New Plan' which created a virtual state monopoly over foreign trade. A series of agreements were made with states in south-eastern Europe and Central and South America in which raw materials and agricultural products were exchanged for industrial goods. Within a year Germany had a positive balance of trade.

By the spring of 1936 the arms programme was seriously disrupting the economy, and in April Göring was given the task of boosting rearmament. It was clear that exports had been maximised, that the foreign exchange shortage would continue, and that Germany must therefore rely on its own resources, invest heavily in the production of artificial raw materials like oil and rubber, and arm in breadth rather than depth in preparation for a short and limited war – a Blitzkrieg. This strategy was contained in a memorandum by Hitler in August 1936 in which he ordered that the economy should be on a war footing by 1940. Only a successful war for *Lebensraum* could solve the problems created by the Nazi economy.

The Four Year Plan, designed to increase armaments and achieve autarky, placed an intolerable strain on the economy by concentrating on the exploitation of uneconomic domestic resources, such as low grade iron ore, rather than encouraging foreign trade. German agriculture failed to meet the needs of the people, and valuable foreign exchange had to be spent on food imports. In spite of massive efforts to strengthen the peasantry and to extol the importance of 'blood and soil', between 1933 and 1939 1.4 million people left the countryside in search of better paid jobs in the towns and cities. Despite massive investment, only 5 per cent of rubber demand was met by domestic synthetic production. The Four Year Plan failed to meet its targets but continued full steam ahead, against the advice of Schacht and many industrialists; they approved of large-scale rearmament, but not at such a pace.

A poster advertising the Volkswagen in 1936. The slogan reads: 'You must save five marks per week if you want to drive your own car!' The 'People's Car', designed by Ferdinand Porsche, was a favourite project of Hitler's. The expressed aim was that the car, sponsored by the 'Strength Through Joy' organization which was responsible for leisure activities, should be easily purchased by ordinary Germans. In fact the car was never available to civilians and only used by the military.

Degenerate art

The Reich Chamber of the Visual Arts was founded in November 1933 as a sub-section of the Chamber of Culture, whose president was Josef Goebbels. Hitler's favourite architect, Paul Ludwig Troost, advised him on artistic matters. His criteria for what constituted 'degenerate art' were simple; if artists were praised in Carl Einstein's *Die Kunst des 20. Jahrhunderts*, they were clearly degenerate. Only artists who were accredited Chamber members were permitted to work, and any art deemed 'degenerate' could be seized by the authorities. Modern works were removed from all museums, except for Berlin's, which was kept open until after the Olympic Games.

The president of the Chamber Professor Ziegler – a painter of grim nudes which Hitler found most pleasing – was ordered to mount an exhibition of 'German degenerate art since 1910' to be held in Munich in 1937. The works of 112 artists who were felt to demonstrate the 'madness, impertinence, incompetence, and degeneracy' of modern art were chosen for the exhibition. It was organized into nine sections: technical incompetence; 'pro-Jewish' religious art; social criticism and anarchism; 'Communism' (including the work of George Grosz and Otto Dix); 'Pornography'; glorification of the Negro (the Expressionists); 'art and insanity'; 'Jewish trash'; and finally, 'the height of degeneracy' (Willi Baumeister, Kurt Schwitters).

Some of the finer works were confiscated by Nazi officials, particularly Göring, who had a taste for the Impressionists and Matisse. Over a thousand paintings were burnt, and 125 major items auctioned in Lucerne in 1939, enabling the world's museums to buy works by van Gogh, Modigliani, Gauguin, Chagall, Picasso, and Braque. Germany recovered few after 1945.

The exhibition 'Degenerate Art' in Berlin 1938. Visitors turn their back on 'The Beach' (1927) by Max Beckmann (1884–1950).

SOCIAL LIFE

Social peace was maintained by a policy of carrots and sticks. The trades unions had been destroyed and the social radicals in the Nazi shop floor organizations (NSBOs) and in the German Work Front (DAF) were silenced by the summer of 1934. The DAF, with 20 million members, a permanent staff of 44,000 and 1.3 million volunteers was essentially an organization to order, control, and indoctrinate labour, but it also sought to win over the working-class by an ambitious recreational programme. 'Strength Through Joy' (*Kraft durch Freude* – KdF) provided cheap theatre, film, and concert tickets, built sports facilities, ran evening courses, and gave DAF and other Party members cheap holidays. The most glamorous of these, such as Caribbean cruises or skiing breaks, became heavily subsidized luxuries for the middle class. Holidays were increased from an average of

Two athletes in training epitomize the National Socialist ideal of womanhood. The Nazis emphasized military discipline, a sense of community, vocational training, and sport. Nazi youth organizations for girls also emphasized their future roles as wives, mothers, and housewives.

three days in 1933 to between six and twelve days in 1939, and millions of workers developed a taste for tourism; this was to become a striking feature of the post-war years.

KdF was successful so long as it avoided ideology. Their holidays were popular, but their evening classes were not. Similarly with cinema, theatre, and literature, only works of real artistic merit or popular appeal had any chance of success. Few wanted to see films about the Hitler Youth or the SA, but historical dramas with subtle ideological content about such figures as Frederick the Great or Bismarck were popular. Foreign best-sellers such as Margaret Mitchell's *Gone With The Wind* or Thomas Wolfe's *Look Homeward, Angel* were very successful, but few politically correct works sold well. Goebbels' ambition was to produce a National Socialist *Battleship Potemkin* or *Mr Deeds Goes to Town*, but despite enormous effort and expense was never able to produce films of similar quality. Theatrical productions,

A still from a German film of the 1930s. Despite attempts to purvey Nazi ideology to the general public through entertainment, escapist fantasies proved enduringly popular

particularly during the war years, were outstanding. By concentrating on the classics, companies like Gustav Gründgens' in Berlin maintained the highest artistic standards and avoided ideological control.

Peacetime Berlin was much like the 'Golden Twenties' for those who could afford to visit the cocktail bars and restaurants or listen to the swing music of Teddy Stauffer and the Original Teddies. For all the talk of the 'Racial Community', class distinctions were as crass as ever. The rich wore tails and furs and delighted in the elegant arrangements of the brilliant singing team The Comedian Harmonists. Fanatical Party members coexisted uneasily with dedicated party-goers, but the more perceptive realized that this could not last. It was, as the title of one popular film suggested, a *Dance on a Volcano*. In 1934 the three Jewish Comedian Harmonists were forced to leave the group and replaced by 'Aryans', and swing music was condemned as 'Negro-Jewish'. The battle against American 'Nigger Culture' intensified, but the regime was clever enough to realize that the attractions of jazz were such that it would be folly to wage an all-out war against them.

Improvements in the working class standard of living were modest. By 1937 average real wages had climbed back to the high levels of 1929, helped by longer hours and higher productivity. These increases were most noticeable in the arms factories, but in other industries real wages fell. By 1939 there was widespread discontent and increasing sabotage and absenteeism. The authorities attributed this to Marxist propaganda, but working weeks of up to 65 hours were not unusual and the strain was beginning to tell.

The National Socialist attitude towards women was a further mockery of the Racial Community. In theory a woman's role was to be a wife and mother, so

Hitler at the Nazi Party rally in Nuremberg. The Party rally was an annual event, held in September, for which Albert Speer designed a vast stadium. The Rally lasted for eight days and was a grandiose and minutely choreographed celebration of the Führer cult. Hitler gave between fifteen and twenty speeches and was always the centre of attention, the object of the adulation of the 250,000 participants.

German women were not required to work. On the other hand, the shortage of labour elicited a decree in 1938 that single women under twenty-five do one year of labour service. Even this was not enforced, and only 50,000 of the 950,000 eligible actually participated. Early in the war the number of working women actually declined, their places being taken by foreign workers. After 1941 the number did increase, but almost exclusively from the working class. Göring explained this inequality by claiming that women were like horses – some were best suited for working, others, like thoroughbreds, for breeding; a brood mare should not be harnessed to a plough for she would soon be used up. In the Racial Community, rich, elegant and beautiful women, for whom the Führer had an appreciative eye, were especially privileged. The ideologues in the National Socialist Women's Organization (*Nationalsozialistische Frauenschaft* – NSF) were deeply resentful.

FOREIGN POLICY

Social discontent was kept within bounds largely by Hitler's foreign policy triumphs. The situation he inherited was very favourable for a determined revisionist policy. Reparations had ended with the Hoover moratorium, the disarmament clauses of the Treaty of Versailles had long since been ignored. Collective security was a dead letter when the Japanese invaded Manchuria and withdrew from the League of Nations in 1933. Britain and France were hopelessly weak and the United States was isolationist.

For the first two years of the Nazi regime little changed in foreign policy, but the allied powers viewed Hitler with suspicion. In January 1935 he had his first success: despite all the anti-fascists' efforts, a plebiscite in the Saar polled 91 per cent for unification with Germany. Three months later Hitler introduced compulsory military service to create an army of 550,000 men, and announced the rebuilding of the air force. One month later, Britain, France and Italy formed the Stresa Front in which they reaffirmed the Locarno pact and proclaimed their determination to preserve the status quo.

The Stresa Front was a toothless pact and the British immediately tried to negotiate a naval agreement with Germany, represented with characteristic boorishness by special envoy Joachim von Ribbentrop. Hitler had two clear motives for agreement: first, to get Britain to concede a flagrant breach of the Versailles Treaty by accepting a fleet ratio of 35 German tons to 100 British tons; second, to initiate a comprehensive agreement with Britain that would give him a free hand against the Soviet Union. The agreement was signed on 18 June and Hitler announced it was his happiest day of his life.

On 5 October 1935 Mussolini, confident that after Stresa the British and French needed him to restrain Germany, declared war on Ethiopia. British and French public opinion was outraged at the brutality of Italian troops against a hopelessly inferior army, but their governments made half-hearted protests. At first Hitler supported the Ethiopians, sending three million marks' worth of weapons, but switched his support to Italy when the League of Nations threatened to impose sanctions. He learnt a valuable lesson from the feeble reaction of Britain and France, and seized the opportunity to befriend fascist Italy. Italian-German relations had been badly strained during the Austrian crisis of 1934 when Nazis had murdered Chancellor Dollfuss, and Mussolini feared that Germany would seize Austria, a valuable buffer state.

With the Stresa Front in ruins, Hitler remilitarized the Rhineland on 7 March 1936, claiming that the recently ratified Franco-Soviet pact was a violation of the Locarno treaty, and calling elections on 29 March to test public reaction to his daring move. Hitler's triumph in the Rhineland brought him to the pinnacle of his popularity, 98.8 per cent voting for the 'Führer's List'. France and Britain did nothing; the council of the League condemned the German action, but Hitler could afford to ignore its strictures. Mussolini had already assured him that he had no objections to the move and no longer wished to support the Austrian nationalist Heimwehr against the Nazis.

Germany and Italy drew closer when, without consultation, both countries supported General Franco in the Spanish civil war. Hitler decided to intervene on the spur of the moment, and although Germany secured some valuable Spanish raw materials, his main motive was fear that Spain would fall into the hands of the Marxists, stiffen the French popular front government against Germany, and strengthen ties with the Soviet Union. On 1 November Mussolini first spoke of an 'axis' from Rome to Berlin, but Hitler had mixed feelings about an alliance with Italy; it was a poor alternative to an alliance with England, on which he had set his heart, and which would provide his best springboard for a war of Eastern conquest.

In October 1936 Hitler appointed von Ribbentrop ambassador in London, ordering him to secure an alliance with Britain. Ribbentrop announced on his arrival at Victoria Station that he wanted to negotiate an alliance with Britain that would give Hitler a free hand to destroy Bolshevism in the East. The British were not enthusiastic, knowing full well that a successful campaign against the Soviet Union would leave Germany as the dominant power on the continent, hardly a pleasing prospect for Stanley Baldwin's Conservative government. The abdication of Edward VIII, whose sympathy for the National Socialists was well known, was seen as a victory for the 'anti-German, reactionary, Jewish clique' which Ribbentrop felt was responsible for the failure of his mission. The ambassador became increasingly frustrated, while the British found him impossibly uncouth and christened him 'von Brickendrop'. Having failed to secure an alliance, or even arrange a meeting of Baldwin and Hitler, Ribbentrop began instead to negotiate with Japan. The resulting Anti-Comintern Pact was swiftly concluded and signed on 6 November 1937. Hitler abandoned hope of reaching an agreement with Britain, while Ribbentrop recommended an offensive against Britain should she try to frustrate Germany's eastward expansion.

By this time it was obvious to the more perspicacious among the diplomatic, military, and business elites that German foreign policy was on a new and dangerous course. On 5 November Hitler treated his foreign minister and service chiefs to a four-hour harangue which Colonel Hossbach was later to note down. After a confused diatribe on race and the social-Darwinian struggle for survival, Hitler announced that Germany would have to go to war to secure vital *Lebensraum* at the very latest by 1943–45, initially attacking Austria and Czechoslovakia. For the first time Hitler mentioned the possibility of war with Britain, although he assumed that neither Britain nor France would lift a finger to save Czechoslovakia.

When Lord Halifax, the Lord Privy Seal in Chamberlain's new government, visited Hitler at the Berghof two weeks later, he offered a comprehensive settlement of all of Germany's claims in Austria, Danzig, and Czechoslovakia. Hitler turned the offer down, for it would have frustrated his long-term goals. But the way was open for the revision of the Treaty of Versailles; the appeasers in Britain and France were ready to concede Germany's demands, the ruinous armaments programme could be checked, and social harmony would be restored. This was what the traditional conservative elite in Germany hoped would happen; they were appalled when they heard of Hitler's outburst of 5 November.

The Night of Broken Glass

In November 1938 a young Jew, Herszel Grynspan, murdered a member of the German embassy staff in Paris, Ernst Eduard von Rath. By this time Jews had been excluded from most professions, had identity cards, and were forced to bear the names Israel or Sara, but the anti-Semitic campaign was paralyzed – the ministries were expressing certain legal doubts and demanding clarifications, while radicals called for more drastic action.

On 9 November, when Hitler learned of the assassination, he was in Munich for the anniversary of the putsch of 1923. He discussed it with Goebbels, who made an inflammatory speech warning that the German people would seek revenge for the murder. The party and the SA were ordered 'spontaneously' to express the peoples' outrage at this Jewish crime; the SS was ordered to remain in the background.

The SA took to the streets in uniform and gleefully set to work. On the night of 9–10 November at least ninety-one German Jews were murdered, most synagogues were set on fire, and Jewish property was destroyed. The Gestapo chief, Heinrich Müller, ordered 20,000–30,000 wealthy Jews to be arrested and sent to a concentration camp pending expulsion from Germany. Such was the destruction in the cities and towns on the following day that this appalling pogrom has been memorialized as *Reichskristallnacht*, a term which trivialised the appalling human suffering involved. The pogrom was far from popular, and everyone knew it had been organized from above. Most Germans felt it went too far — not so much out of sympathy for Jews, but rather for fear that the SA's flagrant disregard for private property might soon affect them.

On 12 November a committee chaired by Hermann Göring decided that the 250,000 remaining German Jews should pay a fine of 1,000 million marks and that they were not elegible for insurance payments for their losses. It was agreed that Jewish businesses were to be 'Aryanised' and Jews were forbidden to go to the theatres, cinemas, or swimming pools. German Jews had lost all legal rights and means of support; the way was now open for genocide. The SS journal, *The Black Corps*, announced that the Jews would soon be exterminated. On 30 January 1939 Hitler proclaimed in the Reichstag that if a war broke out in Europe, its Jews would be destroyed.

Streets are cleaned in the aftermath of the Night of Broken Glass.

Hitler was determined to change his team. He was able to dismiss Blomberg when it transpired that his young bride had a criminal record and had posed for pornographic photographs. Blomberg's obvious successor, General von Fritsch, was a reactionary anti-Semite, but he was not a Nazi and had a snobbish dislike of Hitler. Göring and Himmler falsely accused Fritsch of involvement with a male prostitute and Fritsch resigned. Hitler promptly appointed himself commander-in-chief, abolished the war ministry, and appointed the pliant General Keitel head of the Supreme Command of the Armed Forces (OKW). His second-in-command General Jodl was a submissive technician. Fritsch's successor was General von Brauchitsch, a weak-willed toady who was bribed with a handsome divorce settlement. Neurath, an old-style diplomat, was replaced by Ribbentrop. Schacht, who was critical of the rapid rearmament, was replaced as minister of economics by Party stalwart Walter Funk. New ambassadors were appointed to the key posts in Tokyo, Rome and Vienna.

THE ROAD TO WAR

On 12 February 1938, the Austrian chancellor Schuschnigg visited Hitler at the Berghof. He was treated to a long tirade of crude threats and presented with a list of demands including the appointment of a Nazi, Seyss-Inquart, minister of security, an amnesty for Austrian Nazis who had fallen foul of the law, close cooperation between the two countries in foreign and economic policy, and consultation between the two general staffs. Schuschnigg felt he had no alternative but to accept, imagining that he had at least preserved his country's territorial integrity.

With Seyss-Inquart taking instructions directly from Hitler and Frick, Austria plunged into near anarchy as the Nazis provoked a series of violent incidents. On 9 March Schuschnigg announced a national referendum for a 'free, German, independent, social, Christian, and united Austria' to be held on 13 March. Hitler, urged by Göring, acted quickly. He sent the Prince of Hesse to Mussolini assuring him that he would accept the Brenner frontier and never make a claim to the South Tyrol. On 10 March he issued Order Number One, code-named Operation Otto, for the invasion of Austria. Göring demanded Schuschnigg's resignation on the grounds that he no longer enjoyed the confidence of the German government. Schuschnigg made inquiries in Rome, London, and Paris, and, finding no support, resigned on the evening of 11 March. The Austrian President Miklas then refused to appoint Seyss-Inquart in his place. The Austrian Nazis promptly seized all important ministries and at 8.45 p.m. Hitler ordered the invasion. That same evening the Prince of Hesse telephoned to tell Hitler of Mussolini's support. Hitler replied: 'Please tell Mussolini that I shall never forget him...never, never, never, whatever happens.' He was true to his word.

German troops crossed the Austrian border on 12 March and were greeted by a rapturous population. Encouraged by this reception, Hitler decided on annexation. On the following day he addressed the crowds in Vienna and when he announced that Austria was now a German province, their enthusiasm knew no bounds. Hitler was at the height of his popularity; he had realized Bismarck's dream of a greater Germany. In April, 99 per cent of the German electorate voted in favour of the *Anschluss*. Few seemed to be worried by the appalling violence against Austrian Jews and the opposition committed by the German police and SS.

The benefits to Germany were immense. Germany had won more territory than she had lost in 1919 and with it valuable supplies of iron ore and 500,000 unemployed workers who were badly needed in the arms industry. Austria had 1.4 billion marks in gold and foreign currencies in the central bank at a time when the Reichsbank had only 76 million. Czechoslovakia, previously a strategic threat to Germany, was now highly vulnerable to German attack.

Ein Volk, ein Reich, ein Führer!

A poster of 1938–39, with the rallying cry 'One People, One Country, One Leader!' Hitler combined the offices of President and Chancellor, with no constitutional check on his absolute power. Hitler was commander-in-chief of the armed forces. The entire nation was at Hitler's bidding, obediently carrying out his orders as he set about realizing his ideological fantasies.

Two weeks after the *Anschluss* Hitler received the Sudeten German leader Konrad Henlein, and ordered him to make a series of unacceptable demands to the Czech government. One month later he ordered General Keitel to draw up plans for an invasion of Czechoslovakia, code-named Green. The British government made it plain that it would do nothing to help the Czechs, pronouncing that frontier rectifications in Germany's favour were desirable. France was in the middle of yet another political crisis and would not act without British support, while Mussolini had no objections. On 20 May the Czech government therefore decided to seize the initiative and mobilize its forces. Britain, France, and the Soviet Union were shaken out of their torpor and announced that they fully supported the Czechs' move. War looked imminent.

On 28 May 1938, Hitler gave a three-hour speech to the military and diplomatic leadership in which he expressed his determination to crush Czechoslovakia by means of a decisive four-day Blitzkrieg so as to avoid the intervention of Britain and France. He then intended to deal with France, leaving the way open for his expansionist war in the East. He was still uncertain whether this would involve a war with Britain, but now felt that his Eastern goals could not be achieved without first achieving security in the West.

Manoeuvres were held on the Czech border in June, while Britain and France urged the Czechs to negotiate. On 13 September the British prime minister Neville Chamberlain visited Hitler at the Berghof. Hitler demanded the immediate annexation of the Sudetenland. Chamberlain replied that he would have to consult the cabinet, and Hitler promised not to use force for the time being. The British and French governments then urged the Czechs to hand over all areas in the Sudentenland in which more than half the population was German. Chamberlain returned to present this suggestion to Hitler at Bad Godesberg, but Hitler blandly announced that 'considering the developments in the last few days this solution is unacceptable'. Chamberlain returned to London and, on 26 September, the British government announced that it would support France in the event of war over Czechoslovakia. Hitler complained that he was being treated 'like a nigger' and in a massive rally in the Palace of Sports in Berlin told the crowds that the Czechs had to decide whether they wanted war or peace.

On 27 September Hitler ordered the army to prepare for an attack on Czechoslovakia. On 28 September, urged by Mussolini, he reluctantly agreed to meet Chamberlain and the French premier Daladier in Munich. Agreement was reached in the early hours of the morning on 30 September. Germany was to get the Sudetenland and, along with Italy, would guarantee the territorial integrity of the rest of Czechoslovakia.

In one sense Munich was a triumph for Hitler. Czechoslovakia was now defenceless and had lost some important industries, along with 3.6 million people. But he had been denied his triumphal entry into Prague, his timetable had been disrupted, and Britain and France had been given a breathing space in which to rearm. Chamberlain had been greeted by the German crowds as a man of peace, confirming Hitler's concern that his people were not enthusiastic about the prospect of a confrontation. He bitterly complained that 'with these people I cannot fight a war!'

On 21 October, Hitler ordered plans to be drawn up for the destruction of Czechoslovakia and the annexation of the Memel – a German province awarded to Lithuania in 1919. In Czechoslovakia the Slovaks demanded their independence, with the support of Berlin. The Czech president Hacha dismissed the Slovak leader Monsignor Tiso and sent troops into Slovakia. Tiso was persuaded to meet Hitler, who warned him that if he did not declare Slovak independence he would support Hungarian claims to his country. On 14 March 1939 the Slovak parliament passed a declaration of independence.

That evening Hacha and his foreign minister travelled to Berlin, where they were treated to one of Hitler's violent monologues on the outrageous behaviour of the Czechs. Hacha was presented with the alternatives of handing over his country to Germany or facing invasion and the bombardment of Prague. Hacha had a heart attack and was revived by an injection from Hitler's doctor so that he could sign a document which placed 'the destiny of the Czech people and their country confidently into the hands of the Führer of the German Reich' in order to secure 'law, order, and peace'. By 9 a.m. German troops had entered the Czech capital. Hitler arrived that evening and announced the formation of the Protectorate of Bohemia and Moravia which turned the Czech lands into a German satellite. His reception in Prague was very different from that in Vienna. The people were silent, grim, and tearful. Few raised their arm in the Nazi salute.

On 21 March 1939 Hitler demanded that Lithuania hand over the Memel, and boarded the battleship *Deutschland* . By the time he reached Memel, on 23 March, the Lithuanian government had given way. Hitler suffered badly from sea-sickness but had won another bloodless victory. His attention now focused on Poland.

Hitler hoped that Poland would be a junior partner in his war of conquest in the East, joining the anti-Bolshevik crusade and providing rear cover for a campaign in the West. He wanted Danzig and an extraterritorial railway and autobahn through the corridor, but was prepared to guarantee Poland's frontiers for twenty-five years. At the same time, on 25 March, he ordered preparations to be made for an attack, Case White, to be launched as early as 1 September 1939.

Poland had no wish to play second fiddle to Germany and was fearful of Soviet reactions. On 26 March, the Polish foreign minister Beck turned down Ribbentrop's renewed demand for Danzig, and five days later the British government extended a guarantee to Poland and Romania in response to Hitler's seizure of Bohemia and Moravia. Germany and Poland were now on a collision course, and on 28 April Hitler renounced their 1934 neutrality pact.

Fearful that Britain and France might reach an agreement with the Soviet Union, Hitler cast his ideological scruples aside and agreed to Ribbentrop's proposal for a pact with the devil. Stalin was eager to make a deal which he hoped would give him territorial gains in the Baltic and Poland and he invited Ribbentrop to Moscow. Ribbentrop arrived on 23 August and within three hours an agreement was reached on spheres of influence.

Hitler was now determined to go to war, and nothing could stop him. The British government let it be known that they would support the Poles. On the afternoon of 31 August Hitler issued the order for the attack on Poland to begin at 4.45 a.m. the following morning. A phoney assault on a German radio station near the border was staged to provide an excuse for the invasion, but few were fooled.

HITLER'S WAR

The German people showed no enthusiasm for war and there was no repeat of the heady days of August 1914. It was not until 3 September that the British and French declared war on Germany. This came as an unpleasant surprise both to Hitler and to his people. Hitler's attempt to fight separate wars in the East and the West and to keep Britain neutral had failed. Hitler promised that he would not take off his 'sacred and treasured' uniform until his final victory, or death.

Germany invaded Poland without declaring war and the campaign was soon over. On 17 September the Red Army annexed eastern Poland the Baltic states later became Soviet socialist republics. On 19 September Hitler gave a speech in Danzig in which he claimed that Poland was destroyed and would never rise again. What remained after the German/Soviet partition became the General Government, a colony subjected to the most brutal exploitation. Both the Soviet Union and Germany systematically liquidated Poland's ruling class. Thousands of Polish officers were murdered by the NKVD (the Soviet secret police) and buried in mass graves in the forest of Katyn. The Germans were even more thorough: Heydrich had prepared five squads of SS special troops (*Verfügungstruppen*) with orders to kill the Polish intelligentsia. Tens of thousands of professionals were slaughtered, and on 27 September Heydrich proudly announced that at most 3 per cent of the Polish leadership was still alive. At the same time the SS herded Polish Jews into ghettos in Warsaw, Cracow, Lemberg, Lublin, and Radom. Some decent soldiers, prominent among them General Blaskowitz, were appalled at the brutality of the SS and protested to their superiors and even to Hitler. The Führer was disgusted at this 'Salvation Army attitude' and Blaskowitz was posted to the western front.

Himmler, who in October 1939 had appointed himself Reich Commissar for the Strengthening of the German Race, lay down guidelines for German occupation policy in Poland. Poles were to learn 'that it is God's commandment that they obey the Germans, and be honest, industrious and well-behaved'. Children of good blood, and thus capable of becoming Germans, would be educated appropriately. Slav subhumans would provide a 'leaderless work force'. By the summer of 1941 one million Poles had lost their property and been resettled. The land was colonized by Germans on whom fell a terrible retribution in the war's final stages.

Hitler had won another great victory, but Germany's position was far from secure. Italy had declared its neutrality and so had Japan, the armaments industry was not yet on a war footing and Germany was still dependent on imports of strategic raw materials. Most serious of all, the country depended heavily on the Soviet Union, without whose help it could not mount a campaign against France. In this awkward situation Hitler decided to strike a soon as possible. France was to be defeated swiftly. Britain would be excluded from the continent and might agree to the division of the world which Hitler had repeatedly offered. He would then be free to complete his great historical task of carving out an empire in the East.

The offensive was delayed twenty-nine times, the military arguing that the weather conditions were too poor in order to postpone a campaign about which they had serious misgivings. On 9 April 1940 Germany attacked Denmark and Norway, securing supplies of Swedish iron ore and strengthening its strategic position against Britain. The campaign in the West began in May, when Holland was defeated in a brilliant operation lasting five days. The main offensive from the Ardennes to the Channel then trapped the British and Belgian armies and much of the French. The British and some French were able to escape from Dunkirk when Hitler ordered the German tanks to halt. Their left flank was dangerously exposed, with supply lines over-extended, the troops weary, and tanks in need of repair. On 14 June the Germans entered Paris, and on 21 June Hitler sat in Marshal Foch's chair in the same railway carriage in which the 1918 armistice had been signed, dictating his peace terms.

A new French state under the aged defender of Verdun, Marshal Pétain, was created in the south, with its administrative capital in Vichy. Germany took Alsace and Lorraine, although the provinces were not formally annexed. Italy, which against Hitler's wishes had declared war on 10 June, received a small frontier strip. Northern France was placed under military occupation.

Hitler still hoped to come to an arrangement with Britain, but Winston Churchill, who became prime minister in May 1940, steeled his countrymen to continue the fight. On 16 July Hitler ordered preparations for an invasion of the British Isles, code-named Sea-lion. Three days later he made his 'appeal to reason' in a speech in the Reichstag in which he called upon the British government to end hostilities. The air war over England began on 13 August but by 16 September the offensive was halted by heavy losses and bad weather. Hitler, who uncharacteristically had shown no interest in the invasion plan details, realized that air superiority was essential and pressed ahead at the beginning of July with his plans for the invasion of the Soviet Union.

On 19 July President Roosevelt indicated that he would not stand idly by and let Britain be defeated. Hitler now insisted that the Soviet Union had to be conquered in the spring of 1941. With Germany in command of the continent the British would have to abandon the fight, the United States would not have time to rearm,

Opposite: A crossroads in Calais after an attack by the Luftwaffe in May 1940, part of Hitler's frequently postponed western offensive.

and would face a greatly strengthened Japan. The first step was the three-power pact between Germany, Italy, and Japan signed on 27 September. This amounted to very little. The Japanese remained neutral and had no intention of coordinating their strategy with the Germans. The most that Hitler could hope for was that this racially dubious *Volk*, which were proclaimed to be Aryan until further notice, would keep the Americans occupied in the Pacific. Attempts to bring France and Spain into the bloc also failed. Pétain wanted guarantees specified in a formal peace treaty, and Franco sensibly remained aloof.

On 12 November 1940 Molotov travelled to Berlin to present the Soviet Union's war aims. He demanded control of Finland, Romania, Bulgaria, and the Straits of the Bosphorus and Dardanelles, and suggested that Hungary, Yugoslavia, western Poland, and the entrance to the Baltic should later be included in the Soviet empire. One of Hitler's adjutants remarked that 'M has let the cat out of the bag. He [Hitler] is really relieved, now this is not even a marriage of convenience'. The Molotov visit, which coincided embarrassingly with an RAF raid on Berlin, further convinced Hitler that he had to march east as soon as possible. On 18 December he issued Order No. 21 for Case Barbarossa, an attack on the Soviet Union in 1941, even if Britain had not been defeated. Hitler called for a swift campaign so that Germany could fight the United States from a position of strength in 1942. The Soviet Union would be defeated by August 1941 so that German troops could then seize the British positions in the Middle East and Gibraltar and march through Afghanistan into India. Hitler gave Himmler and the SS 'special duties' in this 'battle of two world views' and clearly separated the SS from the army. The army was also told that the concept of soldierly comradeship no longer existed and that they were to defend western civilization against the Asiatic-Muscovite threat and fight a war of extermination against Jewish Bolshevism.

A newly developed anti-tank gun is hauled out of pit where it would be hidden to protect front-line troops from tank attacks.

The Decree of 13 May on Military Law in the Barbarossa Operation Area stated that military personnel could not be brought before a court martial for crimes committed against Soviet citizens. The infamous Commissar Order of 6 June stated that all captured commissars should be executed. By these means the army were made willing accomplices to Nazi crimes. The SS *Einsatztruppen* (task forces) were given the job of weeding out the 'biological roots of Bolshevism' by the systematic murder of Soviet Jews. The army was to provide food, transport, and accommodation for these murderers, and was thus further implicated.

The attack on the Soviet Union began on 22 June 1941 and went like clockwork. On 15 July Himmler unveiled his General Plan East which envisaged the expulsion of thirty-one million people to Siberia, German colonization in the East and the 'waste disposal' (*Verschrotten*) of the racially undesirable; he was put in charge of the realization of Germany's eastern empire. On 21 July Hitler told the Croatian defence minister Kvaternik that he intended to destroy the European Jews, first in the Soviet Union, then in the rest of Europe. If any European state harboured Jews, Hitler warned, they would act as 'incubators for destructive bacteria'. On 31 July Heydrich received orders from Göring to make the necessary preparations for the 'general solution of the Jewish question in Europe'. Göring explained that he was acting on Hitler's orders.

By the end of July the German offensive was running out of steam and in December the Soviets launched a successful counter-offensive in front of Moscow. Hitler dismissed most of his commanders in order to run the war himself. By now, some among the Nazi leadership were convinced that the war was lost. Even Hitler saw the writing on the wall and said: 'If the German people are not strong enough and are not prepared to sacrifice their own blood for their continued existence, then they should vanish and be destroyed by another, stronger power'. To this he added that he would not waste a single tear for his fellow Germans.

Hitler planned a major offensive in the south-eastern sector for 1942, but failed in the summer to encircle the Red Army. He at once ordered Army Group B to take Stalingrad and advance to the Caspian, and Army Group A to push on to Baku. In the northern sector Leningrad was to be seized and destroyed. On 23 October Montgomery launched his offensive at El Alamein which was to lead to the defeat of the Axis troops in North Africa. On 19 November the Soviet counter-offensive began north of Stalingrad and General Paulus' 6 Army was soon cut off. Hitler ordered Stalingrad to be held at all costs. On 2 February 1943 the remains of Paulus' army surrendered and 90,000 men were taken prisoner; few of them survived. Although Hitler's decision to fight on in Stalingrad was strategically correct, allowing the bulk of the German forces to be extricated from the Caucasus so that they could launch a counter-attack on 20 February, Stalingrad was a crushing defeat and Hitler was no longer seen by all as an invincible leader. At home the Hitler myth was beginning to fade and terror was beginning to take its place.

Left: Jews from all over occupied Europe were transported to the Nazi death camps. Ninety per cent of Polish Jews (3,000,000), 56 per cent of the Jews from the Benelux countries (310,000) and one percent of Danish Jews (70) were murdered.

Below: US First Army troops who were liberating the concentration camp of Buchenwald in May 1945 discovered these wedding rings which had been taken from the victims.

In peacetime the National Socialist state was characterized by a confusion over fields of competence, a multiplicity of competing authorities, and a lack of procedural norms. In wartime the situation became even more confused. After 1937 the cabinet never met and the attempt to create a new ministerial council under Göring was sabotaged by Hitler, who saw it as a threat to his absolute power. Its last meeting as a body was in November 1939. Hitler spent most of his time in his remote headquarters. The civilian authorities in the occupied territories acted on their own initiative and could ignore the ministries in Berlin. Within Germany the Gauleiters increased their powers and ruled their fiefdoms with little regard for established administrative practice.

Himmler, the executant of Hitler's racial policy in the East, became immensely powerful. In 1943 he was additionally appointed minister of the interior and in 1944 took command of the reserve army. Göring's star waned correspondingly. The Luftwaffe had failed in the Battle of Britain, his administration of industry was ineffective, and his lifestyle became increasingly grotesque as he sauntered around in theatrical uniforms dripping with jewels. He concentrated on plundering the art galleries of Europe and on hunting. Hitler's architect, Albert Speer, proved a brilliant organizer of armaments manufacture and Göring was pushed aside. Goebbels came into his own after the disaster at Stalingrad, making a famous speech in Berlin's Palace of Sport on 18 February in which he asked the rhetorical question 'Do you want total war?' He successfully forced Hitler's hand at a time when Hitler's reaction to defeat was undecided. After Hess flew to Scotland in 1941, Bormann, Hitler's secretary, took effective control of the Party and in the final stages of the war was virtually the government of Germany, controlling the flow of information to Hitler and issuing orders in Hitler's name. Bormann combined the fanaticism of an ideologue with the precision of a bureaucrat, and was thus the perfect National Socialist.

THE FINAL SOLUTION

The genocide of the European Jews began in the autumn of 1941 in special extermination camps at Auschwitz, Chelmno, Treblinka, Belzec, Majdanek, and Sobibor. Hundreds of thousands of Jews had already been murdered by SS special units, but mass slaughter on the scale that was now envisaged could not be carried out by execution squads or small mobile gas chambers. However, Jews were needed to make up for the shortage of labour in the armaments industry. This contradiction was clearly seen in Auschwitz, the largest of the camps. On arrival, the prisoners were given a cursory examination by doctors. Those deemed fit to work went to the factories, the less robust to the gas chambers.

Countless Jews were murdered in Poland from the very beginning of the German occupation. There can be little doubt that Hitler ordered, probably in the summer of 1941, the extermination of all European Jews. This decision was not an act of desperation by panic-stricken satraps who did not know what to do with the Jews under their command, nor an attempt by Hitler to fulfil his 'historic mission' before it was too late, it was an integral part of the attack on the Soviet Union, the victorious outcome of which was then in prospect.

On 20 May 1941 the RSHA issued an order forbidding the emigration of Jews from France and Belgium on the grounds that 'the final solution to the Jewish question would come without a doubt'. On 31 July Göring ordered Heydrich to make the necessary preparations for the 'general solution to the Jewish question in the parts of Europe under German influence'. In September Jews were obliged to wear a yellow star of David. In the autumn of 1941 the gas chambers were first used at Chelmno and Belzec, under instructions from men who had used similar methods on psychiatric patients and on hereditary disease sufferers in the 'euthanasia programme' known as T4 (so called after Tiergarten 4, the address of Hitler's personal chancellory). The gas chambers at Auschwitz were first used in January 1942.

On 29 November 1941 Heydrich issued invitations for a conference on the final solution to be held at the old Interpol offices at Grossen Wannsee in Berlin. After some delay the Wannsee conference was held on 20 January 1942. It was brief and the language used was ambiguous, its main purpose being to demonstrate to all government departments that Heydrich was the man in charge.

By 1943 the war was no longer represented as a racial crusade but seen as the struggle of European civilization against Bolshevism – 'Europe's Victory is Your Prosperity'.

The 'Final Solution', which resulted in the murder of some six million Jews, defies explanation. Perhaps it is best so, for understanding brings with it a degree of forgiveness. This uniquely horrible event in human history combined ideological fanaticism, cold bureaucratic calculation, primitive and pathological behaviour patterns, and the technical skills of an advanced industrial society. It is fitting that this most monstrous of crimes should be the enduring monument to National Socialism, for in it Hitler's regime reached its apotheosis.

THE HOME FRONT

On the home front the regime was curiously reluctant to call upon the German people to make any great sacrifices for the war effort. Until Goebbels' Berlin speech there was no mention of blood, sweat or tears. Hitler believed Germany had been defeated in 1918 because of the collapse of the home front and he was determined that morale should never be allowed to sink so low. Supplies of food and consumer goods were secured by careful pre-war planning, imports from the Soviet Union, and exploitation of the occupied territories.

In the spring of 1942 the food ration had to be reduced, causing widespread discontent. The summer offensive in the Soviet Union and a good harvest made it possible to overcome these difficulties and in October the weekly meat ration was increased from 300 to 350 grams.

Rather than make German women work the regime preferred to employ foreigners and prisoners-of-war.

In the final stages of the war Germany's only hope was that a secret weapon would turn the tide. The V1 and V2 rockets were mostly aimed at the population around London. The V1 was slow and relatively harmless, but the V2, which travelled faster than the speed of sound, arrived without warning and was thus a powerful weapon.
Above: The VI, known in Britain as the 'Doodlebug'.
Right: The V2, captured by the US 1st Army at Bromskirchen.

Seven million such workers were brought to Germany. One quarter of the workers in the armaments industry and almost half in agriculture were now foreign, mostly 'Slav subhumans', making a mockery of the Nazi ideology of 'blood and soil'. By these means the Nazis avoided total war until Goebbels forced Hitler's hand on 18 February 1943. His speech, before a carefully selected audience, was a rhetorical masterpiece, but it was also an admission of defeat. A year before, the minister of munitions Fritz Todt and his successor Albert Speer, had come to the conclusion that the war was already lost economically. When Todt was killed in an air crash, Speer continued his efforts to rationalize the arms industry. He achieved remarkable success in an increasingly difficult situation, but was opposed by Nazi ideologues who preferred small and inefficient producers to big business, and who had powerful support in Bormann, the Gauleiters, and the SS economist Otto Ohlendorf.

With Hitler at the zenith of his popularity in 1940 and 1941, resistance seemed pointless. By 1942 the situation had changed dramatically but the resistance movement was hopelessly divided. A small group of Communists were isolated and treated with suspicion by the other opposition groups. From August 1939 to June 1941 the German-Soviet alliance put them in an impossible position, and they were given no help from Moscow. They provided valuable information to the Soviets through spy networks such as the Red Orchestra, but their extraordinary efforts were ignored and many of them were sent to the Gulag after the war by their grateful taskmasters. Ultra-conservative opponents of the regime such as Goerdeler, the mayor of Leipzig, or Beck, the former chief of the general staff, were anti-democratic nationalists who imagined that Germany could survive as a dominant power and a bulwark against Bolshevism. The Kreisau Circle were mostly young and devout Christians of both denominations who inclined towards a religious and individualistic form of socialism. A group of young officers, including von Stauffenberg, von Tresckow, and Olbricht were mostly aristocrats who had initially been sympathetic to the Nazis but grown disenchanted after the pogrom of November 1938 and the brutal Eastern war.

Few of the conspirators wanted a return to the Weimar Republic, for they believed National Socialism to be a product of democracy which gave the ignorant masses far too much influence. The more democratic among them dreamt of a popular movement that would transcend the political parties, a 'New Beginning' that would wipe out all traces of National Socialism. All agreed that Hitler would have to be killed, and that this could only be done by means of a military conspiracy.

After a series of aborted attempts on Hitler's life, von Stauffenberg placed a bomb in the Führer's conference room in East Prussia on 20 July 1944. The bomb exploded, four people died as a result, but Hitler survived, shaken, slightly injured, and vengeful. The vast majority of the German people were horrified at the news of the assassination attempt. Clutching at straws, they saw Hitler as their only hope at

German women factory workers in 1943. In fact relatively few German women were required to work in munitions factories as foreign labour was used extensively. By the autumn of 1944 there were about 8 million foreign workers in Germany. One quarter of the industrial workers were foreigners: 2 million were prisoners of war, 2.5 million came from the Soviet Union, 1.7 million from Poland, 1.3 million from France, and 600,000 from Italy. In addition, 650,000 concentration camp inmates, mostly Jews, worked in the armaments industry. About half the Polish and Soviet workers were women, their average age was twenty.

this desperate stage of the war. The Hitler myth, badly tarnished after Stalingrad, was revived and exploited to the full. Hitler heaped terrible retribution on all who were involved in the plot, blaming 'all those "vons" who call themselves aristocrats'. Goebbels was appointed Reich Plenipotentiary for Total War and made frantic efforts to increase armaments output. All remaining males between the ages of fifteen and sixty were conscripted into the *Volksturm*, a rag-tag army of ill-equipped children and feeble old men. Himmler humiliated the officer corps and unleashed a fresh wave of terror. In the People's Court the odious Roland Freisler handed out death sentences with sadistic glee after the public humiliation of his victims. Mercifully, he was killed by an RAF bomb.

DEFEAT

By now the war could not possibly be won. On the eastern front Army Group Centre had suffered a crushing defeat in June 1944 and it was now only a matter of time before the entire front collapsed. At the same time the Allies had landed in Normandy and were advancing. The allied air offensive had reached a new level of intensity. 'Fortress Europe' no longer had a roof and Germany's beautiful cities were reduced to piles of rubble. Half a million civilians died in the the raids and four million homes were destroyed, but it was not until the summer of 1944 that the bombing had a serious impact on transport and industrial production. Speer knew that the end was near.

Hitler retreated into a fantasy world in which he imagined the Allies falling out, and the British joining him against the Soviets. He announced that his new 'miracle weapons', the V1 and V2 rockets, would bring victory. In a desperate gamble he ordered an offensive through the Ardennes to Antwerp and Brussels. The Ardennes attack badly weakened the eastern front and came to a halt after four days of heavy fighting and losses. The Soviet Union's offensive began on 12 January 1945 and the Red Army was soon on the Oder, driving before it millions of terrified refugees who tried to flee the bestial orgy of murder, rape and plunder in which the Soviets wrought their revenge. They meted out similar treatment to the hapless folk they 'liberated' in Poland, Romania and Hungary.

On 16 January Hitler returned to his bunker in the Berlin chancellory, over twenty feet below ground, isolated from the world in a fantasy twilight. The Nazi grandees rejoiced in the senseless destruction of Germany's cities: Goebbels' press proclaimed that the 'so-called achievements of the bourgeois nineteenth century had finally been buried', making way for a revolutionary new National Socialist society. Hitler told Speer that the Allies were doing useful work preparing the way for the rebuilding of the cities according to the plans they had drawn up together. On 19 March Hitler issued his 'Nero Order' calling for a scorched earth policy that would leave the Allies nothing, while Speer did all he could to ensure the Gauleiters did not carry it out.

On 20 April 1945 Hitler celebrated his fifty-sixth birthday with Göring, Goebbels, Himmler, Bormann, Speer, Ribbentrop, Ley and some senior commanders. His mistress Eva Braun travelled to Berlin for the occasion. Two days later Hitler held his last conference. The Russians were already in the suburbs. He screamed at his generals, accusing them of treason, cowardice and insubordination, and then collapsed weeping, muttering that the war was lost and that he would shoot himself. On 29 April he married Eva Braun and wrote his political testament, appointing Admiral Dönitz president and minister of war and Goebbels chancellor. The newly-weds committed suicide the following day and their bodies were burnt. Goebbels and his wife committed suicide, having first murdered their six children. Bormann was killed escaping from the chancellory, his body found many years later. Dönitz prolonged the war as long as possible, enabling three million of his countrymen to escape the clutches of the Soviets. On 9 May the fighting ceased. On 23 May Dönitz was arrested, and on 5 June the Allies formally took control of a vanquished Germany.

Survivors escaping from the ruins of Aachen after an Allied bombing raid. The bomber offensive placed a greater strain on Allied war production than on Germany's, but it had a shattering effect on civilian morale. About 50,000 died in the Hamburg raid of 1943 and it was feared that other cities would meet a similar fate.

CHAPTER 12 *Germany since 1945*

The occupation zones into which Germany was now divided had been decided upon by the European Advisory Commission in September 1944, to which a French zone was added in July 1945 along with a French sector in Berlin. At the Potsdam conference in July and August 1945 the Allies agreed that Nazi war criminals should be brought to trial and that party members should be removed from office. Democratic political parties and trades unions should be permitted, the freedom of the press and religion respected, and local government should be carried out by Germans under allied supervision.

Under the close supervision of the Soviet authorities, the Communist Party of Germany (KPD) re-emerged as early as 11 June 1945 and began to look for coalition partners. In April 1946 the Social Democratic Party (SPD) in the Soviet zone was forced to amalgamate with the KPD and the new party was named the Socialist Unity Party (SED). In the Western zones neither the SPD nor the allied powers would countenance such a shotgun wedding, and the KPD remained a separate party. In the first federal elections in the West the Communists received 5.7 per cent of the popular vote.

The SPD's leader, Kurt Schumacher, had lost an arm in World War I and had been a member of the Reichstag during the Weimar Republic. He had spent ten terrible years in a concentration camp. He was a passionate anti-Communist and, although a thorough-going democrat, he ruled his party with a rod of iron. He was a fervent nationalist who was determined to do everything possible to ensure that Germany was united and restored to its proper place among the nations. It was a hopelessly unrealistic policy given the Allies' suspicions of Germany and the onset of the Cold War. Similarly his advocacy of extensive nationalization and a controlled socialist economy won him little support. In the first parliamentary elections in the West the SPD received 29.2 per cent of the votes and was thus defeated by the Christian Democratic Union (CDU) which had successfully amalgamated a number of centre and right-wing parties and created a solid bourgeois bloc which received 31 per cent.

THE DIVISION OF GERMANY

In these early years the CDU emphasized Christian social thought. The party upheld the principle of private property, but argued that property brought with it responsibilities towards the less fortunate. Initially the party argued that key industries should be nationalized, but these left-wing ideas were soon dropped, and the party was fully committed to the free market economy. Konrad Adenauer, the leader of the CDU, was the outstanding statesman of the early years of the Federal Republic of Germany and gave his name to an era. Born in 1876, he was seventy-three years old when he became chancellor. He had been mayor of Cologne during the Weimar Republic and had fallen foul of the Nazis. As a Rhinelander and a devout Catholic he violently disliked Prussia, which he saw as a militaristic and chauvinistic state which had plunged Germany into misery. His great achievement was the reconciliation between Germany and France, and the formation of an alliance which he hoped would be the cornerstone of the new Europe. After what had happened, Adenauer never really trusted his own country, which he saw as a loose cannon on deck, and he wanted to tie down the Federal Republic to the western alliance. Although violently opposed to all forms of socialism, he was not a dogmatic liberal and was fully committed to the principles of the welfare state. Personally autocratic, he was in the tradition of father figures such as William I, Bismarck, and Hindenburg, but his achievement was greater than any of his predecessors'. He created a decent, stable, level-headed democracy that was free from the elements of fanaticism and over-bearing hubris that had had such disastrous effects on Germany in the past.

A relatively small liberal party, the FDP, was both anti-socialist and anti-clerical. Since both the SPD and CDU had strong liberal elements, and since the SPD

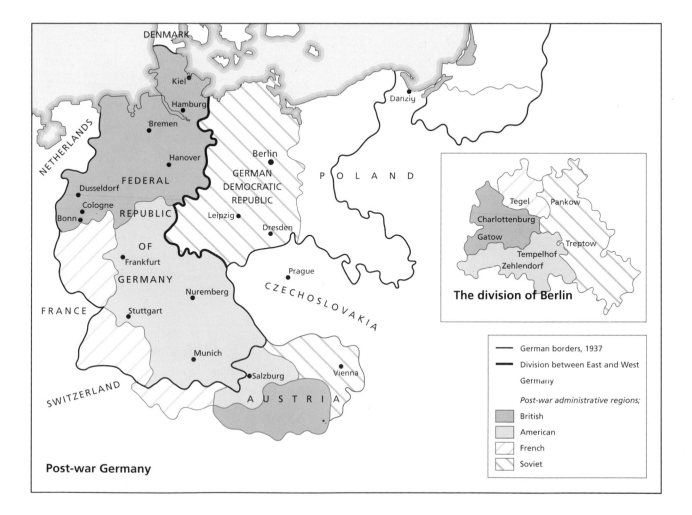

Post-war Germany

The division of Berlin

German borders, 1937

Division between East and West Germany

Post-war administrative regions;

British

American

French

Soviet

The ubiquitous 'Rubble Women' (*Trummerfrauen*) cleared away the debris of Germany's devastated cities with their bare hands. Here, a human chain clears the rubble of Dresden. Allied bombing raids in 1945 destroyed 70 per cent of the city. The police chief reported an estimated 25,000 dead and 35,000 missing.

became increasingly less Socialist and the CDU less clerical, the FDP had considerable difficulty in establishing itself. In the first election it received 11.9 per of the vote. Theodor Heuss led the party from 1948, and Adenauer persuaded him to become the first president of the Federal Republic. He was an amiable Swabian intellectual and principled liberal, although he had made the terrible mistake of voting for Hitler's enabling act.

It soon became very clear that Germany was unlikely to be united. The minister-presidents of the western provinces met twice in Bremen in 1946, and an all-German conference was held in Munich in June 1947, but this conference merely underlined the differences between East and West. The Soviets soon began fundamental reforms in their zone which made unification virtually impossible. Land reform was begun, industry and banking nationalized, and the 'bourgeois educational monopoly' was broken so that middle-class children were excluded from the professions. The Soviets plundered their zone of wealth, resources, and expertise in defiance of the Potsdam agreement, and the western Allies ceased to send industrial equipment from their zones in protest. Soviet attempts to establish a joint allied commission for all of Germany so as to get a say in running the Ruhr were frustrated.

On 6 September 1946 the American secretary-of-state, James F. Byrnes, gave a speech in Stuttgart in which he said that the German people should run their own affairs in freedom and not be subjected to any outside powers. He suggested that to this end the occupation zones should be brought together to form one economic area, and that a new German government should be formed. The Americans knew perfectly well that the Soviets would never accept such a suggestion, and Byrnes was thus proposing a division of Germany. The British were prepared to accept a West German state, the French still had serious objections. Economic support for this scheme was provided by the Marshall Plan, proposed in 1947, which was to facilitate German recovery and integrate Germany into western Europe, thus overcoming French suspicions. The cost of the occupation forces was reduced, and the $17 billion dollars of aid given to western Europe between 1948 and 1952 provided a substantial market for American goods.

With the Marshall Plan the division of Germany was inevitable. The capitalist western sectors enjoyed rapid growth, the Soviet zone, lumbered with a top-heavy socialist bureaucracy, stagnated in Stalinist orthodoxy. On 24 June 1948 the Soviets blocked all land routes to Berlin and the city was supplied by an allied airlift for the next eleven months. It was a splendid display of western solidarity and American efficiency which did much to strengthen America's commitment to Europe, and to steel the resolve of the West to resist Communism. The blockade of Berlin convinced the French that they should accept the integration of the three western zones and a sovereign West German state.

On 1 January 1947 the American and British zones were joined economically to form 'Bizonia'. In June an Economic Council was formed of representatives of the provincial parliaments. In April 1949 the French zone was added to form 'Trizonia'.

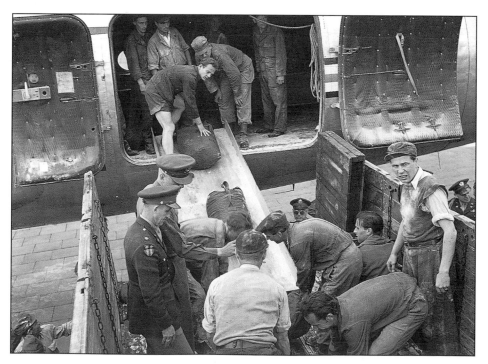

Coal is delivered to Berlin by air on 8 July 1948. Five thousand soldiers' kit-bags, totalling about 200 tons, were carried in twenty-five planes and loaded on to trucks at Tempelhof airport in Berlin.

A further step towards the creation of a West German state was taken in May 1949 with the formation of a Parliamentary Council of 65 members of the provincial parliaments which was called upon to draw up a constitution for the new state. The Fundamental Law was approved by the provincial parliaments and by the western Allies, and the new state, the Federal Republic of Germany, was formed on the basis of this new constitution of 23 May 1949.

The Fundamental Law lessened the plebiscitary elements of the Weimar constitution and greatly strengthened the lower house (Bundestag), which is elected by a combination of direct and proportional representation. Parties which fail to gain 5 per cent of the popular vote are not represented, so that the splinter parties, which played such a sorry role in the Weimar Republic, have less chance of winning seats.

THE FEDERAL REPUBLIC OF GERMANY IN THE ADENAUER YEARS

Elections for the Bundestag were held on 14 August, but the results were disappointing for the framers of the constitution. The three main parties – the CDU and its Bavarian sister party the CSU (Christian Social Union), SPD, and FDP – only managed to attract 70 per cent of the votes. Eight smaller parties were represented. Adenauer formed a majority coalition government made up of the CDU/CSU, FDP, and the German Party (DP), but was only able to become chancellor on 15 September by voting for himself, for which he has been unjustly taken to task. Adenauer so clearly dominated his government that there was soon talk of 'chancellor democracy', and since he was under constant attack from Schumacher he was determined further to strengthen his position.

The Federal Republic was not yet a fully sovereign state. Until 1955 resolutions passed by the Bundestag only became law when countersigned by the Allied High Commission. This obliged Adenauer to pay close attention to matters of foreign policy and to work closely with the western powers. It was fortunate that the imperatives of the political situation coincided with his own convictions.

On 22 November 1949 Adenauer signed the Petersberg Agreement with the western Allies by which the dismantling of factories that had produced armaments was soon to stop and the Federal Republic joined the allied commission which controlled the Ruhr. There followed a fierce debate in the Bundestag in which Schumacher denounced Adenauer as the 'Allies' chancellor', a remark which led to his expulsion from the house for twenty days. The SPD argued that the Federal Republic should make no concessions to the Allies, and should assert its rights as a sovereign power. It was a policy based on a totally unrealistic assessment of the relative power of the two sides, and Adenauer, with his pragmatic and gradual approach, dismissed the opposition as a party of 'the permanent No'.

In the following year Adenauer accepted French foreign minister Schuman's plan for a European Coal and Steel Community consisting of France, the Benelux

Thomas Mann's *Doktor Faustus*

The novel *Doktor Faustus* is the biography of a composer, Adrian Leverkuhn, as told by Dr Serenus Zeitblom. Leverkuhn seeks a way out of his creative crisis by making a pact with the devil in an act which is symbolic of the political, artistic, and social crisis facing Germany in the twentieth century. The novel thus examines how a highly cultivated country like Germany could fall prey to Nazi barbarity.

Leverkuhn, born into a farming family in 1885, was an exceptionally brilliant child with a fascination for the natural sciences. He became passionately interested in music because it combined mathematical rigour with mysterious and ambiguous emotional power. He broke off his theological studies in order to become a composer, even though he had no real creative ability and was convinced that art was in such a state of crisis that the only forms of artistic expression remaining open were parody and eclecticism.

The pact with the devil is not signed in blood as in the traditional story, but is made by copulating with a whore from whom Leverkuhn contracts syphillis. The devil appears in person four years later and promises him that he will be filled with inspiration; in return the devil will have his soul and Leverkuhn has to renounce love. Leverkuhn lives in seclusion for nineteen years, composing a series of major works culminating in the oratorio *Dr Fausti Weheklag* ('Dr Faustus's Cry of Pain'). Having finished his masterpiece, Leverkuhn brings his friends together and confesses all. He then

Thomas Mann (1875–1955), in a portrait taken c.1948.

suffers a stroke which leaves him paralyzed and insane; he dies in 1940.

The figure of Leverkuhn is based on Friedrich Nietzsche and incidents in the novel are from the philosopher's life. The narrator, Zeitblom, writes his biography between 1943 and 1945 so that Thomas Mann can have him comment on the progress of the war and the collapse of National Socialism. Zeitblom, in contrast to Leverkuhn, is a level-headed, pedantic humanist drawn by the author with delicious irony. He represents the decent German bourgeois who refuses any deals with the powers of darkness.

Doktor Faustus is a brilliantly crafted work, but it fails as an analysis of the German malaise and the horrors of National Socialism. Thomas Mann was trapped by his elaborate construction, and the brutal reality of Nazism is allowed to escape.

countries, Italy, and the Federal Republic. The chancellor was convinced that the Federal Republic had the best chance of being accepted as an equal partner in the community of nations through European integration, a vision which had considerable appeal to a youth that had every reason to be suspicious of nationalism. Schumacher and the SPD rejected the Schuman Plan as a plot by French capitalists to control German industry.

There were fierce disagreements over the question of German rearmament. Adenauer had always wanted the Federal Republic to be a member of NATO, which had emerged from the Atlantic Pact of 1949. He was anxious about the security of the Federal Republic, for he took the Communist threat very seriously. Membership of NATO would also be an important step towards making Germany a fully sovereign state. There were many problems to overcome before the country could rearm: a national army was unthinkable five years after the end of Hitler's war, and France had serious reservations about a German army even under strict NATO control.

The SPD rejected the idea of rearmament and argued that it would make the reunification of Germany virtually impossible. The defence of the Federal Republic should be left to NATO, an idea that appealed to young Germans of the 'not me' (*Ohne mich*) generation who had no desire to serve in the army. Once again the SPD failed to comprehend the realities of the Cold War, and their plans for collective security were hopelessly vague and unrealistic. On 10 March 1952 the SPD and those who were opposed to rearmament were given some encouragement when Stalin proposed that Germany could be reunited and could even have a national army if it were to remain neutral. Adenauer rejected the suggestion out of hand. He was determined to continue with his policy of western integration and was convinced that a neutral Germany would become far too dependent on the Soviet Union, and perhaps even become Communist. Passionately attacked at the time, it would now seem that Adenauer was perfectly correct in his assessment of Soviet aims, and that Stalin's offer did not provide a viable basis for German unification. Nor were the USA, Britain and France likely to accept an independent and neutral Germany under the shadow of the Soviet Union. The elections in the autumn of 1953, in which the CDU/CSU got 45.2 per cent of the popular vote and the SPD 28.8 per cent, showed that the majority of West Germans were more interested in their government's economic achievements than in the national question, a fact which generated a great deal of tub-thumping by politicians and journalists.

The currency reform of June 1948 had acted as a stimulus to the economy, although it heightened disparities of wealth, but by early 1950 production was falling and there were almost two million unemployed. On 20 June 1948 a new currency was introduced, the German Mark (DM). The old currency was invalid and every German received forty marks. This clearly benefited those with real estate, goods, and machinery and it certainly did not create a society of equals. As well as the army of the unemployed there were the nouveaux riches who had seized the opportunity of a free market to make spectacular fortunes. Bourgeois conservatives regretted the vulgar materialism of the age, and the SPD saw these developments as proof that the 'social market economy' was both unjust and inefficient; they demanded a planned, socialist economy. The minister of economics, Ludwig Erhard, remained true to his neo-liberal principles and, aided by the economic upswing caused by the Korean War, the economy was soon growing at an annual rate of almost 8 per cent, and maintained this growth throughout the 1950s. Although the gap between rich and poor grew increasingly wide, almost everyone benefited from the 'economic miracle' and the less fortunate were protected by a generous welfare state. The SPD, faced with the obvious success of Erhard's policies, began to distance itself from doctrinaire socialist economics, but could justly complain that his promise of 'prosperity for all' was cruelly empty and that wealth was exceedingly unevenly distributed. On the other hand, the average worker's income rose by 250 per cent between 1950 and 1962, so many who might have been expected to vote for the SPD tended to agree with the CDU electoral slogan 'No Experiments!'

The success and stability of Adenauer's government rested in large part on the remarkable economic achievements of the 'social market economy'. The basis of Erhard's policy was that the state should only interfere indirectly in the economy by encouraging those factors which would stimulate economic growth, especially investment. The state provided investment capital where this could not be provided by ploughing back profits, since in the early years of the Federal Republic the capital market was severely limited. Investments were 22.8 per cent of GNP in 1950 and rose to 28.8 per cent by 1965.

The neo-liberals were concerned that the market should remain competitive and should not be dominated by monopoly concerns. The Law Against the Restriction of Competition, the 'fundamental law of the market economy', was passed in 1957 after lengthy debates, but it was a feeble effort. Germany remained the classic land of cartels and trusts.

Exports of industrial goods formed the basis of the 'economic miracle' which the government encouraged by fiscal measures and an undervalued currency. The Federal Republic soon played a key role in international trade and joined the Organization for European Economic Development (OEEC) in 1949. It joined GATT the following year and the IMF in 1952. The country had a positive balance of trade by 1952, and by 1960 was second to the USA as the world's leading industrial nation.

The social side of the 'social market economy' was anchored in the constitution, even though article 20 is singularly vague: 'The Federal Republic of Germany is a democratic and social federal state'. It was soon accepted that all citizens should be protected by a safety net which would guarantee that they did not fall below a generally accepted minimum standard of living. This reading of the state's obligations was accepted in an early judgment of the constitutional court. It was also agreed that the prosperous had certain obligations towards the less fortunate. This was the thinking behind the burden-sharing law of 1952 in which a special tax provided support for millions of refugees, the victims of Hitler's war and of Soviet oppression. This model was used again to help pay for the immense cost of unification after 1989. In 1957 pensions were

An election poster September 1957 for Konrad Adenauer's Christian Democratic Union. The text attacks the Social Democrats' suggestion that Germany should leave NATO and argues that multilateral disarmament can only come from a position of strength.

CDU

Der Weltfrieden ist in Gefahr!
Auch die Sowjetunion besitzt die furchtbare Atombombe, die Schrecken und Grauen über die gesamte Menschheit verbreitet. Deshalb kann nur eine allgemeine kontrollierte Abrüstung, der auch die Sowjetunion zustimmt, wahren, dauerhaften Frieden garantieren. Die freie Welt hat seither allein durch die NATO der Bundesrepublik Sicherheit, Freiheit, Wohlstand und sozialen Fortschritt ermöglicht.
Die SPD will die Bundesrepublik aus der NATO herauslösen.
Diese Politik führt zum Rückzug der amerikanischen Truppen aus Europa und gibt uns schutzlos der sowjetischen Willkür preis. Diese Politik gefährdet die Abrüstung, zu der die Sowjets nur bereit sind, solange die freie Welt einig und stark ist. Deutsche Wählerin, deutscher Wähler, denkt daran bei der Wahl
AM 15. SEPTEMBER

The unions in post-war Germany were organized on an industrial basis so that only one union was represented in an enterprise. All enterprises with more than 1,000 workers in the coal and steel industries were obliged to have workers' representatives on the supervisory board, and one worker on the board of directors. An expanding economy and responsible union leadership combined to create stable industrial relations to the benefit of both management and labour.

increased by an average of 65 per cent and were indexed to the performance of the economy. Pensioners were thus able to enjoy the benefits of prosperity.

The Allies had established the Bank of the German Provinces (*Bank deutscher Länder*) as a central bank. It continued to function until 1957 when a new central bank, the Bundesbank, was formed. The Bundesbank is almost entirely independent of the government, and has tended to follow a cautious policy that pays no attention to short-term political gain. For this reason relations between the government and the 'Buba' have often been strained. The bank was successful in combating inflation and maintained a strong mark, which was convertible into dollars by 1958 and has remained one of the world's leading currencies.

In 1949 there were sixteen unions in Germany united in the German Trades Union Association (DGB). The DGB had a programme which called for the nationalization of key industries, a planned economy, and industrial democracy. With the economic successes of the Adenauer years this programme was as irrelevant as that of the SPD, and was replaced by a more moderate document in 1963. The unions soon became partners in a pluralistic society, accepting the imperatives of the capitalist system and concentrating on bread and butter issues. Organized labour faced organized management in the German Employers Association (BDA) and the more important Federal Association of German Industry (BDI) which, although they sometimes relapsed into crude red-baiting, were as pragmatic and moderate as their negotiating partners.

In spite of major social legislation on co-determination in industry, compensation of refugees, housing and welfare, the question of rearmament dominated West German politics in these years. The SPD argued that a German contribution to the European Defence Community was irreconcilable with the Fundamental Law. If the constitution were to be changed, the government would have to find a two-thirds majority in the Bundestag and Bundesrat, which they could not do without the support of the SPD. Adenauer managed to get the president to withdraw his request for an expert opinion from the Federal Constitutional Court, and ratified the defence treaties by simple majority in March 1953. The elections in September that year gave Adenauer the two-thirds majority he needed to alter the constitution.

The elections of 1953 showed that the Federal Republic was firmly established as a democratic state. In February reparations were ended when the government accepted the foreign debts of the former Reich. This also established the credit-worthiness of the new state. A generous law on compensation for the victims of National Socialism was an important step in the painful task of reconciliation between Germans and Jews, and was a courageous acceptance of the responsibility of the German people for unimaginable crimes. Various attempts by unrepentant Nazis to organize politically were frustrated by the established parties and by the intervention of the Constitutional Court. The neo-Nazi Socialist Reich Party (SRP) was banned in 1952, and the Communist Party of Germany (KPD) was outlawed in 1956 as unconstitutional, even though it had become an insignificant sect with no parliamentary representation since 1953.

A large number of former Nazis pursued their careers in the Federal Republic and were well represented in the civil service. This certainly hurt the country's reputation abroad, and was used to the full by East German propagandists to discredit the other Germany. There is, however, no evidence that these officials in any way hindered the development of healthy democratic society in the West. The bureaucracy was certainly not antagonistic to the new state, as had been the case in the Weimar Republic, and those with a dubious past became an ever-dwindling minority in a fast-expanding state apparatus. The bureaucracy became so vast that it no longer had the ultra-conservative esprit de corps of its predecessors. It was now a variegated collection of pragmatic specialists administrating a pluralistic society in which serious ideological divisions no longer counted.

The most notorious of these ex-Nazis was Dr Hans Globke, painted by the left as the sinister power behind the throne. He had written the official commentary on the Nuremberg laws, a key document in Nazi racial policy, and was now head of the chancellor's office. As such, Globke was the most powerful and influential civil servant, and it was unfortunate and embarrassing that he had such a disreputable past. Globke was a brilliant administrator who carried out his duties with such efficiency that he was indispensable to Adenauer. There is no evidence whatsoever that he misused his position, and he is generally agreed to have been the outstanding occupant of this high office. The Globke case raised questions of morality, delicacy, and public relations, but it was not evidence of sinister restorative tendencies in the young republic.

Far more serious was the reluctance of judges to condemn their colleagues who had handed down outrageous sentences in the Third Reich. Such judicial crimes were excused on the grounds that they were not illegal at the time, and were consonant with existing legal norms. That sadistic judges had no difficulty in drawing pensions which were often denied to their victims, was in the worst possible tradition of the German legal system. Similarly, Communists were often denied pensions due to them as compensation for persecution under the Nazis. Although the justice system became somewhat more sensitive to such issues, and younger judges had no disreputable pasts to hide, many scandalous cases were later treated with undue leniency.

French objections to German rearmament were finally overcome, in large part due to the skilful diplomacy of the British foreign secretary, Anthony Eden. In October 1954 Germany was accepted as a member of NATO, the occupation statute was to be annulled, and Germany became a fully sovereign state in the Paris treaties. These measures came into effect on 5 May 1955. In order to overcome French suspicions, Adenauer was obliged to accept the proposal for an autonomous Saar under the European Union, subject to a referendum in the region. Adenauer, who had no objections to this solution, was once again attacked for his lack of national spirit, and the opposition claimed that he was selling out the Saar, just as he had sold out the East Germans. The people of the Saar voted overwhelmingly against Europeanization, and the French agreed that the region should return to Germany.

Both Adenauer and his energetic minister of defence, Franz Josef Strauss, were determined that the new German army, the Bundeswehr, should be equipped with the most modern weapons, including delivery systems for atomic weapons. Neither man wanted the atomic weapons themselves, which they believed should remain under the control of the United States. For the opposition, and for many Germans who were deeply concerned about the proliferation of nuclear weapons, this was the first step along a slippery path. Adenauer made a number of unfortunate and misleading statements about tactical nuclear weapons, about which he knew little, and created the impression that the government wanted a nuclear-armed Bundeswehr. A mass movement, the Struggle Against Atomic Death (*Kampf dem Atomtod*), formed in 1958 as the German equivalent to the Campaign for Nuclear Disarmament (CND), was the first large-scale popular political movement in postwar Germany; it combined members of the SPD and trades unions, the churches and pacifists, radical intellectuals and Communists. The need to meet the Soviet nuclear threat was increasingly apparent, and the more level-headed abandoned a movement which rapidly degenerated into a fringe group of idealists and fellow-travellers.

West Berlin youth carrying a wooden cross inscribed 'We Accuse' along the wall, shortly after it was built in 1961. East German police fired water cannon at the demonstrators and West German police retaliated by lobbing tear gas grenades over the wall.

A major reason for the diminution of support for the campaign against nuclear weapons on German soil was the Berlin crisis unleashed by the Soviet leader Khrushchev on 27 November 1958. He demanded that the troops of the western allies be withdrawn from Berlin, and that the city become demilitarized and self-governing. The Soviet leader then threatened that if this were not done traffic to Berlin would be controlled by the GDR, with whom he would sign a separate peace treaty.

The crisis over Berlin continued for almost three years and entered a new phase with the building of the Berlin wall on 13 August 1961. The wall was built to stop people moving to the attractive West, and in this sense was a triumph for the Federal Republic, but it also showed that any hopes of reunification had to be abandoned. The western powers defended their sectors of Berlin, and President Kennedy announced 'ich bin ein Berliner', but the Americans made it clear that the unification of Germany was not a priority and that they were more concerned to maintain the status quo in Europe.

Adenauer disliked the American pursuit of détente, which he believed ruined all chances of German reunification, and he therefore concentrated on improving relations with France. De Gaulle welcomed Adenauer's approach, which he hoped would strengthen his position against the Americans. The Franco-German treaty, signed in Rheims Cathedral on 22 January 1963 was perhaps Adenauer's greatest achievement, and was a turning point in European history. De Gaulle was less pleased. The ratification debate in the Bundestag drew the anti-American teeth from the text of the treaty, and reaffirmed the Federal Republic's commitment to NATO and to the member states of the European Economic Community (EEC).

The Spiegel affair

On 8 October 1962 the weekly magazine *Der Spiegel* published an article on the NATO manoeuvre 'Fallex 62' which pointed out a number of serious deficiencies in West Germany's defences. On the following day the federal prosecutor began preliminary proceedings to investigate whether state secrets had been betrayed and asked the ministry of defence to report on whether there had been a leak. The ministry of defence replied on 19 October that *Der Spiegel* was in possession of secret information, the publication of which had harmed the state. On 23 October the examining magistrate of the federal court issued warrants for the arrest of the magazine's owner, Rudof Augstein, along with members of the editorial staff.

On the night of 26–27 October the editorial offices of the magazine in Hamburg and Bonn were searched and the main office in Hamburg was sealed off until 26 November.

Augstein and several editors were arrested. The military correspondent and deputy editor-in-chief, Conrad Ahlers, who was on holiday in Spain, was arrested by the Spanish police and agreed to be flown back to Germany. His illegal arrest had been ordered by the minister of defence, Franz-Josef Strauss.

The arrest of these prominent journalists in the middle of the night several days after a warrant had been issued caused a public scandal. In a debate which had taken place in the Bundestag on 25 October Strauss had been cleared of charges made by *Der Spiegel* that he had misused his ministerial powers in another affair. It was widely suggested that the arrests were Strauss's revenge against the magazine.

The situation was made worse by a thoughtless speech by Adenauer on 7 November in which he accused *Der Spiegel* of committing high treason in order to make money. It then transpired that the minister of justice had not been informed that the arrests were about to be made, as was required, while the minister of the interior admitted that he had acted 'somewhat outside the law', but had done so for reason of state.

When it became clear that Franz Josef Strauss had lied to the Bundestag about his role in the affair, he refused to resign, as parliamentary custom demanded. Erich Mende announced that the FDP could no longer remain in the government alongside Strauss, and the five FDP ministers then resigned. The CDU/CSU ministers then also resigned, and this enabled Adenauer to form a new coalition government with the FDP that did not include Strauss.

The *Spiegel* affair had both a positive and a negative side. On the one hand it was an attempt to muzzle the critical press using highly dubious means, for which there was a long and unfortunate tradition in Germany. On the other hand the rule of law was upheld, democratic parliamentary practice respected and the executive humiliated by the force of outraged public opinion. Democracy had triumphed and the freedom of the press had been strengthened.

Employees bring laundry baskets full of confiscated papers back into the editorial offices of *Der Spiegel*.

The obvious success of Adenauer's policies and the catastrophic results of the Bundestag elections in 1957 obliged the SPD to rethink their position. In 1959 they produced the Godesberg Programme in which they threw their Marxist relics overboard, accepted Adenauer's policy of western integration, and presented themselves as a broadly based people's party. In 1961 Willy Brandt, who had won widespread admiration at home and abroad for his courageous stand as mayor of West Berlin, took over the leadership of the party. He represented the pragmatic, pro-western and open approach of the renewed party. In the elections of 1961 in which Adenauer led a miserable campaign, stooping as low as to criticize Brandt for having emigrated during the Third Reich and for his illegitimate birth, the CDU/CSU lost the absolute majority. The SPD improved its share of the vote from 31.8 to 36.3 per cent.

Adenauer had great difficulty in forming a new government, for his coalition partners the FDP had fought the campaign under the slogan 'With the CDU/CSU without Adenauer!' The chancellor was now clearly on a downhill path and was unlikely to survive. After the fiasco of the *Spiegel* affair (when the government attempted to muzzle the free press), which led to the resignation of the entire cabinet, Adenauer's days were clearly numbered. His new government was formed on 11 December 1962, and most of the chancellor's efforts were now devoted to the vain task of stopping the minister of economics, Ludwig Erhard, from becoming his successor; Adenauer rightly felt that Erhard lacked any skill in foreign affairs. In April 1963 the party selected Erhard as his successor and the 'Old Man' (*der Alte*) suffered yet another humiliation. On 15 October 1963 he resigned.

CULTURE IN THE ADENAUER YEARS

The cultural achievements of the Adenauer years were considerable, although the preconditions were hardly auspicious. Thomas Mann, in his novel *Doktor Faustus*, published in 1947, pronounced the end of the bourgeois era, of traditional art, philosophy, humanism, of liberalism and capitalism, and the destruction of German culture which had been destroyed by its own demonic subjectivism. The philosopher Theodor W. Adorno who returned from his American exile in 1949, had lost his faith in the proletariat as the 'revolutionary subject', and despaired of the values of the Enlightenment; he announced that there could be no poetry after Auschwitz.

In 1947 a group of writers, soon to be known as the *Gruppe 47* met to discuss the role of literature in post-war Germany. They decided that henceforth they must write clearly and directly, avoiding all the pomposity, literary affectations, and complexities of a language which had been rendered bankrupt by years of misuse, and by the invention of hideous turns of speech which disguised an often horrific reality. Everyday speech revealed the truth behind the sham; literary language all to often served to disguise a reality which could only be revealed by a careful analysis of sub-texts.

Others were not so sure whether it was possible, or even desirable, to abandon the arrogant comforts of the subjective and metaphysical, and face the harsh realities of the world without these familiar defences. Gottfried Benn, the leading poet of the age, articulated this dilemma in works that reached a wide public. Others, like Erich Kästner, looked back nostalgically to a golden age of elegance, wit, and charm that had been utterly destroyed, and which seemed unlikely to return. Günter Eich applied the reductionism of the *Gruppe 47* to produce poetry of great force and immediacy, free from contrivance and false pathos.

The creative genius of the German people was concentrated in these years on the frantic effort to rebuild the economy, and crass material prosperity was beautified with the artistic heritage of the past. Thomas Mann's cultural rubble was soon to be admired as the ancient ruins of a great civilization. Culture was to become, in the words of the Swiss author Max Frisch, an alibi – a means of avoiding a confrontation with the aestheticized barbarity of the Third Reich.

The intellectuals seized upon 'critical theory' whose high priests were Theodor W. Adorno and Max Horkheimer, based at the Institut für Sozialforschung in Frankfurt. Their rarefied reworking of Hegel and Marx provided them with an opaque language with which they imagined they could influence the structure of society from comfortable positions within the infrastructure. By the late 1960s a massive attack, spearheaded by the student movement, was launched against traditional culture, which was seen as anachronistic, affirmative of the status quo, an irrelevant massage of the philistine soul. Opera, theatre, ballet, and orchestras were labour intensive, extremely expensive, and devoted to serving up a dead culture to heavily subsidized middle-class audiences on expense accounts. This was exciting stuff, but it was difficult to see quite how an alternative cultural policy could be implemented. Clearly the culture of the past was not merely an outmoded object of bourgeois snobbery, and much of the avant-garde culture was self-indulgent, irrelevant, and shoddy.

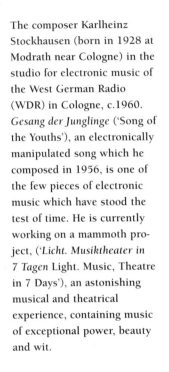

The composer Karlheinz Stockhausen (born in 1928 at Modrath near Cologne) in the studio for electronic music of the West German Radio (WDR) in Cologne, c.1960. *Gesang der Junglinge* ('Song of the Youths'), an electronically manipulated song which he composed in 1956, is one of the few pieces of electronic music which have stood the test of time. He is currently working on a mammoth project, ('*Licht. Musiktheater in 7 Tagen* Light. Music, Theatre in 7 Days'), an astonishing musical and theatrical experience, containing music of exceptional power, beauty and wit.

In the Adenauer era the intellectuals, almost all of whom were on the left, were sharply critical of a man whom they compared to Franco with his authoritarian personality, his clericalism, and his narrow-minded Rhineland patriotism. The Federal Republic seemed to them incurably petit-bourgeois, intolerant, and unenlightened. Adenauer had no interest in art and artists and crudely dismissed most of his finger-wagging critics as fellow travellers in the pay of East Germany. Intellectuals and artists were thus excluded from party politics, but they enjoyed a comfortable martyrdom while denouncing the crass materialism of the economic miracle. Adenauer's greatest failure in the eyes of these high-minded critics was that instead of creating a new Germany, he had simply continued where the Weimar Republic had left off. 'Restoration' was the fashionable word of the day, popularized by Walter Dirks in an influential article in the *Frankfurter Hefte* in 1950.

In fact it was the intellectuals rather than the politicians who were committed to restoration. They were pale echoes of the carping, mocking left-wingers of the Weimar Republic, whose vicious attacks had done much to destroy the democratic process. They signed countless proclamations against nuclear warfare, the censorship of pornography, and Franz Josef Strauss, but were uninvolved in the political process. They remained aloof and disapproving.

In striking contrast to the Weimar Republic there were no outstanding intellectuals on the right. The catastrophic consequences of National Socialism were so obvious that only a few cranks and outsiders could find anything positive in its achievements. Those who had been close to the movement, such as Ernst Jünger, had long since expressed their reservations and were now independent thinkers on the right who accepted the parliamentary system, although often grudgingly. It was not until the 1970s that the right was to seize the intellectual high ground, although some quixotic efforts were made to find the positive aspects of National Socialism.

The key works of the period, such as Günther Grass's hugely successful *Tin Drum*, the novels of Wolfgang Koeppen and Martin Walser, and the poetry of Hans Magnus Enzensberger, were political tracts disguised as literature. Their often heavily underlined political correctness is a poor substitute for literary merit. As time goes by much of this highly acclaimed writing seems intolerably school-masterly, tendentious, and worst of all, tiresome.

The theatre, which had some remarkable achievements in the Nazi period, particularly under Gustav Gründgens in Berlin, continued to thrive, playing mostly German classics and important foreign works. The Wagner festival in Bayreuth had been reopened in 1951 to great acclaim; the master's works were freed of National Socialist trappings and, under his grandsons Wieland and Wolfgang's direction, were presented in a rarified Jungian world of myth and symbolic archetypes, which even sensitive left-wingers allowed themselves to enjoy. Outstanding young composers such as Hans Werner Henze and Karlheinz Stockhausen began their careers in the Adenauer years. American jazz and pop music were enormously popular, and radio stations such as the American Forces Network and Voice of America were greatly appreciated. Popular culture with its freshness and individuality was a healthy influence on the young democracy, not least because it brought blustering reactions from the philistines and cultural pessimists, and helped to underscore Adenauer's western orientation.

The culture of the 1960s was the product of a materially saturated society. The rubble had been cleared and the economic miracle had brought prosperity to almost all. Jean-Luc Godard's 'children of Marx and coca-cola' escaped this bloated world by going into the 'underground'. In this world of sex, drugs, and rock and roll, of eastern meditation and western Marxism, young people imagined that they

Students at the Free
University in Berlin join in a
demonstration organized by
the Socialist German Student
Association (SDS) in July
1966 protesting against
American involvement in the
Vietnam conflict. The placards
read: 'Solidarity with the
National Liberation Front'
and 'Bonn approves of US
genocide in Vietnam'. The
demonstration was attacked
by students sympathetic to
American policy in Vietnam.
The Free University was the
most active centre of the
student protest movement in
the late 1960s.

were living the revolution. The underground was very much above ground and, as the Marxist philosopher, Ernst Bloch, was shrewd enough to fear, was soon packaged and sold to the general public, as wily capitalists made huge profits from 'alternative' culture. The protest movement became more strident as it tried to escape from the clutches of the capitalist Moloch. Sit-ins, teach-ins, strikes, and riots were now the order of the day. Dress and behaviour became increasingly provocative. A new vocabulary made up of words taken from psychoanalysis, Marxism, and philosophy, with a large admixture of the scatological, mounted an attack on what Theodor W. Adorno was pleased to call the 'jargon of the literal' (*Jargon der Eigentlichkeit*) used by those in power.

Before long the philosophers of the Frankfurt School realized that the protest movement was getting out of hand. Adorno was assaulted while lecturing at his university. A younger sorcerer, Jürgen Habermas, issued a frenzied warning about the 'left-wing fascism' of his unruly apprentices. Neither accepted any responsibility for having provided the intellectual justification for much of the nonsense that took place in these years. Not that it really mattered. The students' 'long march through the institutions' achieved very little beyond giving students more say in the running of universities. Those whose heart was on the left soon remembered that their wallets were on the right and pursued careers in the professions, the media, and business and were absorbed into the establishment. With comfortable bank balances, they preached the virtues of their simple lives in Tuscan villages or in Spanish fincas, and could express their concerns about an eco-system which, in their working lives, they did so much to endanger.

By the early seventies the cultural climate was to change drastically. Germany suffered a serious recession and the vast mass of the population did not want any more reforms. They called upon the state to save money and limit its activities. The welfare system was now seen as a new form of feudalism, a crass intrusion by the state into the private sphere of the individual. Subjectivism and the cult of self-awareness were now emphasized at the expense of active politics. The future was no longer seen in terms of a Utopia but of an impending disaster. Prophets announced that the world would end as the result of nuclear war, an ecological apocalypse, or by the exhaustion of all natural resources. The Third World would get poorer, the number of jobless increase, drug addiction and crime would assume increasingly alarming proportions. Politicians and intellectuals could find no answer to these problems.

There can be no doubt that the Federal Republic under Adenauer marked a drastic break with the Nazi past and, as the title of a famous book of the time

The Baader-Meinhof Gang

Meinhof, Ulrike. 7. 10. 34 Oldenburg   **Baader, Andreas Bernd.** 6. 5. 43 München   **Ensslin, Gudrun.** 15. 8. 40 Bartholomae   **Meins, Holger Klaus.** 26. 10. 41 Hamburg   **Raspe, Jan-Carl.** 24. 7. 44 Seefeld

On 2 April 1968, in the year of the students' revolt, there were explosions in two Frankfurt department stores. Four suspects were arrested, among them Gudrun Ensslin, a student, and her boyfriend Andreas Baader. They were defended in the press by Ulrike Meinhof in the left-wing journal *Konkret*. She claimed that the bombs were a heroic attack on the 'terrorism of consumption'. Ensslin and Baader were condemned to three years in jail, but disappeared while their appeal was being heard. Baader was arrested in April 1970 but was sprung from jail in an armed action organized by Ulrike Meinhof in which one of the rescuers was killed.

Ensslin, Baader, Mahler, and Meinhof founded the Red Army Faction (RAF), an organization of urban guerillas. They believed that the capitalist system could best be brought down by murdering policemen and members of the armed forces and by kidnapping prominent figures so as to obtain ransom money and the release of imprisoned comrades. Additional funds could be obtained by robbing banks.

Most members of the Red Army Faction were students, the majority from comfortable middle-class backgrounds. They were disillusioned because the student protest movement had made no impact on society as a whole. They imagined that, by provoking the authorities, they could unmask the state as repressive and fascist and win over the masses to their side. Instead of sympathy they were viewed with repugnance by all but a few intellectuals.

Andreas Baader, Gudrun Ensslin, Ulrike Meinhof, Holger Meins, and Jan-Carl Raspe were eventually arrested in June 1972 and charged with a number of terrorist attacks but the terrorist activity continued. The imprisoned leadership issued orders to their followers, coordinating their efforts with comrades in other prisons. A series of murders and hostage-takings followed, culminating with the hijacking of an Air France plane which was rescued by the Israelis. These spectacular acts of violence strengthened the resolve of the state to combat the terrorists.

In May 1976 a disillusioned Ulrike Meinhof committed suicide, but the murders continued, and in October 1977 terrorists hijacked a Lufthansa jet which was stormed by the crack German anti-terrorist units GSG 9 in Mogadishu. Baader, Ensslin and Raspe committed suicide shortly after the hostages were freed. Isolated terrorist acts continued in the name of the RAF, but it is uncertain whether the organization still exists. With the fall of the wall, terrorists no longer enjoyed the support of the East Germans and their activities dwindled. Their fatal legacy was that the authorities were so obsessed with left-wing terrorism that they tended to ignore the sinister activities of extremist right-wing groups.

The Baader-Meinhof Gang: part of a police Most Wanted poster 1972.

Although West Germany's economy suffered a number of ups and downs, its annual growth rate was consistently higher than most other industrial nations. Agriculture declined and industrial production was the key to the 'economic miracle', doubling in value between 1960 and 1975. Much of this was for export; the value of exports increased from 47,900 million marks in 1960 to 350,000 million by 1980.

claimed, Bonn was not Weimar. Nevertheless for all the talk of 'zero hour', there was an unfortunate continuity in certain areas. The lenient attitude towards Nazis shown in the courts and the correspondingly harsh treatment of Communists and victims of National Socialism is a case in point. The privileges accorded to civil servants and the different social security systems for civil servants, salaried employees, and workers, which dated back to the Wilhelmine era, were criticized by the occupying powers but remained virtually unchanged.

WEST GERMANY AFTER ADENAUER

The new chancellor, Ludwig Erhard, hoped to avoid the political in-fighting and ideological divisions of the Adenauer era and aimed to create what he called a 'formed society', a singularly vague phrase which implied a prosperous society without any crude social distinctions, guided by pragmatic principles, harmoniously enjoying the benefits of a steadily expanding economy. In foreign policy Erhard's foreign minister, Gerhard Schröder, began the first steps to an opening towards the east European countries by concluding trade treaties with Poland, Romania, Hungary, and Bulgaria. This brought a degree of flexibility into German foreign relations that was necessitated by the desire of the Americans to reduce tensions in Europe, including a tacit acceptance of the division of Germany. In March 1966 Erhard addressed a note to most states, excluding the GDR, proposing that they should renounce the use of force and agree to the control and non-proliferation of atomic weapons. This initiative, reminiscent of the Kellog-Briand pact of 1928, was an attempt to gain a little room to manoeuvre within a bipolar world.

Debates over foreign policy threatened to undermine the consensus on which the 'formed society' was to be based. A powerful group of German Gaullists wanted to build a third force that could free itself from the Soviet-American polarity. On the left anti-Americanism, fuelled by an unpopular war in Vietnam, led to demands for an end to the Atlantic alliance which was felt to be a serious threat to European security. Erhard and Schröder argued that there was no viable alternative to the Atlantic alliance, and attempted to strengthen Germany's role in world affairs within that context.

The elections in 1965 returned the Erhard government. The FDP partners lost votes, the SPD made some gains. The chancellor was nonetheless obliged to make considerable concessions to the CSU and the FDP in order to maintain the coalition, and the negotiations showed that Erhard was a weak leader. Provincial elections in North Rhine Westphalia in the following year, which Erhard made into a test of his own popularity, resulted in a serious setback for the CDU, and a new coalition government was formed by the SPD and FDP in Düsseldorf. The economy began to experience increasing difficulties. There was a slowing down in the rate of growth, along with major structural changes and dislocations which caused an increase in unemployment. Disagreements over budgetary proposals obliged the FDP to leave the coalition in October 1966, and Erhard's was now a minority government. The chancellor bowed to the inevitable and resigned, to be replaced by Kurt Georg Kiesinger, the minister-president of Baden-Württemberg.

After lengthy negotiations a 'great coalition' was formed with the SPD with Kiesinger as chancellor. Herbert Wehner, one of the outstanding figures in post-war German politics, argued forcefully that the SPD had to show the electorate that it was able to govern effectively, and he was the leading advocate on the left for the great coalition. The new government, formed on 1 December 1966, was determined to overcome the economic problems that plagued the country and to pursue a more active foreign policy towards the eastern European states.

The minister of economics, Karl Schiller, and the minister of finance, Franz Josef Strauss, set out to reduce the budgetary deficit and at the same time stimulate economic growth through economic planning. They were remarkably successful, but there were acrimonious debates between the coalition partners as to the future course. In foreign policy the Kiesinger government attempted to improve relations with both the United States and France, and resisted de Gaulle's attempts to draw Germany away from the Atlantic alliance to become a junior partner in a French-dominated Europe. Foreign affairs caused less headaches in these years than did domestic politics. The younger generation, sharply critical of American involvement in Vietnam, and of Germany's support for what they felt to be an imperialist war, felt themselves alienated from a capitalist society which they rejected as unjust, inefficient, and materialistic. They found the politics of the Kiesinger government complacent and were outraged when it was revealed that the chancellor had been a member of the Nazi party. Since there was now no serious opposition party they organized the 'Extra-Parliamentary Opposition' (APO) and mounted a series of demonstrations, protest marches, and riots, as did their contemporaries in France, Italy, and the United States. Their worst fears were confirmed by the rise of a radical right-wing party, the New Democratic Party (NDP), and there was much exaggerated talk of a Nazi revival.

The elections of 1969 resulted in an improved showing for the SPD, slight losses by the CDU/CSU and a disaster for the FDP. The NDP received 4.3 per cent of the popular vote and was thus below the 5 per cent required for a party to win seats in the Bundestag. Although the CDU/CSU hoped to continue in a great coalition under Willy Brandt, the SPD opted for a coalition with the FDP.

Willy Brandt's government was determined to undertake far-reaching reforms at home to meet many of the justified criticisms of the alienated youth. He also wanted to pursue a more vigorous policy towards the Communist states, but had a majority of only twelve seats, and his FDP partners had serious reservations about this ambitious programme.

Young people were not placated by the end of the Great Coalition which had seemed so intolerably stuffy. They espoused a carnivalistic form of socialism and preached the doctrine of 'real humans' who were freed from the restraints of convention and bourgeois respectability. In anarchistic communes the works of the young Marx, Mao, and Wilhelm Reich were superficially culled for appropriate slogans. The hedonistic emphasis on self-realization was in fact a rationalization of an irresponsible selfishness, and the attack on authority was a justification for superficiality and indolence. The attacks on existing society became increasingly outspoken until verbal terrorism gave way to actual terrorism.

The government was willing to admit that much of this criticism was justified and announced that it was prepared to 'risk more democracy'. The social services were improved, divorce law was liberalized, equality between men and women in marriage and the family written into the law, and abortion legalized. Education was reformed and made more easily available to the talented, regardless of their social and economic status. These measures were hardly enough to please the radical youth, and were seen as an attack on traditional values and as mindless egalitarianism by vociferous critics on the right.

At least the SPD and FDP could agree on foreign policy objectives. Early in 1970 the government accepted the Soviet invitation of September 1969 to begin negotiations over matters of common concern. A delegation under Egon Bahr, state secretary in the chancellor's office, travelled to Moscow, and agreement was reached in the ten-point 'Bahr Paper' which included a mutual renunciation of the use of force and the Federal Republic's acceptance of the frontiers of the GDR. In the course of further negotiations the Soviet Union accepted that the treaty did not mean that the Federal Republic had abandoned its quest for the unification of the two Germanies, and conceded the Federal Republic's position on West Berlin. The Moscow treaty was signed on 12 August 1970 and was accepted by the three western powers.

Negotiations with Moscow opened up the possibility of treaties with Poland and Czechoslovakia. An agreement was reached with Poland on 7 December 1970 whereby the Germans accepted the Oder-Neisse line as the western frontier of Poland. Most restrictions on the emigration of Germans from Poland were lifted, and Poland accepted the clause on German unification that was included in the Moscow treaty. On 11 December 1973 a similar treaty was concluded with Czechoslovakia which declared the Munich agreement null and void, and diplomatic relations were established.

While the Federal Republic was negotiating with the Soviet Union and Poland, the four powers began discussions over the status of Berlin in March 1970, and the negotiations continued until September the following year. The resulting agreement guaranteed the transit rights of the Federal Republic to West Berlin, and although the Soviets would not accept West Berlin as being part of the Federal Republic, its citizens were acknowledged as being under Bonn's diplomatic protection, and West Berlin was fully integrated into the economy of the Federal Republic.

Relations between the Federal Republic and the German Democratic Republic were clarified in the 'Basis treaty' (*Grundlagenvertrag*) of 21 December 1972 in which the two states agreed to 'normal neighbourly relations on the basis of equality' and the inviolability of their frontiers was guaranteed. Permanent representatives of the two states were exchanged who were ambassadors in all but name. The treaty amounted to an admission that reunification was at best a distant prospect and that the division of Germany had to be accepted. Tensions were greatly reduced in central Europe, the Federal Republic had won considerable freedom of action, and was able to wring certain concessions from the East. The right condemned the eastern treaties as appeasement, but Willy Brandt promised 'change through rapprochement', hoping that the East German dictatorship would be undermined from within, and forced to make further humanitarian concessions.

The socialist-liberal coalition was criticized by the right for increasing the role of the state in the economy and for its openness towards the Communist states. For the left its social reforms were too timid, and *Ostpolitik* did not go far enough. It was a government of the middle which pleased neither the right nor the left, and an increasing number of members of parliament abandoned the coalition and joined the opposition. In August 1972 Brandt's government narrowly survived a vote of no confidence but no longer had a working majority.

Willy Brandt

Willy Brandt was born in Mecklenburg in 1913. As a politically active Social Democrat he was forced to flee Nazi Germany and went to Norway. He joined the Norwegian army to escape the Gestapo. After a brief period as prisoner-of-war in Norway he escaped to Sweden where he worked as a journalist. He became mayor of Berlin in 1957 on the death of the incumbent, and won the election to the office in the following year. He strongly supported Germany's full participation in the western alliance. This put him at odds with the party leadership, but it made him one of the leading spokesmen for the conversion of the SPD into a people's party, free from outmoded ideological baggage.

In 1960 he became his party's candidate for chancellor. He was young, dynamic, and popular. His stature was enhanced by his masterly handling of the crisis when the Berlin wall was built in 1961. Adenauer did not go to Berlin and insulted his rival in the election campaign by referring to him as 'Herr Brandt alias Frahm' (his Norwegian alias, implying that he was a traitor). The CDU/CSU made much of Brandt's illegitimate birth and suggested that he had 'shot at Germans' during the war.

Brandt knew that Germany could not simply rely on the Americans and had to take certain foreign policy initiatives. With his close associate Egon Bahr he began to work out the details of a policy of 'change via rapprochement' (*Wandel durch Annäherung*). In 1964 he became chairman of the SPD and was appointed foreign minister in the Great Coalition of 1966, a move which alienated the left-wing of his party. He set to work energetically on his policy of *Ostpolitik*, arguing in favour of the diplomatic recognition of East Germany and the acceptance of the Oder-Neisse line.

In 1969 Brandt became chancellor in a coalition government with the FDP. He promised to 'risk more democracy', to reform the educational system, to reduce the voting age, to reform family and criminal law, improve the welfare state, have more co-determination in the work-place, and to do everything possible to stop the two Germanies growing apart. His *Ostpolitik* was highly successful, earning him the Nobel prize for peace in 1971. But he was soon under attack for neglecting his duties as party chairman, ignoring domestic affairs, and letting *Ostpolitik* drift. He resigned in May 1974, using as an excuse the fact that a close associate, Günther Guillaume, was a Stasi agent.

Brandt remained a prominent political figure as party chairman, chairman of the Socialist International and of the Independent Commission on International Development Issues, the 'Brandt Commission', which produced a somewhat jejune report in 1980. He died in 1992.

No man was less corrupted by power than Willy Brandt. He remained a thoroughly decent human being and, despite his solidly bourgeois lifestyle, he never lost the common touch. His strength was that he never played the strong man, he sought compromise without sacrificing his principles, and abhorred empty rhetoric and ideological posing. His love for his country was grounded in his love for constitutionally guaranteed freedoms and he gave his often disoriented countrymen an example of true patriotism.

Willy Brandt (1913–92), the chancellor shown giving a speech in 1972.

Elections were held in November and the SPD won 45.8 per cent of the vote, the CDU/CSU 44.9 per cent. The FDP did remarkably well with its 8.4 per cent. The coalition was thus returned with a comfortable majority and continued with its eastern policy in the Conference for Security and Cooperation in Europe (CSCE), preliminary discussions for which began in November 1972 and were concluded with the Helsinki accords in the summer of 1974. The Federal Republic undertook to give the GDR economic assistance and the GDR had to pay a little more attention to humanitarian concerns and to human rights.

The technical military aspects of détente were dealt with in the Mutual Balanced Forces Reduction (MBFR) talks in Vienna which began in the autumn of 1973. These discussions proved fruitless, for the Warsaw Pact was determined to maintain its superiority over NATO. Late in 1979 NATO warned that if the Soviet Union did not reduce the number of medium-range rockets in Europe, the United States would station such weapons on the territory of its allies including Germany. Bilateral discussions on nuclear disarmament began in Geneva in 1981 but were inconclusive. Pershing II rockets were therefore stationed in Germany, a move prompting a massive protest movement which drew its support from a cross section of the community.

In May 1974 Willy Brandt resigned when it was revealed that one of his closest advisors, Günther Guillaume, was an East German spy. His resignation also marked the end of an era of self-confidence and economic growth, as the West desperately tried to tackle the problems caused by the oil crisis of 1973. The new chancellor was Helmut Schmidt, who had served as minister of finance under Brandt. When the FDP foreign minister, Walter Scheel, was elected president, his post was filled by Hans-Dietrich Genscher. Schmidt's government was pragmatic and unideological; it tried in exceedingly difficult circumstances and with limited success to preserve what had been achieved. This was not enough for the left-wing of the SPD who demanded more reforms. The FDP was increasingly disenchanted with what they felt was excessive state intervention in the economy. The large peace movement and the increasingly militant ecologists formed a substantial opposition to a party to which most had formerly been attached. The socialist-liberal coalition survived the elections of 1976 and 1980, but it was only a matter of time before it fell apart. In September 1982 the four FDP ministers in Helmut Schmidt's cabinet resigned in protest at his financial and economic policies, and the FDP began coalition talks with the CDU/CSU. In October Schmidt was toppled by a vote of no confidence and the CDU leader, Helmut Kohl, was appointed chancellor.

CHAPTER 13 *The Reunification of Germany*

Hopes that the Soviet zone of Germany might enjoy a degree of independence from the Soviet Union and develop its own specific form of socialism began to fade in April 1946, when the SPD was forced to amalgamate with the KPD to form the Socialist Unity Party (SED). It was not long before the United Front of Anti-Fascist Parties of July 1946, in which the various political parties worked together as more or less equal partners, became a rubber stamp for Communist policies. By 1948 the SED was a fully Stalinist organization, a fact that was proudly announced by proclaiming it to be a 'new type of party' solidly based on the foundations laid down by Marx and Lenin. The party declared war on 'large farmers' or 'Kulaks' who possessed more than twenty hectares (fifty acres) of land and intensified the 'class struggle' against the bourgeoisie. Proud of its utterly subservient role, the SED announced: 'To learn from the Soviet Union is to learn the way to victory!' Stalin's attempt to destroy Tito and subsequent attack on national forms of Communism, coupled with the outbreak of the Korean war, condemned East Germany to become a Soviet satellite.

THE FOUNDATION OF THE GERMAN DEMOCRATIC REPUBLIC

The party learnt from their Soviet masters that it would be foolish to risk testing their popularity in an election. In the relatively free local elections in the autumn of 1946 the SED had just managed to win a majority of the votes, but by 1949 they had lost much of their popular support. 'United Lists' for the 'Democratic Block', which gave the electorate no choice, were thus used for elections for the 'People's Congress for Unity and a Just Peace' in May. This People's Congress appointed a German People's Council which worked out the details of a constitution for the new state, and on 7 October 1949 the People's Congress was renamed the Provisional People's Chamber of the German Democratic Republic. Minister-president Otto Grotewohl claimed that the foundation of the GDR was 'an expression of the unshakable will of the democratic forces of the German people to overcome the national emergency'.

Not all the decisive moves in the immediate post-war years were carried out against the will of the people. There was considerable popular support for expropriation of big business and banks, which even bourgeois anti-fascists felt had profited excessively from the Nazi dictatorship. In Saxony 77.6 per cent of the electorate voted in favour of seizing the property of 'Nazi activists and war criminals' in the referendum of June 1946. Many also approved of the land reform of 1945 in which estates of more than 100 hectares (247 acres) were divided up and given to the peasantry and refugees. They were not to enjoy the benefits for long,

The East German People's Army (NVA) on parade. The goose-step was an unpleasant reminder of the Nazis, but was in fact copied from the Red Army.

and most of these 500,000 new owners were herded into collective farms. By the generous use of the label 'Nazi activist', to which was soon added the equally flexible 'American spy', the economic basis of the aristocracy and the bourgeoisie was destroyed, and tens of thousands of innocent victims were herded into concentration camps, many of them to be murdered. The Soviet authorities made good use of Nazi camps such as Buchenwald for this purpose, often retaining experienced Nazi thugs as guards. Buchenwald was later cynically converted into an anti-fascist monument.

The new state immediately organized a Ministry for State Security (*Staatssicherheit – Stasi*) with an army of agents and informers. Similarly the justice system was converted into a political instrument according to Marxist-Leninist principles, the judges now being executants of the party's will. In order to overcome the strong regional traditions and loyalties, the old provinces were abolished and the country divided into fourteen new districts. The state was thus centralized and the old federal structure, which had survived even the Nazi dictatorship, was destroyed.

In 1948 a two-year-plan for the economy was introduced. The first five-year-plan of 1950 aimed at a dramatic increase in industrial productivity, but it proved overly ambitious. From 1950 an increasing amount of property was seized by the state, the economic foundations of the bourgeoisie were destroyed, and agriculture was collectivized. These measures were widely unpopular, and the Stalinist emphasis on heavy industry resulted in severe dislocations in the economy, the ruthless exploitation of labour, and a chronic shortage of consumer goods. Grim ideological rigidity, the ever-present secret police, and the drabness of everyday life were not

relieved by any noticeable improvement in the standard of living, and rousing appeals for sacrifices for a socialist future fell on deaf ears.

A number of prominent intellectuals who had emigrated during the Nazi years opted to return to the Soviet zone, attracted by the possibility of building a socialist and anti-fascist Germany. Among their number were Bertolt Brecht and Arnold Zweig. Their hopes were soon to be dashed by the imposition of a Stalinist cultural policy that condemned 'formalism', 'decadence', and 'cosmopolitanism' – umbrella terms that covered most of modern art, particularly American culture. The order of the day was 'socialist realism', the officially-approved paintings of flaxen-haired maidens driving their tractors on the collective farm and muscle-bound steel workers fulfilling their production targets which were reminiscent of Nazi art. Proletarian march music sounded similar to the music which had accompanied the SA. Dreary realistic literature was in the same mould as the blood and soil novels of the Third Reich. Both Nazis and Communists were sternly disapproving of jazz and American popular music, for which there was an insatiable popular demand.

East Germans looked enviously at the exciting culture and rising prosperity of the West. Meat, butter, and sugar were rationed until 1958, citrus fruits and chocolates were virtually unobtainable. The regime called for thrift, vigilance, and further sacrifices. Criticism was construed as treason, minor errors as sabotage. Party members and intellectuals who called for more democracy after Stalin's death were purged and disciplined.

In May 1953 there were a number of wild-cat strikes in Berlin in protest against a raising of the productivity norms in the building trade. These strikes spread to other cities and to other trades. Soon political demands were voiced in addition to the issues of wages, the length of the working week and piece rates. On 17 June there was a widespread revolt throughout the cities and industrial areas of the GDR. The Soviets reacted swiftly and the revolt was violently suppressed on 18 and 19 June. Pockets of resistance remained active until the autumn.

The revolt of 17 June 1953 showed that the SED regime had no popular support, had no idea what to do, and was incapable of governing without the support of Soviet tanks. When the Soviets made the first tentative steps away from Stalinism at the XX Congress of CPSU in 1956, the leadership of the SED was at a loss to know how to react. Devout Stalinists like Walter Ulbricht, the secretary general of the SED, and Wilhelm Pieck, the president, made ritual denunciations of the false teachings of their erstwhile hero and condemned the cult of personality, but they were uncertain what changes in practical policy were implied by this new ideological course, and were concerned that criticism of Stalin could well lead to criticism of the regime.

While the leadership were anxious to stop any further discussions of Stalin and Stalinism, intellectuals demanded more openness and discussion, a freeing of intellectual disciplines from the dead hand of Marxism-Leninism, and an end to the ideological dominance of the SED. A group of intellectuals around the philosopher

Opposite: The Residential Palace in the East German city of Dresden still shows signs of bomb damage. Great efforts have been made to restore the city to its Baroque splendour.

Wolfgang Harich called for a 'Third Way' that avoided the injustices of capitalism and the rigidity of Communist economic planning. Their call for 'humane socialism' met with a wide response, and the Utopian vision of a better world than that known in either East or West was to have a persistent appeal, which remained undiminished, despite the unlikelihood of its ever being achieved. The Harich group had some support within the SED, particularly among those prominent figures who had been released from jail during the brief post-Stalinist thaw, and for a while they enjoyed the support of the leaders in Moscow. The brutal suppression of the Hungarian uprising in October 1956 spelt the end of their hopes, and Ulbricht was once again firmly in charge, steering the old course.

Harich's reforms were emphatically rejected when the GDR formally announced that it was part of the 'socialist camp' in 1957 and in the following year the motto of the V Party Rally of the SED was 'Victory for Socialism!' More socialism, more rigid planning, more control over the economy would, it was claimed, enable the GDR to reach the level of development of West Germany and even to surpass it by 1961. Harich was arrested in 1956 and after a show trial in March the following year was given a ten-year prison sentence. He was released in 1964. In 1990, one of the last acts of the GDR's appeals court was to rehabilitate him.

The rejection of the reformers' ideas was graphically demonstrated in agriculture. In 1956, 70 per cent of agricultural produce came from privately-owned land. An intensified programme of collectivization resulted in 90 per cent being produced in state-run Agricultural Production Cooperatives (LPGs) by 1961. Similarly, much of trade and commerce that had remained in private hands was taken over by the state in these years. Heavy industry consumed vast amounts of capital investment but failed to produce the results that had been anticipated. The GDR lagged hopelessly behind the Federal Republic.

German coal miners. Miners were among the most militant opponents of the Communist regime in the uprising in East Germany in 1953. This uprising was precipitated by the East German leadership's announcement that they were ordering a 10 per cent increase in production targets – an effective wage cut for most workers. Despite attempts to placate increasingly angry workers, between 300,000 and 400,000 people demonstrated in more than 270 locations across the country on 17 June. When the demonstrations began to get out of hand, the Soviets declared a state of emergency, using tanks to disperse the crowds. An estimated 200 civilians were killed.

The president, Wilhelm Pieck, died in 1960 and his office was abolished, his authority now invested in the collective leadership of the Council of State (*Staatsrat*) with Walter Ulbricht as chairman. Ulbricht was also first secretary of the central committee of the SED, and thus an unchallenged dictator, in spite of the constitutional trappings of post-Stalinist collective leadership.

The people still had the option of leaving everything behind and moving to the West. Some 500,000 left between 1949 and 1955. In 1956 280,000 left, the number dropped to 144,000 in 1959, and rose to 200,000 in 1960. Half these refugees were under the age of twenty-five and two-thirds had trades and professions. The GDR was losing its best and brightest young people. The number of refugees rose dramatically in the first half of 1961 and the country's manpower reserves were draining away. The story of *Snow White* had to be rewritten. She now only had three dwarfs. The others had gone to the West.

On 12 and 13 August 1961 the Warsaw Pact met in East Berlin to discuss the situation and it was decided to close the border by building a wall through the centre of the city. The construction of this scandalous 'anti-fascist protective wall' began on 13 August. It was a further declaration of bankruptcy by the regime and a monument to the failure of Soviet Communism. The building of the wall meant that the citizens of the GDR were no longer faced with the difficult choice of whether to stay or to leave for the West. They were now obliged to make do with what they had and either retreated into a private world of family and friends (many of whom later turned out to have been Stasi informants) or tried to reconcile themselves with the regime. A younger generation began slowly to identify with the GDR, proud of the fact that their country appeared to be the most prosperous of the Communist states, and of the remarkable success of their athletes in international events – the GDR became a member of the International Olympic Committee in 1965. The regime tried to sweeten the pill of the Berlin wall by making hollow condemnations of Stalinism and by the 'New Economic System for Economic Planning and Direction' of 1963 which paid slightly more attention to the individual needs of both producers and consumers. Workers were no longer seen as forming politically uniform 'cadres' but rather as a heterogeneous collection of individuals pursuing broadly similar economic goals. One party activist expressed the new ideology in singularly un-Marxist-Leninist terms when he remarked: 'Political consciousness is measured by production figures'.

The more flexible and pragmatic system, combined with the fact that the workforce was no longer steadily draining away through emigration, resulted in an impressive rate of growth between 1961 and 1970 and a marked improvement in the standard of living for the majority of people. Life in the GDR was still drab and grim compared with the Federal Republic, but by Communist standards this was something of an economic miracle. By the mid-1960s, however, Ulbricht decided to emphasize high technology industries in a renewed attempt to overtake the West. It was a disastrous policy as the infrastructure did not exist, capital was desperately needed for investment in less futuristic endeavours, and the necessary expertise was not available. The new policy threatened to lower the standard of living, a fact which was not disguised by talk of a 'socialist community'.

The Soviet Union became increasingly critical of the SED's economic policy and its vision of socialism, but the greatest differences were over relations with the Federal Republic. Willy Brandt's *Ostpolitik* threatened Ulbricht's position since he was not interested in détente, whereas Moscow was prepared to negotiate directly with Bonn. Ulbricht, the loyal Stalinist, the dreary apparatchik, Moscow's faithful henchman, gradually found himself isolated and at odds with his masters. In May 1971, seventy-eight years old and seriously ill, he was obliged to resign. He died in August 1973 and few mourned his passing.

Ulbricht was succeeded by Erich Honecker, a colourless, narrow-minded philistine who was utterly subservient to Moscow, but who was pragmatic enough not to worry too much about a Utopian future and concentrated instead on the problems of the present. Honecker's approach was summed up in the justly derided phrase 'socialism as it really exists', which was seen as a step towards a 'developed socialist society'. Honecker realized that talk of the 'socialist community' could not hide the fact that the GDR was a hierarchical society, and he propagated the curious notion of a 'socialist class society' in which special attention had to be paid to the needs of the working-class. In 1971 8,500 million marks were spent on subsidies for food, industrial goods and wages in the service sector. This amount rose to 50,000 million by 1988. The emphasis now was on a cripplingly expensive welfare state rather than on the dreams of a socialist society dear to ideologues and intellectuals, although there was inspirational talk within the party of the 'victory of socialism' by 1975.

The 'unity of economic and social policy' proclaimed at the VIII SED party congress in 1971 has to been seen against the background of growing unrest in the Communist countries. In December 1970 there had been widespread unrest in Poland in protest against price increases, and this was only two years after the 'Prague Spring' had been crushed. In the GDR housing was made a top priority and large numbers of apartments were built, most of which were of extremely poor quality. Most of the industrial plants and workshops that remained in private hands were nationalized, but their owners were, for the first time, given modest compensation. In education working-class background and social 'activity' were deemed more important than good marks, as had been the case in the 1950s. Half the places at university were reserved for the offspring of workers and peasants.

East Berlin's Stalinallee, formerly Frankfurterallee, which was built between 1949 and 1960. The poster (dated 1952) reads 'National Rebuilding Programme for Berlin. The signing of a peace treaty means a national rebuilding programme for the whole of Germany'.

East Germany's 'Trabant' cars, unreliable, unsafe, and notorious sources of pollution, came to symbolize the failures of the East German economy. This Trabant has broken down on the road from East Berlin to Leipzig.

This ambitious social policy was prohibitively expensive, and the GDR was further affected by the economic crisis of the mid 1970s. The price of raw materials rocketed, while industrial prices made more modest gains. The value of industrial exports rose by 130 per cent between 1970 and 1981, whereas the value of imported raw materials rose by 300 per cent. The regime was reluctant to increase the cost of basic items such as food and housing, fearing the social consequences of such a policy, and raised prices of goods such as cars and washing machines which were already staggeringly expensive. The result was a return to a grim austerity reminiscent of the early years.

By 1982 the SED seemed to have the situation more or less under control. The world economic situation had improved, rigid planning was rendered a trifle more flexible, and the X SED party congress of 1981 stressed the need to keep up with technological and scientific developments in the West and to use modern techniques to make savings in labour and materials. Honecker was soon to become entranced by the prospect of an ultra-modern economy, and made the same mistake as his predecessor, concentrating on high technology which the GDR was ill-suited to develop. Like Ulbricht before him he was also to get out of step with his handlers in Moscow.

HELMUT KOHL'S GERMANY

When Helmut Kohl's government took office in 1982 they were unable to guess that the GDR had reached a hopeless impasse. They could see no hope for any significant change and Honecker seemed to be firmly in the saddle. There were now two German states, a fact which could hardly be disguised by the Federal

Republic's insistence that they formed one nation. Helmut Kohl admitted as much in his statement in 1982 when he said: 'The German nation state is divided. The German nation remains and will continue to exist. We all know that the end to this division can only be conceived in terms of historical epochs'. He said much the same in an after-dinner speech in honour of Erich Honecker who was on a state visit to Bonn: 'The German question remains open, but at the moment its solution is not on the world historical agenda'. Honecker replied in the same vein.

The renewed arms race with medium-range rockets, the cause of widespread alarm to the citizens of both Germanies, made a peaceful understanding between the two countries imperative. This was the message that Helmut Schmidt took to the GDR on his official visit in 1981, and the policy was continued by Helmut Kohl's government. In 1983 the Bavarian minister-president, Franz Josef Strauss, an outspoken critic of socialism in all its forms, and a man particularly reviled in the GDR as an arch-reactionary, was welcomed by Honecker on an official visit. Strauss had lengthy talks with an extremely disreputable individual, Alexander Schalck-Golodowski, who held senior positions in both the ministry of economics and the secret police, and who enriched himself and his cronies at the highest levels of the party through shady currency manipulations and dubious export deals. Strauss helped negotiate a 2,000 million marks credit to the GDR, part of this money almost certainly ended up in private hands on both sides of the wall. The GDR made some concessions in return for this much-needed loan, but border guards were still ordered to shoot anyone trying to escape and severe restrictions on foreign travel remained in force. Strauss was soon under attack, even from within his own party, the CSU, for having given too much and got so little.

Chancellor Helmut Kohl with Prime Minister Margaret Thatcher at a press conference in London on 22 April 1983.

Nuclear rearmament cast a shadow over inter-German relations. The SED regime generously subsidized the peace movement in the West while unleashing the Stasi on their own citizens who protested against Soviet rockets. Similarly, East German ecologists who complained that dangerous waste from the Federal Republic was being dumped in the GDR, and who questioned the safety of nuclear power plants, were condemned as enemies of the state. The churches, which had become more sympathetic to the opposition, were closely monitored and there were frequent arrests of church-goers. The GDR offered protection and training to international terrorist groups, including those active in West Germany. Chancellor Kohl responded to these moves by denouncing the GDR in 1987 as a totalitarian state held together by prisons and concentration camps. It was a reasonably accurate picture, but it did not do a great deal to improve relations between the two countries.

The Federal Republic and its western allies failed to realize that by the mid 1980s the GDR was falling apart. Its leadership was aged and badly out of touch with the people. Opposition groups both inside and outside the SED were growing in strength and self-confidence. Most significant of all, the state was virtually bankrupt with a deficit of 300,000 million marks and no possible means of getting out from under this crippling burden of debt.

Elections were held in the Federal Republic in 1983, the government having taken the unusual step of voting no-confidence in itself in order to oblige the president to dissolve the Bundestag. The result was a resounding victory for the CDU/CSU, who got 48.8 per cent of the vote. The SPD, whom the electorate did not trust to master the economic problems of the day, got 38.2 per cent. For the first time some members of the Green Party were elected. They succeeded in placing important ecological issues on the political agenda but were hopelessly splintered, loosely organized and absorbed in acrimonious debates between 'realists' and 'fundamentalists'.

Franz Josef Strauss reigned in Munich with the support of 60 per cent of the Bavarian electorate and formed what seemed to be to an alternative government that was more exciting and vigorous than the dreary technocrats in Bonn. His startling visit to the GDR and his outspoken advocacy of massive rearmament, left both his supporters and his opponents confused and angered. Strauss made a lot of noise and a lot of money, but it was an extraordinary solo performance on a bare stage. The decisions that really counted were still taken in Moscow and Washington, and Strauss could do little but cause trouble for his rival Helmut Kohl. He appealed to xenophobic, reactionary, and bigoted sentiments, and he found an alarmingly warm response.

The Federal Republic grew steadily in prestige and importance in the 1980s. NATO was keen to have a German as secretary-general when Lord Carrington retired in 1987 and Helmut Kohl secured the appointed of his minister of defence, Manfred Wörner to the post. Relations with the United States and France, the main

President Reagan and Chancellor Kohl's highly controversial visit to the military cemetery at Bitburg in 1985.

allies of the Federal Republic, were strengthened by Kohl and Genscher. President Reagan made a much-publicized visit to Germany in 1985 which was over-shadowed by a foolish decision to pay his respects to the graves of German victims of World War II at the military cemetery of Bitburg, where a number of members of the Waffen-SS were buried.

The visit to Bitburg reopened the debate over how well the West Germans had dealt with the Nazi past. The minute number of unrepentant Nazis were given far more publicity than they deserved. That a handful of eccentrics and attention-seekers should try to make a martyr of the hapless Rudolf Hess who had been condemned to life imprisonment at Nuremberg, and committed suicide in 1987, excited a great deal of journalist comment and much prurient interest. The publication of a clumsy forgery of Hitler's diaries in 1983 was a major event which showed that the Führer still exercised an enduring fascination for many people, not only in Germany.

Small groups of Nazis, paramilitary organizations, and skinheads may well be symptomatic of a general social malaise, but they are not unique to Germany and they are not a serious threat to the democratic system. Brutal murders committed by such elements gave rise to widespread public outrage which was ludicrously condemned by high-minded left-wing intellectuals as sentimental tokenism, but which forced the CDU/CSU out of its complacency to take an active stand against right-wing terrorism.

A more serious threat was posed by the Republicans, a well organized political party of the extreme right, analogous to Le Pen's National Front in France, but with far less popular support. Careful to stay within the law which bans neo-Nazi and racist activities, the Republicans have successfully managed to articulate resentments against foreigners, particularly Turks. They have also stirred up animosity against the hundreds of thousands of asylum-seekers and refugees (many from eastern Europe), the vast majority of whom had fraudulent claims to the generous support of local and state authorities. With exceptionally high levels of unemployment, especially in eastern Germany after 1989, an acute shortage of adequate housing, and a general disenchantment with the established political parties, the Republicans attracted the protest vote, particularly in working class districts. The Republicans won seats in a number of provincial parliaments and in Berlin, but are unlikely to be represented in the Bundestag in the near future. The flood of asylum-seekers has been dammed, robbing the party of its main theme, and the party is seriously split. Lacking respectability and without strong leadership, the Republicans are unlikely to make a serious impact on German politics, but they have helped push the older parties further to the right for fear of losing popular support.

Racism, intolerance, and right-wing radicalism were widespread amid the 'socialism as it really exists' in the GDR, but were forced underground by a regime that chanted the empty slogans of anti-imperialism, international solidarity and anti-fascism. Whereas the Federal Republic has made a sterling effort to educate its youth about the evils of National Socialism and has encouraged a lively debate about recent history, the SED regime made no attempt to confront the past, in part because of the shameful role of the Communist Party and the Soviet Union at that time. The SED proclaimed itself to be the heir of the anti-fascist martyrs of the KPD,

Workers at the AEG factory in Dresden. Thirty four million marks have been invested in its modernization.

and insisted that all the old Nazis lived in the Federal Republic, a state which carried on the traditions of fascism under a new and sinister guise. German fascists were, according to Marxist-Leninist theory, the front men for German capitalists, and these capitalists continued to thrive in the West whereas they had been destroyed in the East.

In the Federal Republic a major source of justified disenchantment with the democratic system has been the abuse of public office for private gain and the means by which the political parties and their officials have enriched themselves. Political parties have made fraudulent tax declarations by hiding contributions made to them. In 1984 it was revealed that the Flick company, a huge international conglomerate which had been involved in similar scandals during the Weimar Republic, was up to its old tricks – Rainer Barzel, the former CDU chairman who was elected president of the Bundestag in 1983, was in Flick's pay. In 1985 it was revealed that Count Lambsdorff, the minister of economics, had fraudulently transferred the party funds of the FDP to avoid the scrutiny of the tax authorities. Although a convicted criminal, Lambsdorff remained in politics as leader of his party, and is given to making Pecksniffian speeches on political morality.

In addition to the further scandals over party finances and corruption in high places, it has gradually been revealed that politicians at both the state and provincial levels have lined their pockets to a truly astonishing extent by giving themselves huge salaries, commissions, fringe benefits and tax breaks, as well as pensions that far exceed those in the private sector. Most of these sordid details have been unearthed by the efforts of a remarkable professor of constitutional law, Hans Herbert von Arnim.

In the Bundestag elections in 1987 the CDU lost a considerable number of votes, in large part because of attacks by Franz Josef Strauss on Chancellor Kohl for being too much of a left-winger. Strauss was also critical of Genscher's foreign policy, which he felt was simply a continuation of the appeasement policies of the socialist-liberal coalition's *Ostpolitik*. Strauss' CSU supporters remained loyal, and the FDP made substantial gains, so that the coalition returned to power. The SPD under Johannes Rau, the minister-president of North Rhine Westphalia, also lost a large number of votes, the electorate having no confidence in the party's abilities to master the economic and social problems which plagued the country. Gross mismanagement and swindles in Co-op chain stores and the huge building and housing concern *Neue Heimat*, both of which were run by the Unions and SPD, were exploited by the CDU/CSU and FDP to show that the SPD was unfit to govern the country.

The general acceptance of *Ostpolitik* by all but a few mavericks meant that by the mid 1980s talk of German unification was merely a pious platitude. It was now considered perfectly acceptable to ignore the aspirations of East Germans to freedom in the interests of West German security. Thus in 1982, the Social Democrat Egon Bahr, one of the principal architects of *Ostpolitik*, asserted that the

Soviets had a perfect right to intervene militarily in Poland to keep the country within the Warsaw Pact.

THE COLLAPSE OF EAST GERMANY

The national question was once again on the agenda because of the gradual collapse of the Soviet Union. Politicians in the West were painfully slow to grasp the opportunities offered, suggesting that their much vaunted intelligence services were exceptionally ill-informed. By 1981 the GDR owed the West more than 10,000 million dollars, and collapse could only be averted by a drastic reduction of imports, an export drive, and large loans from the Federal Republic to help consolidate the debt. The harmful effects of these measures on the average consumer were slightly relieved by permitting a degree of private enterprise and initiative in the economy.

By comparison with other Communist states the GDR was still a consumers' paradise, with twice as many refrigerators and television sets per head of the population as in the Soviet Union. Many of the production figures were shamelessly fudged. In 1988 Honecker handed over the keys of the three millionth apartment to have been built since the housing programme began in 1971 to a happy couple. In fact only two million apartments had been built, and older housing was falling apart.

At the XI SED party congress in 1986 a new five-year plan was unveiled which concentrated once again on the development of high technology industries. The superiority of socialism over capitalism was emphasized with reference to some highly dubious figures on relative rates of economic growth. In the following years this was shown to be a hollow boast. The economy stagnated, the technological gap between East and West widened, and pollution reached totally unacceptable levels in spite of assurances that ecological problems could only be solved by a socialist planned economy. Honecker continued to boast of grand achievements in high technology and managed to fool a large number of people, but the five-year plan was a complete failure, and discontent was reaching a menacing level.

In April an ecumenical congress of the Christian churches in the GDR was held in Dresden which called for a more democratic election law and for an end to the manipulation of the results. Local elections in May 1989 were exposed as a total fraud. Official figures showed that 98.85 per cent of the votes were cast for the official National Front. Since 99.88 per cent had voted for the list in the 1984 local elections, seasoned observers realized that this was a serious defeat for the SED. Observers from the peace and ecology movements estimated that at least 20 per cent had in fact voted against the list, and they began legal action against fraudulent returns. There were demonstrations in Leipzig and a number of other towns, and hundreds of civil rights activists were arrested.

Outrage at the manipulation of the election results was heightened by the rapidly worsening economic situation and by the refusal of the SED to march in step with the reforms taking place in the Soviet Union under Gorbachev, and also in Poland and in Hungary. The regime's support for the brutal suppression of the protest movement in Peking in June further alienated the masses. People who used the slogans of *perestroika* and *glasnost* to attack the regime were arrested, and Rosa Luxemburg's remark that 'freedom is always the freedom to differ' was taken as an unacceptable provocation. Late in 1988 the Soviet magazine *Sputnik* was banned in the GDR, and selected issues of official Soviet journals were also censored.

On 2 May 1989 Hungary opened its borders with Austria and by August 180 GDR citizens were camping in the grounds of the German embassy in Budapest. They were provided with papers by the Red Cross and fled to the West. Hundreds passed over the Hungarian border or sought asylum in the German embassies in Warsaw, Prague and Budapest as well as the Federal Republic's offices in East Berlin. On 10 September the Hungarian authorities allowed GDR citizens freely to cross their border with Austria and by the end of the month 25,000 had taken advantage of this opportunity to reach the Federal Republic.

The opposition forces in the GDR, encouraged by these developments, became more outspoken in their demands. The SED elite was determined not to make any concessions. Honecker's wife, Margot, the minister of education and a dyed-in-the-wool Stalinist, gave a public address in June in which she referred to 'counter-

On 16 October 1989, 120,000 people demonstrated in Leipzig against the Communist regime, finally forcing the Politburo to act, and take steps to remove the East German leader, Erich Honecker.

revolutionaries' and 'enemies of socialism' and ordered teachers to educate youth so that they would be ready to defend socialism by armed force if necessary. In September a number of demonstrators in Leipzig were arrested and some of them given prison sentences.

In July the organization of a new Social Democratic Party in the GDR had begun, and in August an appeal for an end to the political monopoly of the SED was published. A powerful opposition group, New Forum, was formed in September but was promptly declared to be treasonable. New Forum called for an end to state socialism. Another group, Democratic Beginning, formed as a political party in October, was an umbrella organization for a broad spectrum of opposition groups. In September, opposition Marxists formed the United Left which called for democratic reform. A Green Party was formed in October.

On 2 October 1989 20,000 people demonstrated in Leipzig for democratic reform, and two days later the security forces cracked down on 3,000 people in

The steel sculpture 'Berlin' by Brigitte and Martin Matchinsky-Denninghoff. The sculpture symbolizes the divided city. In the background the ruined tower of the Kaiser William Memorial Church is a monument to the destruction caused by the war.

Dresden who hoped to board special trains taking 7,600 asylum-seekers from Czechoslovakia to the Federal Republic. On 4 October the opposition called for free elections supervised by the UN and for an end to the dictatorship of the SED. On the following day demonstrations in Dresden and Magdeburg were dispersed by the police who used excessive force.

Such was the background for the celebrations held on 6 and 7 October for the fortieth anniversary of the foundation of the GDR during which over 1,000 protestors were arrested. A grim-faced Gorbachev attended the celebrations and urged the regime to be more flexible. At a press conference he said that 'He who arrives too late will be punished by history'. The old men around the sickly Honecker were unmoved, even though the Stasi reported that the situation was extremely serious, that there was widespread dissatisfaction even within the SED, that people were leaving the party in droves, and that the political stability of the country was seriously endangered.

In the days after the forty-year celebrations the situation deteriorated rapidly. Thousands left for the West via Czechoslovakia and Hungary. On 9 October 70,000 people demonstrated in Leipzig under the slogan 'We are the people!' It seems likely that Honecker wanted to use violence against the crowd, following the example of the Chinese whom he admired so much, but the Soviets refused to intervene and cooler heads negotiated with the demonstrators. The mayor of Leipzig and three district party leaders, along with the conductor Kurt Masur of the Gewandhaus Orchestra, began discussions with the demonstrators.

Demands for radical change came from all sides – from the churches and intellectuals, from the newly formed parties and opposition groups, and from further mass demonstrations. On 16 October, 120,000 people assembled in Leipzig, finally convincing the Politburo to act. On the following day, discussions began on whether Honecker should be removed. Willi Stoph, the minister-president and chairman of the council of state, told Honecker that the party no longer had confidence in him. Honecker claimed that he had been so sick for the last three months that he had no idea what was going on. He resigned on 18 October and was succeeded by Egon Krenz, for many years head of the Free German Youth (FDJ), a toothy and vacuous party hack who became secretary-general of the SED, chairman of the council of state, and chairman of the council of national defence. This concentration of power in the hands of one man was ratified by the People's Chamber (*Volkskammer*) even though 300,000 people had demonstrated against such a move at the Monday demonstration in Leipzig on 23 October. Clearly the leadership was still completely out of touch with the realities of the situation. Krenz imagined that, with a few corrections, the course could remain the same, when the vast mass of the population would be satisfied with nothing less than the fundamental reform of the entire system.

Krenz telephoned Kohl on 26 October and it was agreed that the two German states would continue to cooperate. Five days later he visited Moscow and together

When the frontier between West and East Berlin was opened on 9 November 1989 a carnival atmosphere gripped the city. Two months later, an East German border guard lifts a child up onto the wall for a view of the West.

with Gorbachev announced that German reunification was 'not on the agenda'. On 4 November about one million people demonstrated in East Berlin, demanding free elections, freedom of expression, freedom to travel, and the unrestricted right of assembly. Similar demonstrations took place throughout the country. The Politburo met on 8 November and a number of prominent figures were removed, including Willi Stoph and the Stasi boss, Erich Mielke. On the following day the frontier to West Berlin was opened. The wall had fallen after almost thirty years. A carnival atmosphere gripped Berlin and Chancellor Kohl, Willy Brandt and the mayor of West Berlin, Hans Momper, addressed the crowd, which was still delirious with joy at this surprising turn of events.

Poverty in East Germany. Although the regime made every effort to provide more consumer goods, and although East Germany enjoyed a higher standard of living than any other communist economy, it lagged hopelessly behind the West.

A visit to West Berlin was enough to convince most people that the GDR could not be reformed'. Krenz had to go and, after fifty days in office, resigned on 6 December, along with the entire Politburo and the central committee of the SED. He was replaced by Hans Modrow, the party boss of Dresden, a colourless figure who had been excluded from the central committee of the SED by Honecker because he was often critical of official policy. Modrow was the last resort for those who hoped that the system could be reformed, but it was now clear that the SED had lost the 'leading role' that it was guaranteed in the constitution. On 1 December this article was removed.

The SED tried to save itself by blaming all its mistakes on the triumvirate of Honecker, Mielke and the economic specialist Günter Mittag, releasing lurid details of their corruption and luxurious lifestyles; but it was obvious to all that the entire structure of the SED state was at fault and that the party elite was corrupt, pampered, and even criminal. The SED was totally discredited and was unable to assert its authority. The Armed Factory Groups had been disbanded, and had refused to fire on the demonstrators. The ministry for state security was dissolved and hastily began to cover its sinister tracks.

On 8 December the SED held a party 'conference' since 'congress' seemed too grand a term for this sad affair. In February 1990 the delegates decided to change the party's name to Party of Democratic Socialism (PDS) and elected as chairman Gregor Gysi, a shrewd lawyer who had skilfully defended a number of prominent dissidents. The one-hundred-man governing body of the party was mostly made up of people who had not been too closely associated with the Honecker regime. Gysi revived Wolfgang Harich's plea for 'a third way between Stalinist socialism and transnational monopolies' and announced that the party was Marxist and socialist, but not Marxist-Leninist, and was committed to democracy, the preservation of the environment, and what he was pleased to call 'solidarity' and 'socialist pluralism'. Few had any idea what all this meant. Only 700,000 people remained in the party and shortly this dwindled to 300,000.

REUNIFICATION

On 7 December the 'Round Table' discussion began between the SED and the satellite block parties, the various opposition parties, and protest groups. They set to work drawing up a draft constitution, and completed the task in April 1990, by which time they were overtaken by events. The SED still hoped to preserve its mass organizations such as the trades unions and the youth movement, but members left en masse. The slogan at the demonstrations was now no longer 'We are the people!' but 'We are one people!' On 15 and 16 December the East German CDU under Lothar de Maizière adopted a new programme which accepted the market economy and called for national unity.

The call for free elections and for national unity grew louder, and on 28 November Kohl published his ten-point programme calling for an end to the division of Europe and of Germany. On 19 December Kohl travelled to Dresden to meet Modrow to discuss the details of a treaty for 'cooperation and good neighbourliness'. In mid January 1990 Modrow announced that the unification of the two German states was not on the agenda. Modrow and the SED/PDS were still clinging desperately to power, but the Round Table demanded that the elections for the People's Chamber be brought forward from 6 May to 18 March. At the end of January Modrow visited Gorbachev, who announced that he had no objections in principle to German reunification. Modrow then drew up his plans for reunification and brought eight members of the opposition into his cabinet.

The elections were held on 18 March 1990, the first free elections in eastern Germany for almost sixty years. The CDU, the German Social Union (DSU) – the East German equivalent of the CSU, and Democratic Beginning joined together in the Alliance for Germany and obtained 48.1 per cent of the vote. The SPD got 21.8 per cent and the PDS 16.3 per cent. 'Alliance 90' (Bündnis 90), made up of those who had led the peaceful revolution, trailed with only 2.9 per cent. The victory of the right-wing parties which campaigned for national unity came as a great surprise, since most experts had predicted a victory for the SPD.

A new CDU government was formed under Lothar de Maizière in a coalition with the SPD. Work began at once on a treaty with the Federal Republic on monetary, economic, and social union; it was completed on 18 May 1990. The difficulties of reunification became immediately apparent. East Germans wanted to exchange their worthless currency at a rate of 1:1 DM, the Federal Republic made the generous offer of 2:1 DM. After lengthy and often acrimonious discussions, savings up to a certain amount were exchanged at par, the rest at 2:1 DM.

The major problem now remaining was to obtain the agreement of the wartime allies to unification. Kohl visited Gorbachev on 10 February and was told that the Soviet Union would accept a united Germany. The Soviet leader hoped to secure massive amounts of aid from Germany to help him stave off his country's economic collapse. The Two Plus Four talks began in May between representatives of the two Germanies and the Soviet Union, the United States, Britain and France. Given the atmosphere of détente, the tactful but forceful handling of the situation by Kohl and Genscher, and the serious weakness of the Soviet Union, the talks were conducted in a constructive atmosphere and were speedily concluded. In June the Bundestag and the People's Chamber formally guaranteed the frontier with Poland. On 14 July Kohl and Genscher visited Gorbachev who told them that he had no objections to a united Germany within the NATO alliance. The Two Plus Four talks concluded on 12 September in Moscow and the powers acknowledged a united Germany as a fully sovereign state. On 2 October the allied commandants in Berlin formally disbanded.

Meanwhile, the process of unification within Germany gave rise to considerable friction. De Maizière's coalition began to fall apart. In the West people became increasingly concerned about the horrendous cost of unification and businessmen were unwilling to invest in a bankrupt country. In the East, there were complaints about the arrogant attitude of westerners, and widespread fears of unemployment and of the loss of East Germany's much-vaunted social services. The Treaty of Unification was signed on 31 August and on 3 October 1990 the German Democratic Republic ceased to exist; the five provinces of Mecklenburg-Hither Pomerania, Brandenburg, Saxony-Anhalt, Thuringia, and Saxony became part of the Federal Republic under article 23 of the basic law.

Elections for the Bundestag were held on 2 December. The CDU/CSU and FDP could claim that reunification was their work and attacked the SPD because its leader, Oscar Lafontaine, had correctly warned of the economic problems of reunification which Kohl had belittled, and seemed unenthusiastic about national unity. Lafontaine felt that nations were outmoded structures that would have no place in a united Europe. The results of the election were broadly similar in both parts of Germany. The CDU got 44.1 per cent of the vote in the West, 43.4 per cent in the East. The FDP did slightly better in the East with 13.4 per cent compared with 10.6 in the West. The SPD was an exception, getting 35.9 per cent in the West but only 23.6 per cent in the East. In the east the PDS got 9.9 per cent and the coalition of *Bündnis* 90 and Greens 5.9 per cent. The constitutional court ruled that the 5 per cent clause for representation in the Bundestag should apply separately in

East and West, thus *Bündnis* 90 and Greens sent eight members to the Bundestag, the PDS seventeen. Had Germany been counted as a whole neither would have had representation in Bonn.

Although the political unification of Germany was completed relatively smoothly, many economic, social, and cultural problems remained. It soon became apparent that Kohl's government had seriously underestimated the costs of reunification, and few realized the parlous state of the East German economy. The people in the former GDR naturally enough wanted to live like their fellow Germans in the West, but were painfully reminded of the tremendous gap between the two societies. High-minded West German intellectuals looked down on such sordid materialism and vulgar consumerism. East Germans were poorly qualified to survive in the highly competitive atmosphere of West German capitalism. Workers were ill-trained, there was no entrepreneurial middle class, and management was completely unfamiliar with the free market economy. West Germany was a cosmopolitan post-national society, fully open to the West. East Germany, behind a veneer of Communist 'internationalism', was a far more narrow-minded and nationalistic society which had miserably failed to come terms with either its Nazi or its Stalinist past. Revelations about the activities of the Stasi, and the fact that a number of leading political figures in the opposition to the SED had been Stasi informers, further poisoned the atmosphere. According to a poll conducted in April 1993, only 22 per cent of West Germans and 11 per cent of East Germans felt 'together as Germans.'

The SED regime was totally discredited in the eyes of the vast mass of East Germans. They wanted to become part of the Federal Republic as soon as possible and enjoy the benefits of a free and prosperous society. For this reason those principled members of the opposition to the SED regime, along with a few left-wing intellectuals in the West who argued for a 'humane socialism', a third way between Communist dictatorship and capitalism, had precious little support. Those, like the novelist Günter Grass, who felt that the division of Germany should be accepted as a just punishment for the crimes of the Third Reich, seemed merely absurd. Concerns of elderly Adenauerians that a united Germany might be a loose cannon on the European deck had a certain resonance, but they underestimated Germany's commitment to Europe and the Western alliance.

Hopefully the enormous courage, idealism, and solidarity that ordinary East Germans showed in their struggle against the SED regime will be channelled into building the new Germany, and will not give way to cynicism, fatalism, and outbursts of mindless violence. East Germans will have to undergo the painful process of dealing with the recent past, as the West Germans have done with reasonable success before them. It will be an unpleasant task, for it involves not merely analyzing the structure of the Communist regime, but also asking uncomfortable questions about the role played by individuals. Dictatorships are not simply abstract structures, nor merely the result of the sinister policies of the

The Brandenburg Gate

In 1788 Frederick William II ordered that the city gate at the end of the avenue Unter den Linden should be replaced. Carl Gothard Langhans' design for the Brandenburg Gate was based on the Propylaeum in Athens and was the first building in the classical style in Germany. This city gate, with a guard house and customs office, was also a triumphal arch at the end of the avenue which led to the royal palace.

The gate was officially opened in 1791 and in 1793 the huge statue of Victory in a chariot, the work of Johann Gottfried Schadow, was placed on the roof. On 27 October 1806 Napoleon made his triumphal entry through the Brandenburg Gate and was welcomed by the crowd along Unter den Linden. The Emperor remarked: '*l'entrée par cette porte est magnifique*', and the chariot was dragged off to Paris.

As public opinion turned against the French and as patriotic sentiments were aroused, the chariot became a national symbol, the empty Brandenburg Gate a reminder of a shameful defeat. In 1814 the chariot was brought back to Prussia on six enormous wagons which were fêted by enthusiastic crowds. On 7 August 1814 Frederick William III and Field Marshal Blücher led the triumphal march through the gate. The square in front of the Brandenburg Gate was renamed Pariser Platz in memory of the defeat of France.

The Brandenburg Gate built by C.G. Langhans 1788–91 in a watercolour by F.A. Calau c.1805.

The Brandenburg Gate with the Berlin Wall.

Victorious Prussian troops marched through the Brandenburg Gate in 1864 and again in 1866. The gate was now no longer a memorial to the victory in the wars of liberation and became a symbol of Prussian military might. On 16 June 1871 42,000 soldiers marched through the gate. The parade was led by the eighty-seven-year-old General von Wrangel who had crushed the Berlin revolution of 1848, followed by Bismarck, Moltke, and Roon, and then by the kaiser. The Brandenburg Gate had become the triumphal arch of the new Reich.

In 1919 President Ebert welcomed the defeated army at the Brandenburg Gate, now a sad reminder of past glories. On 30 January 1933 the SA led a procession by torchlight through the gate to celebrate Hitler's appointment as chancellor. A huge parade was held there for Hitler's fiftieth birthday in 1939 and in 1940 the victory over France was celebrated there with great pomp and ceremony.

In 1945 the victorious Allies paraded through the badly damaged gate. The Brandenburg Gate, seen by some as a symbol of imperialist agression, was now in the Soviet sector. It was restored and was proclaimed to be the 'gate of peace' in the East and became a symbol of a divided nation in the West. On 9 November 1989 the gate was opened and now signifies national unity.

high and mighty, they are made possible by the compliance of ordinary people, and by the daily betrayals of careerists and opportunists.

The reunification of Germany took place not by blood and iron, but by a genuinely democratic process. The overwhelming majority of the people, in the East and in the West, supported the process and only a handful believed there was a viable alternative. Inevitably it will take a long time before the distinctions between 'Wessis' and 'Ossis' are overcome, and Germany becomes genuinely united. It will be a difficult task in which West Germans will have to make enormous efforts both materially and morally to rebuild the five new provinces. The East Germans will also have to play their part. They have to adjust to a democratic and capitalist system to become Europeans and Westerners. Helmut Kohl deserves enormous credit for his single-minded determination to reunite a divided nation. Perhaps it was necessary to brush aside any miserly complaints about the problems that loomed ahead, but his optimism has not made the task of unification any easier.

Christo (Christo Javacheff b.1935) has planned to wrap up a major public building since 1961. He began his first sketches for the Reichstag project in 1972, at a time when it seemed impossible that the building would ever again be the German parliament. The Reichstag was opened in December 1894, destroyed by fire in February 1933, and now this battered symbol of German democracy stands as a monument to German reunification. The wrapping of the Reichstag finally took place in June 1995.

Conclusion

Germans have frequently and often obsessively addressed the 'German question'. Others have spilt a great deal of ink over what they prefer to describe as the 'German problem'. This question or problem is made up of a series of complex issues. Who are the Germans? Should there be a German nation state? Where do its frontiers lie? Can it be formed peacefully, or is war necessary? Should it be a federal or a centralized state? What will be the reaction of Germany's neighbours? In recent years these broader issues have been subsumed by the question of how it was possible for such a highly civilized and advanced nation to give itself up to the National Socialists and to commit two frightful crimes against humanity – World War II and the mass murder of the European Jews.

What are the key components of the German problem that make it different from other European countries? The first immediate answer is the geographical position of Germany in the middle of Europe. This has meant that no European country had so many bordering states, either directly by land or indirectly by sea. This has been the cause of frequent strife, since many of Germany's neighbours were relatively weak. It has also had the effect of making Germany more of a continental power than the other great European nations. Germany's central position resulted in it becoming the meeting place of different cultures: Roman civilization; Christianity; the barbarian east. The great civilizing movements from the south to the north, from the west to the east, ran through the middle of Germany, creating a rich and varied culture, but also many intractable tensions. The cultural differences between north and south Germany remain, but are far less acute than those between west and east, an abiding fact of European history which remains as stubborn as ever despite the collapse of the Soviet empire.

The psychological effects of this central position have been equally profound. For centuries Germans felt culturally inferior to the Italians and the French and materially and politically inferior to England. At the same time they believed themselves to be infinitely superior to the Slavs. German nationalism was bred of hatred both towards those whom they felt in their heart of hearts to be inferior, and towards those whom they were convinced they were superior. Xenophobia, hubris, and self-doubt are at the root of all nationalistic feelings, but Germans have had an unusual difficulty in finding a positive self-image. Today when a German says that something is 'typically German' it is always meant negatively.

Nations and empires rise and fall, but no country has had such a remarkable up and down history as Germany. The great medieval empire collapsed at the end of the twelfth century and for almost seven centuries Germany was a power vacuum until Bismarck offered his solution to the German question in 1871. The country almost fell apart in 1918–19 and reached the height of its power between 1938 and 1942. Then began the collapse and there followed forty-five years as a divided nation. The reunification of Germany in 1989–90 took place within the context of a chronic world recession and the legacy of political chaos caused by the sudden collapse of the Soviet empire.

Extreme nationalists see the foundation of the Second Empire in 1871 as the high point in the history of Germany. Prussia had finally achieved its historical mission in unifying the country and placed its incomparable army, its honest and efficient administration, and its thriving economy at the service of the nation. Left-wing critics, on the other hand, agree with Goebbels' contention that Adolf Hitler was the heir of Frederick the Great, Bismarck, and Hindenburg.

Neither West nor East Germany was able to find a satisfactory historical identity and a fruitful relationship to the past. East German propagandists proclaimed their state to be the apotheosis of all that was progressive in German history and historians were ordered to revise their previously stern judgments of Martin Luther, Frederick the Great, Bismarck, and Moltke and to present them as forerunners of the German Democratic Republic. They had no difficulty in explaining why Hitler came to power. It was all the result of capitalism and thus of no concern to them. The imperialist and militarist tradition lived on in the capitalist Federal Republic, while East Germany cherished the anti-fascist heritage of the Communist party, remaining discreetly silent about the years from 1939–41 when Communists and Nazis were on friendly terms.

West German historians tended either to claim that the Third Reich was an unforeseeable accident or the result of the peculiarities of German history. According to this latter theory Bismarck stifled the democratic and emancipatory movement by his revolution from above, and silenced the liberals by giving them national unity and a token parliament. By arranging a compromise between the aristocratic and agrarian Prussian elite and the liberal bourgeoisie he held both the Catholic Centre Party and the professedly Marxist Social Democrats in check. According to this theory the German nation state was hopelessly flawed and its partition by the Allies in 1945 was thus a blessing. Any thought of reunification had to be banished.

On the left it was frequently argued that the post-war dismemberment of Germany spelt the end of the German nation state. Germany was proclaimed to be a 'post-national society' whose members identified with their regions and with the notion of European union. The state only existed as an institution which collected taxes and in whose name footballers won World Cups. There was something extremely arrogant about this attitude. Germans who adopted this non-national-consciousness felt greatly superior to those less enlightened people who still thought in outmoded and primitive national terms. It also left Germany morally and intellectually ill-prepared to deal with the problem of reunification when it was suddenly raised in 1989. Foreigners saw skin-headed bully-boys and beer hall demagogues and feared a revival of German nationalism. In fact the problem was that there was virtually no national sentiment at all. The criminal excesses of the

Third Reich left most Germans like reformed alcoholics – tee-total and acutely conscious of the dangers of even the slightest regression.

It is to be hoped that German reunification will give an added impetus to the movement towards European unification. Should this be the case in future the emphasis of much historical writing will be less on how Germany became a nation state and will be concerned more with regional studies and the European context of German history. The Third Reich will inevitably, with the passage of time, cease to be a central concern and will not be seen as the culmination of German history. It should not be allowed to go away, and it will always remain as a challenge to our understanding of the past and as a terrible reminder of a world gone desperately wrong. The Third Reich is an essentially German problem, the most ghastly chapter in German history, but it too needs to be seen in a wider context. Foreign sympathizers, appeasers, collaborationists, Quislings, and active supporters should never be allowed to escape their share of responsibility for the most monstrous crime in human history by conveniently shifting all the blame onto Hitler, Himmler, and their lieutenants, or onto the German people at large. Similarly the 'Final Solution' should not be seen purely in terms of Germans and Jews lest its terrible lessons be lost.

No country is more committed to Europe than is Germany, and no country is better suited by its historical traditions to play a key role in creating a united Europe. But the prospects for such a Europe are far from rosy. To many, Europe is little more than an immense and remote bureaucratic apparatus in Brussels, run by faceless technocrats. This horror named Maastricht threatens to destroy national identities and to create in the place of ancient nation states a leviathan that is totally remote from the people with a toothless European parliament at its mercy.

Western Europeans are not in a suitable frame of mind to contribute adequately to the creation of a Europe that is true to its finest traditions – respect for human rights, freedom, and democracy. Used to years of economic growth they are obsessed with individual rights to the point of downright selfishness. They have been encouraged in this individualism and hedonism by their political class, and by that in America, they have lost all sense of their obligations, duties, and responsibilities towards society. At the same time the political parties have become corrupt, concerned solely with gaining power and looking after their own. Having pronounced an end to ideology they are content to mouth mindless denunciations of their opponents and abjure all constructive thought. It is thus small wonder that so many are fed up with politicians, for all the sterling work and honest efforts of many of them, and either cease to be politically active, or support fringe groups.

Western Europe is also faced with chronic problems from outside. European values have failed to take root in most of the post-colonial and post-Communist worlds. The miserable failure of these nations has led millions to seek a better life in Europe. Germany, as the richest of the European states, had naturally been a favourite goal. To the problems of de-industrialization, chronic unemployment, and an uncertain future, East Germans had to pay host to hundreds of thousands of asylum-seekers that had been dumped on them by the Westerners. The result were appalling outbursts of violence against foreigners, first at Hoyerswerda in 1991 and then in Rostock the following year. These alarming exhibitions of proletarian internationalism and solidarity were emulated by neo-Nazi thugs in the west.

Two basic European solutions to this problem have been suggested: either slam the door shut and defend Europe's wealth and culture from importunate foreigners, or open wide the doors and let everyone in. The first solution would be inhumane, the second would invite all the problems and miseries of the world and make it impossible for Europe to play its part in helping to overcome them.

There is every indication that a democratic and federal Germany is fully conscious of its historically determined obligation to play a key role in creating a democratic and humane Europe, devoted to the preservation and enrichment of the best of the European tradition, fully aware that freedom and democracy are not luxuries but absolute essentials. This is only possible if both the Germans and other Europeans are made fully aware of their history, to build on the positive, to learn from the negative, and to realize their common destiny. The old-fashioned nation state has outlived its historical role and nationalism has degenerated into a negative and atavistic tribalism. While nations and states will remain and continue to contribute to the richness of human culture, it is to be hoped they will cease to be the central concern of politicians, and historians.

Let Heinrich Heine, the best of Germans, have the last word. 'German patriotism results in a hardening of the heart, it shrinks like leather in the cold. The German patriot hates everything foreign, he is no longer a citizen of the world, no longer a European, but only wants to be a narrow German. We already saw that in the idealistic uncouthness of Herr Jahn [the nationalist gymnast]. He began the shabby, crude, uncouth opposition to a way of thinking which is the most wonderful and sacred that Germany had produced; that is to say against the humanity, the universal fraternity and cosmopolitanism to which our great minds – Lessing, Herder, Schiller, Goethe, Jean Paul and all educated Germans have always paid homage.' The greatest Germans were great Europeans. May their spirit live on.

Reference guide to The Cambridge Illustrated History of Germany

Chronology
Further Reading

Chronology

AD 9 Romans defeated by Arminius in the 'Teutoburg Forest'.

451 Attila the Hun fails to defeat the Romans at the Battle of the Catalaunian Plains.

453 Death of Attila.

678 Saint Wilfred preached among the Frisians.

718 Saint Boniface begins his missionary work in Germany.

751 Pepin III 'The Short' elected king.

768 Charles the Great (Charlemagne) becomes king.

772 Charles the Great begins his campaign against the Saxons.

800 Charles the Great crowned Emperor of the Romans at Saint Peter's on Christmas Day.

814 Death of Charles the Great.

843 Treaty of Verdun divides Charles the Great's empire.

919 Henry I 'The Fowler' becomes king.

936 On death of Henry I, Otto 'The Great' ascends the throne.

955 Otto defeats the Hungarians at Lechfeld.

962 Otto crowned emperor in Saint Peter's.

1024 Conrad II, the first of the Salians, becomes king.

1039 Death of Conrad II; Henry III ascends the throne.

1056 Death of Henry III; Henry IV becomes king.

1077 Henry IV is humiliated by Pope Gregory VII at Canossa.

1106 Death of Henry IV; Henry V becomes king.

1125 Henry V, the last of the Salians, dies.

1137 Conrad III elected king. Beginning of the Hohenstaufen dynasty.

1152 Frederick I 'Barbarossa' ascends the throne.

1197 Death of Frederick I, Frederick II becomes king.

1250 Death of Frederick II.

1268 The end of the Hohenstaufen dynasty.

1315 Famine in Germany.

1349 Pogrom in Nuremberg; 536 Jews are burnt at the stake.

1351 The plague spreads to Germany.

1439 Frederick III of Habsburg becomes king.

1450 Gutenberg prints the bible.

1493 Maximilian I becomes emperor.

1517 Luther writes the 95 theses attacking common practices in the Roman Catholic Church.

1519 Maximilian I dies and is succeeded by Charles V.

1520 The Diet of Worms, attended by Charles V, initiates reforms to the empire.

1522-23 The Knights' War.

1525 The Peasants' War.

1531 Formation of the Schmalkaldic League, a defensive proteststant group, opposed to the emperor.

1547 Imperial forces defeat the Schmalkaldic League at the battle of Mühlberg.

1555 The Peace of Augsburg.

1556 Abdication of Charles V.

1564 The Council of Trent publishes the *Tridentinum*, a clear statement of the differences between Catholicism and Protestantism.

1618 The beginning of the Thirty Years War (1618–38).

1648 The Peace of Westphalia concludes the Thirty Years War.

1688 Death of Frederick William 'The Great Elector', succession of Frederick III.

1701 Frederick III becomes Frederick I 'King in Prussia'.

1713 Frederick I succeeded by Frederick William 'The Soldier King'.

1740 Frederick William succeeded by Frederick II 'The Great'. Beginning of the First Silesian War.

1745 Peace of Dresden.

1756 The Seven Years War begins.

1763 Peace of Hubertusburg.

1786 Death of Frederick II 'The Great'.

1792 Battle of Valmy; French revolutionary army defeats imperial coalition troops.

1806 Formation of the Confederation of the Rhine. Prussia defeated by Napoleon at Jena and Auerstedt..

1814–15 The Congress of Vienna draws a new map of Europe.

1819 The Karlsbad Decrees impose strict new censorship laws.

1834 The formation of the *Zollverein*, a free trade customs union, joined by eighteen states.

1848 The revolutionary year in Europe; on March 3 violence breaks out in Berlin.

1862 Bismarck is appointed Prussian minister-president.

1864 Prussian and Austrian troops march against Denmark.

1866 Austro-Prussian War.

1870–71 Franco-Prussian War.

1871 January 18, William I proclaimed emperor in Versailles.

1878 Anti-Socialist laws are enacted at the Congress of Berlin.

1888 Accession of William II.

1890 Resignation of Bismarck.

1898 Naval building programme begins.

1914 June 28; Archduke Franz-Ferdinand assassinated in Sarajevo. On 3 August Germany invades Belgium.

1916 Verdun offensive halted. Appointment of Hindenburg and Ludendorff to the High Command.

1918 November 9; the kaiser abdicates and the republic is declared. November 11; armistice.

1919 Treaty of Versailles.

1920 Kapp Putsch.

1923 January; French troops occupy the Ruhr. November; Hitler leads an abortive putsch in Munich.

1933 30 January; Hitler appointed chancellor.

1935 The Nuremberg anti-Jewish laws are enacted.

1936 Germany remilitarizes the Rhineland.

1938 March; *Anschluss* with Austria. September; Munich Conference held with France and Britain.

1939 August 23; Ribbentrop-Molotov Pact. September 1; Germany invades Poland.

1940 June 14; German troops enter Paris.

1941 June 22; Germany attacks the Soviet Union.

1942 February 2; German troops in Stalingrad surrender.

1944 July 20; attempt on Hitler's life.

1945 April 30; Hitler commits suicide. May 9; cease-fire.

1948 June; Berlin Airlift begins.

1949 Formation of the Federal Republic of Germany and the German Democratic Republic.

1953 June 17; Revolt in the German Democratic Republic.

1954 The Federal Republic becomes a member of NATO.

1961 August 13; building of the Berlin Wall.

1963 Adenauer resigns as chancellor; replaced by Ludwig Ehrhardt.

1969 Willy Brandt becomes West German chancellor.

1974 Willy Brandt resigns, Helmut Schmidt becomes chancellor.

1982 Helmut Kohl is appointed chancellor.

1989 November 9; the Berlin Wall breached.

1990 October 3; Germany reunited.

Further Reading

General works

W. Carr, *A History of Germany 1815–1985*, London 1987

F.L. Carsten, *Princes and Parliaments in Germany 1500–1800,*

————, *The Origins of Prussia*, London 1980

G. Craig, *Germany 1866–1945*, Oxford 1981

————, *The Germans*, Harmondsworth 1982

N. Elias, *Über den Prozeß der Zivilisation. Soziogenetische und psychogenetische Untersuchungen*, (2 vols), Frankfurt 1976

F.-W. Henning, *Das vorindustrielle Deutschland 800 bis 1800*, Paderborn 1977

O. Hintze, *Die Hohenzollern und ihr Werk. Fünfhundertjahre vaterländische Geschichte*, Moers 1979

M. Hughes, *Nationalism and Society: Germany 1800–1945*, London 1988

J. Sheehan, *German History 1770–1866*, Oxford 1989

Chapter 1-3
From the Romans to the Middle Ages

W. Abel, *Strukturen und Krisen der spätmittelalterlichen Wirtschaft*, Stuttgart, New York 1980

————, *Stufen der Ernährung. Eine historische Skizze*, Göttingen 1981

H. Angermann, *Die Reichsreform 1410–1555 . Die Staatsproblematik in Deutschland zwischen Mittelalter und Gegenwart*, Munich 1984

B. Arnold, *German Knighthood 1050–1300*, Oxford 1985

G. Barraclough, *The Origins of Modern Germany*, Oxford 1988

H. Boockmann, *Der deutsche Orden. Zwölf Kapitel aus einer Geschichte*, Munich 1982

O. Borst, *Alltagsleben im Mittelalter*, Frankfurt 1983

T. Brady, *Turning Swiss: Cities and Empire, 1450–1530*, Cambridge 1985

F.R.H. Du Boulay, *Germany in the Later Middle Ages*, London 1983

O. Engels, *Die Staufer*, Stuttgart 1984

S. Epperlein, *Bauernbedrückung und Bauernwiderstand im Hohen Mittelalter*, Berlin 1960

J. Fleckenstein, *Early Mediaeval Germany*, Oxford 1978

————, *Investiturstreit und Reichsverfassung*, Sigmaringen 1973

————, *Grundlagen und Beginn der deutschen Geschichte*, Göttingen 1988

H. Fuhrmann, *Germany in the High Middle Ages*, Cambridge 1986

Gillingham, *The Kingdom of Germany in the High Middle Ages*, London 1971

F. Irsigler and A. Lisotta, *Bettler und Gaukler, Dirnen und Henker. Randgruppen und Außenseiter in Köln 1300–1600*, Cologne 1984

J. Leuschner, *Germany in the Later Middle Ages*, Oxford, 1979

K. Leyser, *Mediaeval Germany and its Neighbours, 900–1250*, London 1952

————, *Rule and Conflict in an Early Mediaeval Society*, London 1979

H.K. Schultze, *Vom Reich der Franken zum Land der Deutschen. Merowinger und Karolinger*, Berlin 1987

————, *Hegemoniales Kaisertum. Ottonen und Salier*, Berlin 1991

H. Thomas, *Deutsche Geschichte des Spätmittelalters 1250–1500*, Stuttgart 1983

R. Wiesflecker, *Kaiser Maximilian I. Das Reich, Österreich und Europa an der Wende der Neuzeit*, (4 vols), Munich 1971–81

H. Wolfram, *Das Reich und die Germanen*, Berlin 1990

H. Zimmermann, *Der Canossa Gang von 1077, Wirkungen and Wirklichkeit*, Mainz 1975

Chapters 4-5
From the Reformation to the Thirty Years War

J. Bak, *The German Peasants War of 1525*, London 1976

G. Barudio, *Der teutsche Krieg 1618–1648*, Frankfurt 1985

P. Blickle, *Deutsche Untertanen. Ein Widerspruch*, Munich 1981

————, *Die Reformation im Reich*, Stuttgart 1982

————, *The Revolution of 1525*, London 1981

H. Boockmann, *Stauferzeit und spätes Mittelalter. Deutschland 1517–1648* , Berlin 1987

K. Brandi, *Deutsche Geschichte im Zeitalter der Reformation und Gegenreformation*, Berlin 1967

M. Brecht, *Martin Luther. Sein Weg zur Reformation 1483–1521*, Stuttgart 1981

A.G. Dickens, *The German Nation and Martin Luther*, Glasgow 1976

R. van Dülmen, *Reformation als Revolution. Soziale Bewegung und religiöser Radikalismus in der deutschen Reformation*, Munich 1977

R.J.W. Evans, *Rudolf II and his World*, Oxford 1973

G. Franz, *Der Deutsche Bauernkrieg*, Darmstadt 1977

————, *Der Dreißigjährige Krieg und das deutsche Volk. Untersuchungen zur Bevölkerungs – und Agrargeschichte*, Stuttgart 1979

H.-J. Goertz, *Die Täufer. Geschichte und Deutung*, Munich 1980

M. Heckel, *Deutschland im konfessionellen Zeitalter*, Göttingen 1983

H. Langer, *Kulturgeschichte des 30 jährigen Krieges*, Stuttgart 1978

B. Lohse, *Martin Luther. Eine Einführung in Sein Leben und Werk*, Munich 1981

B. Moeller, *Deutschland im Zeitalter der Reformation*, Göttingen 1988

H.A. Oberman, *Masters of the Reformation*, Cambridge 1981

————, *Luther, Mensch zwischen Gott und Teufel*, Berlin 1983

G. Parker (ed), *The Thirty Years War*, London 1984

H. Schilling, *Aufbruch und Krise. Deutschland 1517–1648*, Berlin 1988

————, *Höfe und Allianzen, Deutschland 1648–1763*, Berlin 1989

G. Schormann, *Der Dreißigjährige Krieg*, Göttingen 1985

R.W. Scribner and G. Benecke, *The German Peasants War 1525: New Viewpoints*, London 1974

R.W. Scribner, *Popular Culture and Popular Movements in Reformation Germany*, London 1987

_____, *The German Reformation*, London 1986

S. Skalweit, *Der Beginn der Neuzeit*, Darmstadt 1982

_____, *Reich und Reformation*, Berlin 1967

R. Wohlfeil, *Der Bauernkrieg 1524–26. Bauernkrieg und Reformation*, Munich 1975

Chapters 6-9
Germany 1700-1848

K.O. von Aretin, *Vom Deutschen Reich zum Deutschen Bund*, Göttingen 1993

T.C.W. Blanning, *The French Revolution in Germany*, Oxford 1983

_____, *Joseph II, Holy Roman Emperor 1741–1790*, London 1994

_____, *Reform and Revolution in Mainz, 1743–1803*, Cambridge 1974

W. Bruford, *Germany in the Eighteenth Century*, Cambridge 1935

J. Bumke, *Höfische Kultur*, (2 vols), Munich 1986

M. Burleigh *Prussian Society and the German Order*, Cambridge 1984

C. Dipper, *Deutsche Geschichte 1648–1789*, Frankfurt 1991

J. Gagliardo, *Reich and Nation. The Holy Roman Empire as Idea and Reality 1763–1806*, Bloomington 1980

S. Haffner, *The Rise and Fall of Prussia*, London 1980

H.-W. Hahn, *Geschichte des deutschen Zollvereins*, Göttingen 1984

C. Ingrao, *The Hessian Mercenary State. Ideas, Institutions and Reform under Frederick II 1760–1785*, Cambridge 1987

H. Lutz, *Zwischen Habsburg und Preußen. Deutschland 1815–1866*, Berlin 1985

H. Möller, *Fürstenstaat oder Bürgernation. Deutschland 1763–1815*, Berlin 1989

T. Nipperdey, *Deutsche Geschichte 1800–1866*, Munich 1983

H. Rosenberg, *Bureaucracy, Aristocracy, Autocracy*, Boston 1966

T. Schieder, *Friedrich der Große. Ein König der Widersprüche*, Berlin 1983

P. Schroeder, *The Transformation of European Politics 1763–1848*, Oxford 1994

J.A. Vann, *The Making of a State: Württemberg 1593–1793*, London 1984

R. Vierhaus, *Germany in the Age of Absolutism*, Cambridge 1988

H. Wagenblaß, *Der Eisenbahnbau und das Wachstum der deutschen Eisen- und Maschinenbauindustrie*, Stuttgart 1973

H.-U Wehler, *Deutsche Gesellschafts-geschichte*, vol.1 1700–1815, vol. 2 1815–1845/49, Munich 1987

Germany 1848-1914

W. Baumgart, *Deutsche Ostpolitik 1918*, Munich 1966

_____, *Deutschland im Zeitalter des Imperialismus 1890–1914*, Frankfurt 1979

V. Berghahn, *Der Tirpitz-Plan. Genesis und Verfall einer innenpolitishcen Krisenstrategie unter Wilhelm II*, Düsseldorf 1971

_____, *Germany and the Approach of War*, London 1973

D. Blackbourn and G. Eley, *The Peculiarities of German History*, Oxford, 1984

K. Borchardt, *Die Industrielle Revolution in Deutschland*, Munich 1972

H. Böhme, *An Introduction to the Social and Economic History of Germany: Politics and Economic Change in the 19th and 20th Centuries*, Oxford 1978

_____, *Deutschlands Weg zur Großmacht*, Cologne 1972

R. Chickering, *We Men Who Feel Most German, A Cultural Study of the Pan German League, 1886–1914*, London 1984

W. Deist, *Militär und Innenpolitik im Ersten Weltkrieg*, (2 vols), Düsseldorf 1970

E. Engelberg, *Bismarck*, Berlin 1985

R.J. Evans (ed), *Society and Politics in Wilhelmine Germany*, London 1978

R.J. Evans, *Death in Hamburg: Society and Politics in the Cholera Years, 1830–1910*, Oxford 1987

L. Gall, *Bismarck: The White Revolutionary*, London 1985

I. Geiss, *German Foreign Policy 1871–1914*, London 1976

H. Grebing, *Arbeiterbewegung, sozialer Protest und kollektive Interessen-vertretung bis 1914*, Munich 1985

D. Groh, *Negative Integration und revolutionärer Attentismus. Die deutsche Sozialdemokratie am Vorarbend des Ersten Weltkrieges*, Frankfurt 1973

T.S. Hamerow, *Restoration, Revolution, Reaction*, Princeton 1966

_____, *The Social Foundations of German Unification, 1858–71*, Princeton 1969

J. Joll, *Origins of the First World War*, London 1984

P.M. Kennedy, *The Rise of Anglo-German Antagonism 1860–1914*, London 1980

P. Kielmansegg, *Deutschland und der Erste Weltkrieg*, Stuttgart 1980

M. Kitchen, *The Political Economy of Germany 1815–1914*, London 1978

_____, *The Silent Dictatorship. The Politics of the German High Command under Hindenburg and Ludendorff, 1916–1918*, London 1976

T. Nipperdey, *Deutsche Geschichte 1866–1918*, (2 vols), Munich 1990

H.-J. Puhle, *Agrarische Interessenpolitik und preußischer Konservatismus im wilhelminischen Reich 1893–1914*, Bonn 1975

G. Ritter, *Frederick the Great*, Berkeley 1968

H. Rosenberg, *Große Depression und Bismarckzeit*, Berlin 1976

J.C.G. Röhl and N. Sombart, *Kaiser William II. New Interpretations*, Cambridge 1982

R. Rürup, *Deutschland im 19 Jahrhundert 1815–1871*, Göttingen 1992

J. Sheehan (ed), *Imperial Germany*, New York 1976

J. Sheehan, *German Liberalism in the Nineteenth Century*, London 1982

R. Stadelmann, *Soziale und politische Geschichte der Revolution von 1848*, Munich 1948

M. Stürmer, *Das ruhelose Reich. Deutschland 1917–1918*, Berlin 1983

H.-U Wehler, *Bismarck und der Imperialismus*, Munich 1976
_____, *The German Empire*, Leamington Spa, 1985

Chapters 10-11
Weimar and Nazi Germany

U. Adam, *Judenpolitik im Dritten Reich*, Düsseldorf 1979

V. Berghahn, *Modern Germany*, Cambridge 1987

R. Bessel and E. Feuchtwanger (eds), *Social Change and Political Development in the Weimar Period 1917–33*, London 1981

K.D. Bracher, *Die Auflösung der Weimarer Republik*, Düsseldorf 1984
_____, *Die deutsche Diktatur*, Cologne 1976

M. Broszat, *The Hitler State*, London 1981

H. Bull (ed), *The Challenge of the Third Reich*, Oxford 1986

W. Carr, *Hitler: A Study in Personality and Politics*, London 1978

F.L Carsten, *The Reichswehr and Politics*, Oxford 1966

T. Childers, *The Nazi Voter*, Chapel Hill 1983

G. Feldman, *Die deutsche Inflation, eine Zwischenbalanz*, Berlin 1982

G. Fleming, *Hitler and the Final Solution*, London 1985

P. Gay, *Weimar Culture*, New York 1968

H. Graml (ed), *The German Resistance to Hitler*, London 1970

S. Haffner, *Anmerkungen zu Hitler*, Munich 1978

K. Hardach, *The Political Economy of Germany in the Twentieth Century*, Berkeley 1980

L. Herbst, *Der Totale Krieg und die Ordnung der Wirtschaft*, Stuttgart 1982

J. Hiden, and J. Farquharson, *Explaining Hitler's Germany*, London 1983

J. Hiden, *The Weimar Republic*, Harlow 1974

K. Hildebrand, *Das Dritte Reich*, Munich 1978

G. Hirschfeld and L. Kettenacher (eds), *The 'Führer State': Myth and Reality*, Stuttgart 1981

P. Hoffmann, *German Resistance to Hitler*, Cambridge 1988

H. James, *The German Slump*, Oxford 1986

E. Jäckel, *Hitlers Herrschaft*, Stuttgart 1986
_____, *Hitlers Weltanschauung*, Stuttgart 1981

I. Kershaw, *Popular Opinion and Political Dissent in the Third Reich*, Oxford 1983
_____, *The Nazi Dictatorship*, London 1985

M. Kitchen, *Nazi Germany at War*, London 1994

K.-J. Müller, *Armee, Politik und Gesellschaft in Deutschland 1933–1945*, Paderborn 1985

A. Nicholls, *Weimar and the Rise of Hitler*, London 1979

R. Overy, *The Nazi Economic Recovery, 1932–38*, London 1982

D. Petzina, *Die deutsche Wirtschaft in der Zwischenkriegszeit*, Wiesbaden 1977

D. Peukert, *Inside Nazi Germany*, London 1987

D. Rebentisch, *Führerstaat und Verwaltung im Zweiten Weltkrieg*, Wiesbaden 1989

A. Rosenberg, *Geschichte der Weimarer Republik*, Frankfurt 1981

G. Schulz, *Deutschland seit dem Ersten Weltkrieg 1918–1945*, Göttingen 1982

H. Schulze, *Weimar. Deutschland 1917–1933*, Berlin 1982

G. Simmel, *Philosophie des Geldes*, Berlin 1958

J. Stephenson, *The Nazi Organization of Women*, London 1981

J.P. Stern, *The Führer and the People*, Glasgow 1975

H.-U. Thamer, *Verführung und Gewalt. Deutschland 1933–1945*, Berlin 1986

B. Weisbrod, *Schwerindustrie in der Weimarer Republik. Interessenpolitik zwischen Stabilisierung und Krise*, Wuppertal 1978

J. Willett, *The New Sobriety: Art and Politics in the Weimar Period, 1917–1933*, London 1978

Chapters 12-13
Germany post-1945

A.M. Birke, *Nation ohne Haus. Deutschland 1945–1961*, Berlin 1989

P. Borowsky, *Deutschland 1963–1969*, Hanover 1983
_____, *Deutschland 1969–1982*, Hanover 1983

R. Dahrendorf, *Society and Democracy in Germany*, London 1968

H. Glaser, *Kulturgeschichte der Bundesrepublik*, (3 vols), Munich 1985–88

A. Grosser, *Geschichte Deutschlands seit 1945*, Munich 1979

K. Köhler, *Adenauer*, Berlin 1994

H. Lilge, *Deutschland 1945–1963*, Hanover 1967

M. McCauley, *The German Democratic Republic since 1945*, London 1983

H.-P. Schwarz, *Adenauer. Der Aufstieg 1876–1952*, Stuttgart 1986
_____, *Adenauer. Der Statsmann: 1953–1967*, Stuttgart 1991

K. Sontheimer, *Die Adenauer-Ära*, Munich 1991

C. Stern, *Ulbricht*, Berlin 1963

Picture Acknowledgements

The following abbreviations have been used:

AKG Berlin: Archiv für Kunst und Geschichte, Berlin

AKG London: Archiv für Kunst und Geschichte, London

BPK: Bildarchiv Preussischer Kulturbesitz, Berlin

Bridgeman: Bridgeman Art Library, London

DPA: Deutsche Presse-Agentur, Bildarchiv Frankfurt

ETA: E.T. Archive, London

Hulton: Hulton Deutsch Collection, London

Magnum: Magnum Photos, London

Mansell: Mansell Collection, London

Mary Evans: Mary Evans Picture Library, London

MM: Mander & Mitchison, Kent

Ullstein: Ullstein Bilderdienst, Berlin

Half title page BPK. **Title page** AKG London/Berlin, Nationalgalerie. 10 Mansell. 15 AKG London. 17 AKG London/Kunsthistorisches Museum, Vienna. 18 Ullstein. 19 AKG London/Sammlung Archiv für Kunsthistorisches & Geschichte, Berlin. 22 AKG London. 23 ETA. 26 *above* ETA. 26 *below* Bridgeman. 27 AKG London/Museum des Kunsthandwerks, Leipzig. 29 AKG London. 30 AKG London/Stift Kremsmunster. 31 Bridgeman/Kunsthistorisches Museum, Vienna. 33 AKG London/Magdeburg, Dom. 34 BPK/New York, Metropolitan Museum of Art. 36 AKG London/Bayerische Staatsbibliothek, Munich/Codex lat. 4453, fol. 24 r. 37 AKG London/Bayerische Staatsbibliothek, Munich/ Codex lat. 4452. 38 Ullstein. 39 *above* BPK/ Hansen/Stalling, 1980. 39 *below* BPK/Speyer. 40 AKG London/Escorial, Codex Vitrinas 17, fol. 65r. 41 ETA. 45 AKG London/Biblioteca Vaticana, Rome. 49 AKG London. 51 VOJ/Landwirtschaft/ Mittelalter. 54 Ullstein. 55 Bridgeman/British Library Roy 2A xxii f.220. 58 AKG London/Lucca, Biblioteca Gover-nativa Statale. 59 AKG London/ Paris, Bibliothèque Nationale, MS. 22495, folio 105. 60 AKG London/Rome, Biblioteca Apostolica Vaticana. 62 AKG London. 63 AKG London/ Rome, Biblioteca Apostolica Vaticana. 64 BPK. 65 AKG Berlin. 67 Ullstein. 70 Mansell. 71 ETA/Manesse Codex. 72 BPK. 76 BPK. 77 Bridgeman/London, V&A. 79 AKG London. 82 AKG London/Augsburg Leihgabe der Bayerischen Staatsgemaldesammlungen. 83 AKG London/ Vienna, Kunsthistorische Museum. 84 *above* AKG London/Coburg, Kunstsammlungen der Veste Coburg. 84 *below* AKG London. 86 *left* AKG London/Berlin, Sammlungen Archiv für Kunst & Geschichte. 86 *right* AKG London. 87 Bridgeman/ City of Bristol Museum & Art Gallery. 88 Bridgeman/Bible Society, London. 89 ETA. 90 Bridgeman/British Library, London. 92 Mary Evans. 94 Mary Evans. 95 AKG London/Munich, Bayerisches Nationalmuseum. 97 AKG London/ Vienna, Graphische Sammlung Albertina. 98 Mary Evans. 100 AKG London. 104 Bridgeman/Private collection, Frankfurt. 105 AKG London/Vienna, Graphische Sammlung Albertina. 106 Mary Evans. 110 Ullstein. 112 BPK. 113 BPK/Zurich, Zentralbibliothek. 114 AKG London. 116 AKG London. 117 BPK/Staatsbibliothek zu Berlin Preussischer Kulturbesitz. 119 BPK. 121 BPK/London, National Gallery. 123 AKG London. 125 AKG London. 128 Bridgeman/Potsdam Staatliche Schlosser und Garten. 130 AKG London/Berlin, Nationalgalerie. 133 ETA. 134 Bridgeman/London, Rafael Valls Gallery. 135 AKG London. 138 *above* BPK/Vienna, Museen der Stadt Wien. 138 *below* AKG London/ London, Royal College of Music. 139 AKG London/Erfurt, Angermuseum. 140 BPK. 142 ETA. 143 AKG London. 146 AKG London. 147 AKG London. 150 AKG London/Versailles, Musée Historique. 151 BPK/Versailles, Musée Historique. 154 AKG London/Winterthur, Sammlung Oskar Reinhart. 155 Bridgeman/Royal Albert Memorial Museum, Exeter. 156 AKG London. 159 ETA. 162 AKG London/Munich, Stiftung Maximilianeum. 165 AKG London. 167 AKG London. 166 BPK. 169 BPK. 170 BPK/Hamburg, Museum für Hamburgische Geschichte. 171 Bridgeman/ Wolverhampton Art Gallery, Staffordshire. 173 Ullstein. 175 *left* Mary Evans. 175 *right* Mary Evans. 178 AKG London/Berlin, Berlin Museum. 179 BPK/Düsseldorf Kunstmuseum. 182 BPK/ Berlin, Staatsbibliothek. 183 AKG London. 185 Mary Evans. 186 Mary Evans. 187 *left* AKG London. 187 *right* AKG London/Munich, Neue Pinakothek. 190 AKG London. 191 AKG London/Nuremberg Germanisches Nationalmuseum. 194 AKG London/Hannover, Niedersachsisches Landesmuseum. 195 Bridgeman/ Private collection. 198 AKG London/Berlin, Sammlung Archiv für Kunst & Geschichte. 202 AKG Berlin. 203 BPK/Berlin, Historisches Museum. 205 BPK. 207 AKG London/Friedrichsruher Bismarck-Museum. 208 AKG London. 210 BPK. 211 AKG London/Berlin, Nationalgalerie. 214 BPK. 215 BPK. 219 AKG London. 221 BPK. 222 BPK/Berlin, Kunstbibliothek Preussischer Kulturbesitz. 224 AKG London. 225 BPK. 226 BPK. 229 Hulton. 230 AKG London/Durck: Kornland & Co., Frankfurt a. M. 231 AKG London. 233 Hulton. 236 Mary Evans. 240 Hulton. 242 ETA. 243 *left* Photo Archive C Raman Schlemmer, Oggebbio, Italy; © 1996 The Oskar Schlemmer Family Estate and Archive, 79410 Badenweller, Germany. 243 *right* AKG London/ Photo by Eric Bohr. 245 AKG London/Berlin, Sammlung Archiv für Kunst & Geschichte. 247 MM/Kevin Mac Donnell. 249 Hulton. 250 *left* Bridgeman/Christie's, London; © DACS 1996. 250 *right* AKG London/Private collection, Konstanz. 251 Bridgeman/Private collection; © DACS 1996. 254 AKG London. 258 Hulton. 259 Hulton. 262 AKG London. 264 Hulton. 266 ETA/Bundesarchiv Koblenz. 267 AKG London. 268 Imperial War Museum. 269 British Film Institute/BFI Stills, Posters & Designs. 270 Hulton. 273 Mary Evans. 274 AKG London. 275 ETA. 279 AKG London. 280 Hulton. 282 *left* AKG London. 282 *right* Hulton. 284 *above* and *below* Hulton. 286 ETA. 287 Hulton. 290 Hulton. 291 Hulton. 293 AKG London. 295 AKG London/Carl Wurm, Frankfurt a. M. 296 Magnum/René Burri. 299 Hulton. 300 DPA. 302 AKG London. 304 DPA. 305 AKG London. 306 Magnum/René Burri. 310 AKG London/Erich Lessing. 313 Magnum/Erich Lessing. 314 ETA. 316 Magnum/Robert Capa. 318 AKG London. 319 Magnum/Raymond Depardon. 320 Hulton. 322 DPA. 323 DPA. 326 Magnum/G. Peress. 327 AKG London/Dieter E. Hoppe. 329 Hulton/Steve Eason. 330 Magnum/Paul Lowe. 334 *above* AKG London/Berlin, Markisches Museum. 334 *below* AKG London/AKG/Bruni Meya. 335 AKG London.

Index